The Rise of Modern Philosophy

A New History of Western Philosophy, Volume 3

Sir Anthony Kenny's engaging new history of Western philosophy now advances into the modern era. *The Rise of Modern Philosophy* is the fascinating story of the emergence, from the early sixteenth to the early nineteenth century, of great ideas and intellectual systems that shaped modern thought. Kenny introduces us to some of the world's most original and influential thinkers, and shows us the way to an understanding of their famous works. The thinkers we meet include René Descartes, traditionally seen as the founder of modern philosophy; the great British philosophers Hobbes, Locke, and Hume; and the towering figure of Immanuel Kant, who perhaps more than any other made philosophy what it is today.

In the first three chapters Kenny tells the story chronologically: his lively accessible narrative brings the philosophers to life and fills in the historical and intellectual background to their work. It is ideal as the first thing to read for someone new to the history of modern philosophy. In the seven chapters that follow Kenny looks closely at each of the main areas of philosophical exploration in this period: knowledge and understanding; the nature of the physical universe; metaphysics (the most fundamental questions there are about existence); mind and soul; the nature and content of morality; political philosophy; and God.

A selection of intriguing and beautiful illustrations offers a vivid evocation of the human and social side of philosophy. Anyone who is interested in how our understanding of ourselves and our world developed will find this a book a pleasure to read.

Sir Anthony Kenny has been President of the British Academy, and Pro-Vice-Chancellor of the University of Oxford. He has written many acclaimed books on the philosophy of mind, the philosophy of religion, and the history of philosophy, including both scholarly and popular works on Aristotle, Aquinas, Descartes, and Wittgenstein.

A New History of Western Philosophy

Anthony Kenny

A NEW HISTORY OF WESTERN PHILOSOPHY

VOLUME III

The Rise of Modern Philosophy

ANTHONY KENNY

CLARENDON PRESS · OXFORD

OXFORD

UNIVERSITY PRESS

Great Clarendon Street, Oxford, OX2 6DP,
United Kingdom

Oxford University Press is a department of the University of Oxford.
It furthers the University's objective of excellence in research, scholarship,
and education by publishing worldwide. Oxford is a registered trade mark of
Oxford University Press in the UK and in certain other countries

First Edition published in 2006
First published in paperback in 2008

Published in the United States of America by Oxford University Press
198 Madison Avenue, New York, NY 10016, United States of America

British Library Cataloguing in Publication Data
Data available

Library of Congress Cataloging in Publication Data
Data available

ISBN 978-0-19-875276-9

SUMMARY OF CONTENTS

CONTENTS

CONTENTS

CONTENTS

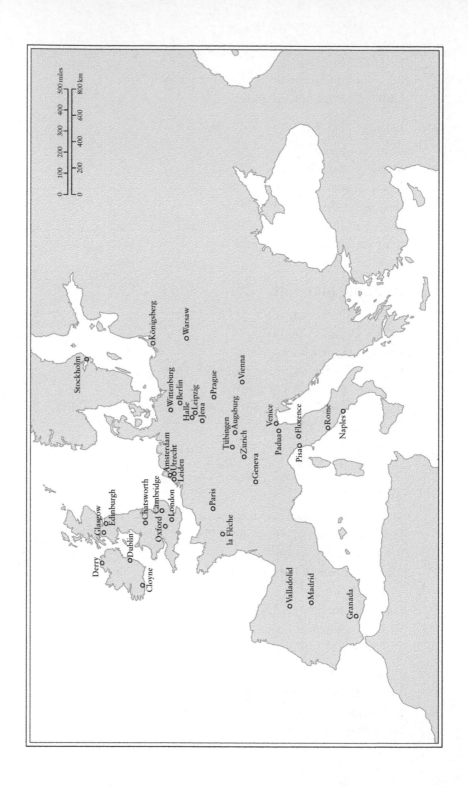

INTRODUCTION

This is the third volume of a projected four-volume history of philosophy from the beginnings to the present day. The first volume, *Ancient Philosophy* (2004), described the early centuries of philosophy in classical Greece and Rome. The second volume, *Medieval Philosophy* (2005), took the story from the conversion of St Augustine to the humanist Renaissance. This volume takes up the narrative from the beginning of the sixteenth century to the beginning of the nineteenth century. A final volume is planned to cover the history of philosophy from the age of Karl Marx and John Stuart Mill up to the present day.

The present volume has the same structure as the two previous volumes. In the first three chapters I offer a chronological survey of the philosophical thinkers of the period. In the remaining chapters I offer a thematic treatment of their contribution to the discussion of particular philosophical topics of abiding importance. Some readers are interested in the history of philosophy principally because of the light it sheds on the people and societies of the past. Other readers study the great dead philosophers in order to seek illumination on themes of current philosophical inquiry. By structuring the book in this way I hope to cater for the needs of both sets of readers. Those whose primary interest is historical may focus on the chronological survey, referring where necessary to the thematic sections for amplification. Those whose primary interest is philosophical will concentrate rather on the thematic sections of my volumes, referring back to the chronological surveys to place particular issues in context.

The audience at which these volumes are primarily aimed is at the level of second- or third-year undergraduate study. However, many of those interested in the history of philosophy are enrolled in courses that are not necessarily philosophical. Accordingly, I try not to assume a familiarity with contemporary philosophical techniques or terminology. Again, with the exception of the original texts of the thinkers of the period I have not included in the bibliography works in languages other than English.

I endeavour also to avoid jargon and to write sufficiently clearly for my history to attract those who read philosophy not for curricular purposes but for their own enlightenment and entertainment.

This has been the easier to do since in the case of many of my historical subjects I write of necessity as an amateur rather than as a professional. In an age when the academic study of past philosophers has expanded exponentially, no one person can read more than a fraction of the vast secondary literature that has proliferated in recent years around every one of the thinkers discussed in this volume. I have myself contributed to the scholarly discussion of some of the great philosophers of the early modern age, in particular Descartes; and I have published monographs on some of the subjects covered by my thematic chapters, such as the philosophy of mind and the philosophy of religion. But in compiling the bibliography for the volume I was made aware how vast was the extent of material I have not read in comparison with the amount that I am familiar with.

Any single author who attempts to cover the entire history of philosophy is quickly made aware that in matters of detail he is at an enormous disadvantage in comparison with the scholars who have made individual philosophers their field of expertise. By compensation, a history written by a single hand may be able to emphasize features of the history of philosophy that are less obvious in the works of committees of specialists, just as an aerial photograph may bring out features of a landscape that are almost invisible to those close to the ground.

To someone approaching the early modern period of philosophy from an ancient and medieval background the most striking feature of the age is the absence of Aristotle from the philosophic scene. To be sure, in the period covered by this volume the study of Aristotle continued in the academic establishment, and at Oxford University there has never been a time since its foundation when Aristotle was not taught. But the other striking characteristic of our period, which marks it off from both the Middle Ages and the twentieth century, is that it was a time when philosophy was most energetically pursued not within universities but outside them. Of all the great thinkers of the seventeenth and eighteenth centuries, none before Wolff and Kant held professorships of philosophy.

Both good and evil consequences resulted when philosophy turned its back on Aristotle. For philosophy in the broad sense—philosophy as it was understood during most of our period, to include the physical sciences as 'natural philosophy'—the removal of Aristotle's dead hand was a great boon. Aristotle's physics was hopelessly erroneous, and had been shown to be so as early as the sixth century of our era; the deference that was paid to it during the Middle Ages was a great brake on scientific progress. But for philosophy in the narrow sense—philosophy as it is now practised as a distinct discipline in universities—there were losses as well as gains resulting from the abandonment of Aristotle.

Our period is dominated by two philosophical giants, one at its beginning and one at its end, Descartes and Kant. Descartes was a standard-bearer for the rebellion against Aristotle. In metaphysics he rejected the notions of potentiality and actuality, and in philosophical psychology he substituted consciousness for rationality as the mark of the mental. Hobbes and Locke founded a school of British empiricism in reaction to Cartesian rationalism, but the assumptions they shared with Descartes were more important than the issues that separated them. It took the genius of Kant to bring together, in the philosophy of human understanding, the different contributions of the senses and the intellect that had been divided and distorted by both empiricists and rationalists.

The hallmark of Cartesian dualism was the separation between mind and matter, conceived as the separation of consciousness from clockwork. This opened an abyss that hampered the metaphysical enterprise during the period of this volume. On the one hand, speculative thinkers erected systems that placed ever greater strains on the credulity of the common reader. Whatever may be the defects of Aristotle's hylomorphism, his substances—things like cats and cabbages—did at least have the advantage of undoubted existence in the everyday world, unlike unknowable substrata, monads, noumena, and the Absolute. On the other hand, thinkers of a more sceptical turn deconstructed not only Aristotelian substantial forms, but primary and secondary qualities, material substances, and eventually the human mind itself.

In the introduction to his lectures on the history of philosophy Hegel warns against dull histories in which the succession of systems are represented simply as a number of opinons, errors, and freaks of thought. In such works, he says, 'the whole of the history of Philosophy becomes a battlefield covered with the bones of the dead; it is a kingdom not merely formed of dead and lifeless individuals, but of refuted and spiritually dead systems, since each has killed and buried the other' (*LHP*, 17).

Though I try to record faithfully the opinions of the successive philosophers of my period, I hope that this volume will not fall under Hegel's censure. I believe that despite handicapping themselves by throwing away some of the most valuable tools that philosophy had forged for itself in Antiquity and in the Middle Ages, the philosophers of this period made many contributions of permanent value, which are identified and described in the thematic chapters. In the course of the book I hope to trace the graph of both the gains and the losses. There is much to be learnt, I believe, from studying even the vagaries of those whom Hegel calls 'heroes of thought'. Great philosophers in every age have engendered great errors: it is no disrespect to them to try to expose some of the confusions to which they appear to have succumbed.

The division into themes in this volume differs from that in the previous volumes in two ways. First, there is no special chapter devoted to logic and language, since philosophers in our period made no contribution in these areas at all comparable to that of the Middle Ages or that of the nineteenth and twentieth centuries. (It is true that the period contains one logician of genius, Leibniz; but his logical work had little impact until the nineteenth century.) Second, there is for the first time a chapter devoted to political philosophy. It is only from the time of Machiavelli and More that the political institutions of the age begin to bear sufficient similarity to those under which we live now for the insights of political philosophers to be relevant to contemporary discussions. The chapter on physics is briefer than in previous volumes, because with Newton the history of physics becomes part of the history of science rather than the history of philosophy, leaving to philosophers, for a while at least, the abstract treatment of the notions of space and time.

I am indebted to Peter Momtchiloff and his colleagues at Oxford University Press, and to three anonymous readers for improving an earlier draft of this volume.

1

Sixteenth-Century Philosophy

Humanism and Reform

The decade beginning in 1511 can well be regarded as the high point of the Renaissance. In the Vatican Raphael was frescoing the walls of the papal apartments, while Michelangelo covered the ceiling of the Sistine Chapel with his paintings. In Florence the Medici family, exiled since the time of the reformer Savonarola, returned to power and patronage. One of the officers of the former republic, Niccolò Machiavelli, now under house arrest, used his enforced leisure to produce a classic text of political philosophy, *The Prince*, which offered rulers frank advice on the acquisition and retention of power. Renaissance art and Renaissance ideas travelled northward as far as Germany and England. A colleague of Michelangelo's designed Henry VII's tomb in Westminster Abbey and the foremost scholar of the age, the Dutchman Desiderius Erasmus, lectured at Cambridge early in the reign of his son Henry VIII. Erasmus was a frequent guest at the house of Thomas More, a lawyer about to begin a political career that would make him, briefly, the most powerful man in England after the king.

Erasmus and More and their friends propounded in Northern Europe the humanist ideas that had taken root in Italy in the previous century. 'Humanism' at that time did not mean a desire to replace religious values with secular human ones: Erasmus was a priest who wrote best-selling works of piety, and More was later martyred for his religious beliefs. Humanists, rather, were people who believed in the educational value of the 'humane letters' *(literae humaniores)* of the Greek and Latin classics. They studied and imitated the style of classical authors, many of whose texts had been recently rediscovered and were being published thanks to the newly developed art of printing. They believed that their scholarship, applied to ancient pagan texts, would restore to Europe long-neglected arts and sciences, and, applied to the Bible and to ancient Church writers, would help Christendom to a purer and more authentic understanding of Christian truth.

Humanists valued grammar, philology, and rhetoric more highly than the technical philosophical studies that had preoccupied scholars during the Middle Ages. They despised the Latin that had been the lingua franca of medieval universities, far removed in style from the works of Cicero and Livy. Erasmus had been unhappy studying at the Sorbonne, and More mocked the logic he had been taught at Oxford. In philosophy, both of them looked back to Plato rather than to Aristotle and his many medieval admirers.

More paid a compliment to Plato by publishing, in 1516, a fictional blueprint for an ideal commonwealth. In More's *Utopia*, as in Plato's *Republic*, property is held in common and women serve alongside men in the army. More, writing in an age of exploration and discovery, pretended that his state actually existed on an island across the ocean. Like Plato, however, he was using the description of a fictional nation as a vehicle for theoretical political philosophy and for criticism of contemporary society.[1]

Erasmus was more sceptical about Plato as a guide to politics. In the teasing *Praise of Folly* that he dedicated to More in 1511 he mocks Plato's claim that the happiest state will be ruled by philosopher kings. History tells us, he says, 'that no state has been so plagued by its rulers as when power has fallen into the hands of some dabbler in philosophy' (M, 100). But when, in the same year as *Utopia*, he published his *Instruction to a Christian Prince*, he did little but repeat ideas to be found in Plato and Aristotle. For this reason his treatise of political philosophy has never achieved the renown of Machiavelli's or of More's.

Erasmus was more interested in divinity than in philosophy, and he cared more for biblical studies than for speculative theology. Scholastics like Scotus and Ockham, he complained, merely choked with brambles paths that had been made plain by earlier thinkers. Among the great Christian teachers of the past his favourite was St Jerome, who had translated the Bible from Hebrew and Greek into Latin. Erasmus worked

---

[1] The political philosophy of Machiavelli and More is discussed at length in Ch. 9 below.

Desiderius Erasmus in Holbein's portrait in the Louvre

for some years annotating the Latin New Testament, and then decided to produce a Latin version of his own to amend corruptions which had crept into the accepted text ('the Vulgate') and, where necessary, to improve on Jerome himself. In 1516 he published his new Latin version along with his annotations, and almost as an appendix, he added a Greek text of the New Testament—the first one ever to be printed. In his Latin version, in striving for fidelity to the Greek original, he did not hesitate to alter even the most beloved and solemn texts. The first words of the fourth Gospel, *In principio erat verbum*, became *In principio erat sermo*: what was in the beginning was not 'the Word' but 'the Saying'.

Erasmus' Latin version was not generally adopted, though passages of it can still be read in the chapel windows of King's College Cambridge. However, the Greek text he published was the foundation for the great vernacular testaments of the sixteenth century, beginning with the monumental German version published in 1522 by Martin Luther.

Luther was an Augustinian monk, as Erasmus had been until released by papal dispensation from his monastic commitments. Like Erasmus, Luther had made a close study of St Paul's Epistle to the Romans. This had made him question fundamentally the ethos of Renaissance Catholicism. The year after the publication of Erasmus' New Testament Luther issued, in the University of Wittenberg, a public denunciation of abuses of papal authority, in particular of a scandalously promoted offer of an indulgence (remission of punishment due to sin) in return for contributions to the building of the great new church of St Peter's in Rome.

Erasmus and More shared Luther's concern about the corruption of many of the higher clergy: they had both denounced it in print, Erasmus pungently in a satire on Pope Julius II, More with ironic circumspection in *Utopia*. But both were alienated when Luther went on to denounce large parts of the Catholic sacramental system and to teach that the one thing needful for salvation is faith, or trust in the merits of Christ. In 1520 Pope Leo X condemned forty-one articles taken from Luther's teaching, and followed this up with an excommunication after Luther had burnt the Bull of Condemnation. King Henry VIII, with some help from More, published an *Assertion of the Seven Sacraments*, which earned him the papal title 'Defender of the Faith'.

Erasmus strove in vain to dampen down the controversy. He tried to persuade Luther to moderate his language, and to submit his opinions for judgement to an impartial jury of scholars. On the other hand, he questioned the authenticity of the papal bull of condemnation and he persuaded the emperor Charles V to give Luther a hearing at the Diet of Worms in 1521. But Luther refused to recant and was placed under the ban of the empire. Pope Leo died and was succeeded by a Dutch schoolfriend of Erasmus, who took the name Adrian VI. The new pope urged Erasmus to take up his pen against the reformers. Very reluctantly, Erasmus agreed, but his book against Luther did not appear until 1524, by which time Pope Adrian was dead.

Sin, Grace, and Freedom

The ground Erasmus chose for battle was Luther's position on the freedom of the will. This had been the subject of one of the theses which had been nailed to the door at Wittenberg in 1517. Among the propositions condemned by Leo X was 'freewill after sin is merely an empty title'. In response, Luther reinforced his assertion. 'Free will is really a fiction and a label without reality, because it is in no man's power to plan any evil or good' (WA VII.91).

In his *Diatribe de Libero Arbitrio* Erasmus piles up texts from the Old and New Testament and from Church doctors and decrees to show that human beings have free will. His constant theme is that all the exhortations, promises, commands, threats, reproaches, and curses to be found in the Scriptures would lose all point if it was necessity, and not free will, that determined good or evil acts. Questions of Bible interpretation dominate both Erasmus' book and Luther's much longer reply, *De Servo Arbitrio*.

Philosophically, Erasmus is unsubtle. He refers to, but does not improve upon, Valla's dialogue on free will. He repeats commonplaces of centuries of scholastic debate which are inadequate responses to the problem of reconciling divine foreknowledge with human freedom—he insists, for instance, that even humans know many things that will happen in the future, such as eclipses of the sun. A theory of free will that leaves us no freer than the stars in their courses is not a very robust answer to Luther. But Erasmus is anxious to avoid philosophical complications. It is a piece of irreligious curiosity to inquire, as the scholastics did, whether God's foreknowledge is contingent or necessary.

Luther, though no friend to the scholastics, finds this outrageous. 'If this is irreligious, curious, and superfluous,' he asks, 'what, then, is religious, serious and useful knowledge?' God, Luther maintains, foresees nothing contingently. 'He foresees, purposes, and does all things according to His immutable, eternal, and infallible will. This thunderbolt throws free will flat and utterly dashes it to pieces' (WA VII.615).

Luther endorses the opinion that the Council of Constance ascribed to Wyclif: that everything happens of necessity. He distinguishes, however, between two senses of 'necessity'. The human will is subject to 'necessity of immutability': it has no power to change itself from its innate desire for evil. But it is not subject to another form of necessity, namely compulsion: a human being lacking grace does evil spontaneously and willingly. The human will is like a beast of burden: if God rides it, it wills and goes where God wills; if Satan rides it, it goes where Satan wills. It has no freedom to choose its rider.

Luther prefers to abandon altogether the term 'free will'; other writers, before and after, have regarded the spontaneity that he accepts as being the only thing that can genuinely be meant by the term.[2] Luther's principal concern was to deny free will in matters that make the difference between salvation and damnation. In other cases he seems to allow the possibility of genuine choice between alternative courses of action. Humans have free will in respect not of what is above them, but in respect of what is below them. The sinner, for instance, can make his choice between a variety of sins (WA VII.638).

The Bible, as Erasmus had copiously shown, contains many passages that imply that human choices are free, and also many passages that proclaim that the fate of humans is determined by God. Over the centuries, scholastic theologians had sought to reconcile these contradictory messages by making careful distinctions. 'Much toil and labour has been devoted to excusing the goodness of God,' Luther says, 'and to accusing the will of man. Here those distinctions have been invented between the ordinary will of God and the absolute will of God, between the necessity of consequence and the necessity of the consequent, and many others. But nothing has been achieved by these means beyond imposing upon the unlearned.' We should not waste time, Luther believes, in trying to resolve the contradiction

---

[2] See vol. I, p. 197, on the distinction between liberty of spontaneity and liberty of indifference.

between different Bible texts: we should go to extremes, deny free will altogether, and ascribe everything to God.

Distaste for scholastic subtlety was not peculiar to Luther: it was shared by Erasmus, and also by More. More himself entered the debate on free will in his controversy with Luther's English admirer, the Bible translator William Tyndale. To counter Lutheran determinism More uses a strategy which goes back to discussions of fate in Stoic philosophy:

One of their sect was served in a good turn in Almayne, which when he had robbed a man and was brought before the judges, he would not deny the deed, but said it was his destiny to do it, and therefore they might not blame him; they answered him, after his own doctrines, that if it were his destiny to steal and that therefore they must hold him excused, then it was also their destiny to hang him, and therefore he must as well hold them excused again. (More 1931: 196)

The claim that if determinism is true everything is excusable would no doubt be rejected by Luther, since he believed that God justly punished sinners who could not do otherwise than sin.

From a philosophical point of view these early Reformation debates on freedom and determinism do no more than rehearse arguments which were commonplaces of ancient and medieval philosophy. They illustrate, however, the negative side of humanist education. Scholastic debates, if sometimes arid, had commonly been sober and courteous. Thomas Aquinas, for instance, was always anxious to put the best possible interpretation on the theses of those he disagreed with. Erasmus shared something of Aquinas' eirenic spirit; but More and Luther attack each other with bitter vituperation made only the more vulgar by the elegant Latin in which it is phrased. The pugnacious conventions of humanist debate were a factor which led to the hardening of positions on either side of the Reformation divide.

Authority and Conscience

The debate on free will continued and ramified through and beyond the sixteenth century, and, as we shall see in later chapters, more sophisticated controversialists were to bring new subtlety into the philosophical treatment of the topic. For the present the most important new element introduced into the debate by Luther was a general hostility not just to scholasticism but to philosophy itself. He denounced Aristotle, and in particular his *Ethics*, as 'the vilest enemy of grace'. His contempt for the powers of unaided reason was the outcome of his belief that in Adam's Fall human nature had become totally corrupt and impotent.

In one way, Luther's scepticism about philosophical speculation was a continuation of a tendency already strong in late medieval scholasticism. Since the time of Scotus philosophers had become ever more reluctant to claim that reason alone could establish the nature of the divine attributes, the content of divine commands, or the immortality of the human soul.[3] The counterweight to their increasing philosophical scepticism had been their acceptance of the authority of the Church, expressed in Christian tradition and the pronouncements of popes and councils. This attitude found expression at the beginning of Erasmus' treatise: 'So great is my dislike of assertions that I prefer the views of the sceptics wherever the inviolable authority of the Scriptures and the decision of the Church permit' (*E*, 6).

The Lutheran Reformation, by taking away this counterweight, gave new impetus to the sceptical trend. To be sure, the Bible was retained and indeed emphasized as a decisive authority: with respect to the teaching of the Scriptures, Luther insisted, the Christian had no liberty to be a sceptic (WA VII.604). But the content of the Bible was no longer to be subjected to professional scrutiny by philosophically trained theologians. Every Christian, Luther said, had the power of discerning and judging what was right or wrong in matters of faith. Tyndale boasted that his translation would make a boy driving the plough understand the Bible better than the most learned divine. Pessimism about the moral capacity of the trained intellect unaided by grace went hand in hand with optimism about the intellectual ability of the untrained mind illumined by faith. Squeezed between the two, philosophy found its role greatly diminished among devout Protestants.

The problem for Luther was that individual consciences, unconstrained by universal authority, and unwilling to submit faith to rational arbitrament, began to produce a great diversity of beliefs. French and Swiss reformers, such as Jean Calvin and Ulrich Zwingli, agreed with Luther in rejecting papal authority but differed from him in their understanding of

---

[3] See vol II, pp. 247, 274.

the presence of Christ in the Eucharist and of the decrees through which God chose the elect. Calvin, like Luther, placed the ultimate criterion of religious truth within the individual soul: every faithful Christian experienced within himself a marvellous conviction of heavenly revelation which was more reassuring than any reasoning could ever be. But how could one tell who were faithful Christians? If one counted only the reformed, then Calvin's criterion was question-begging; on the other hand, if one counted all those who had been baptized, it led to an anarchy of belief.

Protestants argued that the Church could not be the ultimate authority because its claims rested on biblical texts. Catholics, quoting Augustine, claimed that the only reason for accepting the Bible was that it had been given us by the Church. The questions at issue in Europe at the Reformation were in the end settled neither by rational argument nor by interior enlightenment. In country after country conflicting answers were imposed by force of arms or by penal legislation. In England Henry VIII, irked by Vatican refusal to free him from a tedious marriage, broke with Rome and executed More for his loyalty to the pope. The country then lurched from his schismatic version of Catholicism to Calvinism under his son Edward VI, to Counter-Reformation Catholicism under his daughter Mary, and finally to an Anglican compromise under her sister Elizabeth. This chequered history produced hundreds of martyrs, both Protestant and Catholic; but England was spared the sanguinary wars of religion which raged for many decades in continental Europe.

By the mid-sixteenth century doctrinal positions had hardened into a form that they were to retain for some 400 years. Luther's lieutenant Melancthon formulated at Augsburg in 1530 a confession of faith to provide the test of orthodoxy. A concordat agreed in the same city in 1555 provided that the ruler of each state within the Holy Roman Empire could decide whether his subjects were to be Lutheran or Catholic, the principle later known as *cuius regio, eius religio*. Calvin's *Institutes of the Christian Religion* (1536) provided the standard for Protestants in Switzerland, France, and later Scotland. In Rome Pope Paul III (1534–9) promoted a Counter-Reformation, instituting a new religious order of Jesuits, and convening a Council at Trent to reform Church discipline. The council condemned the Lutheran doctrine of justification by faith alone, and the Calvinist doctrine that God predestined the wicked to hell prior to any sin. Free will, it insisted, had not been extinguished by Adam's Fall. It reaffirmed the

The Council of Trent in its final session, as represented in a contemporary Spanish engraving

doctrine of transubstantiation and the traditional seven sacraments. By the time the council had finished its work, in 1563, Luther was dead and Calvin was dying.

The division of Christendom was an unnecessary tragedy. The theological issues which separated Luther and Calvin from their Catholic opponents had been debated many times in the Middle Ages without leading to sectarian warfare; and few twenty-first-century Catholics and Protestants, if not professionally trained in theology, are aware of the real nature of the differences between the contrasting theories of the Eucharist, of grace, and of predestination which in the sixteenth century led to anathema and bloodshed. Questions of authority, of course, are easier to understand and more difficult to arbitrate than questions of doctrine. But the unity of Christendom could have been maintained under a constitutional papacy subject to general councils, such as Ockham had suggested, such as had been the practice in the fifteenth century, and such as even Thomas More, for the greater part of his life, believed to be the divine design for the Church.

The Decline of Logic

The combined effects of the Renaissance and the Reformation made the sixteenth century a barren one in most areas of philosophy. Logic was perhaps the branch of philosophy that suffered most severely. Logic did continue to be taught in the universities, but humanist scholars were impatient of it, regarding its terminology as barbarous and its complexities as pettifogging. Rabelais spoke for them when in *Pantagruel* (1532) he mocked logicians for inquiring whether a chimera bombinating in a vacuum could devour second intentions. Most of the advances in the subject that had been made by Stoic and medieval logicians were lost for four centuries. Instead, a bowdlerized version of Aristotle was taught at an elementary level in popular textbooks.

In the mid-century these began to be published in vernacular languages. The first in English was Thomas Wilson's *The Rule of Reason*, dedicated to Edward VI in 1551: he was the first to use the English words that are now the common terms of logic, such as 'proposition'. Others rejected such Latinisms and did their best to invent a solid Anglo-Saxon terminology. Ralphe Lever thought that logic should be called 'Witcraft'; and when he wanted to explain in his textbook that a contradictory proposition con sisted of two propositions, one affirmative and one negative, with similar subject, predicate and verb, he produced the following: 'Gaynsaying shew-sayes are two shewsayes, the one a yeasaye and the other a naysaye, changing neither foreset, backset nor verbe.'[4]

These English logic texts left little mark. Matters were different in France: Peter Ramus (Pierre de la Ramée, 1515–72) achieved lasting fame

---

[4] W. and M. Kneale, *The Development of Logic* (1979), p. 299.

quite out of proportion to his actual merits as a logician. Legend has it that for his master's degree he defended the thesis that everything Aristotle had ever taught was false. Certainly he went on to publish a short anti-Aristotelian treatise, and after his appointment as professor at the Collège Royale he followed this up with twenty books of Animadversions on Aristotle. His *Dialectic*, which was published in French in 1555, in Latin in 1556, and in English in 1574, was meant to supersede all previous logic texts. For the first time, he maintained, it set out the laws which governed people's natural thinking.

Logic, he tells us, is the art which teaches how to dispute well. It is divided into two parts: invention and judgement, to each of which a book of his text is devoted. Treating of 'invention', he lists nine places or topics to which one may look to find arguments to support a conclusion one wishes to defend. They are cause, effect, subject, adjunct, opposite, comparative, name, division, and definition. He illustrates each of these topics with copious quotations from classical authors, which take up nearly half of his short first book. For instance, Ramus defines 'adjunct' as 'that which has a subject to which it is adjoined, as virtue and vice are called the adjuncts of the body or soul; and to be short all things that do chance to the subject, beside the essence, is called the adjunct'. He then illustrates this with a long quotation from a speech of Cicero's, beginning:

Doth not his very head and over brow altogether shaven and scraped so clean signify that he is malicious and savoureth of knavery? Do they not utter and cry that he is a crafty fox? (*L*, 33)

Despite his official contempt for Aristotle, most of the topics for argument that he lists are taken from various places in the Aristotelian corpus and defined in similar ways. The only novelty is the discussion, at the end of the book, of what he calls 'inartificial' arguments, examples of which are the pronouncements of divine oracles and human testimony in a court of law.

The second book comes closer to the traditional subject matter of logic. Once again Ramus draws heavily on Aristotle in his classification of different kinds of statement and his analysis of syllogisms of different forms. His main innovation is that he devotes much more attention than Aristotle did to arguments containing proper names, such as 'Caesar oppresseth his native country; Tullius oppresseth not his native country; Tullius therefore is not Caesar' (*L*, 37).

Modern historians of logic can find little merit or originality in Ramus' work, but for long after his death debates raged between Aristotelians and Ramists, and there were even groups of semi-Ramists campaigning for compromise. Ramus became a Calvinist in 1561 and was killed in the massacre of Protestants on St Bartholomew's Day in 1572. His status as a martyr gave his writings a prestige they could never have earned in their own right, and his influence lasted through the centuries. John Milton, for instance, published a volume of Ramist Logic five years after the completion of *Paradise Lost*. The popularity of Ramist works impoverished logic for a long period. No further progress was made in formalizing the logic of modality and counterfactuality that had fascinated medieval logicians, and much of their own work passed into oblivion.

Scepticism, Sacred and Profane

It was not only Catholics who killed heretics. In 1553 Michael Servetus, a Spanish physician who had discovered the pulmonary circulation of the blood, was burnt in Calvin's Geneva for denying the Trinity and the divinity of Jesus. A French classicist teaching at Basel, named Sebastian Castellio, was shocked at the execution of Servetus and wrote a treatise *Whether Heretics are to be Persecuted* (Magdeburg, 1554) in which he pleaded in favour of toleration. His arguments are mainly quotations of authoritative texts or appeals to the example of Christ. 'O Christ, when thou didst live upon earth, none was more gentle, more merciful, more patient of wrong ... Art thou now so changed? ... If thou, O Christ, hast commanded these executions and tortures, what hast thou left for the devil to do?'[5] But in a later work, *The Art of Doubting*, Castellio developed more epistemological arguments. The difficulty of interpreting Scripture, and the variety of opinions among Christian sects, should make us very cautious in laying down the law on religious matters. To be sure, there are some truths that are beyond doubt, such as the existence and goodness of God; but on other religious topics no one can be sufficiently certain so as to be justified in killing another man as a heretic. Castellio, in his time, was a lone voice; but later supporters of toleration looked back to him as a forerunner.

---

[5] Quoted by O. Chadwick, *The Reformation* (Harmondsworth: Penguin, 1964), p. 402.

Some contemporaries who regarded Castellio as excessively sceptical about religion began to feel the attractions of scepticism in non-religious areas. This was greatly reinforced when, in mid-century, the works of the ancient Greek sceptic, Sextus Empiricus, were rediscovered after total oblivion in the medieval period. Sextus' sceptical arguments were made popular by the French nobleman Michel Eyquem de Montaigne (1533–92) in an essay which is nominally a commentary on a century-old work of natural theology translated by him at the request of his father. The *Apology for Raimond Sebond* (1569), written in clear and witty French prose, became the classic modern statement of scepticism.[6]

The *Apology* contains much more than a rehearsal of ancient sceptical arguments. Prior to presenting them, Montaigne works hard to induce in his reader a proper degree of intellectual humility. Human beings are inclined to regard themselves as being at the summit of creation; but are men really superior to the other animals who share the earth with them? 'When I play with my cat,' Montaigne asks, 'who knows whether she is passing her time with me no less than I am passing my time with her?' (ME, 2, 119).

Animals of different kinds have individual senses sharper than ours; they can acquire by swift intuition information that humans have to work out laboriously. They have the same needs and emotions as we have, and they display, often to a more remarkable extent, the same traits and virtues that humans take pride in. Montaigne piles up stories of faithful and magnanimous dogs and grateful and gentle lions, to contrast with the cruelty and treachery of human beings. Most of his examples of beasts' ingenuity are drawn from Greek and Latin texts, such as the legendary logical dog, who while following a scent reaches a crossroads, and sniffs out two of the routes, and on drawing a blank charges immediately down the third route without further sniffing. But Montaigne also draws on his own experience, for instance of guide-dogs leading the blind, and some of his examples of animal tool-usage would not look out of place in papers discussed at present-day associations for the advancement of science.

Montaigne was particularly impressed by the skills of migratory birds and fishes:

---

[6] Montaigne's sceptical arguments will be considered in Ch. 4 below. See vol. I, p. 175.

The swallows which we see exploring all the nooks of our houses when spring returns: do they search without judgement, and choose without discretion, that one of a thousand places which is the most commodious for their residence? In the course of building their wonderful and beautiful nests they choose square shapes rather than round, obtuse angles rather than right angles: can they do that without knowing the appropriate conditions and effects? (ME, 2, 121)

Tuna fish, Montaigne assures us, not only compete with humans in geometry and arithmetic, but are actually superior to them in astronomy. They swim in battalions formed into a perfect cube, and at the winter solstice they stop dead where they are and do not move again until the spring equinox (ME, 146).

Montaigne believes that the skilful performances of animals prove that the same thoughts go through their heads as through ours. A fox will cock his ear to listen in order to find the safest way over a frozen river. 'Surely we have therefore reason to judge that there passes through his head the same discourse as would run through ours, reasoning from sensation to conclusion: what makes a noise, moves; what moves, is not frozen; what is not frozen is liquid; what is liquid gives way' (ME, 127).

The two spheres in which above all humans plume themselves on their unique gifts are religion and philosophy. Montaigne makes a gallant attempt to prove that we are not alone in our capacity for worship by describing the funeral rites of ants and the sun-worship liturgy of elephants. He is more persuasive when he shows that humans can take little pride in their theological beliefs and activities, given the variety of contradictory doctrines on offer, and given the often debasing nature of religious practices. As for philosophy, he has no difficulty at all in showing that there has never been a philosopher whose system has been able to withstand the criticism of other philosophers. Like many another after him, he presses into service a dictum of Cicero: 'It is impossible to say anything so absurd that it has not been said already by some philosopher or other' (ME, 211).

Montaigne's deflation of human nature in *Raimond Sebond* is the antithesis of the glorification of mankind in Pico della Mirandola's 1486 *On the Dignity of Man*.[7] The optimism generated by the rediscovery of classical texts and the exuberance of the visual arts in Renaissance Florence gave way to the

---

[7] See vol. II, p. 109.

pessimism natural in a Counter-Reformation France torn by sectarian warfare. Montaigne contrasted the educated and civilized citizens of European states, to their disadvantage, with the simplicity and nobility of the inhabitants of the recently discovered New World.

However, Montaigne's emphasis on the limits of the human intellect does not prevent him from claiming to be quite certain of the truth of Catholic Christianity. On the contrary, he can claim that in his scepticism about philosophy he is following in the footsteps of St Paul in First Corinthians: 'Hath not God made foolish the wisdom of this world? For after that in the wisdom of God the world by wisdom knew not God, it pleased God by the foolishness of preaching to save them that believe.' Pauline texts such as these were painted on the beams of Montaigne's study along with quotations from Sextus such as 'all that is certain is that nothing is certain'.

To reconcile his scepticism with his orthodoxy, Montaigne emphasizes that what he has been attacking are the pretensions of the human intellect to achieve truth by its own efforts. But faith is not an achievement, it is a free gift of God:

It is not by reasoning or understanding that we have received our religion, it is by authority and command from above. The weakness of our judgement is more help than its strength, and our blindness is more help than our clear sight. It is through ignorance, not through knowledge that we become wise with divine wisdom. (ME, 166)

Counter-Reformation Philosophy

Montaigne's exaltation of revelation to the exclusion of reason—'fideism' as it came to be called—was not typical of the Counter-Reformation. In reaction against Luther's insistence that the human intellect and will had been totally corrupted by the sin of Adam, Catholic controversialists tended to emphasize that basic religious truths were within the scope of unaided human intellect, and that faith itself needed the support and defence of reason.

In the forefront of this optimistic thrust of the Counter-Reformation were the Jesuits, the members of the new Society of Jesus. This order was founded by the Spanish ex-soldier Ignatius Loyola and was approved by

The ceiling of the church of S. Ignazio in Rome, painted by Andrea Pozzo, depicts the glorification of the founder of the Society of Jesus

Pope Paul III in 1540. In addition to the vows of poverty, chastity, and obedience taken by all members of religious orders, the Jesuits took a further vow of unquestioning loyalty to the papacy. Its members soon distinguished themselves in educational and missionary work in many parts of the world. In Europe they were happy to risk martyrdom in the Counter-Reformation cause; in America, India, and China they showed more sympathy with indigenous religions than many other Christian proselytizers, Catholic or Protestant. In philosophy and theology in the universities they were soon able to compete with the long-established religious orders such as the Franciscans and Dominicans. They promoted a new and, as they saw it, improved version of scholasticism.

Whereas medieval scholastics had based their university lectures upon canonical texts such as the works of Aristotle and the Sentences of Peter Lombard,[8] Jesuits in universities began to replace commentaries with self-standing courses in philosophy and theology. By the early seventeenth century this pattern was adopted by Dominicans and Franciscans, and this led to a sharper distinction between philosophy and theology than had been common earlier. The pioneer of this movement to reform philosophy into independent textbook form was the Spanish Jesuit Francisco Suarez, whose *Disputationes Metaphysicae* (1597) were the first such systematic treatment of scholastic metaphysics.

Born in Granada in 1548, Suarez joined the Society of Jesus in 1564 and spent the whole of his professional life as a university professor, lecturing at six different universities in Spain and in the Jesuit college in Rome. He was a devout and erudite man, and in terms of sheer intellectual power he has a strong claim to be the most formidable philosopher of the sixteenth century. In the history of philosophy, however, he does not have a place commensurate to his gifts, for two reasons. First, most of his work is a restatement and refinement of medieval themes, rather than an exploration of new territory. Second, as a writer he was not only prolific, leaving behind a corpus that fills twenty-eight volumes, but also prolix and tedious. In so far as he had an influence on subsequent philosophy, it was through the writings of lesser but more readable imitators.

The two areas in which he was, indeed, influential were metaphysics and political philosophy. He had a great reverence for St Thomas Aquinas, but

[8] See vol. II, p. 56.

as a metaphysician he followed in the footsteps of Avicenna and Duns Scotus rather than those of Aquinas himself. Paradoxically, much that was to pass for Thomism during the seventeenth, eighteenth, and nineteenth centuries was closer to Suarezian metaphysics than to the *Summa Contra Gentiles*. In political philosophy Suarez's contribution was the *De Legibus* of 1621, which was the unacknowledged source of many of the ideas of better-known thinkers. In his own day he was most famous for his controversy with King James I about the divine right of kings, in which he attacked the theory that temporal monarchs derived their sovereignty directly from God. King James had his book publicly burnt.[9]

Of the philosophical issues dividing the Catholic and Protestant camps in the sixteenth century none was more thorny than human free will, which had been proclaimed at the Council of Trent in opposition to Lutheran determinism and Calvinist predestinarianism. The Jesuits made themselves champions of the libertarian account of human freedom. Suarez and his Jesuit colleague Luis de Molina offered a definition of free agency in terms of the availability of alternative courses of action—'liberty of indifference' as it came to be known. 'That agent is called free which in the presence of all necessary conditions for action can act and refrain from action or can do one thing while being able to do its opposite.'

Such a definition did ample justice to humans' consciousness of their own choices and their attribution of responsibility to others. But by comparison with more restrictive accounts of freedom, it made it very difficult to account for God's foreknowledge of free human actions, to which both Catholics and Protestants were committed. Molina, in his famous *Concordia* (1589), presented an elaborate solution to the problem, in terms of God's comprehensive knowledge of the actions of every possible human being in every possible world.[10] Ingenious though it was, Molina's solution was unpopular not only among Protestants but also among his Catholic co-religionists.

Dominican theologians, of whom the most vociferous was the Thomist Domingo Banez (1528–1604), thought that the Jesuit theologians were excessively exalting human freedom and derogating from divine power. The dispute between the two religious orders became so bitter that in 1605

[9] Suarez's metaphysics is discussed at greater length in Ch. 6 and his political theory in Ch. 9.
[10] Molina's theory of 'middle knowledge' is reported in detail in Ch. 10.

Pope Clement VIII, without resolving the question at issue, imposed silence on both sides. Ironically, within the reformed camp, a Leiden divine named Arminius propounded views which were similar to, if less sophisticated than, those of Molina. The Synod of Dort in 1619 declared them incompatible with Calvinist orthodoxy.

Giordano Bruno

The most colourful philosopher of the latter part of the sixteenth century operated far outside the bounds of orthodoxy, whether Catholic or Protestant. Giordano Bruno (1548–1600) was born near Naples and became a Dominican there in 1565. By 1576 he was already suspected of heresy and expelled from the order. He fled northwards to Geneva, but there became equally unpopular with the Calvinists. He had better success in France, studying and lecturing in Toulouse and Paris and enjoying, for a time, the favour of King Henri III.

Bruno's first major work, *On the Shadows of Ideas,* combined an elaborate Neoplatonic metaphysical system with practical advice on the art of memory. There is a hierarchy of ideas with human ideas at the lowest level and at the topmost level the divine Ideas forming a unity in God's mind. These are, in themselves, impenetrable to us; but they are expressed in Nature, which is the universal effect of God. Images of the celestial world are closer to God than images of our sublunar world; hence, if we wish to organize our knowledge in such a way that we can recall it systematically we should mentally dispose our thoughts within the pattern of the signs of the zodiac.

In 1583 Bruno moved to England and visited Oxford, where he gave some lectures. His stay there was not a success. He was not to be the last continental philosopher to visit the university and find himself treated as a charlatan, and in his turn to regard his philosophical hosts as more interested in words than in ideas. He expressed his disdain for Oxford pedantry, along with ideas of more universal philosophical concern, in a series of dialogues in 1584 beginning with *Supper on Ash Wednesday (La cena de le ceneri)*. He seems to have written these while acting as a double agent in London for both the French and the English secret services.

Bruno's dialogues are not easy reading. They are peopled by beings of grand but mysterious status, like Wagner's gods and Tolkien's creatures, with powers of uncertain limits and motives of slender intelligibility. Although bearing the names of classical deities, they operate at some distance from Homer and Vergil. The Latin Mercury, for instance, corresponds not only to the Greek Hermes, but to the Egyptian god Thoth: he represents often the teachings of the fashionable Hermetic cult. This was based on recently discovered documents believed to go back to the Egypt of Moses' time. Hermetism, in Bruno's view, was superior to Christianity and was destined to supersede it.

In the system propounded in the dialogues, the phenomena we observe are the effects of a world-soul which animates nature and makes it into a single organism. The world of nature is infinite, with no edge, surface, or limit. But the world's infinity is not the same as God's infinity because the world has parts that are not infinite, whereas God is wholly in the whole world and wholly in each of its parts. This difference perhaps suffices to distinguish Bruno's position from pantheism, but the relation between God and the world remains obscure. It is not really clarified by Bruno's august formulation that God is the Nature making Nature *(natura naturans)* while the universe is the Nature made by Nature *(natura naturata)*.

Two features of Bruno's system have caught the attention of historians and scientists: his adoption of the Copernican hypothesis, and his postulation of multiple universes. Bruno accepted that it was the earth that went round the sun, and not the sun that went round the earth. He went on to develop Copernicus' ideas in a bold and dramatic manner. The earth was not the centre of the universe: but neither was the sun. Our sun is just one star among others, and in boundless space there are many solar systems. No sun or star can be called the centre of the universe, because all positions are relative.

Our earth and our solar system enjoy no unique privilege. For all we know, there may be intelligent life at other times and places within the universe. Particular solar systems come and go, temporary phases in the life of the single infinite organism whose soul is the world-soul. Within the universe each intelligent being is a conscious, immortal atom, mirroring in itself the whole of creation. If in his interfusing of God and Nature Bruno anticipated Spinoza, in his account of rational atoms he anticipated Leibniz.

Bruno's championship of Hermetism and his theory of multiple universes challenged the orthodox teaching that God was incarnate uniquely in Jesus and that Christianity was the definitive divine revelation. Nonetheless,

21

The discovery of the moons that revolved around Jupiter in its planetary orbit had already disposed of one of the strongest arguments urged against heliocentrism, namely that the moon would only be able to orbit the earth if the earth itself was stationary.

Galileo was initially cautious in publicly expressing the conclusions he drew from his astronomical discoveries. However, after an ecclesiastical commission in Rome had taken official notice of his major observations, he began to propagate heliocentric ideas to a wide circle of friends, and in 1613, in an appendix to a book on sunspots, he declared his adherence to Copernicus. A Dominican friar in Florence, in a sermon on Acts 1: 11 ('Ye Galileans, why stand ye gazing up to heaven?') denounced heliocentrism as being in conflict with biblical texts, such as the one in which Joshua tells the sun to stand still so that the Israelites may complete their victory over the Philistines. Galileo decided to travel to Rome to clarify his theological status.

In advance he wrote to the powerful Jesuit cardinal, St Robert Bellarmine, urging that the sacred authors who spoke of the sun as moving were merely using popular idiom and were not intending to teach geometry. Bellarmine referred the matter to a committee of the Inquisition who determined that the opinion that the sun was the centre of the cosmos was heretical, and the opinion that the earth moved was at the least erroneous. On the instructions of Pope Paul V, Bellarmine instructed Galileo that he must not hold or defend either of these opinions. If there was a real proof of heliocentrism, he told one of Galileo's friends, then we would have to re-examine the biblical texts which appeared to contradict it; but as matters stood, Copernicus' theory was only an unproved hypothesis. And indeed, Galileo's own heliocentric system, though it fitted the phenomena better, was almost as complicated as the geocentric system of his opponents, demanding constant appeal to epicycles.[12] The evidence he had discovered did not justify the degree of certainty with which he maintained his thesis.

It is often said that in this exchange Bellarmine showed a sounder grasp of the philosophy of science than the age's greatest scientist and Galileo showed a sounder grasp of biblical exegesis than the age's most famous theologian. The paradox is an agreeable one, but it is not really a fair

---

[12] Galileo did not incorporate Kepler's discovery of the elliptical orbits of the planets, which was needed to achieve the appropriate simplification of heliocentrism.

representation of the debate on either side. And whatever the merits of the case, the upshot was that while Galileo's writings were not condemned, he was silenced for several years to come.

In 1624 Galileo travelled to Rome once more. Paul V and Bellarmine were now dead, and there was a different pope wearing the tiara: Urban VIII, who as Cardinal Barberini had shown himself an admirer of Galileo's astronomical discoveries. Galileo was given permission to write a systematic treatment of the Ptolemaic and the Copernican models, on condition that he presented them both impartially without favouring heliocentrism.

In 1632 Galileo published, with the approval of the papal censor, *Dialogue on the Two Chief World Systems*. In the book one character, Salviati, presents the Copernican system, and another, Simplicius, defends the traditional one. 'Simplicius' was an appropriate name for the defender of Aristotelianism, since it had been borne by the greatest of Aristotle's Greek commentators. However, it could also be interpreted as meaning 'simpleton' and the pope was furious when he found some of his own words placed in the mouth of Simplicius. He concluded that Galileo had presented the Copernican system in a more favourable light than its opponent, and had therefore deviated from the terms of his licence to publish. In 1633 Galileo was summoned to Rome, tried by the Inquisition, and under the threat of torture forced to abjure heliocentrism. He was condemned to life imprisonment, a sentence that he served out until his death in 1642, in confinement in the houses of distinguished friends and eventually in his own home at Bellosguardo outside Florence.

While under house arrest he was allowed to receive visitors. Among them was John Milton, who in *Areopagitica* recorded: 'I found and visited the famous Galileo grown old, a prisoner of the Inquisition, for thinking in Astronomy otherwise than the Franciscan and Dominican licensers thought.' The newly founded college at Harvard in the commonwealth of Massachusetts made an offer of a visiting professorship, which was politely declined. Even though going blind, Galileo continued to write, and incorporated the fruit of his lifetime's work in *Discourses and Mathematical Demonstrations Concerning Two New Sciences*. This was published in Leiden in 1638 and became the most widely influential of his works.

Galileo was treated more humanely than Bruno and many another prisoner of the Inquisition, but the evil effects of his condemnation were felt throughout Europe. Scientific investigation in Italy went into decline:

'nothing has been there written now these many years,' Milton could complain, 'but flattery and fustian.' Even in Protestant Holland, Descartes was for many years deterred by Galileo's fate from publishing his own scientific cosmology. When in 1992 Pope John Paul II publicly acknowledged the injustice the Church had done to Galileo, the apology came 350 years too late.

Bacon

An English contemporary of Galileo, Francis Bacon, shared his antipathy to Aristotle, but was more interested in the theory than in the practice of scientific method. Born in London in 1561, Bacon was educated at Trinity College, Cambridge, and studied law at Gray's Inn. He entered Parliament in 1584 and later became a client of Queen Elizabeth's favourite, the Earl of Essex. When, in 1598, Essex plotted an insurrection, Bacon took a leading part in his prosecution for treason. On the accession of James I he became solicitor-general and was knighted. In 1606 he published the first of his major philosophical writings, *The Advancement of Learning*, a systematic classification of scientific disciplines.

The climax of Bacon's career was his appointment in 1618 as Lord Chancellor with the title Lord Verulam. He planned a massive work, the *Instauratio Magna (The Great Instauration)*, which was to take all knowledge for its province. Only two parts of this were completed: the first was a revision of *The Advancement of Learning*, and the second was the *Novum Organum* which was his principal work on scientific method. In 1621, in the course of a parliamentary inquiry, he pleaded guilty to charges of accepting bribes, and was disgraced and briefly imprisoned. He wrote other scientific and historical works and also the essays for which he is nowadays best remembered. He died at Highgate in 1626. Legend represents him as a martyr to science, offering his life in the cause of experimental refrigeration; for he died, it is said, from a chill caught stuffing a hen with snow to see whether the cold would preserve the meat.

'The parts of human learning', Bacon says in Book Two of *The Advancement*, 'have reference to the three parts of Man's Understanding, which is the seat of learning: History to his Memory, Poesy to his Imagination, and Philosophy to his reason' (*AL*, 177). Poesy, which includes not only poetry

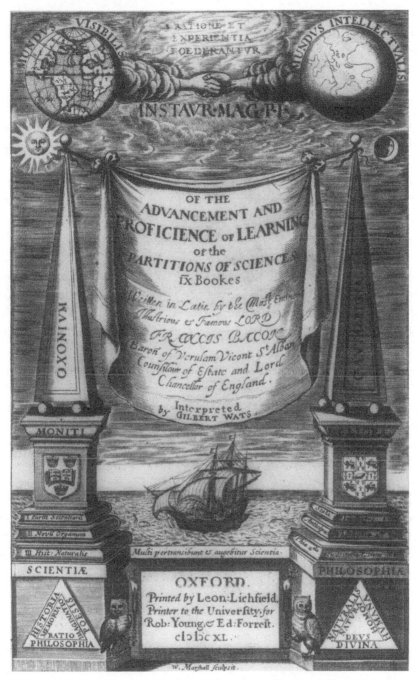

The title page of the Oxford edition of Bacon's *Advancement of Learning* (1640)

but prose fiction, is treated only perfunctorily by Bacon: the kind of poesy he most admires is a story with a moral message, like Aesop's fables. But history and philosophy are addressed at length, and given further subdivisions.

The most important parts of history are Natural and Civil. 'Civil history' is what we would nowadays call history: Bacon himself contributed to it a narrative of the reign of Henry VII. 'Natural history' is a discipline of broad scope with three subdivisions: the history of 'nature in course, of nature erring or varying, and of nature altered or wrought'. It will include, then, treatises of natural science, records of extraordinary marvels, and manuals of technology. Bacon's own contribution to natural history consisted of two compilations of research material, a History of the Winds, and a History of Life and Death. The 'history of nature erring', he thought, should include records of superstitious narrations of sorceries and witchcrafts, in order to ascertain how far effects attributed to superstition could be attributed to natural causes. But the third subdivision, 'history mechanical', was the most fundamental and useful for natural philosophy, whose value, according to Bacon, was above all in its practical application and utility.

In his classification of philosophy, Bacon first puts on one side 'divine philosophy' or natural theology: it suffices, he tells us, to refute atheism but not to inform religion. He then divides philosophy into natural and human. Natural philosophy may be speculative or operative: the speculative kind includes both physics and metaphysics, and the operative kind includes both mechanics and magic. Mechanics is the practical application of physics, and magic is the practical application of metaphysics.

This brisk and provocative anatomy of philosophy is not as neat as it seems, and many of the names Bacon gives to the various disciplines are employed in idiosyncratic ways. His 'natural magic', he tells us, must be sharply distinguished from the 'credulous and superstitious conceits' of alchemy and astrology. It is not at all clear what he has in mind: the one thing he seems to offer as an example is the mariner's compass. Why, we may ask, is this a matter of 'magic' rather than 'mechanics'?

An answer suggests itself when we read that physics deals with the efficient and material causes of things, while metaphysics deals with the final and formal causes. So the sail, which gives the boat its motion, operates in the realm of physics, while the compass, which guides the boat's direction, operates in the realm of metaphysics. Bacon admits candidly that he is using 'metaphysics' in a novel way. What others call metaphysics he calls 'first philosophy' or 'summary philosophy': it is a receptacle, he tells us, for all the universal principles that are not exclusive to particular disciplines. (An example is 'If equals be added to unequals the result will be unequal,' an axiom which he believes applies in law as well as in mathematics.)

But the distinction made between physics and metaphysics on the basis of the Aristotelian four causes is itself misleading. Bacon's scheme for natural magic leaves no real room for teleology: 'inquiry into final causes', he tells us, 'is sterile, and like a virgin consecrated to God, produces nothing.' And when he speaks of 'forms' he is not thinking of Aristotle's substantial forms—such as the form of a lion, or of water—because these, he believes, are too varied and complicated to be discovered. Instead of studying these, we should look rather for the simpler forms which go into their composition, in the way that letters go to make up words. The task of metaphysics is to investigate the simpler forms which correspond to individual letters:

To enquire the forms of sense, of voluntary motion, of vegetation, of colours, of gravity and levity, of density, of tenuity, of heat and of cold, and all other natures and qualities, which like an alphabet are not many, and which the essences (upheld by matter) of all creatures do now consist. (AL, 196)

Bacon's elementary forms are obscure characters in comparison with the mathematical shapes and symbols which Galileo declared to be the alphabet in which the book of the world is written. But most probably when he talked of forms he had in mind hidden material structures underlying the overt appearance and behaviour of things.

So much for natural philosophy. Human philosophy, the other great branch of the subject, has two parts, Bacon tells us, one which considers 'man segregate' and another which considers 'man congregate'. The first part corresponds to anatomy, physiology, and psychology, and the second embraces what would nowadays be called the social sciences. The detailed subdivisions Bacon enumerates appear arbitrary and haphazard. The sciences of the body include medicine, 'cosmetic', 'athletic', and the 'Arts Voluptuary', which include practical joking. The study of the nature of the soul is a matter for theology, but there is a human science which studies the operations of the soul. These fall into two classes, one set belonging to the understanding or reason, whose function is judgement, and the other set belonging to the will or appetite, whose function is action or execution. What of the imagination, which had a privileged place in Bacon's initial classification of human faculties?

The Imagination is an agent or *nuncius* in both provinces, both the judicial and the ministerial. For sense sendeth over to Imagination before Reason have judged: and Reason sendeth over to Imagination before the Decree can be acted; for Imagination ever precedeth Voluntary Motion: saving that this Janus of Imagination hath differing faces; for the face towards Reason hath the print of Truth, but the face towards Action hath the print of Good. (*AL*, 217)

But imagination is no mere servant of the other faculties, Bacon insists: it can triumph over reason, and that is what happens in the case of religious belief.

It is clear that Bacon envisioned the mind as a kind of internal society, with the different faculties enshrined in a constitution respecting the separation of powers. When he comes to treat of the social sciences themselves he offers another threefold division, corresponding to associations for friendship, for business, and for government. Political theory is a part of civil philosophy, that branch of human philosophy that concerns the benefits that humans derive from living in society.

Having finished his classification, Bacon can boast 'I have made as it were a small globe of the intellectual world' (*AL*, 299). The various sciences which appear in his voluminous catalogue are not all at similar stages of development. Some, he thinks, have achieved a degree of perfection, but others are deficient, and some are almost non-existent. One of the most deficient is logic, and the defects of logic weaken other sciences also. The problem is that logic lacks a theory of scientific discovery:

Like as the West-Indies had never been discovered if the use of the mariner's needle had not been first discovered, though the one be vast regions and the other a small motion; so it cannot be found strange if sciences be no further discovered if the art itself of invention and discovery hath been passed over. (*AL*, 219).

Bacon set out to remedy this lack and to provide a compass to guide scientific researchers. This was the task of his *Novum Organum*.

Bacon's project of introducing discipline into research had a negative and a positive component. The researcher's first, negative, task is to be on his guard against the factors that can introduce bias into his observations. Bacon lists four of these, and calls them 'idols' because they are fetishes which can divert us from the pursuit of truth: there are the idols of the tribe, the idols of the den, the idols of the marketplace, and the idols of the theatre. The idols of the tribe are temptations endemic in the whole human race, such as the tendency to judge things by superficial appearances, the tendency to go along with popular belief, and the tendency to interpret nature anthropomorphically. The idols of the den, or cave, are features of individual temperaments which hamper objectivity: some people, for instance, are too conservative, others too ready to seize on novelties. Each person has 'a certain individual cavern of his own, which breaks and distorts the light of nature'. The idols of the marketplace (or perhaps 'idols of the courts'—*idola fori*) are snares lurking in the language we use, which contains meaningless, ambiguous, and ill-defined words. Finally the idols of the theatre are false systems of philosophy which are no more than stage plays, whether 'sophistical', like Aristotle's, or 'empirical', like contemporary alchemists, or 'superstitious' like the Neoplatonists who confuse philosophy with theology.

The positive task of the researcher is *induction*, the discovery of scientific laws by the systematic examination of particular cases. If this is not to be rash generalization from inadequate sampling of nature, we need a carefully schematized procedure, showing us how to mount gradually from particular instances to axioms of gradually increasing generality. Bacon offers a series of detailed rules to guide this process:

Suppose that we have some phenomenon X and we wish to discover its true form or explanation. We must first make a table of presences—that is to say, we list the items A, B, C, D . . . which are present when X is present. Then we make a table of absences, listing items E, F, G, H . . . which are present when X is absent. Thirdly, we make a table of degrees, recording that J, K, L, M . . . are present to a greater degree when X is present to a greater degree, and present to a lesser degree when X is present to a lesser degree.

This is only the preparatory step in the method. The real work of induction comes when we start the process of eliminating candidates for being the form of X. To be successful a candidate must be present in every case occurring in the table of presences, and absent in every case occurring in the table of absences. Bacon illustrates his method with the example of heat. We list cases when heat is present (e.g. the rays of the sun and the sparks of a flint) and cases in which it is absent (e.g. in the rays of the moon and the stars). Since light is present in cases listed in the table of absence, we can eliminate light as being the form of heat. After some further eliminative moves, and making use also of the table of degrees (e.g. that the more exercise animals take the hotter they get), Bacon concludes that heat is a special kind of motion ('an expansive motion held in check and pushing its way through tiny particles').

Bacon never completed the series of guidelines that he set out to present in the *Novum Organum*, and it cannot be said that his system adds up to a 'logic of induction'. However, he did establish the important point that negative instances are more significant, in the process of establishing laws, than positive ones. Twentieth-century philosophers have been willing to give him credit for being the first person to point out that laws of nature cannot be conclusively verified, but can be conclusively falsified.

Bacon's insistence on the importance of precise and repeated observations went hand in hand with an appreciation that natural science could make progress only by a massive cooperative endeavour. In the *New Atlantis*, an unfinished fragment published posthumously, a ship's crew in the South Seas land on an island containing a remarkable institution known as Salomon's House. This turns out to be a research establishment, where scientists work together to embody Bacon's utilitarian ideal of science as the extension of men's power over nature for the betterment of the human race. Their projects include plans for telephones, submarines, and aeroplanes. The president of the institute described its purpose thus:

The End of our Foundation is the knowledge of Causes, and secret motions of things, and the enlarging of the bound of Human Empire, to the effecting of all things possible. (*B*, 480)

Salomon's House was a Utopian fantasy; but it was given a counterpart in the real world when, thirty-five years after the *New Atlantis*, Bacon's compatriots of the next generation founded the Royal Society of London.

2

Descartes to Berkeley

Descartes

The seventeenth century, unlike the sixteenth century, was fertile in the production of philosophers of genius. The man who is often considered the father of modern philosophy is René Descartes. He was born in 1596, about the time when Shakespeare was writing *Hamlet*, in a village in Touraine which is now called after him La-Haye-Descartes. A sickly child, he was exempted at school from morning exercises and acquired a lifelong habit of meditating in bed. From his eleventh to his nineteenth year he studied classics and philosophy at the Jesuit college of La Flèche. He remained a Catholic throughout his life, but chose to spend most of his adult life in Protestant Holland.

In 1616, having taken a degree in law at Poitiers, Descartes gave up his studies for a while. In the wars of religion that divided Europe, he enlisted in both camps. First, he was an unpaid volunteer in the army of the Protestant Prince of Orange; later he served in the army of the Catholic Duke Maximilian of Bavaria, who was then at war with the Palatine Elector Frederick, son-in-law of King James I of Britain. After he left the army he did not adopt a profession. Unlike the great philosophers of the Middle Ages he was a layman in both the ecclesiastical and the academic sense. He never lectured in a university, and he lived a private life as a gentleman of means. He wrote his most famous work not in the Latin of the learned world, but in good plain French, so that it could be understood, as he put it, 'even by women'.

While serving in the army, Descartes acquired a conviction that he had a call to philosophy. He spent a winter's day of 1619 huddled beside a stove, engrossed in meditation. He conceived the idea of undertaking, single-handed, a reform of human learning that would display all disciplines as branches of a single wonderful science. His conviction of vocation was reinforced when, that night, he had three dreams that he regarded as prophetic. But it was not until some years later that he settled permanently to philosophical studies.

From 1620 to 1625 he travelled in Germany, Holland, and Italy, and from 1625 to 1627 he mixed in society in Paris, gambling heavily and becoming involved in a duel over a love affair. His surviving early writings show his interest in mechanical and mathematical problems, and include a brief treatise on music. In 1627 he intervened impressively in the discussion of a grand public lecture in Paris: a cardinal who was present exhorted him to devote himself to the reform of philosophy.

A year later Descartes left for Holland, where he lived until 1649, shortly before his death. He chose the country for its climate and its reputation for tolerance: he looked forward to a life free from the distractions of the city and from morning callers. He dwelt in thirteen different houses during his twenty-year sojourn and kept his address secret from all but close friends. Amid Protestant surroundings, he continued to practise as a Catholic.

Descartes kept in touch with the learned world by letter. His principal correspondent was a Franciscan friar, Father Marin Mersenne, who was the centre of an erudite international network. Mersenne acted as Descartes' literary agent, handling the publication of his works and keeping him informed of recent scientific discoveries. Of the ten volumes of the standard edition of Descartes' works, five are taken up by his letters, which are a highly important source for the development of his thought.

In Holland Descartes lived comfortably and quietly; he was not wholly without company, and in 1635 he had an illegitimate daughter, Francine, who lived only five years. He brought a few books with him from Paris, including the *Summa Theologiae* of Thomas Aquinas. He claimed that he spent very little time reading: he had no great admiration for classical languages and he boasted that he had not opened a scholastic textbook once in twenty years. When a stranger asked to see his library, he pointed to a half-dissected calf. Besides purchasing carcasses from the butcher for dissection, he ground his own lenses in order to make experiments in optics. He trusted experiment rather than learning, but more than either he trusted his own philosophical reflection.

During his first years in Holland his work was mainly mathematical and physical. He laid the foundations of analytical geometry: the Cartesian coordinates that every schoolchild learns about derive their name from the Latin form of his surname, Cartesius. He studied refraction and propounded the law of sines, the result of careful theoretical and experimental work on the nature of light and of the eye. He also worked on meteorology, trying to ascertain the true nature of rainbows.

By 1632 Descartes had in mind to publish a substantial volume which would explain 'the nature of light, the sun and the fixed stars which emit it; the heavens which transmit it; the planets, the comets and the earth which reflect it; all the terrestrial bodies which are either coloured or transparent or luminous; and Man its spectator'. The system that it propounded was a heliocentric one: the earth was a planet, moving around the sun.

The treatise was entitled *The World* and it was ready for the press when Descartes learned that Galileo had been condemned for upholding the Copernican system. Anxious to avoid conflict with ecclesiastical authority, he returned the treatise to his desk. It was never published in his lifetime, although much of its material was incorporated twelve years later in a textbook called *Principles of Philosophy*.

Instead of publishing his system, in 1637 Descartes decided to make public 'some specimens of his method': his dioptrics, his geometry, and his meteorolgy. He prefaced them with 'a discourse on the right way to use one's reason and seek truth in the sciences'. The three scientific treatises are nowadays read only by specialists in the history of science, but the *Discourse on Method* has a claim to be the most popular of all philosophical classics. In significance it compares with Plato's *Republic* and with Kant's *Critique of Pure Reason*, but it has the advantage of being much briefer and more readable than either.

Among other things, the *Discourse* is a witty and urbane piece of autobiography, as the following extracts illustrate:

Good sense is the most fairly distributed thing in the world; for everyone thinks himself so well supplied with it, that even those who are hardest to satisfy in every other way do not usually desire more of it than they already have....

As soon as my age allowed me to pass from under the control of my instructors, I entirely abandoned the study of letters, and resolved not to seek after any science but what might be found within myself or in the great book of the world.... I spent nine years in roaming about the world, aiming to be a spectator rather than an actor in all the comedies of life.

Amidst a great and populous nation, extremely industrious and more concerned with their own business than curious about other people's, while I do not lack any conveniences of the most frequented cities, I have been able to live a life as solitary and retired as though I were in the most remote deserts. (AT VI. 2, 9, 31; *CSMK* I.111, 115, 126)

But the *Discourse* is much more than Descartes' intellectual autobiography: it presents in minature a summary of his philosophical system and his scientific method. Descartes had an extraordinary gift for presenting complicated philosophical doctrines so elegantly that they appear fully intelligible on first reading and yet can provide material for reflection to the most expert philosophers. He prided himself that his works could be read 'just like novels'.

There are two key ideas that are presented in the *Discourse* and elaborated in later works. First: human beings are thinking substances. Second: matter is extension in motion. Everything in his system is to be explained in terms of this dualism of mind and matter. If we nowadays tend naturally to think of mind and matter as the two great mutually exclusive and mutually exhaustive divisions of the universe we inhabit, that is because of Descartes.

Descartes reaches these conclusions by the application of a method of systematic doubt. To prevent being ensnared in falsehood, the philosopher must begin by doubting whatever can be doubted. The senses sometimes deceive us; mathematicians sometimes make mistakes; we can never be certain whether we are awake or asleep. Accordingly:

I decided to feign that everything that had entered my mind hitherto was no more true than the illusions of dreams. But immediately upon this I noticed that while I was trying to think everything false, it must needs be that I, who was thinking this, was something. And observing that this truth 'I am thinking, therefore I exist' was so solid and secure that the most extravagant suppositions of sceptics could not overthrow it, I judged that I need not scruple to accept it as the first principle of philosophy that I was seeking. (AT VI. 32; *CSMK* I.127)

This is the famous *Cogito, ergo sum*, which achieves the second task of the philosopher, that of preventing the systematic doubt from leading to scepticism. But from it Descartes goes on to derive the principles of his system. If I were not thinking, I would have no reason to believe that I existed; hence I am a substance whose whole essence is to think; being a body is no part of my essence. The same goes for every other human being. So Descartes' first main thesis is established.

What assures me that the *Cogito* is correct? Only that I see clearly that it is true. Whenever I conceive something clearly and distinctly, I am assured of its truth. But when we turn to material objects, we find that of all their properties the only ones we clearly and distinctly perceive are shape, size, and movement. So Descartes gains his second main thesis, that matter is extension in motion.

But what guarantees the principle that whatever I see clearly and distinctly is true? Only the truthful nature of the God to whom I owe my existence as a thinking thing. So establishing the existence of God is a necessary part of Descartes' system. He offers two proofs that there is a God. First, I have in myself the idea of a perfect being, and this idea cannot be caused in me by anything less than a being that is itself perfect. Second, to be perfect a being must include in itself all perfections; but existence is a perfection, and therefore a perfect being must exist.[1]

Like Bacon, Descartes compared knowledge to a tree, but for him the tree's roots were metaphysics, its trunk was physics, and its fruitful branches were the moral and useful sciences. His own writings, after the *Discourse*, followed the order thus suggested. In 1641 he wrote his metaphysical *Meditations*, in 1644 his *Principles of Philosophy*, which is a pruned version of the physical system of *The World*, and in 1649 a *Treatise on the Passions*, which is largely an ethical treatise.

The *Meditations* contain a full statement of the system sketched in the *Discourse*. Before publication the text was sent to Mersenne to circulate for comment to a number of scholars and thinkers. Six sets of objections were received. They were printed, with replies from Descartes, in a long appendix to the first edition of 1641, which thus became the first peer-reviewed work in history. The objectors were a varied and distinguished group: apart from Mersenne himself they included a scholastic neighbour in Holland, an Augustinian theologian from Paris, Antoine Arnauld, plus the atomist philosopher Pierre Gassendi, and the English materialist and nominalist, Thomas Hobbes.

Criticisms of the *Meditations* continued to come in after publication, and critical reaction was not only literary. The rector of Utrecht University, Gisbert Voetius, denounced Descartes to the magistrates as a dangerous

---

[1] Descartes' natural theology is considered in detail in Ch. 10.

Princess Elizabeth of
Bohemia, one of
Descartes' first readers
and shrewdest critics

propagator of atheism, and the University of Leiden accused him of the
Pelagian heresy. Descartes wrote two tracts, which survive, to defend his
orthodoxy; but it was really the intervention of influential friends that
prevented him from being arrested and having his books burnt.

One of his most supportive friends was Princess Elizabeth, the daughter
of the Elector Frederick against whom he had once soldiered. He corre-
sponded with her from 1643 until his death, answering (and sometimes
failing to answer) her acute criticisms of his writings. He gave her much
medical and moral advice, and consoled her on the execution of her uncle
King Charles I. It was to her that he dedicated *The Principles of Philosophy*. The
first part of that book summarizes the metaphysics of the *Meditations* and its
three remaining parts deal with physical science, propounding laws of
motion and explaining the nature of weight, heat, and light. The account
given of the solar system is disguisedly heliocentric and discreetly

evolutionary. Descartes explains that he is describing not how the world was actually made, but how God might have made it otherwise, if he had so pleased.

Descartes' correspondence with Princess Elizabeth led him to reflect further on the relationship between the body and the soul, and to construct an ethical system resembling ancient Stoicism. He developed these reflections into *The Passions of the Soul*. When the treatise was published, however, it was dedicated not to Elizabeth, but to another royal lady who had interested herself in philosophy, Queen Christina of Sweden. The queen was so impressed that she invited Descartes to be her court philosopher, sending an admiral with a battleship to fetch him from Holland. Descartes was reluctant to sacrifice his solitude and the appointment proved disastrous. He felt lonely and out of place: he was employed in writing a ballet and forced to rise at 5 a.m. to instruct the queen in philosophy.

Descartes had immense confidence in his own abilities, and still more in the method he had discovered. Given a few more years of life, he thought, and given sufficient research funding, he would be able to solve all the outstanding problems of physiology and learn thereby the cures of all diseases. At this point he fell a victim to the rigours of the Swedish winter. While nursing a sick friend he caught pneumonia, and died on 11 February 1650. There was an ironic fittingness about the motto which he had chosen for himself as an epitaph:

> No man is harmed by death, save he
> Who, known too well by all the world,
> Has not yet learnt to know himself.

Descartes was a man of extraordinary and versatile genius. His ideas on physiology, physics, and astronomy were superseded within a century: they enjoyed a much shorter currency than the Aristotelian system they were designed to replace. But his work in algebra and geometry entered into the abiding patrimony of mathematics; and his philosophical ideas remain—for better or worse—enormously influential to the present day. No one can question his claim to rank among the greatest philosophers of all time.

We should not, however, take him altogether at his own valuation. In the *Discourse* he insists that systems created by an individual are to be preferred to those created by communities:

As a rule there is not such great perfection in works composed of several parts, and proceeding from the hands of various artists, as in those on which one man has worked alone. Thus we see the buildings undertaken and carried out by a single architect are generally more seemly and better arranged than those that several hands have sought to adapt, making use of old walls that were built for other purposes. Again, those ancient cities which were originally mere boroughs, and have become towns in process of time, are as a rule badly laid out, as compared with those towns of regular pattern that are laid out by a designer on an open plan to suit his fancy. (AT VI. 11; *CSMK* I.116)

This is not merely the expression of a taste for classical rather than Gothic architecture: laws too, Descartes goes on, are better if devised by a single legislator in a single code. Similarly, he thought, a true system of philosophy would be the creation of a single mind; and he believed himself to be uniquely qualified to be its creator.

It is true that Descartes initiated a new, individualistic, style of philosophizing. Medieval philosophers had seen themselves as principally engaged in transmitting a corpus of knowledge; in the course of transmission they might offer improvements, but these must remain within the bounds set by tradition. Renaissance philosophers had seen themselves as rediscovering and republicizing the lost wisdom of ancient times. It was Descartes who was the first philosopher since Antiquity to offer himself as a total innovator; as the person who had the privilege of setting out the truth about man and his universe for the very first time. Where Descartes trod, others followed: Locke, Hume, and Kant each offered their philosophies as new creations, constructed for the first time on sound scientific principles. 'Read my work, and discard my predecessors' is a constant theme of seventeenth- and eighteenth-century thinkers and writers.

With medieval philosophers like Aquinas, Scotus, and Ockham, a student has to read the texts closely to realize the great degree of innovation that is going on: the new wine is always decanted so carefully into the old bottles. With Descartes and his successors, the difficulty is the opposite: one has to look outside the text to realize that much that is presented as original insight is in fact to be found stated in earlier authors. There is no need to doubt the sincerity of Descartes' repeated statements that he owed nothing to his scholastic predecessors. He was not a plagiarist, but he had no appreciation of how much he had imbibed from the intellectual atmosphere in which he grew up.

When Descartes tried to doubt everything, the one thing he did not call into question was the meaning of the words he was using in his solitary meditation. Had he done so, he would have had to realize that even the words we use in soliloquy derive their meaning from the social community which is the home of our language, and that therefore it was not, in fact, possible to build up his philosophy from solitary private ideas. Again, Descartes thought that it was not possible to call into question propositions that he was taught by natural light—the clear and distinct perceptions that form the basic building blocks of his system. But in fact, as we shall see in detail in later chapters, too often when he tells us that something is taught by the natural light in our souls, he produces a doctrine that he had imbibed from the Jesuits at La Flèche.

There is no doubt of the enormous influence Descartes has exercised from his own day to ours. But his relation to modern philosophy is not that of father to son, nor of architect to palace, nor of planner to city. Rather, in the history of philosophy his position is like that of the waist of an hourglass. As the sand in the upper chamber of such a glass reaches its lower chamber only through the slender passage between the two, so too ideas that had their origin in the Middle Ages have reached the modern world through a narrow filter: the compressing genius of Descartes.

Hobbes

Of those who had been invited to comment on Descartes' *Meditations* in 1641, the most distinguished was Thomas Hobbes, the foremost English philosopher of the age. At that time Hobbes was fifty-three years old, having been born in 1588, the year of the Spanish Armada. He had been educated at Oxford and had served as a tutor to the Cavendish family and as an amanuensis to Francis Bacon. In 1629 he had published an English translation of Thucydides' *History of the Peloponnesian War*. During a visit to Paris in the 1630s he had met Descartes' Franciscan friend Marin Mersenne, whom he described as 'an outstanding exponent of all branches of philosophy'. In 1640 he had written a treatise in English, *Elements of Law, Natural and Political*, which contained in essence the principles of his philosophy of human nature and human society. He fled in the same year to Paris, anticipating the Civil War which was heralded by the activities of the

Long Parliament. He remained there more than ten years, and was, for a period, tutor to the exiled heir to the throne, the future King Charles II. In 1642 he presented a number of the ideas of the *Elements of Law* in a Latin treatise, *De Cive*, which established his reputation in France.

Hobbes' comments on Descartes show little comprehension of the *Meditations*, and the two thinkers have traditionally been regarded as standing at opposite poles of philosophy. In fact they resembled each other in several ways. Both, for instance, were fired by a passion for mathematics. Hobbes' most lively biographer, the gossipy John Aubrey, described his first encounter with geometry:

He was 40 years old before he looked on geometry; which happened accidentally. Being in a gentleman's library, Euclid's *Elements* lay open, and 'twas the 47th Element at Book I. He read the proposition. 'By G——' said he, 'this is impossible!' So he reads the demonstration of it, which referred him back to such a proposition; which proposition he read. *Et sic deinceps* [and so on], that at last he was demonstratively convinced of that truth. This made him in love with geometry. (Aubrey 1975: 158)

He did not, however, grasp the importance of Descartes' analytic geometry, which he thought 'lacked bite'. He thought even more poorly of his philosophy, in particular his physics or natural philosophy. 'Mr Hobbes was wont to say,' Aubrey tells us, 'that had Des Cartes kept himself wholly to Geometrie that he had been the best Geometer in the world, but that his head did not lye for Philosophy.' There is an irony here. When, later in life, Hobbes betook himself to the serious study of geometry, he wasted years debating with the mathematical professors of Oxford in a futile attempt to square the circle.

Descartes and Hobbes had much in common. They shared a contempt for Aristotle and the Aristotelian establishment in the universities. Both were solitary thinkers who spent significant parts of their lives in exile— each, for a time, beholden to banished Stuart courts. Both of them had very modest libraries, and were contemptuous of book-learning. Those who rely on reading, Hobbes said, 'spend time in fluttering over their books; as birds that entering by the chimney, and finding themselves enclosed in a chamber, flutter at the false light of a glass window, for want of wit to consider which way they came in' (*L*, 24). Hobbes, like Descartes, was a master of vernacular prose, and wrote for popular reading as well as for the learned world.

The most significant philosophical agreement between the two men was that each of them was convinced that the material world was to be explained solely in terms of motion. 'The causes of universal things (of those, at least, that have any cause) are manifest of themselves, or (as they say commonly) known to nature; so that they need no method at all; for they have all but one universal cause, which is motion,' wrote Hobbes (*De Corpore* VI.5). Like Descartes, Hobbes denied the objective reality of secondary qualities such as colour, sound, and heat, and indeed of all real accidents. 'Whatseover accidents or qualities our senses make us think there be in the world, they are not there, but are seemings and apparitions only. The things that really are in the world without us, are those motions by which these seemings are caused' (*Elements of Law* I.10). Like Descartes, Hobbes regarded the science of optics as being a key to the understanding of the true nature of sensation.

However, while Hobbes was close to one half of Descartes' philosophy, his philosophy of matter, he was strongly opposed to the other half, his philosophy of mind. Indeed he denied the existence of mind in the sense in which Descartes understood it. There was, for Hobbes, no such thing as a non-bodily substance, unextended and unmoving. There were no incorporeal spirits, human, angelic, or divine. The very expression 'incorporeal substance', he said, was as absurd as 'round quadrangle'. Historians disagree whether Hobbes' materialism involved a denial of the existence of God, or implied that God was a body of some infinite and invisible kind. It is unlikely that he was an atheist; but he certainly denied the dualism of mind and matter in human beings.

Hobbes' materialism justifies his reputation as a great opponent of Descartes, despite the many attitudes and prejudices they shared. But in addition to the metaphysical contrast between materialism and dualism, the two are often treated by historians of philosophy as founders of opposing schools of epistemology: British empiricism and continental rationalism. In Chapter 4 I will argue that the difference between these two schools is not as great as it appears on the surface.

Hobbes outlived Descartes by nearly thirty years, but he did not remain long in France after Descartes' death in 1650. He found the position of a Protestant in Paris uncomfortable: he had resisted Mersenne's attempts to convert him to Catholicism, and when suffering from a life-threatening illness he had insisted on receiving the sacrament according to the Anglican rite. In

The title page of the first edition of *Leviathan*, probably designed by Hobbes himself. The sovereign, whose body is composed of those of his subjects, bears both civil and ecclesiastical power, represented by the sword and the crozier

his last years in Paris he wrote the work that was to give him immortality, *Leviathan, or the Matter, Form and Power of a Commonwealth Ecclesiastical and Civil.*

Starting from the premiss that in a state of nature, outside any commonwealth, there would be nothing but a mere war of all against all, Hobbes argues that principles of rational self-interest would urge men to give up some of their unfettered liberty in return for equal concessions by others. Such principles would lead them to transfer their rights, save that of self-defence, to a central power able to enforce laws by punishment. A covenant of every man with every man sets up a supreme sovereign, himself not a party to the covenant and therefore incapable of breaching it. Such a sovereign is the source of law and property rights, and it is his function to enforce, not just the original covenant that constitutes the state, but individual covenants that his subjects make with each other.[2]

Leviathan was published in London in 1651. Despite its eloquent presentation of the case for absolute sovereignty, the work was not well received by Charles II's entourage when copies were brought across the Channel. Banished from court and deprived by death of his best Catholic friends, Hobbes decided to return to England, now, since the execution of Charles I, a commonwealth under a Protector.

During the Protectorate Hobbes lived quietly in London and wrote no political philosophy. He published his physical philosophy under the title *De Corpore (On Body)* in Latin in 1655 and in English in 1656. He engaged in controversy with Bishop Bramhall of Derry on the topics that Milton tells us engaged the devils of *Paradise Lost,* 'Providence, Foreknowledge, Will and Fate, / Fixed Fate free will, foreknowledge absolute'. The disputation was inconclusive, like that of the devils 'who found no end, in wand'ring mazes lost'. In 1658 he published a Latin work, *De Homine,* which, like the earlier *De Cive,* presented for an international readership some of the ideas of *The Elements of Law.*

Hobbes was reinstated in the favour of Charles II on his restoration to the throne in 1660. He was awarded a pension and made welcome at court, though much teased by the courtiers. 'Here comes the bear to be baited,' the King is reported to have said on seeing him; but he was able, we are told, to give as good as he got in wit and drollery. *Leviathan,* however, remained an object of suspicion. 'There was a report,' Aubrey tells us, 'that in Parliament,

---

[2] Hobbes' political philosophy is considered in detail in Ch. 9 below.

not long after the King was settled, some of the bishops made a motion to have the good old gentleman burn't for a heretic.'

From 1660 to his death Hobbes lived mainly at the houses of the Earl of Devonshire in London and at Chatsworth and Hardwick. He wrote no more philosophy, but translated the *Iliad* and the *Odyssey*, and wrote a history of the Civil War entitled *Behemoth* which, at the request of the King, he withheld from publication. He died at Hardwick Hall in December 1679, at the age of ninety-one, full of energy to the last in spite of Parkinson's disease. He attributed his vigorous old age to three things: regular tennis until the age of seventy-five, abstinence from wine from the age of sixty, and the continued exercise of the voice in singing. 'At night,' Aubrey tells us, 'when he was abed, and the doors made fast, and was sure nobody heard him, he sang aloud (not that he had a very good voice) but for his health's sake: he did believe it did his lungs good and conduced much to prolong his life.'

Hobbes' fame in the history of philosophy rests above all on his contribution to political philosophy. He himself, however, attached great importance to his philosophy of language. The invention of printing, he observes, was no great matter compared with the invention of writing, and that in its turn is insignificant compared to the invention of speech, which is what marks us off from beasts and makes us capable of pursuing science. Without words 'there had been amongst men, neither commonwealth, nor society, nor contract, nor peace, no more than amongst lions, bears, and wolves' (*L*, 20).

The purpose of speech is to transfer the train of our thoughts into a train of words, and it has four uses:

First, to register, what by cogitation we find to be the cause of any thing, present or past; and what we find things present or past may produce, or effect: which in sum, is aquiring of arts. Secondly, to show to others that knowledge which we have attained; which is, to counsel and teach one another. Thirdly, to make known to others our wills and purposes, that we may have the mutual help of one another. Fourthly, to please and delight ourselves, and others, by playing with our words, for pleasure or ornament, innocently. (*L*, 21)

There are four abuses corresponding to the four uses of words, and great pains are needed to avoid such abuses. 'For words are wise men's counters, they do but reckon by them; but they are the money of fools' (*L*, 21).

Hobbes is a thoroughgoing nominalist: all words are names, and names refer only to individuals. Names may be proper, such as 'Peter', or common, such as 'horse'; and they may also be abstract, such as 'life' or 'length'. They may even be descriptions (which Hobbes calls 'circumlocutions'), such as 'he that writ the Iliad'. But whatever form a name takes, it never names anything other than one or more individuals. Universal names like 'man' and 'tree' do not name any universal thing in the world or any idea in the mind, but name many individuals, 'there being nothing in the word Universall but Names; for the things named, are every one of them Individual and Singular'.

For Hobbes, names are put together to make sentences. If we say 'Socrates is just', the semantic relationship of the word 'just' to the man Socrates is exactly the same as the relationship of the word 'Socrates': both are names, and the predicate term in the sentence signifies in the same way as the subject tem does. Sentences are true when the two names they contain are both names of the same thing. 'A man is a living creature' is true because 'living creature' is a name of everything that is signified by 'man'. 'Every man is just' is false because 'just' is not a name of every man, the greater part of mankind deserving the name 'unjust' (L, 23; G, 38).

The two-name theory is a naïve piece of semantics which would not survive serious logical criticism such as it had received in the medieval period and as it was to receive in the nineteenth century in the work of Gottlob Frege. Hobbes' version of the theory is a particularly crude one by comparison with that of its leading medieval proponent, William Ockham.[3] It remained influential, however, among the British empiricists whom many have seen as the heirs of the tradition of Ockham and Hobbes.

The Cambridge Platonists

A group of half a dozen English philosophers in the mid-seventeenth century occupied a position at odds with both Hobbes and Descartes. Five of them, of whom the most important was Ralph Cudworth (1617–88), were graduates of Emmanuel College, Cambridge, and one of them, Henry

---

[3] See vol. II, pp. 127–8.

More (1614–87), was a graduate of Christ's College, Cambridge, of which Cudworth was for thirty years master. All of them shared an admiration for Plato, Plotinus, and their followers among the early Church Fathers. Hence the group is commonly called the 'Cambridge Platonists'.

Despite their Cambridge affiliation, the members of the group were hostile to the Puritanism that prevailed in that town and university during the Civil War. They rejected Calvinist doctrines of predestination, affirmed human freedom, and preached the merits of religious toleration. Their toleration, however, did not extend to atheists, and the focus of their hostility was Hobbes, whose materialism they regarded as tantamount to atheism. During the reign of Charles I Puritan hostility to the Anglican hierarchy had been followed by the deposition and execution of the king. For the Cambridge Platonists the political slogan 'No Bishop, No King' had a philosophical counterpart: 'No Spirit, no God'. One could not be a materialist and a theist at the same time.

Up to this point, the Cambridge Platonists sided with Descartes against Hobbes in emphasizing the distinction of mind from matter. They devoted themselves to proving the immortality of the human soul and the existence of a spiritual God in such treatises as More's *Antidote Against Atheism* and *The Immortality of the Soul*, and Cudworth's *True Intellectual System of the Universe*. For More, a human being is 'a created spirit endowed with sense and reason, and a power of organizing terrestrial matter into human shape'.[4] Like Descartes, Cudworth argues that God's existence can be proved by the presence in us of the idea of God: 'Were there no God, the idea of an absolutely or infinitely perfect Being could never have been made or feigned, neither by politicians, nor by poets, nor philosophers, nor any other.' The idea of God is a coherent one, 'therefore must it needs have some kind of entity or other, either an actual or a possible one; but God, if he be not, is not possible to be, therefore he doth actually exist.'[5]

Like Descartes, the Cambridge Platonists believed in innate ideas: the mind is not a blank page on which the senses write, but a closed book, which the senses merely open. Innate ideas, More said, are present in our minds in the way that melodies are present in the mind of a musician while

---

[4] *The Immortality of the Soul* (1659), bk 1, ch. 8.
[5] *The True Intellectual System of the Universe* (1678), II.537, III. 49–50.

he is sleeping upon the grass (*Antidote*, 17). Among the innate ideas immediately evident to the human mind are fundamental and undeniable moral principles, of which More was prepared to list, in a handbook of 1668, no fewer than twenty-three. Hobbes, Cudworth maintained, was quite wrong to think that justice and injustice arose as a result of a merely human compact. There was no way in which individual humans could confer upon a sovereign a power of life and death which they did not themselves possess.

The Cambridge Platonists parted company with Descartes when they came to explain the basis of fundamental ethical principles. It was quite wrong, Cudworth complained, to say that moral and other eternal truths depended on the omnipotent will of God and were therefore in principal variable. 'Virtue and holiness in creatures', he told the House of Commons in a 1647 sermon, 'are not therefore Good because God loves them, and will have them be accounted such; but rather, God therefore loves them because they are in themselves simply good.'[6]

The Platonists' disagreement with Descartes was much sharper when they came to consider his account of the material world. They were not opposed to new developments in science—both Cudworth and More were members of the Royal Society—but they denied that the phenomena could be accounted for mechanistically in terms of matter and motion. Unlike Descartes, they believed that animals had consciousness and sensitive souls; and even the fall of a heavy body, they believed, needed to be explained by the action of an immaterial principle. This did not mean that God did everything directly, as it were with his own hands, but rather that he had entrusted the physical world to an intermediary, 'a plastic nature' akin to a world-soul, that acted regularly and teleologically. Those like Descartes who rejected teleology were mere 'mechanic theists' and were little better than the materialist Hobbes.

Locke

Hobbes was a pioneer of modern empiricism, but his fame has been eclipsed by that of a more polished practitioner, John Locke. Locke was

---

[6] Quoted in C. Taliaferro, *Evidence and Faith* (Cambridge: Cambridge University Press, 2005), 11.

born in Somerset in 1632, the son of a minor gentleman who fought in the parliamentary cavalry. He was educated at Westminster School, not only in Greek and Latin but also in Hebrew, and went on to a closed studentship at Christ Church, Oxford, whence he took his MA in 1658. After the restoration of Charles II in 1660 he wrote several Latin pamphlets in defence of Anglican orthodoxy, taught Greek in the university, became a college tutor, and held a number of college offices. He became interested in chemistry and physiology, and spent seven years studying to qualify in medicine.

In 1667 Locke left Oxford to become physician and political adviser to Anthony Ashley Cooper, a member of Charles II's inner cabinet, shortly to become the Earl of Shaftesbury. Soon after arriving in London he wrote a brief *Essay on Toleration* advocating, in contradiction to his earlier tracts, the removal of doctrinal constraints on all except Roman Catholics. The years 1676–8 he spent in France, meeting a number of followers of Descartes and making a serious study of his philosophy.

As his reign progressed, Charles II became unpopular, particularly after the conversion to Catholicism of his brother and heir, James, Duke of York. Protestant dissatisfaction came to a head in 1679 when many Catholics were tried and executed for alleged complicity in an imaginary popish plot to kill the king and place his brother on the throne. Shaftesbury became leader of the Whig Party, which sought to exclude James from the succession; his attempts to secure the passing of an Exclusion Bill were defeated when Charles dissolved Parliament in 1681. After being implicated in a plot against the royal brothers in 1682, Shaftesbury had to flee to Holland, where he died in 1683.

Locke was sufficiently identified with Shaftesbury's projects to find it necessary to go into exile during the Tory revival at the end of Charles II's life and during the short reign of his brother James II (1685–8). Around the time of the popish plot and the exclusion crisis he had written *Two Treatises on Government*. In the first he made a devastating attack on a work by Sir Robert Filmer in defence of the divine right of kings. In the second he presented an account of the state of nature—a much more optimistic one than Hobbes'—and argued that governments and commonwealths are created by a social contract in order to protect the property of individuals. He argued that if a government acts arbitrarily, or if one branch of government usurps the role of another, the government is dissolved and rebellion is justified.[7]

While in Holland, Locke worked on the composition of his greatest philosophical work, the *Essay Concerning Human Understanding*. Notes for this work date back to his early days in London, but it was not published until 1690, after which it went through four editions during Locke's lifetime.

The *Essay* consists of four books. The first and shortest, entitled 'Of Innate Notions', argues that there are no innate principle in our minds, whether speculative or practical. All our ideas are derived, either directly or by combination or reflection, from experience. Even in the case of *a priori* disciplines such as geometry, the ideas that we employ are not innate. The thirty-three chapters of the second book treat exhaustively of ideas, 'idea' being the catch-all term that Locke employs to characterize our mental skills and the concepts of our minds:

Every Man being conscious to himself, That he thinks, and that which his Mind is employ'd about whilst thinking, being the Ideas that are there, 'tis past doubt, that Men have in their Minds several ideas, such as those expressed by the words *Whiteness, Hardness, Sweetness, Thinking, Motion, Man, Elephant, Army, Drunkenness,* and others. (*E*, 104)

Locke classified ideas in various ways: there are simple ideas and complex ideas; there are clear and distinct and obscure and confused ideas; there are ideas of sensation and ideas of reflection. In dealing with simple ideas, Locke divides the qualities to be found in bodies into two categories, primary qualities such as solidity, motion, and figure, which are in bodies 'whether we perceive them or no', and secondary qualities such as colours, which 'are nothing in the objects themselves, but powers to produce various sensations in us by their primary qualities'. Among the ideas of reflection the first and most important is the idea of perception, for this is the first exercise of the mind upon ideas. Perception is a purely passive experience, and everyone knows what it is by looking within himself. The passive experiences of perception are the bedrock on which Locke builds his philosophy.

The second book of the *Essay* presents an empiricist philosophy of mind and will, but it contains much else: reflections on time, space, and number, for instance, and a catalogue of human passions. It deals with causal and

---

[7] Locke's political philosophy is considered in detail in Ch. 9.

other relations, and it contains an elaborate and highly influential discussion of the nature of personal identity.

Although Locke believes that we can recognize simple ideas within ourselves unaided, and that if we cannot recognize them no words will help us to do so, he does in practice identify the ideas that he is talking about by means of the words that express them. He admits that 'our abstract ideas, and general words, have so constant a relation one to another, that it is impossible to speak clearly and distinctly of our Knowledge, which all consists in propositions, without considering, first, the Nature, Use and Signification of Language' (*E*, 401).

To that topic, then, he devotes his third book. The most famous sections of this book are the discussion of abstract ideas and the theory of substance. The mind, Locke says, observing likenesses among natural objects, sorts them under abstract general ideas, to which it attaches general names. These general ideas have, he tells us, remarkable properties: the general idea of a triangle, for instance 'must be neither oblique nor rectangle, neither equilateral, equicrural nor scalenon, but all and none of these at once'. Substances in the world possess various qualities and powers which we make use of when we define things of different kinds; but the definitions we give them do not reveal their real essences, but only a 'nominal essence'. Of substance in general the only idea we have is of 'something we know not what' in which properties inhere.

Epistemological considerations are ubiquitous throughout the *Essay*, but it is the fourth book that is officially devoted to the topic of knowledge. Because the real essences of things are unknown to us, we cannot have true science about items in the natural world, but only probable belief. We can have genuine knowledge of our own existence and of the existence of God; and provided we keep within the bounds of actual sensation, we can have knowledge of the existence of other things. The love of truth should prevent us from entertaining any proposition with greater assurance than the evidence we have for it: 'Whoever goes beyond this measure of assent, it is plain, receives not truth in the love of it, loves not truth for truth's sake, but for some other by end' (*E*, 697).

During his exile, perhaps in 1685 when King Louis XIV revoked the Edict of Nantes which had hitherto given toleration to French Protestants, Locke wrote a Latin letter on toleration (*Epistola de Tolerantia*) advocating to a European audience, as he had earlier done to an English one, the acceptance by Christians of a wide variety of doctrinal beliefs. When, in 1688, the 'Glorious Revolution' drove out James II and replaced him with the Dutch Protestant William of Orange, the English monarchy was placed on a new legal basis, with a Bill of Rights and a much enhanced role for Parliament. The way was now free for Locke to return and to publish works which it had hitherto been too dangerous to print. In 1689 and 1690 there appeared *Two Treatises on Government*, the first edition of the *Essay*, and an English version of the letter on tolerance. In response to controversy Locke published two further letters concerning toleration, the third of which appeared in 1692.

Locke had been deprived of his studentship at Christ Church by Charles II in 1684 and on his return from exile he spent much of his time in London. He held a number of posts in the civil service, notably as a commissioner of the Board of Trade. He found time to write *Some Thoughts on Education* (1693), two papers on the nature of money (1691 and 1695), and *The Reasonableness of Christianity* (1695). The form of Christianity which Locke considered reasonable was a very liberal one, and he had to defend himself against conservative critics in two *Vindications* of his treatise (1695 and 1697). Between 1696 and 1698 he was engaged in controversy with Bishop Stillingfleet of Worcester, who regarded the *Essay* as too rationalistic for the comfort of religion. Most of these controversial works were published anonymously; of Locke's principal works only the *Essay* appeared under his own name in his lifetime.

Since 1691 Locke had been given accommodation at Oates, the Essex manor house of Sir Francis Masham, who had married Damaris, the daughter of the Cambridge Platonist Ralph Cudworth. As the years went on Locke spent more and more time at Oates, and from 1700 until his death in 1704 it was his home. He spent the last years of his life, partly incapacitated by ill health, in writing a devout, if critical, commentary on the Epistles of St Paul. He died on 28 October 1704, while Lady Masham was reading the Psalms to him.

Pascal

Hobbes and Locke saw themselves as opponents of Descartes, one during his lifetime and one after his death. In fact, as I have tried to show in the present

Charles R

Right Reverend Father in God, and Trusty
and Wellbeloved We greet you well. Whereas
We have received information of the factious
and disloyall behaviour of   Lock,
one of the Students of that Our Colledge, We
have thought fit hereby to signify Our Will
and Pleasure to you, that you forthwith
remove him from his said Students Place,
and deprive him of all the Rights and
Advantages thereunto belonging. For
which this shall be your Warrant. And
so We bid you heartily farewell. Given
at Our Court at Whitehall the 11th day
of November 1684 in the Six & thirtieth
Yeare of Our Reigne

By his Majtis command
Sunderland

Deane & Chapter of Christ church.

Instruction from King Charles II to the Dean and Chapter of Christ Church to deprive Locke of his studentship and in later chapters, both of them shared many of his fundamental assumptions. The same is true of the French philosophers of the generation after Descartes, whether they presented themselves as critics or continuators of his work. The most distinguished of the former group was Blaise Pascal; the most distinguished of the latter was Nicholas Malebranche.

Born in 1632, Pascal was the son of a royal official in the Auvergne. A precocious child, educated at home, he was already publishing on the geometry of conic sections at the age of sixteen, and he invented a rudimentary computer to assist his father in tax assessment. He inspired a series of experiments which proved the empirical possibility of a vacuum, which had been denied *a priori* by Descartes. Later in life he took a significant part in the development of the mathematical study of probability, and he can claim to be one of the founders of game theory.

In his own mind, his work in mathematics and physics came to seem a matter of secondary importance. In 1654 he had a religious experience which led him to make devotion and theology his main concern. He became a close associate of a group of ascetics which centred on the convent of Port Royal, where his sister Jacqueline had become a nun in 1652. Members of the group were called 'Jansenists' because they revered the memory of the Dutch Bishop Jansenius who had written a famous treatise on St Augustine, which defended a pessimistic and rigorist version of Catholicism. Jansenism stressed the corruption of fallen human nature, and held out hope of salvation only to a small minority of the human race. In our present state, some divine commands were impossible for human beings to obey, even with the best will in the world. There was little scope for free will: on the one hand, sin was unavoidable, and on the other hand, grace was irresistible.

Such teaching was condemned by Pope Innocent X in 1653, but the Jansenists fought a long rearguard battle, and their influence on Pascal remained profound. In accord with their devaluation of the powers of fallen human nature, Pascal was sceptical of the power of philosophy, especially in relation to knowledge of God. 'The true way to philosophise', he once wrote, 'is to have no time for philosophy'; as for Descartes, he was 'useless and uncertain' (*P*, 445,671). Because the Jansenists took a poor view of the freedom of the will, they were constantly at war with its principal Catholic defenders, the Jesuits. Pascal joined the battle by writing a book, *The Provincial Letters*, in which he attacked Jesuit moral theology as excessively lax and indulgent to sinners.[8] When he died in 1662 a paper was found stitched into his coat with the words 'God of Abraham, God of Isaac, God of Jacob, not of the philosophers and scholars'.

At his death Pascal left behind a series of brief remarks which were published in 1670 as *Pensées* (thoughts). He was a master of aphorism, and many of his sayings have become familiar quotations: 'The eternal silence of the infinite spaces terrifies me'; 'Had Cleopatra's nose been shorter, the whole face of the world would have been changed', 'We die alone'. One of the most striking is this:

Man is only a reed, the frailest thing in nature; but he is a thinking reed. To crush him it does not take the whole universe in arms: a breath of wind, a drop of water is enough to kill him. But were the universe to crush him, man would still be nobler than his killer. For he knows that he is dying and that the universe has the better of him. But the universe knows nothing of this. (*P*, 231)

Many of the remarks were designed to form part of an apology for the Christian religion, and to convert unbelievers and reform worldly believers. The project, however, was never completed and no consensus has been reached among scholars about the form it was intended to take. Two themes, however, recur in the surviving fragments: the misery of humanity without God, and the happiness promised by the religious life:

The wretchedness of our condition is made clear by the philosophical debate between sceptics and rationalists. The sceptics are right that we cannot even be certain whether we are awake or asleep; the rationalists are right that there are some natural principles we cannot doubt. But whether these principles are true or not, depends on whether we come from a good God or from an evil demon. And we cannot know, without faith, whether there is a God: nature offers no satisfactory proof that he exists. The best we can do, if we do not accept revelation, is to bet on his existence.[9] (*P*, 38,42)

Human nature as we know it is a mass of contradiction. We have an ideal of truth, and yet we possess only untruth. We have a yearning for happiness, and we cannot achieve it. Humanity is something monstrous: 'Chaotic, contradictory and prodigious; judge of everything and mindless earth—worm, storehouse of truth and cesspool of error; the glory and refuse of the universe.' Pascal anticipates Pope's *Essay on Man*:

---

[8] The moral philosophy of the *Provincial Letters* is discussed in Ch. 10 below.

[9] Pascal's wager is considered in Ch. 10 below.

Chaos of thought and passion, all confused;
Still by himself abused or disabused;
Created half to rise and half to fall;
Great lord of all things, yet a prey to all;
Sole judge of truth, in endless error hurled—
The glory, jest, and riddle of the world!   (*P* II,13)

The solution to this riddle is contained in the Christian doctrine of the Fall. It is as clear as day that the human condition is twofold. If humans had never been corrupted they would have enjoyed in their innocent state both truth and happiness. If they had never been other than corrupted, they would never have any notion of either truth or happiness. But the Fall, which is the key to understanding of ourselves, is of all Christian teachings the one most shocking to reason:

What is more contrary to the laws of our wretched justice than eternally to damn a child with no will of its own for a sin in which the child had so small a part to play that it was committed six thousand years before the child came into existence? Certainly, nothing shocks us more deeply than this doctrine. Nevertheless without this most incomprehensible of all mysteries we are incomprehensible to ourselves. (*P*, 164)

But if reason revolts at the idea of the Fall, reason can also establish the idea's truth. The starting point is nothing other than human misery:

The greatness of man is so evident that it can be inferred even from his wretchedness. For that which is nature in animals we call wretchedness in man. And by this we recognize that his nature being now like that of the animals, he is fallen from a better nature which formerly was his. For who is unhappy at not being a king, except a deposed king? (Ibid.)

Although Pascal believed that only faith could lead us to saving truth and that only grace could give us lasting happiness, in his philosophical writing he was not the enemy of reason that he is often made out to be. His best-known aphorism, of course, is 'the heart has its reasons of which reason knows nothing'. But if we study his use of the word 'heart' we can see that he is not placing feeling above rationality, but contrasting intuitive with deductive reasoning—rather as we speak of learning mathematical tables 'by heart'. We can see this when he tells us that it is the heart that teaches us the foundations of geometry. In this he was not at all at odds with Cartesian rationalism.

Malebranche

Nicolas Malebranche, the son of one of Louis XIV's secretaries, was born in 1638, the year in which Descartes published *The Discourse on Method*. At the age of twenty-six, in 1664, he was ordained a priest of the French Oratory, founded by Descartes' patron Cardinal Berulle, and in the same year he came across the posthumously published *Treatise on Man*. He was so ravished by this book, his biographer tells us, that he felt 'such violent palpitations of the heart that he was obliged to leave the book at frequent intervals'. He became the most enthusiastic of all Cartesians, and devoted his life to the pursuit of clear and distinct ideas.

In 1674–5 Malebranche published his most significant philosophical work, *The Search after Truth* (*De la recherche de la Vérité*), and in 1688 he summarized his system in *Entretiens sur la Metaphysique*. Most of his other writings were works of theological controversy, beginning with his *Treatise on Nature and Grace* of 1680. He fell foul of many of the leading theologians of the age, quarrelling with Arnauld about grace and with Fénelon about the right way to love God: his *Treatise* was placed on the index in 1690. Shortly before his death in 1715 he found himself the target of a posthumously published polemic of John Locke.

The account of sensation, imagination, intellect, and will presented in Malebranche's works is essentially the same as that of Descartes. The main new item is an explanation of the association of ideas in terms of networks of fibres in the brain. Some of these networks are inborn: from birth, for instance, the brain fibre corresponding to the idea of a steep cliff is linked to the brain fibre corresponding to the idea of death. Other networks are created by experience: if you attend some historic event, for instance, a brain network will be created linking together ever afterward the persons, times, and places involved (*R de V* 2.1, 5).

Malebranche accepted Cartesian dualism: minds were thinking substances and the essence of matter was extension. But he tried to improve upon Descartes' account of the relationship between mind and body, long recognized as the weakest point in the Cartesian system. More consistently than Descartes, Malebranche argued that if mind was pure thought, and matter was pure extension, neither could act upon the other. Mind and body run parallel, but do not interact. 'It seems to me quite certain that the will of spiritual beings is incapable of moving the smallest body in the world.

It is evident, for example, that there is no necessary connection between our will to move our arm and our arm's movement.' Sure, my arm moves *when* I will, but not *because* I will. If it was really myself moving my arm, I would know how I do it; but I cannot even explain how I wiggle my finger.

If I do not move my arm, who does? God does, answers Malebranche. God is the only true cause. From all eternity he has willed all that is to happen and when it is to happen. So he has willed the act of my will and the simultaneous movement of my arm. My willing is not the cause, but only provides an occasion for God to do the causing. (For this reason, Malebranche's system is called 'occasionalism'.) Not only can minds not act on body; neither can bodies act on bodies. If bodies collide and move away from each other, what really happens is that God wills each of them to be in the appropriate places at the appropriate moments. 'There is a contradiction in saying that one body can move another' (*EM*. 7, 10).

If minds cannot act on bodies, and bodies cannot act on bodies, can bodies act on minds? Normally we imagine that our minds are constantly being fed information from the world via our senses. Malebranche denies that our ideas come from the bodies they represent, or that they are created by ourselves. They come directly from God, who alone is capable of acting causally on our intellects. If I prick my finger with a needle, the pain does not come from the needle: it is directly caused by God (*EM*, 6). We see all things in God: God is the environment in which minds live, just as space is the environment in which bodies are located. It was this teaching which particularly aroused the indignation of John Locke.

Many Christian thinkers, from St Augustine onwards, had held that human beings see the eternal truths and the moral laws by contemplating, in some manner, ideas in the mind of God. In making this claim Malebranche could claim august authority. But it was a novelty to say that our knowledge of changeable material objects depends on immediate divine illumination. God, after all, is not himself material or changeable: all there is to be seen in God is the pure idea of intelligible extension. How does contemplation of the eternal divine archetype of extension convey to us any knowledge of the contingent history of bodies moving and changing in the world about us?

The answer that Malebranche gives is that in seeing the archetype of extension we are also made aware of all the laws of Cartesian physics that govern the behaviour of the material world. If this is to be sufficient to predict the actual course of the universe the laws must fulfil two conditions: they must be simple laws and they must be general laws. This is the theme of Malebranche's *Treatise on Nature and Grace*:

God, discovering in the infinite treasures of his wisdom an infinity of possible worlds (as the necessary consequences of the laws of motion which he can establish) determines himself to create that world which could have been produced and preserved by the simplest laws, and which ought to be the most perfect, with respect to the simplicity of the ways necessary to its production or to its conservation. (*TNG*, 116)

Two simple laws of motion, according to Malebranche, suffice to explain all physical phenomena—the first, that bodies in motion tend to continue their motion in a straight line; the second, that when two bodies collide, their motion is distributed in both in proportion to their size.

Malebranche's belief in the simplicity and generality of fundamental laws not only solves the epistemological problem about our knowledge of the external world, but also the moral problem of the presence of evil among the creatures of a good God. God could have made a world more perfect than ours; he might have made it such that rain, which makes the earth fruitful, fell more regularly on cultivated ground than on the sea, where it serves no purpose. But to do that he would have had to alter the simplicity of the laws. Moreover, once God has established laws it is beneath his dignity to tinker with them; laws must be general not only for all places but for all times:

If rain falls on certain lands, and if the sun roasts others; if weather favourable for crops is followed by hail that destroys them; if a child comes into the world with a malformed and useless head growing from his breast, it is not that God has willed these things by particular wills; it is because he has established laws for the communication of motion, of which these effects are necessary consequences. (*TNG*, 118)

It is not that God loves monsters or devises the laws of nature to engender them: it is simply that he was not able, by equally simple laws, to make a more perfect world. The key to the problem of evil is to realize that God acts by general laws and not by particular volitions.

Once again, we have ideas that were later summarized in Pope's *Essay on Man*. We are tempted, Pope says, to see nature as designed for our individual benefit. But here we meet an objection, and receive an answer:

But errs not nature from this gracious end,
From burning suns when livid deaths descend
When earthquakes swallow, or when tempests sweep
Towns to one grave, whole nations to the deep?
'No' ('tis replied) 'the first almighty cause
Acts not by partial, but by general laws.'   (I. 140–5)

Malebranche's teaching that God acts by general laws of nature, rather than by particular acts of providence, was what angered the theologians, who regarded it as incompatible with biblical and traditional accounts of the occurrence of miracles. The error was regarded as sufficiently wicked to be denounced by the greatest preacher of the age, Bishop Bossuet, in his funeral oration for Queen Maria Theresa of France in 1683.

Spinoza

Meanwhile, in Protestant Holland, a Jewish philosopher had developed Descartes' ideas in a way even more adventurous than that of Malebranche. Baruch Spinoza was born in Amsterdam in 1632, into a prosperous merchant family which had migrated from Portugal at the end of the previous century. His father, Michael Spinoza, a respected member of the Jewish community, ensured that he acquired a knowledge of Hebrew and a familiarity with the Bible and the Talmud at the local rabbinic school. When Michael died in 1654 Baruch took over the commercial firm in partnership with his brother, but he took much greater interest in philosophical and theological speculation. Having spoken Portuguese, Spanish, and Dutch from childhood, he now learnt Latin from a Christian physician, Francis Van den Enden, who introduced him to the writings of Descartes and had a considerable influence on the development of his thought.

By his teens, Spinoza had become sceptical of Jewish theology and on becoming an adult he gave up much of Jewish practice. In 1656 he was excommunicated from the synagogue and devout Jews were forbidden to talk to him, to write to him, or to stay under the same roof as him. He trained himself to grind lenses, and manufactured spectacles and other optical instruments. This profession gave him leisure and opportunity for scientific reflection and research; it also made him the first philosopher since Antiquity to have earned his living by the work of his hands.

The frontispiece of Thomas Sprat's *History of the Royal Society*

In 1660 he moved from Amsterdam to the village of Rijnsburg near Leiden. In the same year the Royal Society was founded in London, and shortly after its foundation its secretary, Henry Oldenburg, wrote to Spinoza inviting him to enter into a philosophical correspondence about the Cartesian and Baconian systems. The Royal Society, he told him, was a philosophical college in which 'we devote ourselves as energetically as we can to making experiments and observations, and are much occupied with putting together a History of Mechanical Arts' (*Ep*, 3).

A Dutch traveller who visited Rijnsburg in 1661 reported that in the village there lived:

somebody who had become a Christian from a Jew and now was nearly an atheist. He does not care about the Old Testament. The New Testament, the Koran and the fables of Aesop would have the same weight according to him. But for the rest this man behaves quite sincerely and lives without doing harm to other people, and he occupies himself with the construction of telescopes and microscopes.[10]

There is no evidence that Spinoza ever became a Christian after his excommunication by the Jews, but in his writings on religion he does give Jesus a place above the Hebrew prophets.

At this time Spinoza had already begun to write his first work, a treatise on the improvement of the understanding (*Tractatus de intellectus emendatione*) which he did not complete and which was not published until after his death. This resembled Descartes' *Discourse on Method* in recounting an intellectual conversion and setting out a research agenda. It was probably also in this period that Spinoza wrote a Dutch treatise for private circulation, a *Short Treatise on God, Man, and Happiness*, which was not discovered until 1851.

In 1663 Spinoza published a solemn exposition 'in geometrical form' of Descartes' *Principles of Philosophy*. Descartes himself had praised the merits of the geometrical method of deducing truths from definitions and axioms, and in his response to the second set of objections to his *Meditations* he had set out ten definitions, five postulates, and ten axioms, from which he proved four propositions establishing the existence of God and the real distinction between mind and body (AT VII. 160–70; *CSMK* II. 113–19). Spinoza had taken this project further in teaching Cartesian philosophy to a private pupil, and at the request of a friend, Dr Lodewijk Meyer of Leiden University, he worked up his dictation notes into a complete formalization of the first two books of the *Principles*.

Spinoza took over and enlarged Descartes' set of definitions and axioms, and proved fifty-eight propositions, of which the first is 'We can be

---

[10] Quoted by W. N. A. Klever in *CCS*, p. 25.

absolutely certain of nothing, so long as we do not know that we ourselves exist', and of which the last is 'If a particular body A can be moved in any direction by a force however small, it is necessarily surrounded by bodies all moving with an equal speed.' The exposition is generally very faithful to the *Principles*, but in a preface to the publication Meyer warned the reader against thinking that Spinoza's own views coincided in all respects with those of Descartes. Spinoza, for instance, had already departed from Descartes' philosophy of mind: he did not believe that the intellect and the will were distinct from each other, and he did not believe that human beings enjoyed the degree of freedom which Descartes attributed to them (*Ep*, 8). A number of salient points of Spinoza's own developing philosophy were expounded in an appendix to the geometrical exposition, entitled 'Thoughts on Metaphysics'.

In 1663 Spinoza moved to Voorburg near The Hague, where he was visited in 1665 by the astronomer Christiaan Huygens, with whom he discussed microscopes and telescopes and made observations of the planet Jupiter. In 1665 he decided to write an apologia justifying his departure from Judaism: this grew into a much more general work of biblical criticism and political theory, the *Tractatus Theologico-Politicus*, which was published anonymously in 1670.

The *Tractatus* concludes from a careful examination of the texts that the Hebrew Bible as we have it is a compilation, from more ancient material, made no earlier than the fifth century BC. There was no canon of sacred books earlier than the time of the Maccabees, and it is foolish to regard Moses as the author of the Pentateuch or David as the author of all the Psalms (*E* I. 126, 146). It is clear that the sacred writers were ignorant human beings, children of their time and place, and full of prejudices of various sorts. If a prophet was a peasant he saw visions of oxen; if a courtier, he saw a throne. 'God has no particular style in speaking, but according to the learning and capacity of the prophet he is cultivated, compressed, severe, untutored, prolix, or obscure' (*E* I. 31).

The defects of the prophets did not hinder them from carrying out their task, which was not to teach us truth but to encourage us to obedience. It is absurd to look to the Bible for scientific information; anyone who does so will believe that the sun revolves round the earth, and that the value of π is 3. Science and Scripture have different functions, and neither is superior to the other; theology is not bound to serve reason, nor reason theology (*E* I. 190).

How a passage in the Bible is intended must be determined only by examining the biblical context itself: one cannot argue from the fact that a statement is unreasonable that therefore it must be meant metaphorically. God is the author of the Bible only in the sense that its fundamental message—to love God above all things and one's neighbour as oneself—is the true religion, common to both Old and New Testaments. The Jews were God's chosen people only while they lived in Israel under a special form of government: at the present time 'there is absolutely nothing which the Jews can arrogate to themselves beyond other people' (E I. 55).

If you believe all the stories in the Bible but miss its message, you might as well be reading Sophocles or the Koran. On the other hand, a man who lives a true and upright life, however ignorant he is of the Bible, 'is absolutely blessed and truly possesses in himself the spirit of Christ' (E I. 79). But the Bible should not be a stumbling block, once one understands how to read it. Jews, Spinoza says, do not mention secondary causes, but refer all things to the Deity; for instance, if they make money by a transaction, they say God gave it to them. So when the Bible says that God opened the windows of heaven, it only means that it rained very hard; and when God tells Noah that he will set his bow in the cloud, 'this is but another way of expressing the refraction and reflection which the rays of the sun are subjected to in drops of water' (E I. 90).

The *Tractatus* is carefully argued and courteously expressed, and in drawing critical attention to the literary genres of Scripture, Spinoza was merely anticipating what devout Protestants were to say in the nineteenth century ('the Bible must be read like any other book') and what devout Catholics were to say in the twentieth century (the interpreter of the Bible must 'go back in spirit to those remote centuries of the East'). Nonetheless, the book's liberal interpretation of the Old Testament drew a storm of protest not only from Jews but from the Dutch Calvinists, who condemned the work in several synods. Other contemporaries, however, admired the book and when its authorship became generally known it gave Spinoza an international reputation.

This led, in 1673, to an offer from the Elector Palatine of a chair in philosophy at Heidelberg University. 'You will have', the Elector's secretary promised, 'the most ample freedom in philosophical teaching, which the prince is confident you will not misuse to disturb the religion publicly established.' But Spinoza was wary, and politely declined the offer:

I think, in the first place, that I should abandon philosophical research if I consented to find time for teaching young students. I think, in the second place, that I do not know the limits within which the freedom of my philosophical teaching would be confined, if I am to avoid all appearance of disturbing the publicly established religion. (*Ep*, 48)

Spinoza never occupied an academic post, and never married. He continued to live a retired but comfortable life, welcoming from time to time visiting scholars who came to pay their respects, such as G. W. Leibniz in 1676. He worked quietly on his major work, *Ethics Demonstrated according to the Geometrical Order*. He had it finished by 1675 and took the text to Amsterdam with the intention of having it printed; but he was warned by friends that he might risk persecution as an atheist if he did so. He returned the book to his desk and began work on a *Political Treatise*; but it, like several of his other projects, remained incomplete at his death. He died in 1667 of phthisis, due in part to the inhalation of glass dust, an occupational hazard for a lens-grinder. A volume of posthumous works—including the *Ethics*, the *Political Treatise*, plus the early *Improvement of the Intellect* and a number of letters—was published in the year of his death. Within a year the volume was banned by the States of Holland.

The *Ethics* sets out Spinoza's own system in the way he had earlier set out Descartes, on the model of Euclid's geometry. It is in five parts: 'Of God'; 'Of the Nature and Origin of the Mind'; 'Of the Origin and Nature of the Passions'; 'Of Human Bondage'; and 'Of Human Freedom'. Each part begins with a set of definitions and axioms and proceeds to offer formal proofs of numbered propositions, each containing, we are to believe, nothing that does not follow from the axioms and definitions, and concluding with QED. The geometrical method cannot be regarded as a successful method of presentation. The proofs often offer little understanding of the conclusions, and provide at best a set of hypertext links to other passages of the *Ethics*. The philosophical meat is often packed into scholia, corollaries, and appendices.

There is no doubt, however, that Spinoza was doing his best to make his philosophy utterly transparent, with no hidden assumptions and none but logical connections between one proposition and the next. If the Euclidean clothing often wears thin, the work remains geometrical in a more profound sense: it tries to explain the entire universe in terms of concepts and relationships that can be mastered by the student of elementary

geometry. If the project ultimately fails, it is not the fault of the philosopher but of the nature of philosophy itself.

As the titles of the different parts show, the treatise deals with many
other things besides ethics. The first book is a treatise of metaphysics and
also a treatise of natural theology: it expounds a theory of the nature of
substance which is at the same time an ontological argument for the
existence of God. Whereas for Descartes there were two fundamental
kinds of substance, mental and material, for Spinoza there is only a single
substance (which may be called either 'God' or 'Nature') which possesses
both the attribute of thought and the attribute of extension. The human
mind and the human body, therefore, do not belong in two different
worlds: the mind, as is explained in the second book, is man considered
as a mode of the attribute of thought, and the body is man considered as a
mode of the attribute of extension. Mind and body are inseparable: the
human mind is in fact simply the idea of the human body. On this
foundation, Spinoza builds up an epistemological theory of three levels
of knowledge: imagination, reason, and intuition.[11]

It is in the third book that we approach the topic of the book's title.
Human beings, like all other beings, strive to maintain themselves in
existence and to repel whatever threatens their destruction. The consciousness of this drive in humans is desire, and when the drive operates freely we
feel pleasure, and when it is impeded we feel pain. All the complex
emotions of humans are derived from these basic passions of desire,
pleasure, and pain. Our judgements of good and evil, and therefore our
actions, are determined by our desires and aversions; but the last two books
of the *Ethics* teach us how to avoid being enslaved by our passions (human
bondage) by an intellectual understanding of them (human freedom).

The key to this is the distinction between active and passive emotions.
Passive emotions, like fear and anger, are generated by external forces;
active emotions arise from the mind's own understanding of the human
condition. Once we have a clear and distinct idea of a passive emotion it
becomes an active emotion; and the replacement of passive emotions by
active ones is the path of liberation. In particular we must give up the
passion of fear, and especially the fear of death. 'A free man thinks of

---

[11] Spinoza's metaphysics is considered in detail in Ch. 6, his natural theology in Ch. 10, and
his epistemology in Ch. 4.

nothing less than death; and his wisdom is a meditation not on death but on life' (*Eth*, 151).

Moral liberation depends, paradoxically, on the appreciation of the necessity of all things. We will cease to feel hatred for others when we realize that their acts are determined by nature. Returning hatred only increases it; but reciprocating it with love vanquishes it. What we must do is to take a God's eye view of the whole necessary natural scheme of things, seeing it 'in the light of eternity'.[12]

Spinoza's unique system can be looked at historically in several different ways. We can, if we wish, situate his theory of substance in relation to Locke's. Both Locke and Spinoza eliminate the Aristotelian notion of substance: for Locke, individual substances vanish to a virtual zero, for Spinoza substance expands so far that a single substance encompasses the universe. But if we take Descartes as our point of comparison, we can say that in drawing out the implications of Cartesian assumptions Spinoza overtook Malebranche. Malebranche drew the conclusion that God was the only agent in the universe; Spinoza went further and claimed that he was the only substance. But when Spinoza says that this single substance is 'God or Nature', does this mean that he is a pantheist or an atheist? He has been taken with equal justification to be alleging that 'God' is just a code word for the order of the natural universe, and to be claiming that when scientists speak of 'Nature' they are all the time talking of God.

In philosophy the seventeenth century is the age of the revolt against Aristotle. This revolt is carried to its ultimate length by Spinoza. The hallmarks of Aristotelian scholasticism are the distinctions it makes and the pairs of concepts with which it operates to explain human beings and the material world: actuality and potentiality; form and matter; disposition and activity; intellect and will; natural and rational powers; final and formal causes. All these distinctions are collapsed by Spinoza. Of Aristotle's repertoire we are left with the distinction between substance and accident, and of the scholastic apparatus we are left with the distinction between essence and existence. These are applied once, and once only, by Spinoza in order to mark the relation between finite and infinite being. Spinoza's system is at the furthest point from the medieval Aristotelianism of an Aquinas.

---

[12] Spinoza's ethics is considered in detail in Ch. 8.

Paradoxically, Spinoza and Aristotle meet at just one point—the highest of all. The intellectual love of God that Spinoza presents in the last book of his *Ethics* as the highest human activity is very similar to the joyful contemplation of the divine that Aristotle holds out, in the tenth book of his *Ethics*, as the supreme constituent of human well-being. In each case, the beatific activity to which we are invited has seemed elusive to most subsequent philosophers.

Spinoza's philosophy is often regarded as the most extravagant form of rationalism. He spelt out his system in Euclidean terms not just to elucidate the logical relations between its various theses: for him logical sequences were what held the universe together. He made no distinction between logical and causal connections: for him, the order and connection of ideas are the same as the order and connection of things. Yet this arch-rationalist exercised great influence during the Romantic era. It was the German Romantic poet Novalis who proclaimed him a 'God-intoxicated man' and thus endeared him, later, to Kierkegaard. Wordsworth and Coleridge used to discuss his philosophy together in Somerset in 1797 and were nearly arrested for their pains: a government informer sent to investigate whether the two poets were French revolutionary agents was perturbed to overhear them referring to Spy Nozy.[13]

Spinoza's identification of God and Nature left a mark on the verse of both poets at this period. Wordsworth described himself as a worshipper of Nature, and in his 1798 'Lines above Tintern Abbey' he famously wrote:

> I have felt
> A presence that disturbs me with the joy
> Of elevated thoughts; a sense sublime
> Of something far more deeply interfused
> Whose dwelling is the light of setting suns,
> And the round ocean, and the living air,
> And the blue sky, and in the mind of man,
> A motion and a spirit, that impels
> All thinking things, all objects of all thought
> And rolls through all things.

In the same year Coleridge, in 'Frost at Midnight', predicts for his baby son a life amid the beauties of sandy lakes and mountain crags, and tells him:

---

[13] Coleridge, *Biographia Literaria*, Ch. 10.

So shalt thou see and hear
The lovely shapes and sounds intelligible
Of that eternal language, which thy God
Utters, who from eternity doth teach
Himself in all, and all things in himself.

Leibniz

Gottfried Wilhelm Leibniz straddles the boundary between the seventeenth and eighteenth centuries. Fifty-four of the seventy years of his life were passed in the seventeenth, but his principal philosophical works were composed and published in the eighteenth. Indeed, many of his most significant texts were not published until after his death, sometimes long afterwards. He was not a systematic writer, and historians of philosophy have struggled to construct a coherent and comprehensive system out of brief pamphlets, occasional pieces, and fragmentary notes. But the power of his intellect has never been questioned, and many subsequent philosophers have acknowledged themselves to be in his debt.

Leibniz was the son of a professor of philosophy at Leipzig, who died in 1652, when he was six. He spent much of his childhood in the library left by his father, reading precociously and voraciously. In adult life he showed himself to be one of the best-read philosophers ever to have lived. His interests were wide, including literature, history, law, mathematics, physics, chemistry, and theology. From the age of thirteen, however, logic and philosophy had become his dominant passion. Already in his early teens, he tells us, he found Suarez as easy to read as a novel, and while hiking he would balance in his mind the rival merits of Aristotelianism and Cartesianism.

In 1661 Leibniz entered Leipzig University. After being awarded the baccalaureate in 1663 for a scholastic dissertation on the principle of individuation (G IV. 15–26), he migrated first to Jena to study mathematics, and then to Altdorf to study law. As a sideline, at the age of nineteen he published a small logical treatise, *De Arte Combinatoria,* in which he offered some improvements to standard Aristotelian syllogistic and proposed a method of representing geometrical notions by an arithmetical code. His method of resolving complex terms into simple ones would, he hoped, produce a deductive logic of discovery, something that had so far eluded logicians (G IV. 27–102).

Leibniz took his doctorate at Altdorf in 1667, writing a thesis on 'Hard Cases in Law'. He was offered a chair, but preferred to pursue a career as a courtier and diplomat. He entered the service of the Archbishop of Mainz, one of the electors of the Holy Roman Empire. He dedicated his next academic publications to the archbishop: proposals for the rationalization of German law and a new method of teaching jurisprudence. At the archbishop's suggestion he republished a forgotten fifteenth-century treatise denouncing scholastic philosophy; but he accompanied it with his own defence of Aristotle against Descartes (G I. 15–27, 129–76). A Protestant in a Catholic court, he wrote a number of theological works of an ecumenical cast, concentrating on doctrines that were held in common by all Christian denominations (G IV. 105–36).

In 1672 Leibniz was sent on a mission to Paris, to persuade Louis XIV to lead a crusade into Egypt. Diplomatically his trip was abortive, but philosophically it was fruitful. He met Arnauld and Malebranche, and began a serious reading of Descartes and Gassendi. He was briefly attracted by Gassendi's atomism and materialism, a flirtation that he later regretted. 'When I was a youth,' he wrote in 1716, 'I too fell into the snare of atoms and the void, but reason brought me back' (G VII. 377).

On a further diplomatic visit in the following year, this time to London, Leibniz was introduced to Boyle and Oldenburg. He exhibited a model of a calculating machine to the other members of the Royal Society, who were sufficiently impressed to make him a Fellow. He returned to Paris and remained there until 1676, in which year he invented the infinitesimal calculus, unaware of Newton's earlier but as yet unpublished discoveries. On his way back to Germany he visited Spinoza in Amsterdam, and studied the *Ethics* in manuscript, writing substantial comments. But after the *Ethics* had been published, and Spinoza was a target of general obloquy, Leibniz played down their former intimacy.

From 1676 until his death Leibniz was a courtier to successive rulers of Hanover, employed in many capacities, from librarian to mining engineer. He resumed the ecumenical endeavours he had started at Mainz, and began writing a book of non-sectarian Christian apologetic, for which he sought advice from Arnauld and approval from the Vatican. In 1677 he wrote under an alias a book which claimed, *inter alia*, that the Christian states of Europe made up a single commonwealth of which the emperor was the temporal head and the pope the spiritual head.

This ecumenical project stalled when the duke who sponsored it died in 1680. Leibniz's new employer was Duke Ernst August of Brunswick, whose wife Sophia was the granddaughter of King James I and the sister of Descartes' Princess Elizabeth. He set Leibniz to compile the history of his ducal house, an endeavour which involved archival searches throughout Germany, Austria, and Italy. Leibniz took the task very seriously, tracing the history of the region back to prehistoric times. The only part of the work that was finished at his death was a prefatory description of the soil and minerals of Saxony, a work of geology rather than genealogy.

It was in the winter of 1685 that Leibniz wrote the first of his works which became lastingly popular, *The Discourse on Metaphysics*. As soon as he had written it he sent a summary to Arnauld, who gave it a frosty welcome; perhaps for this reason he did not publish any of it for ten years. He regarded it as the first statement of his mature philosophical position. Brief and lucid, it serves to this day as the best introduction to Leibniz's philosophical system, and contains many of his characteristic doctrines.

The first of these is that we live in the best of all possible worlds, a world freely chosen by God who always acts in an orderly manner according to reason. God is not, as Spinoza thought, the only substance: there are also created individuals. Each individual through its history has many predicates true of it, predicates whose totality defines it as the substance it is. Each such substance, we are told, 'expresses the universe after its own manner', encapsulating the world from a particular viewpoint. Human beings are substances of this kind: their actions are contingent, not necessary, and depending on free will. Our choices have reasons, but not necessitating causes. Created substances do not directly act upon each other, but God has so arranged matters that what happens to one substance corresponds to what happens to all the others. Consequently, each substance is like a world apart, independent of any other thing save God.

The human mind contains, from its origin, the ideas of all things; no external object, other than God, can act upon our souls. Our ideas, however, are our own ideas and not God's. So too are the acts of our will, which God inclines without necessitating. God conserves us continually in being, but our thoughts occur spontaneously and freely. Soul and body do not interact with each other, but thoughts and bodily events occur in correspondence because they are placed in liaison by the loving providence of God. God has so ordered things that spirits, the most precious items in the universe, live for ever in full self-consciousness; and for those that love him he has prepared unimaginable felicity.

It will be seen from this brief summary that the *Discourse* embeds itself in Aristotelian metaphysics and traditional Christianity, and that it includes elements from recent continental philosophers carefully modified to cohere with each other. Its main ideas were published in a learned journal in 1695 under the title *New System of Nature and of the Interaction of Substances*. Many savants published criticisms of it, to which Leibniz responded with vigorous rebuttals. In 1698 he followed up with another journal article, 'On Nature itself', which clearly marked out his own system in contrast to those of Descartes, Malebranche, and Spinoza, on which he had drawn for his synthesis.

Having failed to bring together Catholics and Protestants (in spite of his *Systema Theologicum* of 1686, which set out common ground between the various confessions), Leibniz set himself the potentially easier task of achieving a reconciliation between Calvinist Protestants and Lutheran Protestants. This again proved beyond his powers of argument and persuasion. So too was his grandiose project of a European confederation of Christian states, in which he tried in vain to interest successively Louis XIV of France and Peter the Great of Russia. But his passion for ecumenism was undiminished, and in the last year of his life he was encouraging those Jesuits who were seeking an accommodation between Catholic Christianity and the traditional beliefs and rituals of Chinese Confucians. He remained a Protestant himself until his death, although he sometimes carried a rosary, which on one occasion prevented him being thrown overboard as a heretical Jonah during a storm on an Adriatic crossing.

Locke's rejection of innate ideas in his *Essay concerning Human Understanding* provoked Leibniz into an all-out attack on empiricism. This was completed by 1704 but in that year Locke died, and Leibniz decided not to publish. It saw the light some fifty years after his own death, under the title *New Essays on Human Understanding*. The longest work published during Leibniz's lifetime was *Essays in Theodicy*, a vindication of divine justice in the face of the evils of the world, dedicated to Queen Charlotte of Prussia. 'Theodicy' is a pseudo-Greek word coined to express the project of justifying the works of God to man. The book argues that in spite of appearances we do indeed live in the best of all possible worlds. Its message was summed up by Alexander Pope in his *Essay on Man*:

Drawing by Jonathan Richardson of Alexander Pope, whose *Essay on Man* must be the most philosophical long poem in English

Of Systems possible, if 'tis confest
That Wisdom infinite must form the best....
Respecting Man, whatever wrong we call,
May, must be, right, as relative to all...
All Nature is but Art, unknown to thee:
All Chance, Direction which thou canst not see;
All Discord, Harmony, not understood;
All partial Evil, universal Good:
And, spite of Pride, in erring Reason's spite,
One truth is clear, 'Whatever is, is RIGHT'.

Pope wrote that in 1734. A quarter of a century later Voltaire, shocked out of optimism of this kind by the disaster of the Lisbon earthquake, responded with his satirical *Candide*. In that novel the Leibnizian Dr Pangloss responds to a series of miseries and catastrophes with the incantation: 'All is for the best in the best of all possible worlds.' Candide replies: 'If this is the best, what must the others be like?'

In 1714 two of Leibniz's most important short treatises appeared: the *Monadology* and *The Principles of Nature and of Grace*. The *Monadology* contains a developed and polished form of the system adumbrated in the *Discourse*. Whatever is complex, it argues, is made up of what is simple, and whatever is simple is unextended, for if it were extended it could be further divided. But whatever is material is extended, hence there must be simple immaterial elements. These soul-like entities Leibniz called monads—these are the 'worlds apart' of the *Discourse*. Whereas for Spinoza there was only one substance, with the attributes of both mind and extension, for Leibniz there are infinitely many substances, with the properties only of souls.

Like Malebranche, Leibniz denied that creatures could be causally affected by other creatures. 'Monads', he said, 'have no windows, by which anything could come in or go out.' Their life is a succession of mental states or perceptions, but these are not caused by the external world. A monad mirrors the world, not because the world shines into it, but because God has programmed it to change in synchrony with the world. A good clockmaker can construct two clocks which will keep such perfect time that they forever strike the hours at the same moment. In relation to all his creatures, God is such a clockmaker: at the very beginning of things he pre-established the harmony of the universe.

In the same year as Leibniz wrote the *Monadology*, Queen Anne of Britain died. The British Act of Settlement of 1701 had settled the succession on the heirs of Sophie, the Electress of Hanover, and her son, the Elector Georg Ludwig, became King George I of England. Leibniz did not follow his employer to London but was left behind in Hanover. He might well have been unwelcome in England, because of his quarrel with Newton over the ownership of the infinitesimal calculus. The Royal Society had intervened in the dispute and awarded the priority to Newton in 1712.

Leibniz died in 1716, leaving behind a mass of unpublished papers and a number of incomplete projects, the most ambitious of which was a comprehensive encyclopedia of human knowledge. This was to be the combined work of religious orders, such as the Benedictines and the Jesuits, and the recently founded learned societies, such as the Royal Society, the Académie des Sciences in Paris, and the Prusssian Academy of which Leibniz had himself been the first president. Nothing came of the project, and now, nearly 300 years later, the German Academy is still not halfway through the programme, begun in 1923, of a complete publication of Leibniz's own works.

Berkeley

During the last years of Leibniz's life several works were published which marked the appearance of a gifted young thinker. George Berkeley was born near Kilkenny in Ireland in 1685, the most talented philosopher from that island since John Scotus Eriugena in the ninth century.[14] When fifteen he entered Trinity College, Dublin, and having taken his BA in 1704 he was made a Fellow of the College on the strength of two mathematical papers. Unlike Leibniz, he wrote his best philosophical works when young, between the ages of twenty-four and twenty-eight.

An Essay towards a New Theory of Vision appeared in 1709. This offered an account of how we judge the distance, and size, of seen objects. Distance, it is argued, is not itself visible, being 'a line endwise to the eye': we judge it by the degree of distinctness of a visual appearance, and by the feelings we experience as we adjust our eyes for optimum vision. When we consider the visual perception of size, we have to distinguish between visible magnitude and tangible magnitude. 'There are two sorts of objects apprehended by sight, each whereof has its distinct magnitude or extension—the one properly tangible, i.e. to be perceived and measured by touch, and not immediately falling under the sense of seeing; the other, properly and immediately visible, by mediation of which the former is brought into view.' The visible magnitude of the moon, for instance, varies in accordance with its distance from the horizon; but its tangible magnitude remains constant. It is, however, by means of visual magnitude that we normally judge tangible magnitude. In the case both of size and distance Berkeley's discussion leads to an empiricist conclusion: our visual judgements are based on the experience of connections between sensations:

As we see distance, so we see magnitude. And we see both in the same way that we see shame or anger in the looks of a man. Those passions are themselves invisible, they are nevertheless let in by the eye along with colours and alterations of countenance, which are the immediate object of vision: and which signify them

---

[14] See vol II, pp. 30–3.

for no other reason than barely because they have been observed to accompany them. Without experience we should no more have taken blushing for a sign of shame than of gladness. (*BPW*, 309)

The connection between shape as judged by vision and shape as judged by touch is something learnt only by experience. Intrinsically, seen roundness and felt roundness have nothing in common. A man born blind, who had learnt to tell a cube from a sphere by touch, would not, if his sight were suddenly restored, be able to tell by looking alone which of two objects on a table in front of him was a cube and which was a sphere. So Berkeley affirmed, following Locke.

It will be seen that the *New Theory* was a contribution to experimental psychology as well as to philosophy of mind. The thesis just stated, for instance, is not a piece of conceptual analysis, but a thesis which could be tested by experiment.[15]

Berkeley's next work, the *Principles of Human Knowledge* of 1710, was something very different: it presented and ingeniously defended the astonishing thesis that there is no such thing as matter. Even Leibniz, who read the book as soon as it appeared, was a little shocked. 'Many things that are here seem right to me,' he wrote in a review. 'But they are expressed rather paradoxically. For there is no need to say that matter is nothing. It is sufficient to say that it is a phenomenon like a rainbow.'[16]

Berkeley's immaterialism was presented again in 1713 in *Three Dialogues between Hylas and Philonous*, a brief work which is one of the most charming pieces of philosophy to be written in English. In the dialogue Philonous, the lover of mind, debates with Hylas, the patron of matter, and emerges triumphant. The argument proceeds in four stages. First, it is argued that all sensible qualities are ideas. Second, the notion of inert matter is tested to destruction. Third, a proof is offered of the existence of God. Finally, ordinary language is reinterpreted to match an immaterialist metaphysics. In the end, Hylas agrees that trees and chairs are nothing but bundles of ideas, produced in our minds by God, whose own perception of them is the only thing that keeps them in continuous existence.

[15] And indeed, when tested in 1963, was found to be false: a man who recovered his sight after a corneal graft was immediately able, from experience of feeling the hands of his pocket watch, to tell the time visually. R. L. Gregory, *The Oxford Companion to the Mind* (Oxford: Oxford University Press, 1987), p. 95.

[16] Written in Leibniz's copy of the *Principles*; quoted in S. Brown, *Leibniz* (Brighton: Harvester Press, 1984), p. 42.

Berkeley's final work of theoretical philosophy was a Latin treatise on motion, published in 1712. By that time he had been for two years a priest of the Protestant Church of Ireland. From time to time he visited London, where he became a friend of Alexander Pope and was presented at court by Jonathan Swift. In 1714 he made a grand tour of the continent, taking the Alpine route in the middle of winter in an open chair; he was suitably terrified by Mont Cenis, 'high, craggy and steep enough to cause the heart of the most valiant man to melt within him'.

In 1724 he became Dean of Derry, and resigned his Fellowship of Trinity. Shortly afterwards he conceived the plan of founding a college in Bermuda to educate and give religious instruction to the sons of British colonists from mainland America alongside native Americans. He foresaw that the leadership of the civilized world would one day pass to America, and in a poem 'On the Prospect of Planting Arts and Learning in America' he wrote:

> Westward the course of empire takes its way
> The four first acts already past
> A fifth shall close the drama with the day:
> Time's noblest offspring is the last.

Berkeley obtained a charter for his college and the promise of a parliamentary grant of £20,000. He set sail across the Atlantic in 1728. Having reached Newport, Rhode Island, he soon determined that this would be a more suitable venue for his academy. But the promised grant did not in the end materialize, and he returned to England in 1731 without having achieved anything. The citizens of the United States, however, did not forget his care for the education of their ancestors, and named after him a college at Yale and a university town in California.

In 1734 Berkeley was appointed Bishop of Cloyne. Although he was a conscientious bishop, his pastoral task was not a heavy one, and he devoted himself to propagating the virtues of tar-water, which he advertised as a panacea for most human diseases. Tar-water was a concoction from the bark of pine trees which Berkeley had seen used in America as a remedy for smallpox. It is, he wrote in his treatise *Siris,* 'of a nature so mild and benign and proportioned to the human constitution, as to warm without heating, to cheer but not inebriate'. His words were later purloined by the poet Cowper and used in praise of tea.

In 1749 Berkeley wrote *A Word to the Wise* in which he exhorts the Roman Catholic clergy in his diocese to join with him in endeavouring to stir their countrymen out of their hereditary laziness and to improve the wretched economic condition of Ireland. Three years later the government offered him a more lucrative Irish see, but he refused the offer and retired to Oxford. He spent the last year of his life in a modest house in Holywell Street. He died at the beginning of 1753, while listening to his wife reading from the Bible; he was buried in Christ Church Cathedral where his monument may still be seen.

Berkeley was long remembered, and not only in philosophical circles, for his paradoxical thesis that matter does not exist and that so-called material objects are only ideas that God shares with us, from time to time. His slogan *esse est percipi*—to be is to be perceived—was widely quoted and widely mocked. Some people, such as Dr Samuel Johnson, thought the doctrine was incredible; others, such as the poet Arthur Hugh Clough, thought that it made no real difference to life.

James Boswell describes how he discussed Berkeley's immaterialism with Johnson in a churchyard. 'I observed, that though we are satisfied his doctrine is not true, it is impossible to refute it. I never shall forget the alacrity with which Johnson answered, striking his foot with mighty force against a large stone, till he rebounded from it, "I refute it *thus*."

In Clough's *Dipsychus* the young hero professes an austere ideal of lonely communion with God. His interlocutor, the voice of worldly wisdom, finds this hard to take seriously:

> To these remarks so sage and clerkly,
>   Worthy of Malebranche or Berkeley
> I trust it won't be deemed a sin
>   If I too answer with a grin.
> These juicy meats, this flashing wine,
>   May be an unreal mere appearance;
> Only—for my inside, in fine,
>   They have a singular coherence.
> This lovely creature's glowing charms
>   Are gross illusion, I don't doubt that;
> But when I pressed her in my arms
>   I somehow didn't think about that.

> (*Poems* (Oxford: Oxford University Press, 1974), p. 241)

3

Hume to Hegel

Hume

Shortly after Berkeley, in Dublin, gave the world his empiricist meta-physics, there was born in Edinburgh a philosopher who was to take empiricist principles to an anti-metaphysical extreme, David Hume. Hume was born in 1711 into a junior branch of a noble Scottish family. As the younger son of a mother widowed early he had to make his own way in the world. Between twelve and fifteen he studied literature and philosophy at Edinburgh University, falling in love, he tells us, with both subjects. He then set out to prepare himself for a legal profession, but soon gave up because, in his own words, he found 'an insurmountable Aversion to anything but the pursuits of Philosophy and General Learning'.

Despite this, he did attempt a commercial career with a sugar firm in Bristol; but four months of clerking there convinced him that a life in business was not for him. He decided to live frugally on his small inher-itance, and went across to France where life in a country town need not be expensive. From 1734–7 he lived at La Flèche in Anjou, where Descartes had been educated at the Jesuit college. Making use of the college library, Hume wrote his first work, a substantial *Treatise of Human Nature*.

On returning to England he found some difficulty in getting this work published, and when it appeared he was disappointed by its reception. 'Never Literary Attempt was more unfortunate than my Treatise,' he wrote in his autobiography. 'It fell *dead-born from the Press*.' After his death, how-ever, it was to achieve enormous fame. German idealists in the eighteenth century and British idealists in the nineteenth took it as the target of their criticisms of empiricism: they detested it, but at the same time they revered

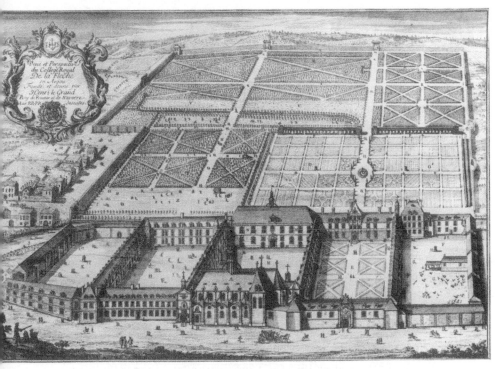

A seventeenth-century engraving of the college of La Flèche

it. British empiricists in the twentieth century extolled it as the greatest work of philosophy in the English language. Certainly the book, along with Hume's later more popular presentations of its ideas, came to exercise a greater influence than the work of any philosopher since Descartes. The town of La Flèche can be proud of its contribution to philosophy.

The *Treatise* was published in three volumes, the first two ('Of the Understanding' and 'Of the Passions') in 1739, and the third ('Of Morals') in 1740. The aim of the work was stated in the subtitle of the first edition, *An Attempt to introduce the experimental method of reasoning into Moral Subjects.* Hume saw himself as doing for psychology what Newton had done for physics, by applying the experimental method to moral subjects. He set out to provide an account of the relationships between ideas which would be a counterpart of the gravitational attraction between bodies. Notions like causation and obligation, which had been obfuscated by the metaphysicians, would for the first time be brought into clear light. All the sciences would benefit: instead of taking small forts on the frontiers of knowledge, we would now be able to 'march up directly to the capital or centre of these sciences, to human nature itself' (*T*).

The first book of the *Treatise* begins by setting out an empiricist classification of the contents of the mind ('perceptions'). This covers much of the same ground as Locke and Berkeley's epistemology, but Hume divides perceptions into two classes, impressions and ideas. Impressions are more forceful, more vivid, than ideas. Impressions include sensations and emotions; ideas are perceptions involved in thinking and reasoning. Hume treats in detail ideas of memory and imagination, and the association between them. He endorses and reinforces Berkeley's criticism of Locke's abstract ideas.

After a second part devoted to the ideas of space and time[1] Hume presents, in a section entitled 'Of Knowledge and Probabilty', his most original and influential thoughts. All knowledge that extends beyond the immediate deliveries of the senses, Hume argues, depends upon the notions of cause and effect: it is through those ideas that we discover what happened in the past and conjecture what will happen in the future. We must therefore examine closely the origin of these ideas.

The idea of causation, he says, cannot arise from any inherent quality of object, because objects of the most different kinds can be causes and effects. We must look, instead, for relationships between objects; and we find that causes and effects must be contiguous to each other, and that causes must be prior to their effects. Moreover, contiguity and succession are not enough for us to pronounce two objects to be cause and effect, unless we see that objects of the two kinds are found in constant conjunction. But that is not enough: if we are to infer an effect from its cause, we feel, there must be a necessary connection between a cause and its effect.

After many pages of artful argument, Hume leads us to an astonishing conclusion: it is not our inference that depends on the necessary connection between cause and effect, but the necessary connection that depends on the inference we draw from one to the other. Our belief in necessary connection is not a matter of reasoning, but of custom; and to wean us from the contrary doctrine Hume presents his own analysis of the relationship between reason and belief. He rounds off the book on

---

[1] See Ch. 4 below.

understanding with a Part that places his novel scepticism in the context of other versions of scepticism, ancient and modern. The Part ends with a celebrated section in which Hume denies the existence of the self as conceived by philosophers.[2]

In devoting the second book of the *Treatise* to a disquisition on the passions or emotions, Hume was following in the footsteps of Descartes and Spinoza. But the topic is much more important for him than it was for those rationalist thinkers, since his philosophy of mind attributes to the passions many of the operations which they regarded as activities of reason—causal inference being only the most striking example of many.

Passions, Hume tells us, are a special kind of impression. Having divided perceptions into impressions and ideas, he makes a further division between original and secondary impressions: sense impressions and physical pains and pleasures are the original impressions, and the secondary impressions are the passions which form the topic of the book. Particular passions, such as pride and humility, or love and hatred, are discussed in quaint detail. The book's most striking conclusion is that the much discussed conflict between passion and reason is a metaphysician's myth. Reason itself, we are told, is impotent to produce any action: all voluntary behaviour is motivated by passion. Passion can never be overcome by reason, but only by a contrary passion. This thesis should not perturb us: 'reason is and ought only to be the slave of the passions, and can never pretend to any other office than to serve and obey them' (*T* II. 3. 3).

By the end of Book Two it is already clear that Hume's ethical system is going to be something rather different from any traditional moral philosophy. Since reason cannot move us to action, moral judgements cannot be the product of reason because the whole purpose of such judgements is to guide our behaviour. Reason is concerned either with relations of ideas or with matters of fact, but neither of these leads on to action. Only the passions can do that, and reason can neither cause nor judge our passions. 'Tis not contrary to reason to prefer the destruction of the whole world to the scratching of my finger.' All that reason can do its to determine the feasibility of the objects sought by the passions and the best methods of achieving them. Hume concludes his remarks on reason and passion with a famous paragraph:

---

[2] Hume's treatment of causation is discussed in detail in Ch. 6 and his treatment of the self in Ch. 7.

In every system of morality, which I have hitherto met with, I have always remark'd that the author proceeds for some time in the ordinary way of reasoning, and establishes the being of a God, or makes observations concerning human affairs; when of a sudden I am surpriz'd to find, that instead of the usual copulations of propositions, *is*, and *is not*, I meet with no proposition that is not connected with an *ought* or *ought not*. The change is imperceptible; but is, however, of the last consequence. (*T* III.1.1)

An 'ought' cannot be derived from an 'is' and the conclusion we must draw is that distinctions between good and evil, right and wrong, are the product not of reason but of a moral sense.

From this basis Hume goes on in the second part of the book to discuss justice and injustice, and in the third book other natural virtues such as benevolence and greatness of mind. He concludes that the chief source of moral distinctions is the feeling of sympathy with others. Justice is approved of because it tends to the public good; and the public good is indifferent to us, except in so far as sympathy interests us in it. 'Virtue is consider'd as a means to an end. Means to an end are only valued so far as the end is valued. But the happiness of strangers affects us by sympathy alone' (*T* III. 3.6).

The *Treatise of Human Nature* is a very remarkable achievement for a man in his twenties, and it was no wonder that Hume was disappointed by its reception. He recovered from his initial depression, and decided that the faults in the book were a matter of presentation rather than substance. Accordingly, in 1740 he published anonymously a brief abstract of the work, especially its theory of causation. After two further anonymous volumes, *Essays Moral and Political* (1741–2), which were well received, he rewrote in popular form much of the content of the *Treatise*. An *Enquiry Concerning Human Understanding*, corresponding to the first volume, appeared (under a slightly different title) in 1748 and (in a definitive edition) in 1751. This omitted the earlier consideration of space and time, but included a chapter on miracles which gave great offence to orthodox readers of the Bible. Also in 1751 Hume published *An Enquiry Concerning the Principles of Morals*, which was an abridged and revised version of the third part of the *Treatise*.

In 1745 Hume had applied for a philosophy professorship at Edinburgh. He was unsuccessful, but he did obtain a post as tutor to the young Marquis of Annandale. Next he was taken into the entourage of a distant cousin,

General St Clair, under whom he served on a naval expedition to Brittany during the War of the Austrian Succession. Towards the end of that war, in 1747, he accompanied the general on diplomatic missions to Vienna and Turin. At last he began to taste prosperity: he boasted that he had amassed savings of £1,000 and he was described by a contemporary as resembling 'A Turtle Eating Alderman'. In 1751 he was made librarian to the Faculty of Advocates in Edinburgh, and set up house in the city with his sister.

In the 1750s Hume's philosophical works began to sell well and to achieve fame or at least notoriety. 'Answers by Reverends and Right Reverends', he tells us, 'came out two or three in a year.' But his own work took a new turn. Between 1754 and 1761 he wrote a six-volume history of England with a strong Tory bias. During his lifetime, indeed, he was much better known as a historian than as a philosopher.

In 1763, at the end of the Seven Years War, Hume became secretary to the British Embassy in Paris, and during a six-month period between one ambassador and another he served as *chargé d'affaires*. He found the environment most congenial, consorting with philosophers such as Diderot and d'Alembert, and engaging in an elegant flirtation with the Comtesse de Boufflers, continued in a series of love letters after his return to Britain. He brought back with him to London the Swiss philosopher, Jean-Jacques Rousseau, who feared persecution on the continent. Rousseau's difficult temperament was proof against Hume's kindly efforts to befriend and protect him, and in 1767 the two philosophers parted after a well-publicized quarrel.

Hume's career in government service ended with two years as undersecretary for the northern department from 1767–9 in the administration of the Duke of Grafton. He retired to Edinburgh where he lived until his death in 1776. He spent some time revising a set of *Dialogues Concerning Natural Religion*, a philosophical attack on natural theology, which was published posthumously in 1779. To the disappointment of James Boswell (who recorded his final illness in detail) he died serenely, having declined the consolations of religion. He left a brief autobiography which was brought out in 1777 by his friend Adam Smith, the economist. Smith himself wrote of Hume: 'Upon the whole, I have always considered him, both in his life-time and since his death, as approaching as nearly to the

Hume's draft of a letter to Rousseau inviting him to England

idea of a perfectly wise and virtuous man, as perhaps the nature of human frailty will admit.'

Smith and Reid

Adam Smith's own place is in the history of economics rather than that of philosophy, but he did hold chairs of logic and moral philosophy at Glasgow University, and in 1759 he published a *Theory of Moral Sentiments*. In this work

he carried further Hume's emphasis on the role of sympathy as a fundamental element in our moral judgements, presenting a more complex
analysis of sympathy itself and of its relationship to morality. Whereas, for
Hume, sympathy was essentially a sharing of pleasure or pain with another,
for Smith sympathy has a broader scope and can arise from the sharing of
any passion. Thus, our concern for justice arises from sympathy with
a victim's resentment of harm. Our approval of benevolence arises from
sympathy both with the benefactor's generosity and with the beneficiary's
gratitude. Because of the role of sympathy in generating moral judgement,
the motive of an action matters more to us than outcome; hence utility,
though of the first importance in economics, is not the ultimate criterion
for morality. 'The usefulness of any disposition of mind is seldom the first
ground of our approbation, and the sentiment of approbation always
involves in it a sense of propriety quite distinct from the perception
of utility' (*TMS*, 189).

Moral judgement, he insists, is essentially a social enterprise: a person
brought up on a desert island 'could no more think of his own character,
of the propriety or demerit of his own sentiments and conduct, of the
beauty or deformity of his own mind than of the beauty or deformity of his
own face' (*TMS*, 110). We need the mirror of society to show us ourselves:
we cannot form any judgement of our own sentiments or motives unless
we can somehow distance ourselves from them. Hence:

I divide myself, as it were, into two persons...The first is the spectator, whose
sentiments with regard to my own conduct I endeavour to enter into, by placing
myself in his situation, and by considering how it would appear to me, when seen
from that particular point of view. The second is the agent, the person whom
I properly call myself, and of whose conduct, under the character of a spectator,
I was endeavouring to form some opinion. (*TMS*, 113)

This character, the impartial spectator whom Smith thus introduces into
ethics, was to make a frequent appearance in the pages of subsequent moral
philosophers.

While Adam Smith admired Hume and developed some of his philosophical ideas in an amicable manner, his successor at Glasgow as professor of
moral philosophy, Thomas Reid, (1710–96), was one of the earliest and fiercest
critics not only of Hume but of the whole tradition to which he belonged. In
1764 he published an *Inquiry into the Human Mind on the Principles of Common Sense* in

response to Hume's *Treatise,* and he followed this up in the 1780s with two essays on the intellectual and active powers of man. The paradoxical conclusions to which Hume's investigations led made Reid call in question the basic principles from which he began, and in particular the system of ideas common to both the British empiricists and the continental Cartesians:

When we find the gravest philosophers, from Des Cartes down to Bishop Berkeley, mustering up arguments to prove the existence of a material world, and unable to find any that will bear examination; when we find Bishop Berkeley and Mr Hume, the acutest metaphysicians of the age, maintaining that there is no such thing as matter in the universe—that sun, moon, and stars, the earth which we inhabit, our own bodies, and those of our friends, are only ideas in our minds, and have no existence but in thought; when we find the last maintaining that there is neither body nor mind—nothing in nature but ideas and impressions—that there is no certainty, nor indeed probability, even in mathematical axioms: I say, when we consider such extravagancies of many of the most acute writers on this subject, we may be apt to think the whole to be only a dream of fanciful men, who have entangled themselves in cobwebs spun our of their own brain.

The whole of recent philosophy, Reid maintains, shows how even the most intelligent people can go wrong if they start from a false first principle.

Reid puts his finger accurately on the basic error of Descartes and Locke, arising from the ambiguity of the word 'idea'. In ordinary language 'idea' means an act of mind; to have an idea of something is to conceive it, to have a concept of it. But philosophers have given it a different meaning, Reid says, according to which 'it does not signify that act of the mind which we call thought or conception, but some object of thought'. Ideas which are first introduced as humble images or proxies of things end up by supplanting what they represent and undermine everything but themselves: 'Ideas seem to have something in their nature unfriendly to other existences.'

Ideas in the philosophical sense—postulated intermediaries between the mind and the world—are, in Reid's view, mere fictions. We do of course, have conceptions of many things, but conceptions are not images, and in any case it is not conceptions that are the basic building blocks of knowledge, but propositions. Followers of Locke think that knowledge begins with bare conceptions ('simple apprehensions'), which we then put together to form beliefs and judgements. But that is the wrong way of looking at things. 'Instead of saying that the belief or knowledge is got by putting together and comparing the simple apprehensions, we ought rather to say that the simple apprehension is performed by resolving and analysing a natural and original judgement' (*I.* 2, 4). This thesis that concepts are logically subsequent to propositions, and result from their analysis, was an anticipation of a doctrine popular with some analytic philosophers in the twentieth century.

When I see a tree, Reid argues, I do not receive a mere idea of a tree; my vision of the tree involves the judgement that it exists with a certain shape, size, and position. The initial furniture of the mind is not a set of disconnected ideas, but a set of 'original and natural judgements'. These make up what Reid calls 'the common sense of mankind'. 'Common sense', before Reid, was commonly used by philosophers as the name of an alleged inner sense which discriminated between, and brought together, sense data from different exterior senses. It was Reid who gave the expression the meaning which it has borne in modern times, as a repository of commonly shared unreasoned principles. In the greatest part of mankind, Reid says, no higher degree of reason is to be found, but it is a universal gift of heaven.

Among the common principles that Reid regards as the foundation of reasoning are a number that had been called in question by the British empiricists. Against Berkeley, he insists that size, shape, and motion inhere in material substances. Against Locke, he insists that secondary qualities also are real qualities of bodies: a colour I see is not identical with my sensation of it, but is that sensation's cause. Against Hume, he insists that our conscious thoughts 'must have a subject which we call mind'. And he reaffirms the principle that whatever begins to exist must have a cause which produced it (*Essays on the Active Powers of the Human Mind*, 8.3, 6).

Hume often wrote with a degree of contempt about the beliefs of 'the vulgar'—the belief, for instance, that objects continue to exist unperceived. Reid believes that philosophers despise the vulgar at their peril, and that they can discount their beliefs only because they have surreptitiously changed the meaning of words. 'The vulgar have undoubted right to give names to things which they are daily conversant about; and philosophers seem justly chargeable with an abuse of language, when they change the meaning of a common word, without giving warning.'

Reid said that 'in the unequal contest betwixt common sense and philosophy the latter will always come off both with dishonour and loss' (*I*, 1, 4). These should not be taken as the words of a philistine Luddite opposed to science and technology. Like the ordinary language philosophers of whom he was a precursor, he thought that it was only with respect to the meaning of words, not with respect to the truth or falsehood of propositions, that the man in the street had the final say. And when he talks of 'common sense' he does not mean popular beliefs about nature, or old wives' gossip, but rather the self-evident principles which other philosophers presented as intuitions of reason. Science itself was not a matter of simple common sense, but rather of rational inquiry conducted in the light of common sense; and the outcome of scientific investigation may well trump individual prejudices of the vulgar.

Reid himself was an experimental scientist, who produced original results in the geometry of visible objects, some of them anticipating the development of non-Euclidean geometries. What he wanted to show in his philosophy was that the realism of the common man was at least as compatible with the pursuit of science as the sophisticated and sophistical philosophy of the rationalists and the empiricists.

The Enlightenment

Adam Smith and Thomas Reid were two distinguished ornaments of what later came to be known as the Scottish Enlightenment. Throughout the Europe of the eighteenth century members of the intelligentsia saw themselves as bringing the light of reason into regions darkened by ignorance and superstition, but it was France which was seen by itself and others as the home of the Enlightenment *par excellence*. The high point of the French enlightenment was the publication in the 1750s and 1760s of the seventeen volumes of the *Encyclopédie, ou Dictionannaire raisonné des arts et des métiers,* edited by Denis Diderot and Jean d'Alembert. But the ground for this manifesto had been prepared for more than half a century by other French thinkers.

Pierre Bayle (1647–1706) had brought out a *Dictionnaire Historique et Critique* in which he showed, by detailed studies of biblical and historical personages, the inconsistency and incoherence of much of natural and revealed theology. The moral of his *tour d'horizon* was that religious faith was only tenable if accompanied by general toleration, and that the teaching of ethics should be made independent of religious instruction. Belief in human immortality, or in the existence of God, was not something necessary for virtuous living.

Bayle's scepticism was controverted by many, most notably by Leibniz in his *Theodicy*. But his negative attitude to religious authority set the tone for Enlightenment thinkers in Germany as well as in France. The positive element in the Enlightenment—the attempt to achieve a scientific understanding of the human social and political condition—owed more to another, more systematic thinker, Charles de Secondat, Baron de Montesquieu (1689–1755).

Montesquieu's great work was *The Spirit of the Laws* (1748), which built up a theory of the nature of the state upon a mass of historical and sociological erudition. This work, which took many years to write, had been preceded by two shorter works—the *Persian Letters* of 1721, a satire on French society, and a more ponderous treatise on the causes of the greatness and decadence of the ancient Romans (1734).[3]

Montesquieu spent a period in England and acquired a great admiration for the English Constitution. His Anglophile passion was shared by later Enlightenment philosophers, who saw themselves as heirs of Bacon, Locke, and Newton rather than of Descartes, Spinoza, and Leibniz. The first philosophical publication of Voltaire (born in 1694 as François Marie Arouet), the *Philosophical Letters* of 1734, is full of enthusiasm for the comparative freedom and moderation of English political and ecclesiastical institutions. His admiration for British tolerance was all the more sincere, since before being exiled to England in 1726 he had already been imprisoned twice in the Bastille in punishment for libellous pamphlets about senior noblemen.

Locke, Voltaire says in his thirteenth letter, is the first philosopher to have given a sober account of the human soul in place of the romantic fantasies woven by earlier philosophers. 'He has displayed to mankind the human reason just like a good anatomist explaining the machinery of the human body.' In the years before the appearance of the *Encyclopédie* Voltaire made himself a lively publicist for English science and philosophy, publishing in 1738 his *Philosophy of Newton*. The very idea of an encyclopedia came from England, where in 1728 one Ephraim Chambers had produced, in two volumes *Cyclopaedia; or, an Universal Dictionary of Arts and Sciences*.

The two editors of the *Encyclopédie* were men of different talents and temperaments. D'Alembert was a gifted mathematician with original work in fluid dynamics to his credit. He aimed to bring to all the sciences the

---

[3] Montesquieu's political philosophy is treated in detail in Ch. 9.

Engraving by Hubert of Voltaire dining with fellow *philosophes*

clarity and accuracy of arithmetic and geometry. He was an early proponent of the ideal of a single great unified science. 'The Universe', he wrote in
the introduction to the *Encyclopédie*, 'would be only one fact and one great
truth for whoever knew how to embrace it from a single point of view.'
Diderot was more interested in the biological and social sciences than in
physics, and while d'Alembert was being fêted by academies, he spent a
term in prison because of a *Letter on the Blind* which questioned the existence
of design in the universe. The two men shared a faith in the inevitability
of scientific progress, a belief that the Christian religion was a great obstacle
to human betterment, and a fundamentally materialist view of human
nature. They gathered a group of like-minded thinkers as contributors to
the *Encyclopédie*, including, besides Montesquieu and Voltaire, Julien de La
Mettrie, a medical doctor who had recently published *L'Homme Machine*, the
Baron d'Holbach, an atheist who presided over a lavish philosophical salon,
and Claude Helvétius, a determinist psychologist who became notorious
for a book arguing that human beings had no intellectual powers distinct
from the senses.

While the Enlightenment philosophers were all anti-clerical, they were not all atheists. Voltaire, for instance, thought that the world as explained by Newton manifested the existence of God just as much as a watch shows the existence of a watchmaker. When he published his own *Philosophical Dictionary* in 1764 he wrote, in the entry on atheism:

Atheism is a monstrous evil in those who govern; and also in learned men even if their lives are innocent, because from their studies they can affect those who hold office; and that, even if not as baleful as fanaticism, it is nearly always fatal to virtue... Unphilosophical mathematicians have rejected final causes, but true philosophers accept them; and as a well-known author has said, a catechism announces God to children, and Newton demonstrates him to wise men. (*PD*, 38)

If God did not exist, Voltaire famously said, it would be necessary to invent him—otherwise the moral law would carry no weight. But he did not himself believe in a God who had freely created the world. Such a God would have to bear responsibility for catastrophic evils similar to the earthquake which struck Lisbon in 1755. The world was not a free creation, but a necessary, eternal, consequence of God's existence. To reject any accusation of atheism, Voltaire called himself a 'theist', but the standard philosophical term for those who believe in his type of divinity is 'deist'.

Although they are often seen as precursors of the French Revolution, the *philosophes* were not necessarily radical or even democratic. Diderot accepted the patronage of Catherine the Great of Russia, and Voltaire was for three years a chamberlain to Frederick II of Prussia. Their ideas of liberty resembled those of the English revolutionaries of 1688 more than those of the French revolutionaries of 1789. Freedom of expression was the freedom they most treasured, and they had no objection in principle to autocracy, although each of them was to find that their chosen despots were less enlightened than they had hoped. At home, both men were willing to take risks in protesting against abuses by government, but they did not call for any fundamental political changes. Least of all did they want an empowerment of the common people—the 'rabble', to use Voltaire's favourite term.

Rousseau

One encyclopedist was willing to go much further—Jean-Jacques Rousseau, who had contributed several articles on musical topics. Born in Geneva in

1712, the son of a watchmaker, Rousseau was brought up a Calvinist, but at the age of sixteen, a runaway apprentice, he became a Catholic in Turin. This was at the instigation of the Baronne de Warens, with whom he lived on and off between 1729 and 1740. After short spells as a singing master and a household tutor, he obtained a post as secretary to the French ambassador in Venice in 1743. Dismissed for insubordination, he went to Paris where he became close to Diderot, whom he visited regularly during his imprisonment. He was also for a while on good terms with d'Alembert and Voltaire. But he shocked the *philosophes* when in 1750 he published a prize essay which gave a negative answer to the question whether the progress of the arts and sciences had had a beneficial effect on morality. He followed this up four years later by a *Discourse on the Origin and Foundation of Inequality among Men*. The theme of both works was that humanity was naturally good, and corrupted by social institutions. The ideal human being was the 'noble savage' whose simple goodness put civilized man to shame. All this was, of course, at the opposite pole from the encyclopedists' faith in scientific and social progress: Voltaire called the *Discourse* 'a book against the human race'.

Rousseau exhibited his contempt for social convention in a practical form by a long-standing liason with a washerwoman, Therese Levasseur. By her he had five children whom he dumped, one after the other, in a foundling hospital. Having written an opera, *Le Devin du village*, which was performed before Louis XV at Fontainebleau, he returned to Geneva in 1754 and became a Calvinist again, in order to regain his citizenship there. Voltaire had returned from Berlin and was now settled in the Geneva region, but the two philosophers were not destined to be good neighbours: their mutual distaste became public with Rousseau's *Letter on Providence*, published in 1756. When, in 1757, d'Alembert published an encyclopedia article on Geneva in which he deplored the city's refusal to allow the peformance of comedies, Rousseau published in reply a *Letter to d'Alembert* in which he discoursed, in the style of Plato's *Republic*, on the morally corrupting influence of theatrical peformances. Rousseau had already quarelled with Diderot for leaking an amatory confidence, and his break with the *philosophes* was complete when he published his *Lettres Morales* of 1861.

The period 1758 to 1761 was very productive for Rousseau, who spent the years in retirement in a small French country house. He wrote a novel, *La Nouvelle Héloïse*, which was an immediate best-seller when it appeared

in Paris in 1761 He wrote also two philosophical treaties, one on education entitled *Émile,* and one on political philosophy, *The Social Contract.*
Émile narrated the life of a child educated apart from other children, as
an experiment; *The Social Contract* began with the memorable words 'Man is
born free, and is everywhere in chains.'[4] These two works were published in
1762 and immediately caused an uproar because of their inflammatory
doctrines. *Émile* was condemned by the Archbishop and Parliament of Paris
and it and *The Social Contract* were burnt in Geneva. With a warrant out for
his arrest in both cities, Rousseau fled to Switzerland (of which Geneva was
not at that time a part). After seeking refuge in various continental cities
he was given sanctuary in England through the good offices of David
Hume, who secured him a pension from King George III. But his paranoid
ingratitude turned Hume against him, and he returned to France, spending
the last years of his life (1770–78) in Paris. The main achievement of this
period was a book of autobiographical *Confessions,* which was published some
years after his death.

The year 1778 was also the time of Voltaire's death. In his later years his
writings had become more explicitly anti-Christian. From his safe haven
at Ferney, near Geneva, he published his irreverent *Pocket Philosophical
Dictionary* (1765) and *The Profession of Faith of Theists* in 1768. He wrote also
historical works and dramas, and he died just after returning to Paris for
the triumphant first night of his play *Irène.* Rousseau and Voltaire, enemies
in life, now lie side by side in the crypt of the Pantheon, the mausoleum in
Paris dedicated to the great men of France.

The philosophers of the French Enlightenment, and Rousseau especially, have been regarded by many as responsible for the revolutionary
convulsions into which France and Europe were plunged soon after their
deaths. Thomas Carlyle, author of *The French Revolution,* was once reproached
by a businessman for being too interested in mere ideas. 'There was once a
man called Rousseau', Carlyle replied, 'who wrote a book containing
nothing but ideas. The second edition was bound in the skins of those
who laughed at the first.'[5]

---

[4] Rousseau's political philosophy is discussed in detail in Ch. 9.
[5] Quoted in Alasdair MacIntyre, *A Short History of Ethics* (London: Routledge, 1976), p. 182.

A Female Philosopher in Extasy at solving a Problem

Rousseau, like the author of this cartoon, held the view that women were made for emotion, not for philosophizing

Wolff and Lessing

In Germany, the Enlightenment took a form that was less threatening to the existing establishment—partly, no doubt, because it enjoyed for a while the patronage of Frederick the Great, King of Prussia from 1740–86. In the first half of the eighteenth century the leading German philosopher was Christian Wolff (1679–1754), who began his career as a professor of mathematics at Halle, a post he was offered on the recommendation of Leibniz. When he first ventured into philosophy he aroused the hostility of devout Lutherans, who influenced the then monarch to deprive him of his chair and banish him from Prussia. Such an experience of persecution was almost the only thing Wolff had in common with the *philosophes*; unlike them, he was solemn, academic, systematic, and accurately erudite. His rationalism was at the opposite pole from Rousseau's romanticism.

Wolff taught for seventeen years in a Calvinist university in Marburg, but when Frederick the Great came to the throne he was restored to his chair in Halle, which he held until his death. Later, he became vice-chancellor of the university and was made a baron of the Holy Roman Empire. His philosophical system was eclectic and capacious, embracing elements from classical Aristotelianism, Latin scholasticism, Cartesian rationalism, and Leibnizian metaphysics. He took over from Leibniz the principle of sufficient reason, which he regarded as the fundamental basis of metaphysics in conjunction with the principle of identity. The sufficient reason for the existence of the world is to be found in a transcendent God, whose existence can be established by the traditional ontological and cosmological arguments. The world we live in is the best of all possible worlds, freely chosen by God's wisdom.

There was little that was original in Wolff, except for the system which he imposed upon his borrowings from earlier authors. He perceived it as his task, for instance, to impose order on what he saw as the chaos of Aristotle's metaphysics. He regimented the different branches of philosophy, popularizing such distinctions as those between natural theology and general metaphysics ('ontology'), which had been absent from medieval discussion. His definition of ontology as 'the science of all possible things insofar as they are possible', with its emphasis on possible essences rather than actual existents, was a continuation of a line begun by Avicenna and Duns Scotus. He introduced a novel distinction between physics (the experimental study of the contingent natural laws of this world) and cosmology (an *a priori* investigation of every possible material world).

Like Descartes, Wolff accepted the existence of a human soul that was a simple substance available to self-consciousness; but the relation between this soul and the body he explained by appeal to a Leibnizian pre-established harmony. In Wolff's ethical system the key notion is that of perfection. Good is what increases perfection, and evil what diminishes it. The fundamental human motivation is self-perfection, which includes the promotion of the common good and the service of God's honour. Although living bodies, including human bodies, are machines, nonetheless we enjoy free will: rational choice can, and should, overcome all the pressures of sensibility.

Wolff is nowadays hardly ever read by English readers. His importance in the history of philosophy is that his system became accepted in Germany as the paradigm of a rationalist metaphysics, and that later writers defined their own positions in relation to his. This is particularly true of Immanuel Kant, who in his magisterial critique of metaphysics often has Wolff's doctrines immediately in his sights.

A thinker who was much closer to the Enlightenment as understood in France and Britain was Gotthold Ephraim Lessing (1729–81). The son of a Lutheran pastor, he was initially destined for the Church, but he abandoned theology for a literary career, in which he supported himself by acting as librarian to the Duke of Brunswick. Like the *philosophes* he expressed his thoughts in essays and dramas in preference to academic textbooks. His first publication was an essay written jointly with the Jewish philosopher Moses Mendelssohn entitled '*Pope a Metaphysician!*', which was partly an attack on the Leibnizian views expressed in Pope's *Essay on Man*, but also a plea for a sharp separation between philosophy and poetry as two quite different spiritual activities. In *Laocoon* of 1776 he pleaded for a similar separation between poetry and the visual arts: the artistic effect of Virgil's description of the death of Laocoon is quite different, he argued, from that of the famous classical statue in the Vatican. In each case Lessing, taking as his starting point Aristotle's *Poetics* ('as much an infallible work as the *Elements of Euclid*'), delineated a special, semi-prophetic role for the poet. In doing so he foreshadowed one of the principal themes of Romanticism.

Like the Romantics, Lessing admired Spinoza. He regarded the world as a single unified system whose components were identical with ideas in the mind of God. He was willing to accept that determinism was true and that freedom was an illusion; on the other hand, he was willing to admit contingency in the world, with the consequence that some among God's ideas were contingent also. He praised Spinoza for realizing that liberation from anxiety is only to be achieved by accepting the inevitability of destiny. 'I thank my God', he said, 'that I am under necessity, that the best must be.'

Lessing's most important philosophical work was *The Education of the Human Race* (1780). The human race, like the human individual, passes through different stages, to which different kinds of instruction are appropriate. The upbringing of a child is a matter of physical rewards and punishment: the childhood of the human race was the era of the Old Testament. In our youth, educators offer us more spiritual rewards for good conduct; eternal rewards and punishments for an immortal soul. This corresponds to the period of history dominated by the Christian religion. However, as Lessing endeavoured to show in a number of critical studies of the New Testament, the evidence for the divine origin of Christianity is uncompelling. Even the strongest historical evidence about contingent facts, Lessing went on to argue, cannot justify any conclusion to necessary truths about matters of divinity.

The Christian religion, therefore, can be no more than a stage in the education of the human race, and its dogmas can have no more than symbolic value. Human nature, come of age, must extract from Christianity a belief in the universal brotherhood of man, and must pursue moral values for their own sake, not for the sake of any reward here or hereafter (although Lessing toys with the idea of a transmigration of souls into a new incarnation after death). Like the leaders of the French Enlightenment, Lessing was a passionate advocate of religious toleration; he gave fullest expression to this advocacy in his drama *Nathan the Wise* (1779). One reason for toleration that Lessing offers is that the worth of a person does not depend on whether his beliefs are true, but on how much trouble he has taken to attain the truth. This novel argument was presented in a vivid paragraph often quoted since:

If God held all truth in his right hand and in his left the everlasting striving after truth, so that I should always and everlastingly be mistaken, and said to me, Choose, with humility I would pick on the left hand and say, Father, grant me that; absolute truth is for thee alone. (*Gesammelte Werke*, ed. Lachmann and Muncker, XIII. 23)

Kant

One man who devoted his whole life to the pursuit of absolute truth was Immanuel Kant: indeed, apart from this pursuit, there is little to tell about his biography. Born in 1724 in Königsberg, which was then in the eastern part of Prussia, he lived all his life in the town of his birth. From 1755 until 1770 he was a *Privatdozent* or lecturer in Königsberg University, and from 1770 until his death in 1804 he held the professorship of logic and metaphysics there. He never travelled or married or held public office, and the story of his life is the story of his ideas.

Kant was brought up in a devout Lutheran family, but he later became liberal in his theological views, though perforce regular in religious observance. He was always a man of strict life and constant habit, notorious for exact punctuality, rising at five and retiring at ten, lecturing in the morning from seven to eight, and then writing until a late and ample luncheon. The citizens of Königsberg used to joke that they could set their watches by his appearance for his afternoon constitutional. As a university student he was taught by a disciple of Wolff, but his own early interests were more scientific than philosophical, and as a *Privatdozent* he lectured not only on logic and metaphysics but on subjects as diverse as anthropology, geography, and mineralogy. His first books, too, were written on scientific subjects, most notably the *General History of Nature and Theory of the Heavens* of 1755.

From 1760 onwards he began to devote himself seriously to philosophy, but for the next twenty years the works he published were of a cautious and conventional kind. In 1762 he wrote a short and rather superficial essay on the traditional syllogistic, criticizing the unnecessary subtlety ('Die falsche Sptizfindigkeit', as the essay's title has it) of its customary presentation. In the same year he wrote *The Only Possible Ground for a Demonstration of God's Existence*, in which, while rejecting three of the standard proofs of God's existence, he argued, in the spirit of Wolff and Duns Scotus, that if there are any possible beings at all there must be a perfect being to provide the ground of this possibility.

In 1763 the Berlin Academy set as a prize question 'whether metaphysical truths can be demonstrated with the same certainty as truths of geometry'. Kant's (unsuccessful) entry for the prize underlined a number of crucial distinctions between mathematical and philosophical method. Mathematicians start from clear definitions which create concepts which they then go on to develop; philosophers start from confused concepts and analyse them in order to reach a definition. Metaphysicians rather than aping mathematicians should follow Newtonian methods, by applying them not to the physical world but to the phenomena of inner experience.

The programme that Kant lays out here for the philosopher closely resembles that which Hume had set himself, and later Kant was to credit Hume with having woken him from the 'dogmatic slumber' of the years when he accepted the philosophy of Leibniz and Wolff. It is not certain when Kant began the serious study of Hume, but during the 1760s he became increasingly sceptical of the possibility of a scientific metaphysics. The anonymous, skittish *Dreams of a Ghost Seer* of 1766 compared metaphysical speculations with the esoteric fantasies of the visionary Immanuel Swedenborg. Among other things, Kant emphasized, in the wake of Hume, that causal relations could be known only through experience and were never matters of logical necessity. However, his inaugural dissertation as professor in 1770 (*On the Form and Principles of the Sensible and Intelligible World*) still shows the strong influence of Leibniz.

The first eleven years of his professorship were spent by Kant in developing his own original system, which was published in 1781 in *The Critique of Pure Reason*, a work which at once put his pre-critical works in the shade and established him as one of the greatest philosophers of the modern age. He followed it up with a briefer and more popular exposition of its ideas, the *Prolegomena to any Future Metaphysics* (1783), and republished it in a second edition in 1787.

Kant's aim in his critical philosophy was to make philosophy, for the first time, fully scientific. Mathematics had been scientific for many centuries, and scientific physics had come of age. But metaphysics, the oldest discipline, the one which 'would survive even if all the rest were swallowed up in the abyss of an all-destroying barbarism', was still far from maturity. Metaphysical curiosity was inherent in human nature: human beings could not but be interested in the three main objects of metaphysics, namely, God, freedom, and immortality. But could metaphysics become a true science?

Hume and others, as we have seen, had tried to do for the philosophy of mind what Newton had done for the philosophy of bodies, making the association of ideas the psychic counterpart of gravitational attraction between bodies. Kant's programme for rendering metaphysics scientific was on a more ambitious scale. Philosophy, he believed, needed a revolution like that of Copernicus who had moved the earth from the centre of the universe to put the sun in its place. Copernicus had shown that when we think we are observing the motion of the sun round the earth what we see is the consequence of the rotation of our own earth. Kant's Copernican revolution will do for our reason what Copernicus did for our sight. Instead of asking how our knowledge can conform to its objects, we must start from the supposition that objects must conform to our knowledge. Only in this way can we justify the claim of metaphysics to possess knowledge that is necessary and universal.

Kant distinguishes between two modes of knowledge: knowledge *a priori* and knowledge *a posteriori*. We know a truth *a posteriori* if we know it through

An engraving of Kant at the age when he published his first *Critique*

experience; we know it *a priori* if we know it independently of all experience. Kant agreed with Locke that all our knowledge begins with experience, but he did not believe that it all arose from experience. There are some things that we know *a priori*, fundamental truths that are not mere generalizations from experience. Among the judgements that we make *a priori* some, Kant says, are analytic, and some are synthetic. In an analytic judgement, such as 'all bodies are extended', we are merely making explicit in the predicate something that is already contained in the concept of the subject. But in a synthetic judgement the predicate adds something to the content of the subject: Kant's example is 'all bodies are heavy'. All *a posteriori* propositions are synthetic, and all analytic propositions are *a priori*. Can there be propositions that are synthetic, and yet *a priori*? Kant believes that there are. For him, mathematics offers examples of synthetic *a priori* truths. Most importantly, there must be propositions that are both *a priori* and synthetic if it is ever going to be possible to make a genuine science out of metaphysics.

The philosopher's first task is to make plain the nature and limits of the powers of the mind. Like medieval and rationalist philosophers before him, Kant distinguishes sharply between the senses and the intellect; but within the intellect he makes a new distinction of his own between understanding (*Verstand*) and reason (*Vernunft*). The understanding operates in combination with the senses in order to provide human knowledge: through the senses, objects are given us; through the understanding, they are made thinkable. Experience has a content, provided by the senses, and a structure, determined by the understanding. Reason, by contrast with understanding, is the intellect's endeavour to go beyond what understanding can achieve. When divorced from experience it is 'pure reason', and it is this which is the target of Kant's criticism.

Before addressing pure reason, Kant's *Critique* makes a systematic study of the senses and the understanding. The senses are studied in a section entitled 'Transcendental Aesthetic', and the understanding in a section entitled 'Transcendental Logic'. 'Transcendental' is a favourite word of Kant's; he used it with several meanings, but common to all of them is the notion of something which (for better or worse) goes beyond and behind the deliverances of actual experience.

The transcendental aesthetic is largely devoted to the study of space and time. Sensations, Kant says, have a matter (or content) and a form. Space is the form of the outer senses, and time is the form of the inner sense. Space and time are not entities in the world discovered by the mind: they are the pattern into which the senses mould experience. In expounding his transcendental aesthetic, Kant offers his own novel solution to the age-old question 'Are space and time real?'[6]

When we move from the transcendental aesthetic to the transcendental logic we again encounter a twofold division. The logic consists of two major enterprises, which Kant calls the *transcendental analytic* and the *transcendental dialectic*. The analytic sets out the criteria for the valid empirical employment of the understanding; the dialectic exposes the illusions that arise when reason tries to operate outside the limits set by the analytic. In his analytic Kant lays out a set of *a priori* concepts which he calls 'categories', and a set of *a priori* judgements which he calls 'principles'. Accordingly, the analytic is again subdivided, into two main sections, containing 'The Deduction of the Categories' and 'The System of Principles'.

The first section presents the deduction, or legitimation, of the categories. Categories are concepts of a particularly fundamental kind: Kant gives as instances the concepts of 'cause' and 'substance'. Without these categories, he argues, we could not conceptualize or understand even the most fragmentary and disordered experience. His aim here is to meet the empiricist's challenge on the empiricist's own ground. He agrees with the empiricist that all our knowledge begins with experience, but he denies that all of it arises from experience. He seeks to show that without the metaphysical concepts that Hume sought to dismantle, Hume's own basic items of experience, impressions, and ideas would themselves disintegrate.

The second section of the analytic, the system of principles, contains a number of synthetic *a priori* propositions about experience. Experiences, Kant maintains, must possess two kinds of magnitude—extensive magnitude (of which an instance is the distance between two points) and intensive magnitude (of which an instance is a particular degree of heat) Moreover, Kant maintains, experience is only possible if necessary connections are to be found among our perceptions. Hume was wrong to think that we first perceive temporal succession between events, and then go on to regard one as cause and another as effect. On the contrary, we could not establish an

---

[6] Kant's account of space and time is considered at greater length in Ch. 5.

objective time sequence unless we had already established relationships between causes and effects.[7]

While Kant is hostile to empiricism, he attacks rationalism no less vigorously. At the end of his analytic he insists that the categories cannot determine their own applicability, the principles cannot establish their own truth. Understanding alone cannot establish that there is any such thing as a substance, or that every change has a cause. All that one can establish *a priori* is that if experience is to be possible, certain conditions must hold. But whether experience is possible cannot be established in advance: the possibility of experience is shown only by the actual occurrence of experience itself.

The analytic shows that there cannot be a world of mere appearances, mere objects of sense that do not fall under any categories or instantiate any rules. But we cannot conclude from this that there is a non-sensible world that is established by the intellect alone. To accept the existence of extra-sensible objects that can be studied by the use of pure reason is to enter a realm of illusion, and in his 'transcendental dialectic' Kant explores this world of enchantment.

'Transcendental', as has been said, means something that goes beyond and behind the deliverances of actual experience, and in his dialectic Kant has three principal targets: metaphysical psychology, metaphysical cosmology, and metaphysical theology. 'Pure reason', he tells us, 'furnished the idea for a transcendental doctrine of the soul, for a transcendental science of the world, and finally for a transcendental knowledge of God.' In turn he tests to destruction the three notions of an immaterial immortal soul, of a surveyable cosmic whole, and of an absolutely necessary being.

Rationalist psychology, as practised by Descartes, started with the premiss 'I think' and concluded to the existence of a substance that was immaterial, incorruptible, personal, and immortal. Kant argues that this line of argument is littered with fallacies—he lists four of them which he calls 'the paralogisms of pure reason'. These paralogisms are not accidental: in principle, any attempt to go beyond empirical psychology must be guilty of fallacy.

In order to dismantle *a priori* cosmology, Kant sets up four antinomies. An antinomy is a pair of contrasting arguments which lead to contradictory

---

[7] Kant's account of the relation between time and causation is discussed in Chapter 6.

conclusions (a thesis and an antithesis). The first of the four antinomies has as its thesis 'The world has a beginning in time and is limited in space,' and as antithesis 'The world has no beginning in time and no limits in space.' Kant offers proofs of both these propositions. He does not, of course, mean us to conclude that both contradictories are true: the moral is that reason has no right to talk at all about 'the world' as a whole.

In each of the antinomies the thesis states that a certain series comes to a full stop and the antithesis states that it continues for ever. The second antinomy concerns divisibility, the third concerns causation, and the fourth concerns contingency. In each case Kant presents the series as a series of entities that are conditioned by something else—an effect, for instance, is in his terms 'conditioned' by its cause. In each of the antinomies, the thesis of the argument concludes to an unconditioned absolute. Both sides of each antinomy, Kant believes, are in error: the thesis is the error of dogmatism and the antithesis the error of empiricism. The point of constructing the antinomies is to exhibit the mismatch between the scope of empirical inquiry and the pretensions of pure reason. The thesis represents the world as smaller than thought (we can think beyond it); the antithesis represents it as larger than thought (we cannot think to the end of it). We must match thought and the world by trimming our cosmic ideas to fit the empirical inquiry.[8]

In his fourth antinomy Kant proposes arguments for and against the existence of a necessary being, and then in a later section of the *Critique* he goes on to consider the concept of God as held out by natural theology. He classifies arguments for God's existence into three fundamental types, and shows how arguments of every type must fail. If God is to have a place in our thought and life, he believed, it is not as an entity whose existence is established by rational proof.

The Critique of Pure Reason is not an easy book to read, and not all the difficulty is due to the profundity of its subject matter or the originality of its thought. Kant (as must already be apparent) was excessively fond of inventing technical terms and (as will appear elsewhere in this book) was too anxious to force ideas into rigid schematisms. But any reader who perseveres through the difficult text will enjoy a rich philosophical reward.

---

[8] A further account of the antinomies will be found in Ch. 5.

In his sixties, Kant turned his attention to ethics and aesthetics in three seminal works: *Fundamental Principles of the Metaphysics of Morals* (1785); *The Critique of Practical Reason* (1788); and *The Critique of Judgement* (1790). In the first two of these he aimed to set out critically the synthetic *a priori* principles of practical reason just as he had, in his first *Critique*, set out the synthetic *a priori* principles of theoretical reason.

The starting point of Kant's moral theory is that the only thing that is good without qualification is a good will. Talents, character, and fortune can be used to bad ends and even happiness can be corrupting. It is not what a good will achieves that matters; good will, even if frustrated in its efforts, is good in itself alone. What makes a will good is that it is motivated by duty: to act from duty is to exhibit good will in the face of difficulty. Some people may enjoy doing good, or profit from doing good, but worth of character is shown only when someone does good not from inclination, but for duty's sake.

To act from duty is to act out of reverence for the moral law, to act in obedience to a moral imperative. There are two sorts of imperative, hypothetical and categorical. A hypothetical imperative says: if you wish to achieve a certain end, act in such-and-such a way. The categorical imperative says: no matter what end you wish to achieve, act in such-and-such a way. There are as many sets of hypothetical imperatives as there are different ends that human beings may set themselves, but there is only one categorical imperative which is this: 'Act only according to a maxim by which you can at the same time will that it shall become a universal law.' Whenever you are inclined to act in a certain way—for instance, to borrow money without any intention of paying it back—you must always ask yourself what it would be like if everyone acted in that way.

Kant offers another formulation of the categorical imperative: 'Act in such a way that you always treat humanity, whether in your own person or in the person of any other, never simply as a means, but always at the same time as an end.' As a human being, Kant says, I am not only an end in myself, I am a member of a kingdom of ends, a union of rational beings under common laws. In the kingdom of ends, we are all both legislators and subjects. A rational being 'is subject only to laws which are made by himself and yet are universal'.[9]

[9] Kants's moral philosophy is discussed at length in Ch. 8.

In his third critique, the *Critique of Judgement*, Kant sought to apply to aesthetic notions such as beauty and sublimity the kind of analysis that in the earlier critiques he had applied to scientific and ethical concepts. Judgements of aesthetic taste rest on feeling, and yet they claim universal validity. But it is a mistake to think that they concern some objective universal, Kant argues: what can be universally shared is rather the particular internal relationship between the imagination and the understanding which is characteristic of a contemplative judgement of taste.

In the 1890s, with his critical philosophy firmly established, Kant ventured into areas that were not just philosophically adventurous. In 1793 he published a semi-theological work, entitled *Religion within the Bounds of Reason Alone*, which offered a reinterpretation of several Christian doctrines, and in 1795, in the midst of the French revolutionary wars, he wrote a pamphlet *On Perpetual Peace*. The first of these works gave offence to the new King of Prussia, Frederick II, who saw it as an unjustified attack on the authority of the Bible. Kant refused to recant his views, but agreed not to write or lecture further on religious topics. He kept this promise until 1798, after the king's death, when he published *The Conflict of the Faculties* on the relationship between theology and philosophy. In 1797 he amplified his moral system in *The Metaphysic of Morals*. This was divided into two parts, one treating of individual virtue and the other of legal theory. It was a more substantial but much less influential treatise than the earlier *Groundwork*.

Kant died in 1804. On his tombstone was inscribed a sentence from the conclusion of his *Critique of Practical Reason*. 'Two things fill the mind with ever new and increasing admiration and awe, the more often and steadily we reflect upon them: the starry heavens above me and the moral law within me.'

Fichte and Schelling

Until his last days Kant was working on an ambitious philosophical project that was published only after his death (the *Opus Postumum*). This shows that in his last days he had begun to have some misgivings about some aspects of the system of the first *Critique*. These were occasioned by criticisms aired by some of his own most devoted admirers and pupils. Foremost among these was Johann Gottlieb Fichte, who was forty-two in the year of Kant's death, and at the apogee of his own philosophical career.

Fichte was born into a poor family and was employed at an early age to herd geese. His intellectual gifts caught the attention of a philanthropic baron, and he was able to study theology at the University of Jena, where he came to admire Lessing, Spinoza, and Kant. His first publication was a *Critique of All Revelations* (1792), written in the style of Kant so successfully that for a while it passed as the master's own composition. Kant denied authorship, but reviewed the work very favourably. Partly through the influence of Goethe, Fichte was appointed to a professorship at Jena in 1794, where the great poet and dramatist Friedrich Schiller was among his colleagues.

Fichte's lectures were initially popular, but soon they were criticized by the students for being too puritanical and by the faculty for being insufficiently religious. He was forced to leave the university in 1799, and was without a tenured academic post until in 1810 he became dean of the philosophy faculty in the new University of Berlin. He was much involved in the resurgence of German nationalism during Napoleon's European hegemony. His *Addresses to the German Nation*, in 1808, rebuked the Germans for the disunity that led to their defeat by Napoleon at the battle of Jena, and he served as a volunteer in the army of resistance in 1812. He died of typhus in 1814, caught from his wife who was a military nurse.

Fichte's philosophical reputation rests on his *Wissenschaftslehre* of 1804. He saw the task of philosophy in Kantian terms as providing a transcendental account of the possibility of experience. Such an account could start either from pure objectivity (the thing in itself) or free subjectivity ('the I'). The former would be the path of dogmatism, and the latter the path of idealism. Fichte rejected the Kantian solution to the Kantian problem, and abandoned any notion of a thing-in-itself. He sought to derive the whole of consciousness from the free experience of the thinking subject. Thus he made himself the uncompromising originator of German idealism.

What is this I from which all things flow? Is it revealed by introspection? 'I cannot take a pace, I cannot move hand or foot, without the intellectual intuition of my self-consciousness in these actions,' Fichte said. If the theory is that the individual self can create the whole material world, we seem to be faced with an unconvincing and unappetizing solipsism. But this, Fichte insisted, is a misinterpretation. 'It is not the individual but the one immediate spiritual Life which is the creator of all phenomena,

Fichte's relaxed lecturing style marks a contrast with the dense nature of his prose

including phenomenal individuals' (*Sämmtliche Werke*, ed. I. H. Fichte (Berlin, 1845–6), II. 607).

This sounds rather like God, and in his later, popular works Fichte went so far as to say: 'It is not the finite self that exists, it is the divine Idea that is the foundation of all philosophy; everything that man does of himself is null and void. All existence is living and active in itself, and there is no other life than Being, and no other Being than God.' But elsewhere he said that it was superstitious to believe in any divine being that was anything more than a moral order. Clearly, he was more of a pantheist than a theist.

Fichte's philosophy of religion resembles that of Spinoza, as was pointed out by the most devoted of his disciples, F. W. J. Schelling, who had become his colleague on appointment to a professorship in Jena in 1798, at the age of twenty-three. Fichte's philosophy was the critical form, Schelling maintained, of the teaching that Spinoza had presented in dogmatic form. Schelling went on to develop his own less uncompromising form of idealism, a 'Nature Philosophy', according to which an initial absolute gives rise to two co-equal principles existing side by side: a spiritual consciousness and a physical nature. Here too we meet the ghost of Spinoza: the initial absolute is *Natura Naturans*, the system of material nature is *Natura Naturata*.

Schelling's system is rich but difficult, and his works are not much read nowadays in anglophone countries. He is perhaps best known in England because of the influence he exercised on Samuel Taylor Coleridge, who admired and imitated him to the extent of being accused of plagiarizing his works.[10] In most histories of philosophy Schelling is presented as a bridge between the idealism of Fichte and that of G. W. F. Hegel, who collaborated with him as editor of a philosophical journal at Jena in 1802–3.

Hegel

Hegel's first book, indeed, had been a comparison between the philosophies of Fichte and Schelling (1801). Born in 1770, he had studied theology at the University of Tübingen; he became a colleague of the two philosophers when he obtained a post at the University of Jena in 1801. He taught there until Jena's university was closed down after Napoleon's crushing victory over the Prussian army there in 1806. Shortly afterwards Hegel, now almost

---

[10] Coleridge was not, however, an admirer of Fichte, whose idealism he burlesqued in a poem containing the following lines:

> I, I! I, itself I!
> The form and the substance, the what and the why
> The when and the where, and the low and the high,
> The inside and outside, the earth and the sky,
> I, you, and he, and he, you and I,
> All souls and all bodies are I itself I!
>   All I itself I!
>   (Fools! A truce with this starting!)
>   All my I! all my I!
> He's a heretic dog who but adds Betty Martin!

> (*Biographia Literaria*, Ch. 9)

destitute, published his monumental *Phenomenology of Spirit (Die Phanomenologie des Geistes)*.

It was not until 1816 that Hegel became a professor, at the University of Heidelberg; by that time he had published his major work, *The Science of Logic*. A year later he published an encyclopedia of the philosophical sciences—logic, philosophy of nature, and philosophy of spirit. In 1818 he was called to a chair in Berlin, which he held until his death from cholera in 1831. During these years he published little, but his lecture courses were published posthumously. In addition to covering the history of philosophy, they treat of aesthetics, philosophy of religion, and philosophy of history. More readable than his difficult official publications, they exhibit an enormously original and capacious mind at work.

Hegel's greatest contribution to thought was his introduction of a historical element into philosophy. He was not the first historian of philosophy: that honour is Aristotle's. Nor was he the first philosopher of history: when he wrote there were already two classic contributions to that discipline, the *Scienza Nuova* of Giambattista Vico (1725) and the *Ideen zur Philosophie der Geschichte der Menscheit* of J. G. Herder (1784), both of which reflected on historical method and emphasized the developmental evolution of human institutions. But it was Hegel who gave history a special place in philosophy, and the philosopher a special place in historiography.

Hegel believed that the philosopher had a special insight into history that ordinary historians lacked. Only the philosopher really understands that reason is the sovereign of the world, and that the history of the world is a rational process. There are two ways of reaching this understanding: either by the investigation of a metaphysical system, or by induction from the study of history itself. The belief that history is the unfolding of reason corresponds to the religious faith in divine providence; but the metaphysical understanding is deeper than the theological one, because a general providence is inadequate to account for the concrete nature of history. Only the philosopher knows the ultimate destiny of the world, and how it is to be realized.

Cosmic history, according to Hegel, consists in the life story of spirit (*Geist*). The internal development of spirit manifests itself in concrete reality. 'Everything that from eternity has happened in heaven and earth, the life of God and all the deeds of time are simply the struggles of Spirit to know itself and to find itself' (*LHP* I. 23). Spirit is not something given in advance in all its fullness: it proceeds from potentiality to actuality, and the motive force of history is spirit's drive to actualize its potential. Universal history is 'the exhibition of Spirit in the process of working out the knowledge of that which it is potentially.'

Hegel claims that the existence of spirit is a matter of logic, but he uses the word 'logic' in a special sense of his own. Just as he sees history as a manifestation of logic, so he tends to see logic in historical, indeed martial, terms. If two propositions are contradictories, Hegel will describe this as a conflict between them: propositions do battle with one another and will emerge victorious or suffer defeat. This is called 'dialectic', the process by which one proposition (the 'thesis') fights with another (the 'antithesis') and both are finally overcome by a third ('the synthesis').

We pass through two stages of dialectic in order to reach spirit. We begin with the absolute, the totality of reality, akin to the Being of earlier philosophers. Our first thesis is that the absolute is pure Being. But pure Being without any qualities is nothing, so we are led to the antithesis, 'The absolute is Nothing'. Thesis and antithesis are overcome by synthesis: the union of Being and Unbeing is Becoming, and so we say 'The absolute is Becoming'.

The becoming, the life, of the absolute provides the second stage of dialectic. We begin by considering the absolute as a subject of thought, a universal thinker: Hegel calls this 'The Concept', by which he means the totality of the concepts that the intellect brings to bear in thinking. We then consider the absolute as an object of thought: Hegel calls this 'Nature', by which he means the totality of the objects that can be studied by the intellect. Concept and nature are brought together when the absolute becomes conscious of itself, being thus both subject and object of thought This synthesis of self-consciousness is spirit.

Hegel's notion of spirit is baffling on first acquaintance. An attempt at an explanation will be given in later chapters, but we must try to get an initial feel for what he means. We may wonder whether the spirit is perhaps God—identified perhaps with Nature, à la Spinoza. Or we may guess that 'Spirit' is a misleadingly grand way of talking about individual human minds, in the way in which medical textbooks speak of 'the liver' rather than of individual livers. Neither suggestion is quite right.

A better place to start is by reflection on the way we all talk about the human race. Without any particular metaphysical theory in mind, we are happy to say such things as that the human race has progressed, or is in

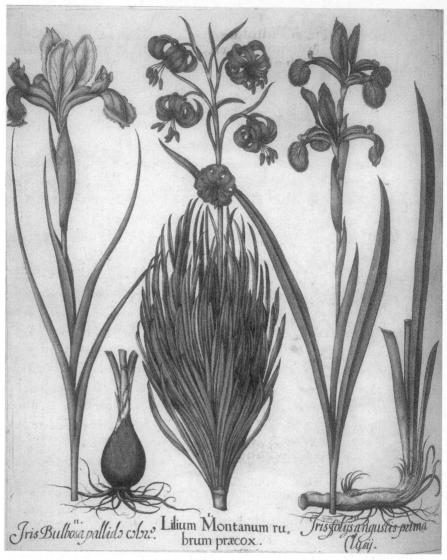

Hegel's Idea of a plant resembles botanical illustrations that show simultaneously various stages of development

decline, or has learnt much of which it was once ignorant. When Hegel uses the word 'Spirit' he is using the same kind of language, but he is adding two layers of metaphysical commitment. First, he is talking not just about human history, but about the history of the whole universe; and, second, he is viewing that universe as an organic whole which has a life cycle mapped out for it.

Hegel invites us to look on the universe as we look on specific organisms in nature. A plant passes through stages of development, producing twigs, leaves, blossom, and fruit; it does so in accordance with a pattern specific to its own kind. Hegel, with a deliberate bow to Plato, calls this the Idea of the plant. A plant, of course, is not conscious of its own Idea. But a human child, as its bodily powers develop, and as its intellectual skills emerge, gradually grows into consciousness of itself and its nature or Idea (*LHP* I. 29). The progress of spirit reproduces this development on a cosmic scale:

Spirit is not to be considered only as individual, finite, consciousness, but as that Spirit which is universal and concrete within itself... Spirit's intelligent comprehension of itself is at the same time the progression of the total evolving reality. This progression is not one that takes its course through the thought of an individual and exhibits itself in a single consciousness, for it shows itself to be universal Spirit presenting itself in the history of the world in all the richness of its form. (*LHP* I. 33)

Thus the history of the world is the history of the ever-growing self-consciousness of spirit. Different stages in the cosmic Idea present themselves at different times to different races. Spirit progresses in consciousness of freedom *pari passu* with the growth of awareness of freedom among human beings. Those who lived under oriental despots did not know that they were free beings. The Greeks and Romans knew that they themselves were free, but their acceptance of slavery showed that they did not know that man as such was free. 'The German nations, under the influence of Christianity, were the first to attain the consciousness that man, as man, is free: that it is the freedom of Spirit that constitutes its essence.'

The freedom of spirit is what marks it off from matter, which is bound by the necessity of laws such as that of universal attraction. The destiny of the world is spirit's expansion of its freedom and of its consciousness of its freedom. Self-interested individuals and nations are the unconscious instruments of spirit working out its destiny: they become conscious of their role in the cosmic drama at the point at which they are formed into a national state. The state is 'the realization of Freedom, i.e. of the absolute final aim, and it exists for its own sake.' The state does not exist for the sake of its citizens; on the contrary, the citizen possesses worth only as a member of the state—just as an eye only has any value as part of a living body.

Different states will have different characteristics corresponding to the folk-spirit of the nation which they incorporate. At different times different folk-spirits will be the primary manifestation of the progress of the world-spirit, and the people to which it belongs will be, for one epoch, the dominant people in the world. For each nation, the hour strikes once and only once, and Hegel believed that in his time the hour had struck for the German nation. The Prussian monarchy was the nearest thing on earth to the realization of an ideal state.[11]

The most important manifestation of spirit, however, was not to be found in political institutions, but in philosophy itself. The self-awareness of the absolute is brought into existence by the philosophical reflection of human beings; the history of philosophy brings the absolute face to face with itself. Hegel firmly believed that philosophy made progress: 'the latest, most modern and newest philosophy is the most developed, richest and deepest', he tells us (*LHP* I. 41). In his lectures on the history of philosophy he displays earlier philosophies as succumbing, one by one, to a dialectical advance marching steadily in the direction of German idealism.

---

[11] Hegel's political philosophy is considered in detail in Ch. 9.

4

Knowledge

Montaigne's Scepticism

In the sixteenth century, several factors contributed to make scepticism enjoy a new popularity. The clash between different Christian sects in Europe, and the discovery of peoples across oceans with different cultures and different religions, had as an immediate effect a surge of proselytizing and persecution; but these encounters also caused some reflective thinkers to question the claim of any human system of belief to hold unique possession of the truth. The rediscovery of ancient sceptical works, such as those of Sextus Empiricus, brought to the attention of the learned a battery of arguments against the reliability of human cognitive faculties. The most eloquent presentation of the new scepticism is to be found in Montaigne's *Apology for Raimond Sebond*.

Montaigne, like Sextus, favoured an extreme form of scepticism, called Pyrrhonian scepticism after its (half-legendary) founder Pyrrho of Elis, who in the time of Alexander the Great had taught that nothing at all could be known. Many of the examples that Montaigne uses to urge the fallibility of the senses and the intellect are drawn from Sextus' works, but the classical quotations that he uses in the course of his argument are taken not from Sextus, but from the great poem *On the Nature of Things* by Lucretius, a Latin follower of Epicurus, itself another great Renaissance rediscovery.

The two most influential philosophies of the classical Latin period were the Epicureans and the Stoics. The Epicureans, Montaigne tells us, maintain that if the senses are not reliable, then there is no such thing as knowledge. The Stoics tell us that if there is any such thing as knowledge it cannot come from the senses, because they are totally unreliable. Montaigne, like Sextus, uses Stoic arguments to show the fallibility of the senses, and Epicurean arguments to show the impossibility of non-empirical knowledge. Using the negative arguments of each sect, he aims to show against both of them that there is no such thing as real knowledge.

Montaigne rehearses familiar arguments to show that the senses mislead us. Square towers look round from a distance, vision is distorted by pressure on the eyeball, jaundice makes us see things yellow, mountains seem to travel past us when we look at them from shipboard, and so on. When two senses contradict each other, there is no way of resolving the difference. Montaigne quotes a famous passage of Lucretius:

> Can ears deliver verdict on the eyes?
> Can touch convict the ears, or taste the touch, of lies?

But he does not go on to conclude, with Lucretius, that the senses are infallible. Lucretius wrote:

> If what the senses tell us is not true
> Then reason's self is naught but falsehood too.[1]

Montaigne accepts this conditional; but he concludes, not that the senses tell us true, but rather that reason is equally false (*ME* II. 253).

Sense and reason, so far from cooperating to produce knowledge, each work on the other to produce falsehood. Terrified sense, when we look down, prevents us from crossing a narrow plank across a chasm, although reason tells us the plank is quite broad enough for walking. On the other hand, passions in our will can affect what we perceive with our senses: rage and love can make us see things that are not there. 'When we are asleep,' Montaigne maintains, 'our soul is alive and active and exercises all its powers neither more nor less than when it is awake.' The difference between sleep and waking is less than that between daylight and darkness (*ME* II. 260–1).

We need some criterion to distinguish between our varying and conflicting impressions and beliefs, but no such criterion is possible. Just as we cannot find an impartial arbiter to adjudicate the differences between Catholic and Protestant, since any competent judge would already be one or the other, similarly no human being could set out to settle the conflicts between the experiences of the young and the old, the healthy and the sick, the asleep and the awake:

---

[1] *De Rerum Natura* 4.484–7; see vol. I, p. 166.

To judge of the appearances that we receive from objects we need some judging instrument; to calibrate such an instrument, we would need an experiment; to verify the experiment, we would need some instrument: we are going round in a circle. (*ME* II. 265)

Montaigne adds some original material to the arsenal of ancient scepticism. Reverting to one of his favourite themes, he points out that some animals and birds have sharper senses than we do. Perhaps they even have senses which we totally lack. (Is it such a sense that tells the cock when to crow?) Our five senses are perhaps only a small number of those that it is possible to have. If so, our view of the universe, compared with a true view, is no less deficient than the view of a man born blind by comparison with that of a sighted person.

Descartes' Response

Descartes, in his *Meditations,* set himself the task of liberating philosophy from the threat of scepticism that had developed in the preceding century. In order to do so, first he had to exhibit the sceptical position that he wanted to refute. In the first of the *Meditations*, he follows in Montaigne's footsteps, but sets out the arguments in brisker and neater form. The deliverances of the senses are called into question initially by considerations drawn from sense-deception, and then by the argument from dreaming:

What I have so far accepted as true *par excellence*, I have got either from the senses or by means of the senses. Now I have sometime caught the senses deceiving me; and a wise man never entirely trusts those who have once cheated him.

But although the senses may sometimes deceive us about some minute and remote objects, yet there are many other facts as to which doubt is plainly impossible, although these are gathered from the same source: e.g. that I am here, sitting by the fire, wearing a winter cloak, holding this paper in my hands and so on . . .

A fine argument! As though I were not a man who habitually sleeps at night and has the same impressions (or even wilder ones) in sleep as these men do when awake! How often, in the still of the night, I have the familiar conviction that I am here, wearing a cloak, sitting by the fire—when really I am undressed and lying in bed! (AT VII. 19; *CSMK* II.13)

But surely even dreams are made up of elements drawn from reality:

Suppose I am dreaming, and these particulars, that I open my eyes, shake my head, put out my hand, are incorrect; suppose even that I have no such hand, no such body; at any rate it has to be admitted that the things that appear in sleep are like painted representations, which cannot have been formed except in the likeness of real objects. So at least these general kinds of things, eyes, head, hands, body must not be imaginary but real objects. (AT VII.20; *CSMK* II.14)

Perhaps these, in their turn, are imaginary complexes; but then the simpler elements out of which these bodies are composed—extension, shape, size, number, place, time—must surely be real. And if so we can trust the sciences of arithmetic and geometry which deal with these objects. 'Whether I am awake or asleep, two and three add up to five, and a square has only four sides; and it seems impossible for such obvious truths to fall under a suspicion of being false' (ibid.).

Even mathematics, however, is not immune to Cartesian doubt. It is not just that mathematicians sometimes make mistakes: it may be that the whole discipline itself is a delusion. God is omnipotent, and for all we know he can make us go wrong whenever we add two and three, or count the sides of a square. But surely a good God would not do that! Well, then:

I will suppose not that there is a supremely good God, the source of truth; but that there is an evil spirit, who is supremely powerful and intelligent, and does his utmost to deceive me. I will suppose that sky, air, earth, colours, shapes, sounds, and all external objects are mere delusive dreams, by means of which he lays snares for my credulity. I will consider myself as having no hands, no eyes, no flesh, no blood, no senses, but just having a false belief that I have all these things. (AT VII.23; *CSMK* II.15)

The second *Meditation* brings these doubts to an end by producing the *Cogito*, the famous argument by which Descartes proves his own existence. However the evil genius may deceive him, he cannot trick him into thinking he exists when he does not:

Undoubtedly I exist if he deceives me; let him deceive me as much as he can, he will never bring it about that I am nothing while I am thinking that I am something. The thought 'I exist' cannot but be true when I think it; but I cannot doubt it without thinking of it. Hence, it is not only true but indubitable, because whenever I try to doubt it I see its truth.

The *Cogito* is the rock on which Descartes' epistemology is built. From his day to ours, critics have questioned whether it is as solid as it looks. 'I am thinking, therefore I exist' is undoubtedly a valid argument, whose validity can be taken in at a single mental glance. But so too is 'I am walking, therefore I exist': so what is special abut the *Cogito?* Descartes responded that the premiss 'I am walking' could be doubted (perhaps I have no body), but the premiss 'I am thinking' cannot be doubted, for to doubt is itself to think. On the other hand, 'I think I am walking, therefore I exist' is a perfectly acceptable form of the *cogito*: the thinking referred to in the premiss can be a thought of any kind, not just the self-reflexive thought that I exist.

A more serious question concerns the 'I' in 'I am thinking'. In ordinary life the first-person pronoun gets its meaning in connection with the body that gives its utterance. Is someone who doubts whether he has a body entitled to use 'I' in soliloquy? Perhaps Descartes was entitled only to say: 'There is thinking going on.' Similar questions can be raised about the 'I' in 'I exist'. Perhaps the conclusion should only have been 'Existing is going on.' Critics have argued that the doubting Descartes has no right to draw the conclusion that there is an enduring, substantial self. Perhaps he should have concluded rather to a fleeting subject for a transient thought, or perhaps even that there can be thoughts with no owners. Is it certain that the 'I' revealed by the methodical doubt is the same person who, unpurified by doubt, answered to the name 'René Descartes'?

Even on its own terms, the *Cogito* does not prove the existence of Descartes as a whole human being. By itself, it proves only the existence of his mind. After the *Cogito* Descartes continues to doubt whether he has a body, and it is only after considerable further reasoning that he concludes that he does indeed possess one. What he is aware of at all times are the contents of his mind, and it is from these that he must rebuild science. From the *Cogito*, Decartes derives much else besides his own existence: his own essence; the existence of God; the criterion of truth. But for our present purposes what is important is to see how he proceeds from this Archimidean point to re-establish the cognitive system that the sceptical arguments appear to have overthrown.

Cartesian Consciousness

The contents of our minds are thoughts. 'Thought' is used by Descartes very widely: a piece of mental arithmetic, a sexual fantasy, a severe toothache, a view of the Matterhorn, or a taste of a vintage port are all, in his terminology, thoughts. Thinking, for Descartes, includes not only intellectual meditation, but also volition, emotion, pain, pleasure, mental images, and sensations. The feature which all such elements have in common, which makes them thoughts, is the fact that they are items of consciousness. 'I use this term to include everything that is within us in such a way that we are immediately conscious of it. Thus, all the operations of the will, the intellect, the imagination and the senses are thoughts' (AT VII. 160; *CSMK* II. 113). 'Even if the external objects of sense and imagination are non-existent, yet the modes of thought that I call sensations and images, in so far as they are merely modes of thought, do, I am certain, exist in me' (AT VII. 35; *CSMK* II. 34). These thoughts, then, are the basic data of Descartes' epistemology.

One passage brings out very strikingly how the word 'thought' for Descartes applies to conscious experience of any kind:

It is I who have sensations, or who perceive corporeal objects as it were by the senses. Thus, I am now seeing light, hearing a noise, feeling heat. These objects are unreal, for I am asleep; but at least I seem to see, to hear, to be warmed. This cannot be unreal, and this is what is properly called my sensation; further sensation, precisely so regarded, is nothing but an act of thought. (AT VII.29; *CSMK* II. 19)

These apparent sensations, possible in the absence of a body, are what later philosophers were to call 'sense-data'. The viability of the Cartesian system depends on whether a coherent signification can be given to such a notion.[2]

In the third *Meditation* Descartes singles out an important class of thoughts, and gives them the name 'ideas': 'Some of my thoughts are as it were pictures of objects, and these alone are properly called "ideas"—for instance, when I think of a man, or a chimera, or the sky, or an angel, or God' (AT VII.37). The word 'idea' is now at home in ordinary language, but it was a new departure to use it systematically, as Descartes did, for the contents of a human mind: hitherto philosophers had commonly used it to refer to Plato's Forms, or to archetypes in the Mind of God. Crudely, we can say that, for Descartes, ideas are the mental counterpart of words. 'I cannot express anything in words, provided that I understand what I say, without its thereby being certain that there is within me the idea of what is signified by the words in question' (AT VII.160).

---

[2] See Ch. 8 below.

Descartes divides ideas into three classes: 'Of my ideas, some seem to be innate, some acquired, and some devised by myself.' As examples of innate ideas, Descartes offers the ideas of *thing, truth,* and *thought.* The ideas that occur when Descartes seems to hear a noise, or to see the sun, or to feel the heat of a fire, appear to originate in external objects. Ideas of sirens and hippogriffs, on the other hand, seem to be creations of Descartes himself. At this stage of the epistemological journey, all this can only be a *prima facie* classification: as yet Descartes knows nothing about the origin of these ideas that occur in his mind. In particular he cannot be sure that the 'acquired' ideas originate in external objects. Even if they do so, he cannot be sure that the objects that cause the ideas also resemble the ideas.

There is, however, one idea that can be shown to originate outside Descartes' own mind. He has an idea of God, 'eternal, infinite, omniscient, almighty, and creator of all that exists beside himself'. While most of his ideas—such as the ideas of thought, substance, duration, number—may well have originated in himself, the attributes of infinity, independence, supreme intelligence, and power cannot be drawn from reflection on a limited, dependent, ignorant, impotent creature like himself. The perfections which are united in his idea of God are so much superior to anything that he can find in himself that the idea cannot be a fiction of his own creation. But the cause of an idea must be no less real than the idea itself. Accordingly, Descartes can conclude that he is not alone in the universe: there is also, in reality, a God corresponding to his idea. God himself is the source of this idea, having implanted it in Descartes from birth:

The whole force of the argument lies in this: I realise that I could not possibly exist with the nature I actually have, that is, one endowed with the idea of God, unless there really is a God; the very God, I mean of whom I have an idea; and he must possess all the perfections of which I can attain any notion, although I cannot comprehend them; and he must be liable to no defects. (AT VII.52; CSMK II.35)

God, then, is the first entity outside his own mind that Descartes recognizes; and God plays an essential role in the subsequent rebuilding of the edifice of science. Because God has no defects, Descartes argues, he cannot be deceitful, because fraud or deceit always depends on some defect in the deceiver. The principle that God is no deceiver is the thread that will enable Descartes to lead us out of the mazes of scepticism.

There are some truths which are so clear and distinct that whenever the mind focuses on them they cannot be doubted. But we cannot keep our minds fixed for long on any one topic; and often we merely remember having clearly and distinctly perceived a particular proposition. But now that we know that God is no deceiver, we can conclude that everything we clearly and distinctly perceive is true. Hence we are entitled to be certain, not just of momentary intuitions such as that of our immediate existence, but of whole *a priori* sciences such as arithmetic and geometry. These remain true and evident to us, Descartes claims, whether we are awake or asleep. So he can count these sciences among his cognitive assets even while he is still, in theory, uncertain whether he has a body and whether there is an external world. He can know a great deal about triangles, without yet knowing whether there is anything in the world that has a triangular shape (AT VII. 70; *CSMK* II.48).

It is not until the sixth meditation that Descartes establishes to his own satisfaction that there are material things and that he does have a body. He calls our attention to the difference between intellect and imagination. Geometry is the work of the intellect, and by geometry we can establish, for instance, the difference between a polygon with a thousand sides and a polygon with a million sides. We cannot, though, by any effort of the imagination, call up a distinct mental picture of either a chiliagon or a myriagon in the way that we can call up a picture of a triangle or a pentagon. The power of imagination appears to be an optional extra to the power of intellect, which alone is essential to the mind. One way of explaining the existence of this extra power would be to postulate some bodily entity in close association with the mind. The difference between imagination and pure understanding would be this: 'in the act of under-standing the mind turns as it were towards itself, and contemplates one of the ideas contained in itself; in the act of imagining, it turns to the body, and contemplates something in it resembling an idea understood by the mind itself.' But this, for the moment, is no more than a probable hypothesis (AT VII. 73; *CSMK* II.50).

What is it that establishes the existence of bodies? Descartes finds in himself a passive power of receiving sense-impressions. Corresponding to this passive power, there must be an active power to produce or make these impressions. In theory these could be produced by God himself, but there is not the slightest clue to suggest this:

The relationship between mind and body illustrated in one of Descartes' diagrams. Motion travels through the nerves from a burnt hand up to the pineal gland, where it is perceived by the soul as pain

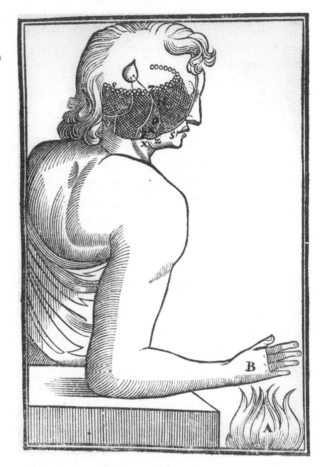

God has given me no faculty at all to detect their origin; on the other hand, he has given me a strong inclination to believe that these ideas proceed from corporeal objects; so I do not see how it would make sense to say that God is not deceitful, if in fact they proceed from elsewhere, not from corporeal objects. Therefore corporeal objects must exist. (AT VII.80; *CSMK*, II.55)

Since God is the author of nature, and God is no deceiver, whatever nature teaches is true. There are two principal things that nature teaches us:

There is no more explicit lesson of nature than that I have a body; that it is being injured when I feel pain; that it needs food, or drink, when I suffer from hunger, or thirst, and so on . . .

Moreover, nature teaches me that my body has an environment of other bodies, some of which must be sought for and others shunned. And from the wide variety of colours, sounds, odours, favours, degrees of hardness and so on, of which I have sensations, I certainly have the right to infer that in the bodies from which these various sense-peceptions arise there is corresponding, though not similar, variety.

Not everything, however, that appears natural to us is actually taught by nature and so guaranteed by the veracity of God—hence the caveat 'though not similar' in the last sentence of the quotation. Only what we clearly and distinctly perceive is really taught us by nature, and if we wish to achieve truth we must carefully restrict our beliefs within those limits. Only thus will a sound science of material objects be built up to replace the superannuated physics of the Aristotelian establishment.

Many philosophers nowadays find Descartes' epistemology quite unconvincing because they regard the existence of God as much more problematic than the everyday and scientific truths that he is called on to guarantee. None of his contemporary critics was willing to question the existence of God, although each was happy to challenge his method of proving it. But there were two different fundamental objections which Descartes had to meet if he was to defend his method of erecting the edifice of science on the basis of God's veracity.

First, if God is no deceiver, how is it that I constantly fall into error? The faculties that I have are given me by the truthful God; how then can they lead me astray? The answer Descartes gives is that, if properly used, our faculties do not ever lead us astray. I have one faculty, the intellect, which offers perceptions of things and of truths; I have a different faculty, the will, by which I judge whether a proposition is true or false. If I restrict the judgements of the will to cases in which the intellect presents a clear and distinct perception, then I will never go astray. Error only arises when I make a precipitate judgement in advance of clear and distinct perception. The whole intellectual exercise of the *Meditations* is designed precisely to give the reader practice in suspending judgement in the absence of clarity and distinctness.

The second objection to Descartes' method became famous under the title 'The Cartesian Circle'. It was Antoine Arnauld, author of the fourth objections, who was the first to point out an apparent circularity in Descartes' appeal to God as the guarantor of clear and distinct perceptions. 'We can be sure that God exists, only because we clearly and distinctly perceive that he does; therefore, prior to being certain that God exists, we need to be certain that whatever we clearly and evidently perceive is true' (AT VII.245; *CSMK* II.170).

Descartes has an answer to this objection, which depends on a distinction between particular clear and distinct perceptions, on the one hand, and the general principle, on the other, that whatever we clearly and distinctly perceive is true. No appeal to God's veracity is necessary to bring conviction of the truth of individual perceptions. Intuitions such as that I exist, or that two and three make five, cannot be doubted as long as I continue clearly and distinctly to perceive them. But although I cannot doubt something I am here and now clearly and distinctly perceiving, I can—prior to establishing God's existence—doubt the general proposition that whatever I clearly and distinctly perceive is true. Again, individual intuitions can be doubted once they are in the past. I can wonder, after the event, whether there is any truth in what I clearly and distinctly perceived while reading the second *Meditation*.

Since simple intuitions cannot be doubted while they are before the mind, no argument is needed to establish them; indeed Descartes regarded intuition as superior to argument as a method of attaining truth. Individual intuitions can only be doubted in the roundabout way I have just illustrated; they cannot be doubted in any way that involves advertence to their content. It is only in connection with the general principle, and in connection with the roundabout doubt of particular perceptions, that the appeal to God's truthfulness is necessary. Hence there is no circularity in Descartes' argument. Undoubtedly, however, in the *Meditations* the mind is *used* to validate itself. But that kind of circularity is unavoidable and harmless.

The Empiricism of Hobbes

Historians of philosophy often contrast British and continental philosophy in the seventeenth and eighteenth centuries: the continentals were rationalists, trusting to the speculations of reason, and the British were empiricists, basing knowledge on the experience of the senses. In order to assess the real degree of difference between British and continental epistemology we should look more closely at the teaching of Hobbes, who has a fair claim to be the founder of British empiricism.

Hobbes' *Leviathan* begins with a chapter 'Of Sense' and offers a resounding manifesto: 'There is no conception in a man's mind, which hath not at first, totally, or by parts, been begotten upon the organs of sense. The rest are derived from that original' (*L*, 9). Other operations of the mind, such as memory, imagination, and reasoning, are wholly dependent on sensation. Imagination and memory are the same thing, namely decaying sense:

> For as at a great distance of place, that which we look at, appears dim, and without distinction of the smaller parts; and as voices grow weak, and inarticulate: so also after great distance of time, our imagination of the past is weak; and we lose (for example) of cities we have seen, many particular streets; and of actions, many particular circumstances. (*L*, 66)

Reasoning, Hobbes says, is nothing but reckoning the consequences of general names agreed upon for the marking and signifying of our thoughts; and thoughts are always, for him, mental images (of names or things) derived from sensation. 'They are every one a representation or appearance of some quality, or other accident of a body without us' (*L*, 66).

There are, according to Hobbes, two kinds of knowledge: knowledge of fact, and knowledge of consequence. Knowledge of consequence is the knowledge of what follows from what: the knowledge that keeps order in the constant succession or train of our thoughts. It is expressed in language by conditional laws, of the form 'If A then B.' Knowledge of fact—the kind of knowledge that we require from a witness—is given by sense and memory. Mere reasoning, or discourse, can never end in absolute knowledge of fact, past or to come (*L*, 42).

It is true, as empiricists claim, that we can never acquire information about the world around us, directly or indirectly, without at some stage exercising our powers of sense-perception. The weakness of British empiricism lies in its naive and unsatisfactory account of what sense-perception actually consists in. Thinkers in the Aristotelian tradition, which Hobbes specifically rejected, had emphasized that our senses are powers to discriminate: the power to tell one colour from another, to distinguish between different sounds and tastes, and so on. They had emphasized that the senses had an active role in experience: any particular episode of sensing (e.g. tasting the sweetness of a piece of sugar) was a transaction between an item in the world (a property of the sugar) and a faculty of a perceiver (the

A portrait of Hobbes from Hardwick Hall, seat of his patron the Duke of Devonshire

power of taste). For Hobbes and his successors, by contrast, sensation is a passive affair: the occurrence of an image or fancy in the mind.

There is indeed, according to Hobbes, an active element in sensation; however, it is not a matter of making discriminations between genuine qualities in the real world, but rather of projecting on to the world items that are illusory fancies:

The cause of sense, is the external body, or object, which presseth the organ proper to each sense, either immediately, as in the taste and touch; or mediately, as in seeing, hearing, and smelling: which pressure, by the mediation of the nerves, and other strings, and membranes of the body, continued inwards to the brain and heart, causeth there a resistance, or counter-pressure, or endeavour of the heart, to deliver itself: which endeavour because *outward*, seemeth to be some matter without. And this *seeming* or *fancy*, is that which men call *sense*; and consisteth, as to the eye, in a light or colour figured; to the ear, in a *sound*; to the nostril, in an *odour*; to the tongue and palate, in a *savour*, and to the rest of the body in *heat, cold, hardness, softness*, and such other qualities, as we discern by *feeling*. All which qualities called *sensible*, are in the object that causeth them, but so many several motions of the matter, by which it presseth our organs diversely. (*L*, 9)

The account of sensation in the empiricist Hobbes turns out to be exactly the same as that of the rationalist Descartes. For both of them, qualities such as colour and taste are nothing more than deceptive experiences, items of private consciousness: 'fancies' for Hobbes; '*cogitationes*' for Descartes. Hobbes uses arguments similar to those of Descartes to urge the subjectivity of such secondary qualities: we see colours in reflections; a bang upon the eye makes us see stars; and so on. For Hobbes as for Descartes, there is no intrinsic difference between our sensory experience and our mental imagery and our dreams. Just as Descartes argued that he could be certain of the content of his thoughts even if he had no body and there was no external world, so Hobbes argues that all our images would remain the same even though the world were annihilated (*L*, 22).

A common error underlies the Descartes–Hobbes attack on the objectivity of sensory qualities: a confusion between relativity and subjectivity. It is true that sensory qualities are relative; that is to say, they are defined by their relationships to sensory perceivers. For a substance to have a certain taste is for it to have the ability to produce a certain effect on a human being or other animal; and the particular effect it produces will vary according to a number of conditions. But the fact that taste is a relative property does not mean that it is not an objective property. 'Being larger than the earth' is a relative property; yet it is an objective fact that the sun is larger than the earth.

Where Hobbes differs from Descartes is that he fails to make any serious distinction between the imagination and the intellect. If the intellect is, roughly, the capacity to use and understand language, then it is something quite different from the flow of images in the mind. Descartes made clear the difference between intellect and imagination in a luminous passage of the sixth *Meditation*:

When I imagine a triangle, I do not just understand that it is a figure enclosed in three lines; I also at the same time see the three lines present before my mind's eye, and this is what I call imagining them. Now if I want to think of a chiliagon, I understand just as well that it is a figure of a thousand sides as I do that a triangle is a figure of three sides; but I do not in the same way imagine the thousand sides, or see them as presented to me. (AT VII.71; *CSMK* II. 50)

Hobbes nowhere makes a similar distinction, and systematically identifies the mind with what Descartes calls the imagination. Hobbes was, indeed, aware of the role of language in intellectual activity, and saw its possession as the main privilege that set mankind above other animals. He wrote, for instance:

By the advantage of names it is that we are capable of science, which beasts, for want of them, are not: nor man, without the use of them: for as a beast misseth not one or two out of her many young ones, for want of those names of order, one, two, three &c, which we call number; so neither would a man, without repeating orally, or mentally, the words of number, know how many pieces of money or other things lie before him. (*L*, 35–6)

He writes, however, as if the fact that a series of images passing through the mind consists of images of names rather than things is sufficient to turn a flow of fancy into an operation of the intellect. But in fact no explanation in terms of mental images can account for our knowledge even of simple arithmetic, Hobbes' favourite paradigm of reasoning. If I want to add 97 to 62, I cannot call upon any mental image of either number; and the mental image of the numerals themselves will be no help either, unless I have been through the long and tedious process of learning to do mental arithmetic. The occurrence of the images does nothing to explain that process, and it is only as a consequence of that process that the images are useful for arithmetical purposes.

Locke's Ideas

Empiricism is not often defended in the crude and blunt form in which it is put forward by Hobbes, so it is time to turn to the better-known and more generally admired presentation by John Locke. Locke and Descartes are often contrasted as the prime exponents of two different philosophical schools, but in fact they share a number of common assumptions. Locke bases his system on 'ideas', and his 'ideas' turn out to be very similar to Descartes' 'thoughts'. Both philosophers make an initial appeal to immediate consciousness: ideas and thoughts are what we meet when we look within ourselves. Both philosophers fail to clear up a fatal ambiguity in their key terms, and this cripples their epistemology and philosophy of mind.

In Locke, for instance, it is often difficult to tell whether by 'idea' is meant an object (what is being perceived or thought about) or an action (the act of perceiving or thinking). Locke says that an idea is 'whatever it is which the mind can be employed about in thinking'. The crucial ambiguity is in the phrase 'what the mind is employed about', which can mean either what the mind is thinking of (the object) or what the mind is engaged in (the action). The ambiguity is damaging when Locke considers such questions as whether greenness is an object in the world or a creation of the mind.

Although Locke often takes issue with Descartes, he adopts much of his philosophical agenda from Descartes, and asks many of the same questions. Are animals machines? Does the soul always think? Can there be space without matter? Are there innate ideas?

This last question is often taken as a deciding issue: the answer a philosopher gives shows whether she is a rationalist or an empiricist. But the question is not a simple one. If we break it down into the different meanings it may have, we find that there is no great gulf fixed between the positions of Locke and Descartes.

First, we may ask: 'Do infants in the womb think thoughts?' Locke, as well as Descartes, believed that unborn infants had simple thoughts or ideas, such as pains and feelings of warmth. Locke mocks the idea that a child who knows that an apple is not a fire will give assent to the principle of non-contradiction (*E*, 61). But Descartes did not believe any more than Locke did that infants had complicated thoughts of a philosophical kind. A child has an innate idea of self-evident principles only in the same way as it may have an inherited propensity to gout (AT VIII. 357; *CSMK* I. 303).

In the light of this, we may take the question to concern not the activity of thinking, but the mere capacity for thought. Is there an inborn, general capacity for understanding which is specific to human beings? Both Descartes and Locke believe that there is. The *Essay* begins with the statement that it is the understanding that sets man above the rest of sensible beings (*E*, 43).

Locke focuses not on the general faculty of understanding, but on assent to certain particular propositions, e.g. 'one and two are equal to three' and 'it is impossible for the same thing to be, and not to be'. Does our assent to such truths depend on experience? No, says Descartes, they are innate principles we recognize. But Locke does not think they depend on experience; he claims that experience is necessary to provide us with the concepts that make up the propositions, not in order to secure our assent to them once formed. 'Men never fail, after they have once understood the Words, to acknowledge them for undoubted Truths' (E, 56). Descartes, on the other hand, does not maintain that all innate ideas are principles assented to as soon as understood: some of them become clear and distinct, and command assent, only after laborious meditation.

Locke devotes much of his treatment of innate ideas to the question whether there are any principles, whether theoretical or practical, which command universal assent. He denies that there are any theoretical principles which are held by all human beings, including children and savages. Turning to practical principles, he enjoys himself piling up examples of violations, in various cultures, of moral maxims which seem fundamental to all civilized Christians—including the most basic: 'Parents preserve and cherish your children' (E, 65–84). Even if there were truths universally acknowledged, this would not be sufficient to prove innateness, since the explanation might be a common process of learning.

Descartes, however, can agree that universal consent does not entail innateness, and he can also retort that innateness does not entail universal consent either. It is a fundamental presupposition of his method that some people, indeed most people, may be prevented by prejudice and laziness from assenting to innate principles that are latent in their minds.

On the topic of innate ideas, the arguments of Locke and Descartes largely pass each other by. Descartes argues that experience without an innate element is an insufficient basis for scientific knowledge; Locke insists that innate concepts without experience cannot account for the knowledge we have of the world. Both contentions may well be correct.

Locke claimed that the arguments of the rationalists would lead one 'to suppose all our ideas of colours, sounds, taste, figure etc. innate, than which there cannot be anything more opposite to reason and experience' (E, 58). Descartes did not believe that our knowledge of the colour or taste of a particular apple was something innate; but he found nothing absurd in the general idea of redness or sweetness being innate—and that for a reason that Locke himself accepted, namely, that our ideas of such qualities are entirely subjective. Once again the surface dispute between rationalism and empiricism masks a fundamental agreement.

Locke's argument for the subjectivity of qualities like colours and tastes begins with a division between those ideas 'which come into our minds by one sense only', and those 'that convey themselves into the mind by more senses than one'. Sounds, tastes, and smells are examples of the first kind; so too 'Colours, as white, red, yellow, blue; with their several Degrees or Shades and Mixtures, as Green, Scarlet, Purple, Sea-green and the rest'. As examples of ideas that we get by more than one sense, Locke gives extension, shape, motion, and rest—items we can detect both by seeing and by feeling.

Corresponding to this distinction between two kinds of ideas is a distinction between qualities to be found in bodies. We should distinguish ideas, as they are perceptions in the mind, and as they are modifications of matter in the bodies that cause these perceptions; and we should not take it for granted that our ideas are exact images of something in the bodies that cause them. The powers to produce ideas in us are called by Locke 'Qualities'. Qualities perceptible by more than one sense he calls 'primary qualities', and qualities perceptible only by a single sense he calls 'secondary qualities'. This distinction was no innovation: it had been customary since Aristotle to distinguish between 'common sensibles' (=primary qualities) and 'proper sensibles' (=secondary qualities) (E, 134–5). Where Locke departed from Aristotle was in denying the objectivity of proper sensibles. In this he had been anticipated by Descartes, who argued that in giving a scientific account of perception only primary qualities needed to be invoked. Heat, colours, and tastes were strictly speaking only mental entities, and it was a mistake to think that in a hot body there was something like my idea of heat, or in a green body there was the same greenness as in my sensation (AT VII.82; *CSMK*, II.56). The bodily events that cause us to see or hear or taste are nothing more than motions of shaped matter. In support of this conclusion Locke offers some of the same considerations as Descartes, but presents a more sustained line of argument.

First, Locke claims that only primary qualities are inseparable from their possessors: a body may lack a smell or a taste, but there cannot be a body without a shape or a size. If you take a grain of wheat and divide it over and over again, it may lose its colour or taste, but it will retain extension, shape, and mobility. Descartes had used a similar argument, taking not wheat but stone as his example, to prove that only extension was part of the essence of a body.

We have only to attend to our idea of some body, e.g. a stone, and remove from it whatever we know is not entailed by the very nature of body. We first reject hardness; for if the stone is melted, or divided into a very fine powder, it will lose this quality without ceasing to be a body. Again, we reject colour: we have often seen stones so transparent as to be colourless.

What are we to make of such arguments? It may be true that a body must have some shape or other, but any particular shape can be lost. As Descartes himself reminds us elsewhere, a piece of wax may cease to be cubical and become spherical. What Locke says of the secondary qualities might also be said of some of the primary qualities. Motion is a primary quality, but a body may be motionless. Indeed, if motion and rest are to be considered, as Locke considers them, as a pair of primary qualities, at any time a body must lack one or other of them.

The argument for the permanence of primary properties seems to depend on taking them generically: a body cannot cease to have some length or other; some breadth or other; some height or other. The argument for the impermanence of other qualities seems to depend on taking them specifically: a body may lose its particular colour or smell or taste. It is true that a body may be tasteless, odourless, and invisible, whereas a body cannot lack all extension. But the fact that such qualities are inessential properties of bodies does not show that they are not genuine properties of bodies, any more than the fact that a body may cease to be cubical shows that a cubical shape, while it lasts, is not a genuine property of the body.

Locke says that secondary qualities are nothing but a power to produce sensations in us. Even if we grant that this is true, or at least an approximation to the truth, it does not show that secondary qualities are merely subjective rather than being genuine properties of the objects that appear to possess them. To take a parallel case, to be poisonous is simply to have a power to produce a certain effect in a living being; but it is an objective matter, a matter of ascertainable fact, whether something is or is not poisonous to a given organism. Here, as in Descartes and Hobbes, we meet a confusion between relativity and subjectivity. A property can be relative while being perfectly objective. Whether a key fits a lock is a plain matter of fact, and as Locke's contemporary Robert Boyle remarked, the secondary qualities are keys which fit particular locks, the locks being the different human senses.

'The particular Bulk, Number, Figure, and Motion of the parts of Fire, or Snow, are really in them,' Locke says, 'whether any ones senses perceive them or no.' Light, heat, whiteness, and coldness, on the other hand, are no more really in bodies than sickness or pain is in food which may give us a stomach ache. 'Take away the sensation of them; let not the Eyes see light, or Colours, nor the Ears hear Sounds; let the Palate not Taste, nor the Nose Smell, and all Colours, Tastes, Odors and Sounds, as they are such particular ideas, vanish and cease' (E, 138). This argument is inconsistent with what Locke has just said, namely, that secondary qualities are powers in objects to cause sensations in us. These powers, to be sure, are only exercised in the presence of a sensing organ; but powers continue to exist even when not being exercised. (Most of us have the power to recite 'Three Blind Mice', but rarely exercise it.)

Locke claims that what produces in us the ideas of secondary qualities is nothing but the primary qualities of the object having the power. The sensation of heat, for instance, is caused by the corpuscles of some other body causing an increase or diminution of the motion of the minute parts of our bodies. But even if this were a true account of how a sensation of heat is caused, why conclude that the sensation itself is nothing but 'a sort and degree of motion in the minute particles of our nerves'? The only ground for this conclusion seems to be the archaic principle that like causes like. But to take an example of Locke's own, a substance can cause illness without itself being ill.

Locke denies that whiteness and coldness are really in objects, because he says there is no likeness between the ideas in our minds and the qualities in the bodies. This statement trades on the ambiguity we noted at the outset in the notion of an idea. If an idea of blueness is a case of the action of perceiving blueness, then there is no more reason to expect the idea to resemble the colour than there is to expect playing a violin to resemble a violin. If, on the other hand, the idea of blueness is what is perceived, then when I see a delphinium the idea is not an image of blueness, but blueness itself. Locke can deny this only by assuming what he is setting out to prove.

Locke's final argument is an analogy between perception and feeling:

He that will consider, that the same Fire, that at one distance produces in us the Sensation of Warmth, does at a nearer approach, produce in us the far different Sensation of Pain, ought to bethink himself, what Reason he has to say, that his Idea of Warmth, which was produced in him by the Fire, is actually in the Fire; and his Idea of Pain, which the same Fire produced in him the same way, is not in the Fire. (E, 137)

The analogy is being misapplied. The fire is painful as well as hot. In saying that it is painful, no one is claiming that it feels pain; equally, in saying that it is hot, no one is claiming that it feels heat. If Locke's argument worked it could be turned against himself. To take an example of his own, when I cut myself I feel the slash of the knife as well as the pain—does that mean that motion, too, is a secondary quality?

Locke insists, drawing on familiar examples, that the sensations produced by the same object will vary with circumstances (lukewarm water will appear hot to a cold hand and cold to a hot hand, what colours we see in porphyry depends on the intensity of the light shining on it, and so on). But the moral of this is not that secondary qualities are not objective. Grass is green, all right; but 'green' is not, as Locke thought it was, the name of a private ineffable experience, and being green is not a simple property, but a complicated one that includes such features as looking blue under certain conditions of lighting.

Spinoza on Degrees of Knowlege

In Spinoza's system epistemology is not as prominent as it is in Locke's, but it presents a number of subtle features. In his early *Improvement of the Understanding* Spinoza describes four levels of knowledge or perception. First, there is knowledge by hearsay: the kind of knowledge I have of when I was born and who were my parents. Second, there is knowledge 'from crude experience': Spinoza is thinking of inductive conclusions such as that water puts out fire and that one day I shall die. Third, there is the kind of knowledge where 'the essence of one thing is inferred from the essence of another, but not adequately'. Spinoza illustrates this rather obscure definition by giving as an example our knowledge that the sun is larger than it looks. Finally, there is knowledge of things by their essences: an instance is the knowledge of a circle we are given by geometry. This fourth kind of knowledge is the only one which gives us an adequate, error-free, grasp of things (E II.11). It is noteworthy that although Spinoza calls all of these forms of knowledge 'perception', raw sense-perception itself does not figure as a kind of knowledge.

In his later work, *Ethics,* Spinoza gives a threefold rather than a fourfold division of knowledge. We are told nothing more about hearsay, an

Geometry, for Spinoza, was the paradigm of knowledge. His presentation of his own system is modelled on Euclid's *Elements*

important topic commonly neglected by philosophers—the honourable exceptions being Hume in the eighteenth century, Newman in the nineteenth, and Wittgenstein in the twentieth. Instead we are told of three levels of knowledge, namely, imagination, reason, and intuition. Hearsay becomes a subdivision of the level of imagination, which is the second item of the earlier classification. Reason and intuition correspond to the last two items of the earlier classification.

Like Descartes and Locke, Spinoza describes knowledge in terms of ideas in our minds, and like them he includes under the under the term 'idea' both concepts (the idea *of* a triangle) and propositions (the idea *that* a triangle has three sides). Concepts and propositions of this kind, he maintains, are inseparable. I cannot affirm that a triangle has three sides without having a concept of a triangle; and I cannot have a concept of a triangle without affirming that it has three sides (*Eth*, 63).

There is often an ambiguity when Spinoza speaks of 'the idea of X': we may wonder whether the 'of' is a subjective or objective genitive; that is to say, is the idea of X an idea belonging to X, or is it an idea whose content is X? When Spinoza tells us that the idea of God includes God's essence and everything that necessarily follows from it, he is clearly speaking of the idea that God has, God's idea, rather than the idea that you and I might have of God (*Eth*, 33). But not every reference to 'the idea of God' is similarly unambiguous. And a corresponding ambiguity attaches to Spinoza's statement that the human mind is the idea of the human body.[3]

However, Spinoza expressly excludes an ambiguity in the term 'idea' that often gives us trouble when reading Descartes and Locke:

A true idea—for we do possess such a thing—is something different from its object (*ideatum*). Thus, a circle is one thing, and the idea of a circle is another. The idea of a circle is not a thing that has a circumference and a centre, as a circle has. Again, the idea of a body is something other than the body itself. (E II. 12)

A man Peter is something real; the idea of Peter is also a real thing, but a different one. We can also have an idea of the idea of Peter, and so on indefinitely.

If we know something, Spinoza maintains, we know that we know it, and know that we know that we know it. Philosophers ask how we know

---

[3] See Chapter 7 below.

when we have knowledge, and look for some criterion to distinguish knowledge from mere belief; without this, they think, we can never achieve certainty. But this, Spinoza says, is to begin at the wrong end. In order to know that we know, we must first know; and in order to achieve certainty we need no special sign beyond the possession of an adequate idea. He who has a true idea knows *eo ipso* that he has a true idea, and cannot doubt its truth (*Eth*, 58). 'How can a man be sure that his idea corresponds to its object?' philosophers ask. Spinoza replies: 'His knowledge arises simply from his having an idea that does in fact correspond to its object; in other words, truth is its own criterion' (*Eth*, 59).

The different stages of knowledge correspond to ideas with different properties. An idea may be true without being adequate, and it may be adequate without being clear and distinct. From the experience of our body coming into contact with other objects, we gather not only ideas of individuals like Peter but also general ideas such as man, horse, or dog. Spinoza explains the origin of such general ideas in the following manner:

> They arise from the fact that so many images, for instance, of men are formed simultaneously that they overpower the faculty of imagination—not entirely, but to the extent that the mind loses count of small differences between individuals (colour, size, and so on) and of their actual number. It imagines distinctly only that which the individuals have in common in so far as the body is affected by them—for that is the point in which each of the individuals principally affected it—and this the mind expresses by the name *man* and it predicates it of infinite individuals. (E II.112)

Other ideas are formed from symbols, from our having read or heard certain words. These ideas, while they are true, are confused and unsystematic. Our repertoire of such notions constitutes our knowledge of the first kind, which we may call 'opinion' or 'imagination'.

There are some ideas, however, which are common to all human beings, which represent adequately the properties of things. Such are the ideas of extension and motion. Spinoza defines an adequate idea as 'an idea which, insofar as it is considered in itself, without relation to the object, has all the properties or intrinsic marks of a true idea' (*Eth*, 32). It is not quite clear how this is to be reconciled with his statement that a true idea needs no mark of its truth. It is tempting to think that Spinoza means merely that adequate ideas express truths that are self-evident and are not derived by deduction from other truths. But in fact adequate ideas are linked by logical connections to each other, forming a system of necessary truths. This is the province of reason (*ratio*) and constitutes knowledge of the second kind (*Eth*, 57). Both the second and third kind of knowledge, then, can give us true and adequate ideas.

Knowledge of the third kind is called by Spinoza 'intuitive knowledge', and it is clearly the form of knowledge that is most to be valued. We are offered little help, however, in understanding its nature. It is clear that reason operates step by step; intuition is an immediate mental vision. More importantly, intuition grasps the essences of things; that is to say, it understands their universal features and their place in the general causal order of the universe. Reason may tell us that the sun is larger than it looks; only intuition can give us a full grasp of why this is so. But Spinoza's formal definition of intuitive knowledge raises as many questions as it solves: 'This kind of knowledge proceeds from an adequate idea of the formal essence of certain attributes of God to the adequate knowledge of the essence of things' (*Eth*, 57). Perhaps only a complete mastery of the whole philosophical system of the *Ethics* would provide us with such knowledge.

Spinoza twice attempts to illustrate the three degrees of knowledge by inviting us to consider the problem of finding the number x which has to a given number c the same proportion as a given a has to a given b. Merchants, he says, will have no difficulty in applying the rule of three that they have gathered from experience or learnt by rote. Mathematicians will apply the nineteenth proposition of the seventh book of Euclid. This illustration distinguishes the first and second degree clearly enough; but we are left in the dark about the intuitive method of solving the problem. Perhaps Spinoza has in mind something like the achievements of Indian mathematicians who can solve such problems instantaneously without calculation.

Spinoza's epistemology has to answer one final question. In the content of any idea, he maintains, there is no positive element other than truth (*Eth*, 53). But if there is no positive element in ideas on account of which they can be called false, how is error possible at all? Descartes had explained error in the following manner: error is wrong judgement, and judgement is an act of the will, not of the intellect; error occurs when the will makes a judgement in the absence of enlightenment from the intellect. Spinoza cannot offer this explanation, since for him the will and the intellect are not distinct; he cannot, therefore, give the advice that in order to avoid error one should suspend judgement whenever the intellect fails to present a clear and distinct idea.

Spinoza's response is to say that error is not anything positive. Error—which occurs only at the first level of knowledge—consists not in the presence of any idea, but in the absence of some other idea which should be present:

Thus, when we look at the sun, and imagine that it is about two hundred feet away from us, this imagination by itself does not amount to an error; our error is rather the fact that while we thus imagine we do not know either the true distance of the sun or the cause of our fancy. (Ibid.)

As for suspension of judgement, that is possible indeed, but not by any free act of will. When we say that someone suspends judgement, we merely mean that she sees that she does not have an adequate perception of the matter in question. Even in dreams we suspend our judgement, when we dream that we dream (*Eth*, 66).

The Epistemology of Leibniz

Spinoza's epistemology consists of a series of attempts to reconcile what we naturally say and think about knowledge and experience with his metaphysical thesis that ideas in the mind and motions in the body are just two aspects of individual items in the life of the single substance which is God and nature. Leibniz's epistemology is likewise an attempt to match ordinary speech and thought to a metaphysical system—but to one diametrically opposite to Spinoza's, in which ideas and motions, so far from being substantially identical with each other, have no interaction at all and belong to two different and wholly independent series of events, linked only by the harmony pre-established in the mind of God.

Given Leibniz's official theory of monads, it is hard to see how he could have, in the normal sense, any epistemology at all. How, for instance, could he give any account of sense-perception, since there are no transactions between the mind and the external world? How could he take an interest in the debate about which of our ideas are innate and which are acquired, since for him every single idea is an internal product of the mind alone? Yet in fact one of the most substantial of Leibniz's works is a work of epistemology: *New Essays on Human Understanding,* in which he offers a detailed critique of Locke's empiricist theory of knowledge. *New Essays* is a 500-page long debate between Philalethes, a spokesman for Locke, and Theophilus, the mouthpiece of Leibniz. Each chapter of the work corresponds to a chapter of Locke's *Essay,* and answers it point by point.

Many of the positions that Leibniz defends in the *New Essays,* and many of the arguments he employs, could in fact be adopted by a philosopher with a much more commonsensical metaphysic. Leibniz is aware of this, and defends himself by saying that for expository purposes he has a right to talk of bodies acting on minds just as a Copernican philosopher goes on talking of the sun rising and setting (G V.67). It is indeed difficult to make everything in the *New Essays* consistent with the official metaphysical system, but this makes the book more rather than less interesting to those who are more interested in epistemology than monadology.

Empiricists claim that there is nothing in the intellect that was not in the senses. Leibniz responds by adding 'except the intellect itself'. Our soul is a being, a substance, a unity, identical with itself, a cause, and the locus of ideas and reasoning. Consequently, the ideas of being, substance and so on can be acquired by the soul's reflection on itself. Moreover, they could never be acquired from the senses (G V. 45, 100–1). These ideas, then, are innate in the fullest sense. This does not mean that a newborn child already thinks of them; but it has more than a mere ability to learn them: it has a predisposition to grasp them. If we want to think of the mind as being initially like an unpainted canvas, we can do so; but it is a canvas already pencil-marked for painting by numbers (G V.45, 132).

Among ideas that are innate in this sense, Leibniz includes the principles of logic, arithmetic, and geometry. But what of truths such as 'red is not green' and 'sweet is not bitter'? Leibniz is prepared to say that 'sweet is not bitter' is not innate in the sense in which 'a square is not a circle' is innate. The feelings of sweet and bitter, he says, come from the senses (G V.79). How can this be reconciled with the denial that the external world acts on the mind and the thesis that all the thoughts and actions of the soul originate internally?

To answer this, we must recall that for Leibniz the human soul is a dominant monad, situated at the top of a pyramid of monads, which are animated entities corresponding to the different parts and organs of the

Leibniz as remembered by admirers in the age of enlightenment.

human body. Translated into monadese, the statement that some feelings come into the mind from the senses appears to mean that some of the ideas of the dominant monad originate from the inferior monads. Perceptions of inferior monads are brought into focus by the apperception, the self-conscious awareness of the dominant monad. Monads are windowless, Leibniz says, and let in nothing from the external world; but perhaps monad can talk to monad by a kind of telepathy.[4]

Leibniz cashes this out in a study of levels of awareness that is one of the most interesting parts of his epistemology. 'There are a thousand indications which lead us to think that there are constantly numberless perceptions in us, but without apperception and without reflection' (G V.46). A man living by a mill or a waterfall soon ceases to notice the noise it makes. Walking by the seashore we hear the roar of the tide coming in, but we do not distinguish the crash of each individual wave. Much of our conscious experience is in this way composed of a multitude of tiny perceptions of which we have no distinct idea. The perceptions characteristic of inferior monads are confused ideas; the apperception of the dominant monad brings clarity and distinction into our ideas. It is because sense-perceptions are confused that they appear to come from outside.

Leibniz uses his distinction between levels of awareness to answer a standard objection to innate ideas, namely, that we learn individual truths long before we are aware of the fundamental laws of logic. 'General principles', he says, 'enter into our thoughts and form the soul of each and the link between them. They are as necessary as muscles and tendons are necessary for walking, even though we don't think of them.' The mind relies on logic all the time, but it takes an effort to identify its laws and make them specific. The Chinese speak in articulate sounds just as Europeans do; but they have not invented an alphabet to express the recognition of this (G V.69–70).

For Locke, the basic building blocks of knowledge were simple ideas presented by the senses. Leibniz regards the notion of a simple idea as an illusion:

I believe that one can say that the ideas of the senses appear to be simple because they are confused: they do not give the mind scope for distinguishing their

---

[4] On perception and apperception, see below, p. 234.

content. It is like the way in which distant objects appear round, because we cannot distinguish their angles, even though we take in some confused impression of them. It is obvious, for instance, that green is made out of blue and yellow, mixed together—so you might well think that the idea of green is composed of those two ideas. And yet the idea of green appears to us as simple as those of blue or warm. So we must believe that the ideas of blue and warm are only apparently simple. (G V.109)

Leibniz also rejected Locke's distinction between secondary qualities, such as colour, which were subjective, and primary qualities, such as shape, which were objective: he regarded both primary and secondary qualities as phenomenal. His position on this issue was to be fully developed by Berkeley (whose early works were read and approved by Leibniz).

Berkeley on Qualities and Ideas

In the first of his *Dialogues between Hylas and Philonous* Berkeley argues for the subjectivity of secondary qualities, using Locke as an ally; then he turns the tables on Locke by producing parallel arguments for the subjectivity of primary qualities. He concludes that no ideas, not even those of primary qualities, are resemblances of objects.

In the dialogue Hylas, the materialist, is hampered in his defence of matter by his acceptance without question of Locke's premiss that we do not perceive material things in themselves, but only their sensible qualities. 'By sensible things,' he says, 'I mean those only which are perceived by sense; and that in truth the senses perceive nothing which they do not perceive immediately, for they make no inferences' (*BPW*, 138). Material things may be inferred, but they are not perceived. Sensible things, in fact, are nothing else but so many sensible qualities. But these qualities are independent of the mind.

Philonous, the idealist in the dialogue, in order to undermine Hylas' belief in the objectivity of sensible qualities, takes him through Locke's argument to show the subjectivity of heat. All degrees of heat are perceived by the senses, and the greater the heat, the more sensibly it is perceived. But a great degree of heat is a great pain; material substance is incapable of feeling pain, and therefore the great heat cannot be in the material substance. All degrees of heat are equally real, and so if a great heat is not something in an external object, neither is any heat.

The argument is full of fallacies that are artfully concealed by Berkeley. The false moves are placed in the mouth of Hylas, not Philonous. Philonous simply asks leading questions, which Hylas then answers with a 'yes' or 'no' when he should be making distinctions. Let us give some instances:

> *Phil. Heat* then is a sensible thing?
> *Hyl.* Certainly.
> *Phil.* Doth the reality of sensible things consist in being perceived? or is it something distinct from their being perceived, and that bears no relation to the mind?
> *Hyl.* To exist is one thing, and to be perceived is another.

Let us accept that we are talking of heat as a perceptible quality, not as a form of energy definable in physical terms. Hylas is right to say that to exist is not the same as to be perceived: the fire in the fireplace may be hot when no one is standing near enough to feel the heat. But he should not have accepted—as he goes on to do—Philonous' equation of 'distinct from being perceived' and 'bearing no relation to the mind'. A shrewder defender of the objectivity of qualities might have admitted that they have a relation to perception, while still insisting that their existence is distinct from their actually being perceived. Another example:

> *Phil.* Is not the most vehement and intense degree of heat a very great pain?
> *Hyl.* No one can deny it.
> *Phil.* And is any unperceiving thing capable of pain or pleasure?
> *Hyl.* No certainly.
> *Phil.* Is your material substance a senseless being, or a being endowed with sense and perception?
> *Hyl* It is senseless without doubt.
> *Phil.* It cannot therefore be the subject of pain?
> *Hyl.* By no means.

To the first question Hylas should have replied with a distinction: the maximum degree of heat *causes* great pain, agreed; the heat is itself a great pain, no. When asked if senseless things are capable of pain, he should have made a corresponding distinction: capable of *feeling* pain, no; capable of *causing* pain, yes. And he should never have admitted that material substances are senseless: some are (e.g. rocks), and some are not (e.g. cats). But here of course the blame rests with Locke for his argument that a material substance cannot have sensation because it is what *has* sensation.

It would be tedious to follow, line by line, the sleight of hand by which Hylas is tricked into denying the objectivity not only of heat, but of tastes, odours, sounds, and colours. Halfway through the dialogue, Hylas concedes that secondary qualities have no existence outside the mind. But he tries to defend Locke's position that primary qualities really exist in bodies. Philonous is now in a strong position to show that the arguments used by Locke to undermine the objectivity of secondary qualities can also be deployed against primary qualities.

Locke had argued that odours were not real properties because things that smell foul to us smell sweet to animals. Can one not equally argue that size is not a real property because what one of us can hardly discern will appear as a huge mountain to some minute animal (*BPW*, 152)? If we argue that neither heat nor cold is in water, because it can seem warm to one hand and cold to another, we can just as well argue that there are no real sizes or shapes in the world, because what looks large and angular to a nearby eye looks small and round to a distant eye (*BPW*, 153).

At the end of the first dialogue, Hylas, accepting that material objects are in themselves imperceptible, still maintains that they are perceived through our ideas. But Philonous mocks this: how can a real thing, in itself invisible, be like a colour? Hylas has to concur that nothing but an idea can be like an idea, and that no idea can exist without the mind; hence he is unable to defend the claim that ideas give us any information about anything outside the mind.

In the next chapter we will follow the course of the argument in the second and third dialogues in which Berkeley seeks to establish his metaphysical immaterialism. But to complete our account of his epistemology we have to consider what he has to say not only about the ideas of the senses, but also about the universal ideas that have traditionally been regarded as the province of the intellect. Locke had said that the ability to form general ideas was the most important difference between humans and dumb animals. Unlike animals, humans use language; and the words of language have meaning by standing for ideas, and general words, such as sortal predicates, correspond to abstract general ideas. In his *Principles of Human Knowledge* Berkeley mounted a destructive attack on Locke's theory of abstraction. Abstract ideas are said to be attained in the following manner:

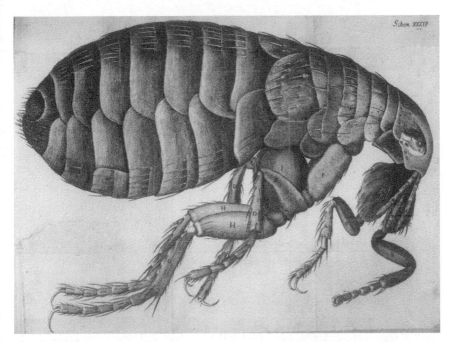

Berkeley used the discoveries of the microscope (such as Hooke's representation of a flea) to cast doubt on the objectivity of primary qualities

The mind having observed that Peter, James and John resemble each other in certain common agreements of shape and other qualities, leaves out of the complex or compound idea it has of Peter, James, and any other particular man, that which is peculiar to each, retaining only what is common to all, and so makes an abstract idea, wherein all the particulars equally partake; abstracting entirely from and cutting off all those circumstances and differences which might determine it to any particular existence. And after this manner it is said we come by the abstract idea of *Man*. (*BPW*, 48)

Thus, the abstract idea of man contains colour, but no particular colour; stature but no particular stature; and so on.

Berkeley thinks this is absurd. 'The idea of man that I frame myself must be either of a white or a black, or a tawny, a straight, or a crooked, a tall, or a low or a middle-sized man. I cannot by any effort of thought conceive the abstract idea.' He is surely wrong about this. If by 'idea' we mean a concept, then there is no doubt that the concept 'man' applies to human beings irrespective of their colour or size, and anyone who possesses the concept knows that. If, as seems more likely, Berkeley is thinking of an idea as an image, he still seems mistaken: mental images do not need to contain all the properties of that of which they are images. My mental image of Abraham does not make him either tall or short; I have no idea which he was. Berkeley conceives mental images very much on the pattern of real images; but even allowing for this, he is mistaken. A portrait on canvas need not specify all the features of a sitter, and a dress pattern need not specify a colour, even though any actual dress must have some particular colour.

At one point Locke writes that it takes skill to form the general idea of a triangle, 'for it must be neither oblique nor rectangle, neither equicrural nor scalenon, but all and none of these at once'. Berkeley is right to say that this is a piece of nonsense. But he should really be attacking Locke for believing that the possession of images of any kind was sufficient to explain our acquisition of concepts. That is what is really wrong with Locke's theory of language, not that he has chosen the wrong images or described them in self-contradictory terms.

To use an image, or a figure, to represent an X, one must already have a concept of an X. An image does not carry on its face any determination of what it represents. An image of an oak leaf, like a drawing of an oak leaf, may represent a leaf, an oak, a tree, a boy-scout achievement, a military rank, or many other things. And concepts cannot be acquired simply by stripping off features from images. What does one strip off from an image of blue in order to use it as an image of colour? In any case there are concepts to which no image corresponds: logical concepts, for instance, such as those corresponding to 'some' or 'not' or 'if'. There are other concepts that can never be unambiguously derived from images, for instance, arithmetical concepts. One and the same image may represent four legs and one horse, or seven trees and one copse.

Berkeley was correct, against Locke, in separating the mastery of language from the possession of abstract general images. But he retained the idea that mental images were the key to language: for him, a general name signified not a single abstract images but 'indifferently a great number of particular images'. But once concept-possession has been distinguished from image-mongering, mental images become unimportant for the philosophy of language and mind. Imaging is no more essential to thinking than illustrations are to a book. It is not our images that explain our possession of concepts, but our concepts that confer meaning on our images.

Hume on Ideas and Impressions

The empiricist identification of thinking and imaging is carried to an extreme point in the philosophy of Hume. Hume does, however, attempt to improve on Locke and Berkeley by making a distinction between two classes of perceptions, impressions and ideas, instead of calling them all 'ideas'. Everyone, Hume says, knows the difference between feeling and thinking. Feeling is a matter of impressions: sensations and emotions. Thinking involves ideas: the sort of things that come into one's head while reading the *Treatise*, for instance (*T*,1).

It becomes quite clear that Hume's 'ideas' are mental images. They are, he says, like impressions except by being less forceful and vivid. Moreover, simple ideas are copies of impressions. This looks at first like a definition of 'idea', but Hume appeals to experience in support of it. From time to time he invites the reader to look within himself to verify the principle and challenges him to produce a counter-example. He supports the principle by telling us that a man born blind has no idea of colours. In the case of colour ideas, however, he is himself willing to produce a counter-example. Suppose that a man has encountered all colours except one particular shade of blue:

Let all the different shades of that colour, except that single one, be placed before him, descending gradually from the deepest to the lightest; it is plain that he will perceive a blank where that shade is wanting, and will be sensible that there is a greater distance in that place between the contiguous colours than any other. Now I ask, whether it be possible for him, from his own imagination, to supply this deficiency, and raise up to himself the idea of that particular shade, though it had never been conveyed to him by the senses? I believe there are few but will be of opinion that he can. (*E* II.17)

Hume is prepared to accept this thought experiment as providing an exception to his principle that all ideas are derived from impressions. 'This instance is so singular,' he continues, 'that it is scarcely worth our observing, and does not merit that for it alone we should alter our general maxim'. This cavalier dismissal of a counter-example must call in question the genuineness of Hume's commitment to 'the experimental method' in the study of the mind. Undeterred, he puts the principle 'no idea without antecedent impression' to vigorous use whenever he wishes to attack metaphysics.

Having used vivacity as the criterion for differentiating between ideas and impressions, Hume makes a further distinction on the basis of vivacity between two different kinds of ideas: ideas of memory and ideas of imagination. 'Tis evident at first sight', he tells us, 'that the ideas of the memory are much more lively and strong than those of the imagination, and that the former faculty paints its objects in more distinct colours than any which are employ'd by the latter.' In accordance with his general principle, Hume says that both kinds of ideas must have been preceded by the corresponding impression, but he also notes a difference between them: the ideas of the imagination, unlike the ideas of the memory, are not tied down to the order in time and space of the original impressions.

We are given, then, two criteria for distinguishing memory from imagination: vivacity and orderliness. It is not clear, however, how these criteria are to be used. It is, no doubt, to enable us to distinguish genuine from delusory memory ('Do I remember that I posted the letter, or am I only imagining it?'). The second criterion would make the distinction, but could never be applied in a case of doubt; the first criterion could be used by a doubter, but would be unreliable, since fantasies can be more forceful and obsessive than memories.

Hume thinks of memory as reliving in the mind a series of past events; but of course remembering the date of the Battle of Hastings, remembering how to make an omelette, or remembering the way to Oxford from London, are very different from each other. So are many other different kinds of memory. Similarly, the word 'imagination' covers much more than the free play of mental imagery: it includes misperception ('Is that a knock at the door, or am I only imagining it?'), hypothesizing ('imagine what the world would be like if everyone behaved in that way!'), and creative originality ('*The Lord of the Rings* is a work of extraordinary imagination'). Hume's treatment of memory and imagination tries to pack a great variety of mental events, capacities, activities, and errors into a single empiricist straitjacket.

There are cases which seem to fit Hume's account reasonably well. I hear a bird sing and then try to recapitulate the melody mentally; I gaze at a patterned wallpaper, and see an after-image after I have closed my eyes. But even in these cases Hume misrepresents the situation. On the face of it, the difference between the impressions and the ideas is that whereas the bird and the wallpaper are external to me, the after-image and the subvocal humming are interior events. But Hume accepts the empiricist thesis that all we ever know are our own perceptions. My hearing the bird sing is not a transaction between myself and the bird, but my encounter with a vivid bird-like sound. For Hume, everyone's life is just one introspection after another.

It has to be by introspection, then, that we tell the difference between our memories and our imaginings. The difference between the two, one might think, could best be made out in terms of *belief*. If I take myself to be remembering that *p*, then I believe that *p*; but I can imagine *p*'s being the case without any such belief. As Hume himself says, we conceive many things that we do not believe. But his classification of mental states makes it difficult for him to find a suitable place for belief.

The difference between merely having the thought that *p* and actually believing that *p* cannot be a difference of content. As Hume puts it, belief cannot consist in the addition of an extra idea to the idea or ideas which constitute *what* is believed. One argument for this is that we are free to add any ideas we like, but we cannot choose to believe whatever we please. A more convincing reason would be that if belief consisted in an extra idea, someone who believes that Caesar died in his bed and someone who does not believe that Caesar died in his bed would not be in conflict with each other because they would not be considering the same proposition (*T*, 95).

In the *Enquiry*, Hume says that belief is a conception 'attended with a feeling or sentiment, different from the loose reveries of the fancy'. But such a feeling would surely be an impression; and in an appendix to the *Treatise*, Hume argues forcefully that this would be directly contrary to experience—belief consists only of ideas. But he still insists that 'An idea assented to *feels* different from a fictitious idea,' and he offers various names to describe the feeling: 'force, vivacity, solidity, firmness, steadiness'. He ends by confessing that ''tis impossible to explain perfectly this feeling or manner of conception' (*T*, 629). But he urges us to accept his account on the implausible ground that history books (which we believe to be factual) are much more vivid to read than novels (which we are well aware are fiction) (*T*, 97).

Some of the difficulties in Hume's account of vivacity as a mark of belief are internal to his system. We observe his embarrassment at discovering a perception that is neither quite an idea nor quite an impression. We may wonder how we are to distinguish the belief that Caesar died in his bed from a memory of Caesar dying in his bed, since vivacity is the mark of each. But other difficulties are not merely internal. The crucial problem is that belief need not involve imagery at all (when I sit down, I believe the chair will support me; but no image or thought about the matter enters my mind). And when a belief does involve imagery, an obsessive fantasy (of a spouse's infidelity, for instance) may be livelier than a genuine belief.

There is something pitiable about Hume's delusion that in presenting his few scattered remarks about the association of ideas he was doing for epistemology what Newton had done for physics. But it is unfair to blame him because his philosophical psychology is so jejune: he inherited an impoverished philosophy of mind from his seventeenth-century fore-bears, and he is often more candid than they in admitting the gaps and incoherences in the empiricist tradition. The insights that make him great as a philosopher can be disentangled from their psychological wrapping, and continue to provoke reflection. His treatment of causation, of the self, of morality, and of religion will be treated in the appropriate chapters. His main contribution to epistemology was the presentation of a new form of scepticism.

This begins from the distinction, which we have met in several philosophers, between propositions expressing relations of ideas, and propositions expressing matters of fact. The contrary of every matter of fact is possible, Hume says, because it can never imply a contradiction. That the sun will not rise tomorrow is as intelligible and coherent as the affirmation that it will rise. Why then do we believe the latter but not the former (E II. 25–6)?

All our reasonings concerning matters of fact, Hume argues, are founded on the relation of cause and effect. But how do we arrive at our knowledge of causal relations? The sensible properties of objects do not reveal to us either the causes that produced them or the effects that will rise from them. Merely looking at gunpowder would never tell you that it was explosive; it takes experience to learn that fire burns things up. Even the simplest regularities of nature cannot be established a priori, because a cause and an effect are two totally different events and the one cannot be inferred from another. We see a billiard ball moving towards another, and we expect it to communicate its motion to the other. But why? 'May not both these balls remain at absolute rest? May not the first ball return in a

A

TREATISE

OF

Human Nature :

BEING

An ATTEMPT to introduce the experimental Method of Reaſoning

INTO

MORAL SUBJECTS.

Rara temporum felicitas, ubi ſentire, quæ velis ; & quæ
ſentias, dicere licet. TACIT.

VOL. I.

OF THE

UNDERSTANDING.

LONDON:
Printed for JOHN NOON, at the *White-Hart,* near
Mercer's-Chapel, in *Cheapſide.*

MDCCXXXIX.

The title page of the first
edition of Hume's *Treatise*
which 'fell dead-born
from the Press'

straight line, or leap off from the second in any line or direction? All these
suppositions are consistent and conceivable' (*E* II. 30).

The answer, obviously enough, is that we learn the regularities of nature
from experience. But Hume carries his probe further. Even after we have
experience of the operations of cause and effect, he asks, what ground is there

in reason for drawing conclusions from that experience? Experience gives us information only about past objects and occurrences: why should it be extended to future times and objects, which for aught we know resemble past objects only in appearance? Bread has nourished me in the past, but what reason does this give me for believing that it will do so in the future?

These two propositions are far from being the same, *I have found that such an object has always been attended with such an effect* and *I foresee, that other objects, which are in appearance, similar, will be attended with similar effects*. I shall allow, if you please, that the one proposition may justly be inferred from the other: I know, in fact, that it always is inferred. But if you insist that the inference is made by a chain of reasoning, I desire you to produce that reasoning. (*E* II. 34)

No demonstrative argument is possible: there is nothing at all self-contradictory in the supposition that the next time I put the kettle on the stove the water will refuse to boil. But no argument from experience is possible; for if we countenance the possibility that the course of nature may change we cannot regard experience as a reliable guide. Any argument from experience to prove that the future will resemble the past must manifestly be circular. Clearly, therefore, it is not reasoning that makes us believe that it will.

At the level of argument, then, scepticism is victorious. But Hume tells us not to be cast down by this discovery: we are led to believe in the regularity of nature by a principle stronger than reasoning. This principle is custom or habit. No one could infer causal relationship from a single experience, because causal powers are not something observable by the senses. But after we have observed similar objects or events to be constantly conjoined, we immediately infer one kind of event from the other. And yet, a hundred instances have given us no more reason to draw the conclusion than the single one did. 'After the constant conjunction of two objects—heat and flame, for instance, weight and solidity—we are determined by custom alone to expect the one from the appearance of the other' (*E* II. 43). It is custom, not reason, that is the great guide of human life.

Kant's Synthetic a priori

Many readers have regarded Hume's conclusion as small comfort in return for his devastating demolition of any reasoned ordering of our experience over time. No one was more perturbed by Hume's sceptical challenge than Immanuel Kant, and no one worked harder to meet the challenge and to re-establish the function of the intellect in the ordering of our perceptions.

Just as Hume started his argument with a contrast between matters of fact and relations of ideas, Kant begins his response by making distinctions between different kinds of propositions. But instead of a single distinction, he has a pair of distinctions to make, one epistemological and one logical. First, he distinguishes between two modes of knowledge: knowledge derived from experience, which he calls *a posteriori* knowledge, and knowledge independent of all experience, which he calls *a priori* knowledge. Next, he makes a distinction between two kinds of judgement, analytic and syn-thetic. He explains how to decide to which kind a judgement of the form 'A is B' belongs:

Either the predicate B belongs to the subject A, as something that is contained (though covertly) in the concept A, or it lies quite outside the concept A even though it is attached to it. In the first case, I call the judgement analytic, in the second synthetic. (A, 6)

He gives as an example of an analytic judgement 'all bodies are extended', and as an example of a synthetic judgement 'all bodies are heavy'. Extension, he explains, is part of the concept 'body', whereas weight is not.

Kant's distinction between analytic and synthetic propositions is not wholly satisfactory. It is clearly intended to be universally applicable to propositions of all kinds, yet not all propositions are structured in the simple subject–predicate form he uses in his definition. The notion of 'containing' is metaphorical and although the distinction is clearly intended to be a logical one, Kant sometimes speaks of it as if it were a matter of psychology. Some later philosophers tried to tighten up the distinction, and others tried to break it down; but it retained a permanent place in subsequent philosophical discussion.

What is the relation between the epistemological distinction *a priori/a posteriori* and the logical distinction *analytic/synthetic*? The two distinctions are made on different bases, and they do not, according to Kant, coincide in their application. All analytic propositions are *a priori*, but not all *a priori* propositions are analytic. There is no contradiction in the notion of a synthetic *a priori* proposition, and indeed there are many examples of such propositions. Our knowledge of mathematics is *a priori* because mathematical truths are universal and necessary, whereas no generalization from experience can have those properties. Yet many truths of arithmetic and geometry are synthetic, not analytic. 'That a straight line between two points is the shortest one is a synthetic proposition. For my concept of *straightness* contains no notion of size, but only of quality' (B, 16). Physics, too, contains synthetic *a priori* principles, such as the law of conservation of matter. Finally, a genuine metaphysics is not possible unless we can have *a priori* knowledge of synthetic truths.

How such synthetic *a priori* judgements are possible is the principal problem for philosophy. Its solution is to be found by reflection on the way that human knowledge arises from the combined operation of the senses and the understanding. It is the senses that present us with objects; it is the understanding that makes objects thinkable. Our senses determine the content of our experience; our understanding determines its structure. To mark the contrast between content and structure, Kant uses the Aristotelian terms 'matter' and 'form'. The matter of sensation would include what makes the difference between a splash of blue and a splash of green, or the sound of a violin and the sound of a trumpet. If we isolate sensation from everything that really belongs to the understanding, we find that there are two forms of pure sensory awareness, space and time: the common structure into which our perceptions are fitted. But in real life human beings never have purely sensory awareness.

For human knowledge, both senses and understanding are necessary:

Neither of these faculties has a priority over the other. Without the senses no object would be given to us, and without the understanding no object could be thought. Thoughts without content are empty, awareness without concepts is blind . . . The understanding is aware of nothing, the senses can think nothing. Only through their union can knowledge arise. (A, 51)

In human experience any object of sense is also an object of thought: whatever is experienced is classified and codified; that is to say, it is brought by the understanding under one or more concepts.

In addition to the understanding, Kant tells us, human beings have a faculty of judgement. The understanding is the power to form concepts, and the judgement is the power to apply them. The operations of the understanding find expression in individual words, while judgements are expressed in whole sentences. A concept is nothing other than a power to make judgements of certain kinds. (To possess the concept 'plant', for instance, is to have the power to make judgements expressible by sentences containing the word 'plant' or its equivalent.)

There are many different kinds of judgement: they may, for instance, be universal or particular, affirmative or negative. More importantly, as Kant illustrates by examples, they may be categorical ('there is a perfect justice'), or hypothetical ('if there is a perfect justice, the obstinately wicked are punished'), or disjunctive ('the world exists either through blind chance, or through inner necessity, or through an external cause'). Corresponding to the different kinds of judgement there are different fundamental types of concepts.

Concepts and judgements may be empirical or *a priori*: *a priori* judgements are called principles and *a priori* concepts are called categories. In an elaborate, and not wholly convincing, 'deduction of the categories' Kant relates each category to a different kind of judgement. For instance, he relates the category of substance to categorical judgements, hypothetical judgements to the category of cause, and disjunctive judgements to the category of interaction. Whether or not we are convinced by these specific links, we cannot deny the importance of Kant's general claim that there are some concepts that are indispensable if anything is to count as the operation of understanding. Is the claim true?

It may be easier to answer the question if we put it in linguistic form. Are there any concepts that must find expression in any fully-fledged language? The answer seems to be that any genuine language-users, however alien they may be to us, need to have a concept of negation, and the ability to use quantifiers such as 'all' and 'some'. These are the concepts corresponding to Kant's distinction between affirmative and negative judgements, and his distinction between universal and particular judgements. Again, any rational language-user will need the ability to draw conclusions from premises, and this ability is expressed in the mastery of words like 'if', 'then', and 'therefore', which are related to Kant's class of hypothetical judgements. So, whatever we think of particular details of the transcendental deduction of the categories, it seems to be correct to link concepts with judgements and to claim that certain concepts must be fundamental to all understanding.

Kant goes on to argue that not only are there *a priori* concepts that are essential if we are to make sense of experience, but there are also *a priori* judgements, the ones that he calls 'principles'. Some of these are analytic, but the principles that are really interesting are the ones that underlie synthetic judgements.

One such principle is that all experiences have extension. Whatever we experience is extended—that is to say, has parts distinct from other parts, either in space or in time. It is this principle that underpins the synthetic *a priori* axioms of geometry, such as the axiom that between two points only one straight line is possible.

Another principle is that in all appearances the object of sensation has intensive magnitude. For instance, if you feel a certain intensity of heat, you are aware that you could be feeling something hotter or less hot: what you are feeling is a point on a scale that extends in two directions. A colour, too, is of its nature located on a spectrum. When I have a sensation I know *a priori* the possibility of similar sensations at another point upon a common scale. Kant calls this 'an anticipation of perception', but the term is unfortunate—he does not mean that you can tell what feeling is going to come next; as he says himself, 'sensation is just that element which cannot be anticipated'. A better word than 'anticipation' might be 'projection'.

Realism vs Idealism

In later chapters we will explore in greater detail other categories and other principles that Kant derives in the course of his transcendental analytic. But the epistemological question that is raised by his brilliant exposition of the *a priori* elements in our experience is this: if so much of what we perceive is the creation of our own mind, can we have any genuine knowledge at all of the real, extra-mental world? A reader of the first *Critique* begins to worry about this long before the transcendental analytic, when he is told at the end of the transcendental aesthetic that space and time are empirically real, but transcendentally ideal. 'If we take away the subject,' Kant tells us, there 'space and time disappear: these as phenomena cannot exist in themselves, but only in us.'

If space and time are subjective in this way, can anything be more than mere appearance? We commonly distinguish in experience, Kant explains in response, between that which holds for all human beings and that which belongs only to a single viewpoint. The rainbow in a sunny shower may be called a mere appearance, while the rain is regarded as a thing-in-itself. In this sense, we may grant that not everything is mere experience. But this distinction between appearance and reality, Kant continues, is something merely empirical. When we look more closely, we realize that 'not only are the drops of rain mere appearances, but that even their round shape, nay even the space in which they fall, are nothing in themselves, but merely modifications or fundamental forms of our sensible awareness, and that the transcendental object remains unknown to us' (A, 46).

Passages such as this make it sound as if Kant is an idealist, who believes that nothing is real except ideas in our mind. In fact, Kant is anxious to distance himself from previous idealists, whether they are, like Descartes, 'problematic idealists' ('I exist' is the only indubitable empirical assertion), or, like Berkeley, 'dogmatic idealists' (the external world is illusory). Kant fastens on the point that is common to both versions of idealism, namely, that the inner world is better known than the outer world, and that outer substances are inferred (correctly or incorrectly) from inner experiences.

In fact, Kant argues, our inner experience is only possible on the assumption of outer experience. I am aware of changing mental states, and thus I am conscious of my existence in time, that is to say, as having experiences first at one moment and then at another. But the perception of change involves the perception of something permanent: if there is to be change, as opposed to mere succession, there has to be something which is first one thing and then another. But this permanent thing is not myself: the unifying subject of my experience is not an object of experience. Hence, only if I have outer experience is it possible for me to make judgements about the past—even about my own past inner experience (B, 275–6).

Philosophers, Kant says, make a distinction between phenomena (appearances) and noumena (objects of thought). They divide the world into a world of the senses and a world of the intellect. But as the transcendental analytic has shown, there cannot be a world of mere appearances, mere sense-data that do not fall under any categories or instantiate any rules. Nor can there be, in any positive sense, pure noumena, that is to say, objects of intellectual intuition independent of sensory awareness. However, if we are to talk of appearances at all, we must think that they are appearances of *something*, a something that Kant calls 'the transcendental object'. It is, however, only an unknown X, 'of which we know, and with the present constitution of our understanding can know, nothing what-soever'. We cannot say anything about it: to do so we would have to bring it under a category, and the categories are applicable only to sensory awareness. The concept of noumenon can only be understood in a negative sense, as a limiting concept whose function is to set the bounds of sensibility (A, 255–6; B, 307–10). But it is fundamental to Kant's claim that while he is a transcendental idealist he is, at the empirical level, a realist and not an idealist like Berkeley.

Kant took great pains to distinguish his own position from that of other philosophers in the early modern period. It may be instructive, finally, to compare his position with an earlier philosopher whom he resembles more closely than he resembles Berkeley or Descartes: St Thomas Aquinas. Kant and Aquinas agree that knowledge is possible only through a cooperation between the senses and the intellect. According to Aquinas, in order not only to acquire but also to exercise concepts the intellect must operate upon what he calls 'phantasmata', which correspond to Kant's 'sensory manifold'—the deliverances of inner and outer senses. For Aquinas, as for Kant, concepts without experience are empty, and phantasms without concepts are unintelligible.

We may ask whether, in the last analysis, Aquinas and Kant are idealists: do they believe that we never know or understand the real world, but only ideas of the mind? It is easier to give a straight answer in the case of Aquinas. For him, ideas were universals, and universals, as such, were creations of the mind; there was no such thing as a universal in the real world. But this does not mean that he was an idealist in the sense defined. Universal concepts were not the objects of intellectual knowledge: they were the tools by which the intellect acquired knowledge of the nature of the material substances of the world around us. All thought, therefore, made use of ideas, but not all thought was about ideas. Natural objects had a reality of their own, of which, through experience, we could acquire a piecemeal and partial knowledge, though the essences of much of the natural world remained unknown to us.[5]

Kant, however, can distinguish his position from that of Berkeley only by claiming that there exists a noumenon, a thing-in-itself underlying the

[5] See vol. II, pp. 236–8.

appearances, to which we have no access either by sense or by intellect, and which cannot be described under pain of uttering nonsense. He is emphatic that it is false to say that there is nothing other than appearance; but to many of his readers it has seemed that a nothing would do just as well as a something about which nothing can be said.

Idealist Epistemology

No sooner was Kant dead than his system was subject to fundamental criticism. Fichte argued that there was a radical inconsistency in the *Critique of Pure Reason*. How could it simultaneously be true that our experience was caused by things in themselves and that the concept of cause could only be applied within the sphere of phenomena? The way to avoid this contradiction, Fichte claimed, was to abandon the idea of an unknown, mind-independent cause of phenomena, and to accept wholeheartedly the idealist position that the world of experience is the creation of a thinking subject.

Fichte convinced few of the possibility of deriving the universe from the subjectivity of the individual ego, and German idealism was given a more plausible and influential form by Hegel, who concurred in the elimination of the thing-in-itself, but who saw the creative activity of the mind occurring on a cosmic scale rather than at the level of individual consciousness.

Nonetheless, *The Phenomenology of Spirit*, however metaphysical in intent, contains some acute reflection on the nature of everyday knowledge and perception. In his customary fashion, Hegel sees human cognitive faculties as threefold, an ascending hierarchy of consciousness, self-consciousness, and reason. Consciousness in its turn proceeds through three stages: there is first sense-awareness (*Die sinnliche Gewissheit*), then there is perception (*Wahrnehmung*), and finally there is understanding (*Verstand*).

Immediate sense-awareness, the reception of crude sense-data, has seemed to many philosophers, before and after Hegel, the richest and firmest form of knowledge. Hegel shows that it is in fact the thinnest and emptiest level of consciousness. If we try to express what we experience, stripped of the categories of the understanding, we are reduced to impotent silence. We cannot even pin down our sense-datum as 'this, here, now'; all these indexical expressions are really universals, capable of being used on different occasions for quite different experiences, times, and places.

It is at the level of perception that consciousness can first claim to be knowledge. At this stage, we take the objects of sense to be things possessing properties. But this too is an illusory form of knowledge. Hegel proceeds, in Kantian style, to show that if we are to reconcile the multiplicity of sense-experience with the unity of properties in a substance we have to rise to the level of understanding, which invokes scientific, non-sensible, categories to confer order on sensory phenomena. Thus we appeal to the notion of force, and construct natural laws to regulate its operation. But reflection shows that these laws are the creation of the understanding itself, rather than some super-phenomenal objective system. Thus consciousness must return upon itself and become self-consciousness.

Consciousness and self-consciousness in their turn yield to the higher faculty of reason, which sees both the nature which is the object of consciousness and the mind which is the object of self-consciousness as manifestations of a single infinite spirit. At this point epistemology turns into metaphysics. Reason's task is no longer to observe or know the world, but to create it and fashion it. For reason is itself an episode in the life of the all-embracing spirit.

Throughout the period that we have been considering, epistemology was the discipline that occupied the centre of philosophical attention: 'What can we know, and how can we know it?' became the key philosophical question. Indeed, the major philosophical schools are given names— 'empiricist' and 'rationalist'—that define them in epistemological terms. This makes an important difference between the early modern period and the ancient and medieval periods, and also between the early modern period and the post-Hegelian age. In the Hegelian tradition epistemology merged with metaphysics; in another tradition that was to become dominant in many parts of the world in the twentieth century, the study of logic and language superseded epistemology as the master philosophical discipline. This we shall see in our next and final volume.

5

Physics

Natural Philosophy

The period at the end of the sixteenth century and the beginning of the seventeenth was one of great importance in the philosophy of the natural world. What had been, up to this point, a single discipline of 'natural philosophy' gradually split into two different endeavours: the philosophy of natural science and the science of physics. Both disciplines share a common subject matter, but they have different purposes and operate in different ways. The philosophy of nature seeks an understanding of the concepts we employ in describing and accounting for natural phenomena: concepts such as 'space', 'time', 'motion', and 'change'. Scientific physics seeks to establish and explain the phenomena themselves, not by *a priori* reasoning or conceptual analysis, but by observation, experiment, and hypothesis. The two disciplines are not in competition, and indeed each needs the other; but it is of prime importance to keep in mind the difference between their goals and methods.

The separation of the two was achieved, in this early modern period, in the course of a battle about the authority of the natural philosophy of Aristotle, which contains elements of both disciplines indiscriminately entwined. That philosophy remained dominant in universities both Catholic and Protestant throughout the period, and its influence undoubtedly acted as a brake on the development of sciences such as mechanics and astronomy. These sciences gathered impetus only to the extent that the Aristotelian yoke was thrown off, and this was due above all to three philosophers who attacked the system from outside the academic mainstream: Galileo, Bacon, and Descartes. Sadly, the liberation of physics was

Susterman's portrait of the ageing Galileo

accompanied by an impoverishment of philosophy. Though Aristotle's scientific physics was shown to be very largely mistaken, his conceptual scheme retained much of its value. All too often, both bad and good were thrown overboard together.

The establishment which persecuted Galileo has long been denounced by historians as hidebound, protectionist, and obscurantist. In particular, the scholastic professors have been blamed for preferring *a priori* speculation to observation and experiment. Not only were they reluctant to conduct research themselves, the charge goes, but they were unwilling to take account of the research of others. They rejected observation, even when it was handed to them, as when a Paduan professor refused to look through Galileo's telescope.

The charge is basically just, though overdrawn. Some of Galileo's Jesuit adversaries were respectable astronomers in their own right. More importantly, we must remember that the anti-empiricist bias of these latter-day Aristotelians was not typical of Aristotle himself. In a famous passage, Aristotle had affirmed the primacy of fact over speculation: 'We must trust observation rather than theory, and trust theories only if their results conform with the observed phenomena.'[1] Indeed, that passage was often quoted by Galileo's critics: heliocentrism was only a theory, but the motion of the sun was something we could see with our own eyes.

Aristotle's own works are full of original and careful observation, and it is no disgrace to him if his physics was shown to be mistaken after a lapse of eighteen centuries. It is paradoxical that one of the greatest scientists of the ancient world should have turned out to be the greatest obstacle to scientific progress in the early modern world. The explanation, however, is simple. When Aristotle's works were rediscovered in the Latin West they were introduced into a society that was predominantly text-based. Christianity, like Judaism and Islam, was a 'religion of a book'. Supreme authority rested with the Bible: the function of the Church was to preserve, proclaim, and interpret the messages contained in that book, and to promote the ideals and practices that it presented. Once Aristotle's texts secured acceptance in Latin academia, instead of being read as stimuli to further research, they were treated with the reverence appropriate to a sacred book. Hence Galileo's genuine contradictions of Aristotle caused as much scandal as his imagined contradictions of the Bible.

Scientific method, as it has been commonly understood in recent centuries, consists of four principal stages. First, systematic observation is undertaken of the phenomena to be explained. Second, a theory is proposed which would provide an explanation of these phenomena. Third, from this theory is derived a prediction of some phenomenon other than those already included in the survey. Fourth, the prediction is tested empirically: if the prediction turns out false, than the theory is to be rejected; if it comes true, then the theory is so far confirmed, and should be put to further test. At each of these stages, mathematics plays a crucial role: in the accurate measurement of the phenomena to be

---

[1] See vol. I, p. 73.

explained and of the result of the test experiment, and in the formulation of the appropriate hypotheses and the derivation of their expected consequences.

During our period four philosophers, through their writings, contributed features of the eventual consensus: Aristotle, Galileo, Bacon, and Descartes. Each of them, however, was guilty of a failure to appreciate one or other element that was needed for the synthesis, and for most of them a key deficiency was a misunderstanding of the relationship between science and mathematics.

Aristotle, while an admirable empirical investigator in practice, presented in his *Posterior Analytics* an unrealistic model of science based on geometry, the most advanced branch of mathematics in his day. He believed that a completed science could be presented as an axiomatic *a priori* system such as was later developed by Euclid. Descartes, himself a distinguished mathematician, thought that science should imitate mathematics not by adopting its methods of ratiocination and calculation, but by looking for truths which had the immediate intuitive appeal of propositions of simple arithmetic and basic geometry.

Bacon, while devoting more care than either of these philosophers to describing procedures for the systematic collection of empirical data and the formation of appropriate hypotheses, had little appreciation of the importance of mathematics in these two tasks. He thought of mathematics as a mere appendix to science, and he complained about 'the daintiness and pride of mathematicians, who will needs have this science almost domineer over physic' (*De Augmentis*, 476).

Of our quartet only Galileo fully appreciated the essential role of mathematics. The book of the universe, he famously said, 'is written in the language of mathematics, and its characters are triangles, circles and other geometric figures, without which it is humanly impossible to understand a single word of it' (*Il Saggiatore*, 6). His weakest point was precisely the one insisted on by his Aristotelian opponents: he failed fully to appreciate that a hypothesis is only confirmed, not proved with certainty, by the success of a prediction. It is this point which was seized on by twentieth-century philosophers of science, such as Pierre Duhem and Karl Popper, who judged Bellarmine the victor in the debate on heliocentrism. They were perhaps over generous in attributing to the cardinal a full grasp of the hypothetico-deductive method.

Cartesian Physics

Like Galileo, and unlike Bacon, Descartes thought that mathematics was the key to physics, though he did not have Galileo's grasp of the use of mathematics in the construction and verification of experiments. In the *Principle of Philosophy* he wrote:

I recognize no kind of matter in corporeal objects except that matter susceptible of every sort of division, shape, and motion which geometers call quantity and which they presuppose as the subject matter of their proofs. Further, the only properties I consider in it are those divisions, shapes and motions; and about them I accept only what can be derived from indubitable true axioms with the sort of self-evidence that belongs to a mathematical proof. All natural phenomena, as I shall show, can be explained in this way: I therefore do not think any other principles in physics are either necessary or desirable. (AT VIII. 78; *CSMK* I. 247)

Descartes' physical system is mechanistic; that is to say it assumes that all natural phenomena can be explained by the motion of geometrical matter. It is not just a matter of seeing everything, outside the mind, as being merely clockwork. Even the simplest form of clock, as naturally explained, is not a mechanistic system, since it involves the notion of *weight*, and for Descartes weight, as distinct from motion or extension, is just one of many properties which are to be dismissed as subjective or secondary:

I observed ... that colours, odours, savours and the rest of such things, were merely sensations existing in my thought, and differing no less from bodies than pain differs from the shape and motion of the instrument which inflicts it. Finally, I saw that weight, hardness, the power of heating, attraction, and of purging, and all other qualities which we experience in bodies, consisted solely in motion or its absence, and in the configuration and situation of their parts. (AT VII. 440; *CSMK* II. 397)

To prove that the essence of matter is constituted by extension, Descartes argues that a body, without ceasing to be a body, can lose any of its properties with the exception of extension. Consider our idea of a stone. Hardness is not essential to it: it may be ground into a fine powder. Colour is not essential: some stones are transparent. Weight is not essential to a body: fire is bodily but light. A stone may change from being warm to being cold and yet remain a stone. 'We may now observe that absolutely no element of our idea remains, except extension in length, breadth and depth.'

One might agree that properties such as colour and warmth are not essential to a body, and yet claim that they are genuine, objective properties. Such was the position of Descartes' scholastic predecessors, who regarded such things as 'real accidents' of substances—'real' because they were objective, and 'accidents' because they were not essential. Descartes offers several arguments against this position.

First he points out that such properties are perceived only by a single sense, unlike shape and motion which are perceived by several senses—warmth and colour are, in Aristotelian jargon, 'proper sensibles' not 'common sensibles'. This seems a poor argument. It is true that judgements, if they are to be objective, must be capable of assessment and correction, and that a judgement of a single sense cannot be corrected by the operation of any other sense. But any individual's sense-judgement can be corrected by his own further, closer, investigation by the same sense, or by the cooperation of other observers using the same faculty.

Descartes' main argument for the subjectivity of proper sensibles is a negative one: the scholastic notion of 'real accidents' is incoherent. If something is real, it must be a substance; if it is an accident, it cannot be a substance. If, *per impossible*, there were such things as real accidents, they would have to be specially created by God from moment to moment (AT III.505, VII.441; *CSMK* II. 298, III. 208).

Possibly some of Descartes' scholastic contemporaries were vulnerable to this argument. But Thomas Aquinas, centuries earlier, had pointed out that the idea that accidental forms must be substances rested on a misunderstanding of language:

Many people make mistakes about forms by judging about them as they would about substances. This seems to come about because forms are spoken of in the abstract as if they were substances, as when we talk of whiteness or virtue or suchlike. So, some people, misled by ordinary usage, regard them as substances. Hence came the error of those who thought that forms must be occult and those who thought that forms must be created. (*Q. D. de Virt* in *Comm.*, ed. R. Pession (Turin: Marietti, 1949), 11)

Descartes saw no need for the accidents and forms of scholastic theory because he claimed to be able to explain the whole of nature in terms of motion and extension alone. Because matter and extension are identical, he argued, there cannot be any empty space or vacuum, and the only possible movement of bodies is ultimately circular, with A pushing B out of its place and B pushing C and so on, until Z moves into the place vacated by A. In the beginning God created matter along with motion and rest: He preserves the total quantity of motion in the universe as constant, but varies its distribution in accordance with the laws of nature. Descartes claims to deduce these laws *a priori* from the immutability of God. The first law says that every body, if unaffected by extraneous causes, perseveres in the same state of motion or rest; the second states that simple or elementary notion is always in a straight line. On the basis of these laws Descartes constructed an elaborate system of vortices, that is to say whirlpools of material particles varying in size and velocity. This system, he maintained, was adequate to explain all the phenomena of the natural world (AT VIII. 42–54, 61–8; *CSMK* I.224–33; 240–5).

Descartes' physical system enjoyed a limited popularity for a period, but within a century it had been totally superseded. It was, in fact, internally incoherent, as can be shown in many ways. Inertia provides the simplest example. According to Descartes' first law everything tends, so far as it can, to remain in the same state of motion or rest in which it is. But if a moving body's tendency to continue moving is not a genuine property of a body, then it cannot explain physical effects. If, on the other hand, it is a genuine property of the body, then it is untrue that bodies have no properties except motion and geometrical properties. For a tendency to move cannot be identified with actual motion; the one may be present without the other. Descartes is badly served here by his contempt for the Aristotelian categories of potentiality and actuality.

Experimental observation during his own lifetime exhibited the weaknesses in Descartes' system. Descartes incorporated into his account of the human body the circulation of the blood recently discovered by William Harvey, but he attempted to explain it purely mechanistically in terms of rarefaction and expansion. This involved him in an account of the movement of the heart that was in total conflict with Harvey's own results, because, unlike Harvey, he believed that it was the expansion of the heart, rather than its contraction, that was responsible for the expulsion of blood.

Again, because he identified matter with extension, Descartes denied the possibility of a vacuum. If God took away all the matter inside a vessel without allowing it to be replaced, he said, then the sides of the vessel would touch each other (AT VIII.51; *CSMK* I. 231). Because of his rejection of the vacuum, he also opposed the atomic hypothesis. Matter, being identical with extension, must be infinitely divisible, and there was no such thing as a void for the atoms to move about in. Descartes sought to explain away the evidence for the existence of a vacuum that had been provided in 1643 by Evangelista Torricelli's invention of the barometer.

The Atomism of Gassendi

When Descartes published his *Principles,* atomism was being revived by Pierre Gassendi, on the model of the ancient theories of Democritus and Epicurus, whose ideas had recently become familiar to the learned world through the discovery and wide dissemination of Lucretius' great Epicurean poem, *De Rerum Natura.*[2] A Catholic priest, who held both a professorship of mathematics and the deanship of a cathedral, Gassendi sought to show that the philosophy of the pagan Epicurus was no more difficult to reconcile with Christianity than was the philosophy of the pagan Aristotle. Both pagan philosophers had erred in teaching that the world was eternal and uncreated; but from a philosophical point of view the explanation of physical phenomena in terms of the behaviour of atoms was to be preferred to an account in terms of substantial forms and real accidents. Gassendi attacked Aristotle in his earliest treatise, and in a series of works between 1647 and his death in 1655 Gassendi defended not only the atomism, but also the ethics and character, of Epicurus.

Natural bodies, said Gassendi, following Epicurus, are aggregates of small units of matter. These units are atoms, that is to say, they are indivisible. They possess size, shape, and weight, and solidity or impenetrability. These atoms, according to Gassendi, possess motion under the constant influence of the divine prime mover: they move in a straight line unless they collide with other atoms or get incorporated into a larger unit (which he called a 'molecule'). All bodies of whatever size are composed of molecules of atoms, and the motions of atoms are the origin and cause of all motions in nature.

Philosophical objections against atomism, Gassendi argued, rested on a confusion between physics and metaphysics. One could accept that any

[2] See vol. I, pp. 179–80.

magnitude must be theoretically capable of further division—no matter
how short a line may be, it always makes sense to talk of a line only half as
long—and yet maintain that there are some physical bodies which cannot
be divided by any power short of the omnipotence of God. A distinction
between the two kinds of divisibility is ruled out only if one accepts
Descartes' identification of matter with extension. But Gassendi rejected
this identification, and was willing to accept the Aristotelian term 'prime
matter' to describe the ultimate constituents of his atoms.

Against both Aristotle and Descartes, but again following Epicurus,
Gassendi maintained that there could be no motions, whether of atoms
or of composite bodies, unless there was a void or vacuum for them to
move through. When air is compressed, for instance, the air atoms move
into the empty spaces that were hitherto between them. Empty space, he
believed, would exist even if there were no bodies in existence; it existed
before creation, and so too did time:

Even if there were no bodies, there would remain a steady place and a flowing
time; so time and place do not seem to depend on bodies or be accidents of
bodies...Place and time must be considered real things, or actual entities, for
although they are not the kind of thing that substance and accident are commonly regarded, they do actually exist and do not depend on the mind like
a chimaera, for whether mind thinks of them or not place stays put and time flows
on. (1658, 182–3)

Space, according to Gassendi, is immense and immovable, and spatial
regions are also incorporeal—not in the sense of being spiritual, but in
the sense of being penetrable in a way that solid bodies are not.

Newton

Subsequent thinkers more often agreed with Gassendi than with Descartes
about the nature of matter and the possibility of a vacuum. Nonetheless, in
the mid-seventeenth century Gassendi's system was not a serious competitor to Descartes' theories. The death blow to Descartes' physics was given
by the publication in 1687 of Sir Isaac Newton's *Principia Mathematica*. Newton
established a universal law of gravitation, showing that bodies are attracted
to each other by a force in direct proportion to their masses and in inverse
proportion to the square of the distance between them. The force of

gravity was something above and beyond the mere motion of extended matter which was all that was allowed in Cartesian physics. Descartes had considered the notion of attraction between bodies, but had rejected it as too like Aristotelian final causes, and as involving the attribution of consciousness to inert masses.

What is it, Newton asks, that glues together the parts of homogeneous hard bodies? Descartes tells us that it is nothing but lack of motion; Gassendi talks of the hooks and eyes of atoms. The first answer explains nothing; the second merely puts the question back. 'I had rather infer from their cohesion', Newton said, 'that their particles attract one another by some force, which in immediate contact is exceedingly strong.' It was this same power of attraction which, operating upon bodies not in immediate contact, was the force of gravity. Was this then a case of action at a distance? At first Newton denied this; but by the time of his *Opticks* (1706) he seemed to be willing to accept that gravity, magnetism, and electricity were indeed forces or powers by which the particles of bodies could act at a distance. He seems to have remained agnostic whether the laws that he had discovered could eventually be explained without appeal to action across a vacuum— e.g. by the postulation of some medium such as an aether.[3]

By accepting the existence of forces in nature which may, for all we know, have no explanation in terms of matter and motion, Newtonian physics made a complete break with the mechanism of Descartes. And by bringing under a single law not only the motion of falling bodies on earth, but also the motion of the moon round the earth and the planets round the sun, Newton put to rest for ever Aristotle's idea that terrestrial and celestial bodies were totally different from each other. His physics was quite different from the competing systems it replaced, and for the next two centuries physics simply *was* Newtonian physics.

The Labyrinth of the Continuum

The separation of physics from the philosophy of nature, set in train by Galileo, was now complete. However, Newton left one problem for philosophers to chew upon for a century or more: the nature of space. On

---

[3] See Steven Nadler, 'Doctrines of Explanation', in *CHSCP*, pp. 342–6.

the basis of the experiments with a vacuum, Newton believed that space was an absolute entity, not a mere set of relations between bodies. In this Newton resembled Gassendi, but he went further than him when he described space as 'the sensorium of God'. It is not quite clear what he meant by this—he probably did not wish to attribute organs to God—but undoubtedly he thought of space as some kind of divine attribute. 'God endures for ever and is present everywhere,' he wrote, 'and by existing always and everywhere he constitutes space, eternity, and infinity' (Newton 1723: 483).

These views of Newton were criticized by Leibniz in 1715 in a letter to Caroline, Princess of Wales. This led to a famous exchange of letters with Newton's admirer Samuel Clarke. Leibniz argued that space was not real, but simply ideal: 'I hold space to be something merely relative, as time is; I hold it to be an order of coexistences as time is an order of successions. For space denotes, in terms of possibility, an order of things which exist at the same time, considered as existing together' (A, 25–6). An empty space, he maintained, would be an attribute without a subject, and he offered many arguments against the idea that space was a substance or any kind of absolute being.

Clarke replied by reaffirming Newton's idea of time and space as belonging to God:

Space is not a Substance, but a Property . . . Space is immense, and immutable, and eternal: and so also is Duration. Yet it does not at all from hence follow, that anything is eternal hors de Dieu. For Space and Duration are not hors de Dieu, but are caused by, and are immediate and necessary consequences of his existence: And without them, his Eternity and Ubiquity (or omnipresence) would be taken away.

The identification of space with the immensity of God is not plausible, since God has no parts and it is essential to the notion of space that one part of it is distinct from another. On the other hand, Leibniz's own view contradicts not just an absolute notion of space, but denies any reality to space at all. For the only real substances in his system are monads, and these are not in any spatial relationship to each other, being each a world of its own. He adopted this position because he could see no coherent way of accepting the reality of the continuum. 'The geometers', he wrote, 'show that extension does not consist of points, but the metaphysicians claim that matter must be made up of unities or simple substances' (G II.278).

The problem seemed to be this. Since space is infinitely divisible, bodies that occupy space must be infinitely divisible too. They must, therefore, contain an infinite number of parts. How big are these parts? If they lack any size, like a point, then even an infinite number of them will lack size too, and no body will have any extension. On the other hand, if they have size, then any body containing an infinite number of them will itself be infinite in extension.

Aristotle had long ago shown that the way to avoid this problem was to make a distinction between two senses of infinite divisibility. 'Divisible to infinity', he insisted, means 'unendingly divisible', not 'divisible into infinitely many parts'. However often a magnitude has been divided, it can always be divided further—there is no end to its divisibility. But that does not mean that the continuum has infinitely many parts: infinity is always potential, never actual.[4] Gassendi had shown that this metaphysical infinite divisibility need not conflict with the atomistic theory that some physical objects are indivisible by any physical power.

The 'labyrinth of the continuum', as Leibniz called it, is an illusion that rests on two bases: the rejection of the Aristotelian metaphysic of actuality and potentiality; and the acceptance of the Cartesian identification of matter with extension. Without the former, there is no reason to see any contradiction in the notion of infinite divisibility. Without the latter, there is no reason to believe that bodies must be infinitely divisible because space is infinitely divisible. Matter may be atomic without extension being lumpy.

Throughout the eighteenth century, however, the continuum was regarded as one of the greatest conundrums of philosophy. David Hume took a robust way out: he simply denied the infinite divisibility of space and time, mocking it as one of the strangest and unaccountable opinions, supported only by 'mere scholastick quibbles'. He based his argument against infinite divisibility upon the finite nature of the human mind:

Whatever is capable of being divided *in infinitum* must consist of an infinite number of parts, and 'tis impossible to set any bounds to the number of parts, without setting bounds at the same time to the division. It requires scarce any induction to conclude from hence, that the *idea*, which we form of any finite quality, is not

---

[4] See vol. I, p. 180.

infinitely divisible, but that by proper distinctions and separations we may run up this idea to inferior ones, which will be perfectly simple and indivisible. In rejecting the infinite capacity of the mind, we suppose it may arrive at an end in the division of its ideas; nor are there any possible means of evading the evidence of this conclusion. 'Tis therefore certain, that the imagination reaches a minimum, and may raise up to itself an idea, of which it cannot conceive any sub-division, and which cannot be diminished without a total annihilation. (*T*, 27)

What goes for ideas, goes also for impressions: 'Put a spot of ink upon paper, fix your eye upon that spot, and retire to such a distance, that at last you lose sight of it; 'tis plain, that the moment before it vanished the image or impression was perfectly indivisible' (*T*, 27).

Kant's Antinomies

Kant had a novel way of dealing with the problems of the continuum. He took over the arguments of his predecessors (for and against infinite extension of time, for and against the infinite divisibility of matter), and instead of taking sides between them he proclaimed that the impossibility of resolving the debate showed that it was a mistake to talk of the universe as a whole or to treat space and time as having reality in themselves. This is the tactic he adopted in the part of the transcendental dialectic called 'the antinomies of pure reason'.

The first antinomy concerns the extension of time and space. If we leave aside space for the moment, the thesis is 'The world had a beginning in time' and the antithesis is 'The world had no beginning in time'. Both propositions had long been discussed by philosophers. Aristotle thought the antithesis could be proved, Augustine thought the thesis could be proved, and Aquinas thought that neither could be proved. Kant now proposes that both can be proved: not, of course, to show that there are two contradictory truths, but to show the impotence of reason to talk about 'the world' as a whole (A, 426–34).

The argument for the thesis is this. An infinite series is one that can never be completed, and so it cannot be the case that an infinite series of temporal states has already passed away. This argument fails, because of an ambiguity in the word 'completed'. It is true that any discrete series which has two termini cannot be infinite; but such a series may be closed at one end and go on for ever in the other. Elapsed time would then be 'completed' by having a terminus in the present, while reaching forever backward.

The argument for the antithesis is equally unconvincing. If the world had a beginning, it goes, then there was a time when the world did not exist. There is nothing to differentiate any moment of this 'void time' from any other; hence there can be no answer to the question 'why did the world begin when it did?' One may agree that it is not possible to date the beginning of the world from outside ('at such a point in void time'), while maintaining that one can locate it from within ('so many time-units before now'). Augustine and Aquinas would have agreed in rejecting the notion of void time: for them, time began when the world began.

The second antinomy concentrates not on time but on space—or rather, the spatial divisibility of substances. The thesis is: 'Every composite substance in the world is made up of simple parts'; the antithesis is: 'No composite thing in the world is made up of simple parts.' The thesis is the affirmation, and the antithesis the denial, of atomism. Once again the arguments Kant presents on each side of the antinomy are inconclusive: they fail to take full account of Aristotle's distinction between something's being divisible into infinite parts, and something's being infinitely divisible into parts.

The antinomies are designed to exhibit the general pointlessness of asking or answering questions about the world as a whole, but in the particular case of space and time Kant had already argued for their unreality earlier in the first *Critique*, in the transcendental aesthetic. He started from an inherited distinction between inner and outer senses. Space, he claimed, is the form of outer sense; it is the subjective condition of our awareness of objects outside ourselves (A, 26). Time, on the other hand, is the form of inner sense, by means of which the mind experiences its own inner states, which have no extension in space but are all ordered in time:

What, then, are space and time? Are they real existences? are they only determinations or relations of things, yet such as would belong to things even if they were not intuited? Or are space and time such that they belong only to the form of awareness, and therefore to the subjective constitution of our mind, apart from which they could not be ascribed to anything whatsoever?

A dogmatic metaphysician, Kant tells us, would say that infinite space and infinite time are presupposed by experience, and that we can imagine space and time without objects but not objects without space and time. But we may ask how it is that we can know truths about space and time which are based on awareness (because they are not analytic) and yet are *a priori* (because they are necessary and universal). Kant's answer is that the knowledge of synthetic *a priori* truths about space and time is only explicable if they are formal elements of sense-experience rather than properties of things in themselves.

Does this mean that they are unreal? Empirically, Kant replies, they are real, but transcendentally they are ideal. 'If we take away the subject, space and time disappear: these as phenomena cannot exist in themselves but only in us.' What things are in themselves, beyond the phenomena, is something that is unknown to us.

During the period covered by this volume, as we have seen, the philosophical study of the material world passed through two stages. In the first phase, the seventeenth century saw the gradual separation of the old

Philosophers over the centuries have debated the reality or otherwise of time. Kant's view of it as a subjective phenomenon contrasts with this personification of it as a causal agent in a sixteenth-century French woodcut

discipline of natural philosophy into the science of physics, whose role was the empirical investigation of actual natural laws, and the philosophy of physics, whose task it was to analyse the concepts presupposed by any physical inquiry. In the second phase, philosophers examined a wide gamut of possible conceptions of space and time, ranging from the extreme realism of Newton and Clarke to the subjective idealism of Kant. In our next and final volume, there will not be a thematic chapter devoted to the philosophy of physics. By the nineteenth century physics was a fully mature empirical science, operating independently of philosophy; the history of physics is now quite separate from the history of philosophy. To be sure, the philosophy of physics continues on its way, as an analysis of the conceptual implications of novel physical theories. Such a discipline, however, can be pursued only by those with more knowledge of the modern science of physics itself than can be presumed in the readership of an introductory history of philosophy.

6

Metaphysics

The Metaphysics of Suarez

It was through the *Disputationes Metaphysicae* of Francisco Suarez, directly or indirectly, that the metaphysics of the medieval scholastics became known to the philosophers of the early modern age. Suarez was well acquainted with the works of his medieval predecessors, and he summarized their views, codified their positions, and built up his own system by choosing options from the menu that they offer. A summary of the main positions of the *Disputationes* accordingly provides a good starting point for a consideration of the metaphysics of our period.

Suarez starts from Aristotle's definition of the subject as the discipline that studies being qua being. He expands on this by offering a classification of different types of being, proceeding by a series of dichotomies. First there is the division between infinite being and finite being, or, as he often says, between *ens a se* (that which has being of itself) and *ens ab alio* (that which has being from elsewhere). The creaturely world of finite being is then divided first of all into substance and accident. Substances are things like stars and dogs and pebbles which subsist on their own; accidents are entities like brightness, fierceness, and hardness which exist only by inhering in substances and have no independent history. We can proceed further if we wish by subdividing substances into living and non-living, and living substances into animal and vegetable and so on; we can also identify at least nine different kinds of accidents corresponding to Aristotle's categories. But such further division will take us outside the scope of general metaphysics, which operates at the most abstract level. All these items are beings, but metaphysics is interested in studying them only *qua beings*. The study of living beings *qua living*, for instance, is for physical rather than metaphysical disciplines—biology, say, and zoology or psychology.

To Aristotle's definition Suarez adds a qualification. The subject matter of metaphysics, strictly speaking, is not any old being, but *real* being. All the items we have considered in the previous paragraph, including items like fierceness and hardness, count as real beings. If so, one might wonder, what other beings are there? In addition, Suarez says, there are creations of the reason (*entia rationis*) that have being only in the mind and not in reality. Blindness is an *ens rationis*: this does not mean that it is something unreal or fictitious; it means that it is not a positive reality, as the power of sight is, but an absence of such a power. Certain types of relation form another class of *entia rationis*: when I become a great-uncle, I acquire a new relationship but there is no real change in myself. Finally, there are the creations of the imagination: chimeras and hippogriffs. So there are three kinds of *entia rationis*: negations, relations, and fictions. These are fringe topics for the metaphysician rather than his principal concern.

Let us return then to the centre: real being. Is there a single, univocal concept of being that applies in the same sense to all the varied kinds of being? Aquinas had said no: 'being' was an analogous term, and God is not a being in the same sense as ants are beings. Scotus had said yes: 'being' could be used about God in exactly the same sense as about creatures. Suarez offers a subtle answer which he believes enables him to take sides with both Aquinas and Scotus. There is a single abstract concept of being which applies to everything alike, and Scotus is so far correct; but this is not a concept that tells us anything real or new about the objects to which it applies, and to that extent Aquinas is right. Sentences like 'this animal is a dog' or 'this dog is white' can be instructive, because the predicate carries information that is not already implicit in the subject. But the predicate '. . . is a being' can never be instructive in the same way: *being* is not an activity or attribute distinct from *being an animal* or *being a dog* (*DM* 2.1, 9; 2.3, 7).

In saying this, Suarez is touching on a dispute much ventilated in the Middle Ages, namely, whether in creatures there is a real distinction between essence and *esse*. The issue is not a clear one, and its significance depends on two decisions. First, it matters whether we take 'essence' as generic essence or individual essence (e.g. as 'humanity' or as 'Peter's humanity'). Second, it matters whether we take *esse* as equivalent to 'existence' or as the all-embracing predicate 'being'. There is one option which gives a clear answer. If we take essence in the generic sense, and *esse* as existence, then there is an undeniable difference between essence and existence: essence is what answers the question 'What is an X?' and existence is what answers the question 'Are there Xs?' The difference between the questions is so enormous that talk of a 'real distinction' seems to fail only by understatement.

Suarez in fact denies that there is a real distinction between essence and *esse*; the distinction, he says, is only mental (*tantum ratione*). We have to look closely to see which of the options he is taking. It becomes clear that by 'essence' he means individual essence; the essence of an individual person, Peter, not anything like humanity in the abstract. And by *esse* he means the all-embracing predicate which delineates the subject matter of metaphysics. In denying the real distinction he is denying that there is any real difference in Peter between *being* and *being Peter*. These are different predicates we can apply to Peter: we can say 'Peter is Peter' and (in Latin, if not idiomatically in English) 'Peter is'. But in using these two forms of speech we are not referring to two different real items in Peter, as we are when we say 'Peter is tall' and 'Peter is wise'.

Some earlier scholastics, notably Thomas Aquinas, would have said that the sentence which tells us the essence of Peter is not 'Peter is Peter' but rather 'Peter is human'. This was because Aquinas believed that the principle of individuation was matter: what makes two peas two rather than one is not any difference between their properties, but the fact that they are two different lumps of matter. According to Aquinas, in an individual human like Peter there was no extra formal element in addition to humanity which gave him his individuality. For Duns Scotus and his school, on the other hand, Peter possessed, in addition to his humanity, a further individuating feature, his *haecceitas* or 'thisness'. Once again, Suarez wants to side with both his great predecessors. 'The adequate principle of individuation is this matter and this form in union, the form being the chief principle and sufficient by itself for the composite, as an individual thing of a certain species, to be considered numerically one' (*DM* 5.6,15). In effect, Suarez comes down definitely on the side of Scotus. There is in Peter a real formal element, a *differentia individualis*, in addition to the specific nature of humanity, which is what makes him Peter and not Paul (*DM* 5.2, 8–9).

Scotus, as we have just seen, adds an extra metaphysical item to the apparatus employed by Aquinas. Suarez, in his turn, adds an extra item of his own. In Peter we have not just the matter and form which all followers of Aristotle accepted, and not just the individuating element that Scotists accepted, but an extra thing, that makes Peter a substance and not an accident. Subsistence, the form of existence peculiar to substance as opposed to accident, adds to an individuated essence a *mode,* and there is a special form of composition which is that of mode-plus-thing-modified. Suarez employed his notion of mode in an attempt to illuminate the difference between a soul existing embodied and a soul existing in separation after death. But his new terminology was to be widely employed, and made popular, especially by Descartes.

Descartes on Eternal Truths

Descartes took over many of the technical terms of scholastic metaphysics—substance, mode, form, essence, and so on—but used many of them in novel ways. His most important innovation in metaphysics was one that was not fully spelt out in his published works and only became clear when his copious correspondence was made public after his death. This was his doctrine of the creation of eternal truths.

In 1630, when he was completing his treatise *The World,* Descartes wrote to Mersenne:

The mathematical truths that you call eternal have been laid down by God and depend on him entirely as much as all other creatures . . . Please do not hesitate to assert and proclaim everywhere that it is God who has laid down these laws in nature just as a king lays down laws in his kingdom. (AT I. 135; *CSMK* III. 23)

As for the eternal truths, I say once more that they are true or possible only because God knows them as true or possible. They are not known as true by God in any way which would imply that they are true independently of Him . . . In God willing and knowing are a single thing, in such a way that by the very fact of willing something He knows it, and it is only for this reason that such a thing is true. (AT I.147; *CSMK* III. 13)

It was a new departure to say that the truths of logic and mathematics depended upon the will of God. Scholastic philosophers agreed that they were dependent on God, but dependent on his essence, not on his will:

they did not believe, as Descartes did, that God was free to make it not be true that the three angles of a Euclidean triangle were equal to two right angles (AT IV. 110; *CSMK*. III.151; Aquinas, ScG II.25). Moreover, scholastics believed that prior to the creation of the world logical and mathematical truths had no reality independent of God; whereas for Descartes these truths were creatures, distinct from God, brought into existence from all eternity by His creative power. 'It is certain that He is no less the author of creatures' essence than he is of their existence; and this essence is nothing other than the eternal truths...I know that God is the author of everything and that these truths are something and consequently that he is their author' (AT I. 151; *CSMK* III.25).

For Descartes, the truths of logic and mathematics had their being neither in the material world nor in the mind of anyone, divine or human. The eternal truths were not truths about material objects: theorems about triangles could be proved even if there was not a single triangular object in existence, and geometry held true even if the external world was a complete illusion. The eternal truths were prior to, and independent of, any human minds, and though they were dependent on, they were distinct from, the mind of God. The eternal truths belonged in a third realm of their own, similar to the domain in which in Antiquity Plato had located his Ideas. St Augustine had relocated the Platonic Ideas in the mind of God, and that had been ever since the standard position among Christian philosophers right up to Suarez. Descartes' novel doctrine makes him the founder of modern Platonism.[1]

The theory of the creation of eternal truths plays a fundamental role in Descartes' metaphysics and physics. At the time when he was explaining his theory to Mersenne, Descartes was writing a sustained attack on the Aristotelian metaphysics of real qualities and substantial forms. Rejection of substantial forms entailed rejection also of essences, since the two are closely connected in the Aristotelian system—essence being identical with form in the case of immaterial beings, and in the case of material beings consisting of form plus the appropriate matter. Descartes did not reject the terminology of essence as firmly as he rejected that of form and quality, but he reinterpreted it drastically. Essences, as he told Mersenne, are nothing but eternal truths.

[1] For Plato, see vol. I, pp. 52–3. Among scholastics, Henry of Ghent (whom Descartes is most unlikely to have read) came closest to anticipating his position (see vol. II, p. 85).

The title page of the first French edition of Descartes' *Meditations*

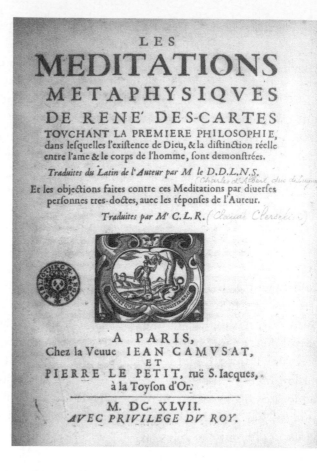

LES
MEDITATIONS
METAPHYSIQVES
DE RENE' DES-CARTES
TOVCHANT LA PREMIERE PHILOSOPHIE,
dans lefquelles l'exiftence de Dieu, & la diftinction réelle
entre l'ame & le corps de l'homme, font demonftrées.

Traduites du Latin de l'Auteur par M le D.D.L.N.S.

Et les objections faites contre ces Meditations par diuerfes
perfonnes tres-doctes, auec les réponfes de l'Auteur.

Traduites par M' C. L. R.

A PARIS,
Chez la Veuue IEAN CAMVSAT,
ET
PIERRE LE PETIT, ruë S. Iacques,
à la Toyfon d'Or.

M. DC. XLVII.
AVEC PRIVILEGE DV ROY.

In the Aristotelian system it was the forms and essences that provided the element of stability in the flux of phenomena—the stability that was necessary for there to be universally valid scientific knowledge. Having rejected essences and forms, Descartes needed a new foundation for physics, and he found it in the eternal truths. If there are no substantial forms, then what connects one moment of a thing's history to another is nothing but the immutable will of God (AT VII.80; AT XI.37).

God has laid down the laws of nature, enshrined in the eternal truths. These include not only the laws of logic and mathematics, but also the law of inertia and other laws of motion. Consequently they provide the foundations of mechanistic physics. But if they are dependent on God's unfettered will, how do we know that they will not change? There can, of course, be no question of God changing his mind; but might he not have decreed from all eternity that at a certain point in time the laws should change? To rule out that possibility, Descartes once again appeals to the notion that God is no deceiver. The veracity of God, in his post-Aristotelian system, is necessary to establish the permanent validity of these clearly and distinctly perceived truths.

The doctrine of the creation of the eternal truths was, as we have said, from one point of view a gigantic innovation. But it can also be looked at as the culmination of a philosophical development which had been taking place throughout the later Middle Ages—the gradual extension of the scope of divine omnipotence. In respect to the determination of moral truths, for instance, Scotus and Ockham had allotted to the divine will a much freer scope than Aquinas had done. In the religious sphere this tendency had been taken to an extreme by Jean Calvin's doctrine of the absolute sovereignty of God, who freely and unaccountably predestines humans to salvation or damnation. Descartes' extension of divine freedom into the realm of logic and mathematics might be seen as the philosophical counterpart of Calvinist absolutism.

Three Notions of Substance

In the Aristotelian system, the notion of substance was all important: all qualities and other properties were accidents belonging to substances, and only substances were real and independent. Descartes, too, assigned to substance a fundamental role. 'Nothing has no qualities or properties,' he wrote, 'so that where we perceive some there must necessarily be a thing or substance on which they depend.' That was a step in the argument from *cogito* to *sum*, to the existence of the first discoverable substance, Descartes' own self. In his *Principles* he offered a definition of substance as 'a thing which so exists that it needs no other thing in order to exist'. Strictly speaking, he observed, only God counted as a substance by this definition, but created substances could be said to be things which need only the concurrence of God in order to exist (AT VIII.24; *CSMK* I.210).

For the Aristotelians, there were many different kinds of substances, each specified by a particular substantial form—humans by the form of humanity and so on. According to Descartes there were no such things as substantial forms, and there were only two kinds of substance: mind, or thinking substance, and body, or extended substance. These did not have substantial forms, but they did have essences: the essence of mind was thought and the essence of body was extension. How particular substances of these two kinds are individuated remains unclear in Descartes' system, and in the case of body he sometimes writes as if there was only one single, cosmic, substance, of which the objects we encounter are simply local fragments engaging in local transactions (AT VIII.54, 61; *CSMK* I.233, 240).

The Aristotelians believed that substances were visible and tangible entities, accessible to the senses, even though it took the intellect to work out the nature of each substance. When I look at a piece of gold, I am genuinely seeing a substance, though only science can tell me what gold really is. Descartes took a different view. 'We do not have immediate awareness of substances,' he wrote in the *Fourth Replies*, 'rather, from the mere fact that we perceive certain forms or attributes, which must inhere in something in order to have existence, we name the thing in which they exist a substance' (AT VII. 222; *CSMK* II.156). So substances are not perceptible by the senses—not only their underlying nature, but their very existence, is something to be established only by intellectual inference.

Locke took much further the thesis that substances are imperceptible. The notion of substance, he says, arises from our observation that certain ideas constantly go together. If, to some idea of substance in general, we join 'the simple Idea of a certain dull whitish colour, with certain degrees of Weight, Hardness, Ductility and Fusibility, we have the Idea of Lead'. The idea of any particular kind of substance always contains the notion of substance in general; but this is not a real idea, certainly not a clear and distinct one, but only a 'supposition of we know not what support of such qualities which are capable of producing simple Ideas in us; which are commonly called Accidents' (*E*, 295).

The operative part of our idea of a distinct kind of substance, then, will be a complex idea made up of a number of simple ones. The idea of the sun, for instance, is 'an aggregate of those several simple Ideas, Bright, Hot, Roundish, having a constant regular motion, at a certain distance from us, and, perhaps some other' (*E*, 299). The ideas of kinds of substance such as *horse* or *gold* are called 'sortal ideas': collections of simple co-occurent ideas plus the confused idea of the unknown substratum. Particular substances are concrete individuals belonging to these different sorts or species.

The substances of different sorts have essences: to be a man, or to be an oak, is to have the essence of man or the essence of oak. But there are, for Locke, two kinds of essence: real and nominal. The real essence is: 'The real, internal, but generally in substances, unknown constitution of things, whereon their discoverable Qualities depend.' The nominal essence is the collection of simple ideas that have been assembled and attached to names in order to rank things into sorts or species. The nominal essence gives the right to bear a particular name, and nominal essences are largely the arbitrary creation of human language.

In the case of a triangle, the real essence and the nominal essence (*three-sided figure*) are the same. Not so in the case of substances. Locke considers the gold ring on his finger:

It is the real constitution of its insensible Parts, on which depend all those Properties of Colour, Weight, Fusibility, Fixedness etc. which are to be found in it. Which Constitution we know not; and so having no particular Idea of it, have no Name that is the sign of it. But yet it is its Colour, Weight, Fusibility and Fixedness etc. which makes it to be Gold, or gives it a right to that Name, which is therefore its nominal Essence. Since nothing can be called Gold, but what has a conformity of Qualities to that abstract complex Idea, to which that Name is annexed. (*E*, 419)

The real essences of things, like the hidden constitution of gold, are generally unknown to us. Even in the case of a human being we have no more idea of his real essence than a peasant has of the wheels and springs which make a church clock strike (E 440).

Essences belong to sorts, not individuals. Individuals have neither real nor nominal essences. 'Nothing I have', Locke says, ' is essential to me. An accident or Disease, may very much alter my Colour, or Shape; a Fever, or Fall, may take away my Reason, or Memory, or both; and an Apoplexy leave neither Sense, nor Understanding no nor Life' (*E*, 440). The real Locke, it seems to follow, is the underlying, impenetrable, substratum of various properties; something quite other than a human being.

Locke maintains that substance itself is indescribable because it is propertyless. But it seems incredible that someone should argue that substance has no properties precisely because it is what *has* the properties. The thesis that individuals have no nominal essence means that one could identify an individual, A, and then go on to inquire whether that individual did or did not have the properties which would qualify it to be called 'man' or 'mountain' or 'moon'. But how is a propertyless individual to be identified in the first place?

In the Aristotelian tradition there was no such thing as a propertyless substance, a something that could be identified as a particular individual without reference to any sortal. Fido is an identifiable individual only so long as he remains a dog, so long as the sortal 'dog' can be truly applied to him. We cannot ask whether A is the same indidividual as B without asking whether A is the same individual F as B, where 'F' holds a place for some sortal: 'man', 'mountain', or whatever. Locke's confused doctrine of substance led him into insoluble difficulties about identity and individuation: we shall meet them again when we come, in Chapter 8, to consider the topic of personal identity.

Single Necessary Substance

While Locke, in England, evacuated the notion of substance of any significant content, Spinoza, in Holland, had made it the basis of his metaphysical system. One of the first definitions in the *Ethics* reads: 'By substance I mean that which is in itself, and is conceived through itself: that of which a concept can be formed independently of the concept of anything else' (*Eth*, 1). Descartes had defined substance as 'that which requires nothing but itself in order to exist'. Such a definition, Spinoza thought, could apply at most to God; finite minds and bodies, which Descartes counted as substances, needed to be created and conserved by God in order to exist.

Spinoza, like Descartes, links the notion of substance with the notions of attribute and of mode. An attribute is a property conceived to be essential to a substance; a mode is a property only conceivable by reference to a substance. Armed with these definitions, Spinoza proves that there can be at most one substance of a given kind. If there are two or more distinct substances, they must be distinguished from each other either by their attributes or by their modes. They cannot be distinguished by their modes, because substance is prior to mode and therefore any distinction between modes must follow, and cannot create, a distinction between substances.

They must therefore be distinguished by their attributes, which they could not be if there were two substances having an attribute in common. Moreover, no substance can cause any other substance, because an effect must have something in common with its cause, and we have just shown that two substances would have to be totally different in kind.

The seventh proposition of Book One of the *Ethics* is 'It belongs to the nature of substance to exist', and its proof runs as follows:

A substance cannot be produced by anything other than itself; it must therefore be its own cause—that is, its essence necessarily involves existence, or it belongs to its nature to exist. (*Eth*, 4)

So far, the word 'God' has not been mentioned in the *Ethics*, except in the introductory definition where it is said to mean infinite substance. By now, however, every reader must suspect where Spinoza is leading him. In the very next proposition we are told that any substance is necessarily infinite. At this point one may feel inclined to object that now that substance has been given such august properties, we cannot take it for granted that there are any substances in existence at all. Spinoza would agree: the first few propositions of the *Ethics* are designed to show that at most one substance exists. Only at proposition 11 does he move on to show that at least one substance exists, namely, God.

Spinoza's treatment of God's existence and nature will be considered in detail in Chapter 10. Here we are concerned with the consequences that he draws for the metaphysics of finite beings. Mind and matter are not substances, for if they were they would present limitations on God and God would not be, as he is, infinite. Everything that there is is in God, and without God nothing else can exist or be conceived. Thought and extension, the defining characteristics of mind and matter, are in fact attributes of God himself, so that God is both a thinking and an extended thing: he is mental and he is bodily (*Eth*, 33). Individual minds and bodies are modes, or particular configurations, of the divine attributes of thought and extension. It is thus that the idea of any individual thing involves the thought of the eternal and infinite essence of God.

All Spinoza's contemporaries agreed that finite substances were dependent on God as their first cause. What Spinoza does is to represent the relationship between God and finite substances not in terms of physical cause and effect, but in the logical terms of subject and predicate. Any

This engraving of Spinoza makes him appear a more observant student of the Bible than he really was

apparent statement about a finite substance is in reality a predication about God: the proper way of referring to creatures like us is to use not a noun but an adjective. Indeed the word 'creature' is not really in place: it suggests a distinction between a creator and what he creates, whereas for Spinoza there is no such distinction between God and nature.

The key element in Spinoza's monism is not the doctrine that there is only one substance; it is the collapsing of any distinction between entailment and causation. There is just a single relation of consequence: it is this which unites an effect with its causes and a conclusion with its premiss. Smoke follows from fire in just the same way as a theorem follows from axioms. The laws of nature, therefore, are as necessary and exceptionless as the laws of logic. From any given cause there necessarily follows its effect, and everything is ruled by absolute logical necessity. For most other thinkers causes had to be distinct from their effects. Not so for Spinoza, given his identification of causation with entailment. Just as a proposition entails itself, God is His own cause and He is the immanent, not the transient, cause of all things.

This system is extremely difficult to understand, and may well be ultimately incomprehensible. It is more profitable to follow another line of thought which Spinoza offers in order to explain the structure of the universe. Our bodies, he remarks, are composed of many different parts, varying in kind from each other; the parts may change and vary, and yet each individual retains its nature and identity. 'We may easily proceed thus to infinity, and conceive the whole of nature as one individual, whose parts, that is, all bodies, vary in infinite ways, without any change in the individual as a whole' (*Eth*, 43). This invites us to see the relationship between finite beings and God not in terms of effect and cause but in terms of part and whole.

We often talk of parts of our body as performing actions and undergoing changes—but it is not too difficult to see that this is an improper way of talking. It is not my eyes which see, or my liver which purifies my blood. My eyes and liver do not have a life of their own, and such activities are activities of my whole organism. Philosophers from Aristotle onwards have pointed out that it is more correct to say that I see with my eyes and that my body uses my liver to purify my blood. If we follow Spinoza's hint we will see that he is inviting us to see nature as a single organic whole, of which each of us is a particle and an instrument.

This vision of nature as a single whole, a unified system containing within itself the explanation of all of itself, is found attractive by many people. Many, too, are willing to follow Spinoza in concluding that if the universe contains its own explanation, then everything that happens is determined, and there is no possibility of any sequence of events other than the actual one. 'In nature,' Spinoza says, 'there is nothing contingent; everything is determined, by the necessity of the divine nature, to exist and operate in a certain manner' (*Eth*, 20).

Making Room for Contingency

Of all Spinoza's contemporaries, the philosopher closest to him was Malebranche. Like Spinoza, Malebranche thought that the connection between a cause and its effect must be a necessary one. 'A true cause as I understand it', he wrote, 'is one such that the mind perceives a necessary connection between it and its effects' (*R de V* 6.2, 3). Many people, having read Hume on causation, believe that before his time it was a unanimous philosophical opinion that there must be a necessary connection between cause and effect. But, in fact, Spinoza and Malebranche were unusual in treating the following of an effect from a cause as being on a par with the following of a conclusion from a premiss. Aquinas, for instance, had insisted that relationship to a cause is no part of the definition of the thing that is caused. He considers an argument purporting to show that things can come into existence without a cause. The argument goes like this:

Nothing prevents a thing's being found without what does not belong to its concept, e.g. a man without whiteness; but the relation of caused to cause does not seem to be part of the concept of existent things: for they can be understood without that. Therefore they can exist without that. (*ST*. 1a, 44. 1)

Aquinas does not accept that things can come into existence without a cause, but he does not find fault with the minor premiss of the argument.

For Spinoza and Malebranche, on the other hand, the necessary connection between cause and effect was indeed a conceptual one. In laying this down as a condition for a true causal relation, both of them realized that they were making it more difficult to find in the world examples of genuine causal relations. Parcels of matter in motion could not be genuine causes. A body could not move itself, because the concept of body did not include that of motion, and no body could move another, for there was no logical relationship between motion in one body and motion in another body. Both Spinoza and Malebranche, in fact, came to the conclusion that there is only one genuine cause operating in the physical world, and that is God.

Malebranche's position, however, was more complicated than Spinoza's. For Spinoza, God was the only cause, not just in the physical world, but in the universe as a whole (since for him mind and extension are two aspects of the same entity). Again, for Spinoza, God is not just the only cause in the universe, but also the only substance, and his existence and his operation are all matters of logical necesssity.

Malebranche, on the other hand, allows that in addition to God and the material world there are finite spirits, which are genuine agents and enjoy a degree of freedom. Human beings, for instance, can direct their thoughts and desires in one direction rather than another. But created spirits are incapable of causing any effect in the natural world. I cannot even move my own arm. It is true that it moves when I will; however, I am not, he says, the natural cause of this movement, but only its occasional cause. That is to say, my internal act of willing provides the occasion for God to cause the movement of my arm in the external world. What goes for parts of my body goes *a fortiori* for other material objects: 'There is a contradiction in saying that you can move your armchair...No power can transport it where God does not transport it or place it where God does not place it' (*EM*, 7, 15).

For Malebranche, unlike Spinoza, there is contingency in the physical universe, therefore, but it derives only from the eternal free decree of God. God wills without any change or succession all that will take place in the course of time. He is not (unlike Spinoza's God) necessitated to will the course of natural history, but other than Him there are no other causal agents to introduce contingency into the material world.

Leibniz took issue here with Malebranche and Spinoza: in order to allow for divine and human freedom he wished to make room for contingency throughout the universe. In the *Monadology* Leibniz makes a distinction between truths of reason and truths of fact. Truths of reason are necessary and their opposite is impossible; truths of fact are contingent and their opposite is possible. Truths of reason are ascertained by a logical analysis parallel to the mathematicians' derivation of theorems from axioms and definitions; their ultimate basis is the principle of non-contradiction. Truths of fact are based on a different principle: the principle that nothing is the case without there being a sufficient reason why it should be thus rather than otherwise (G, 6, 612–13).

Leibniz attached great importance to the principle of sufficient reason, which was his own innovation. It is not immediately obvious how to reconcile the statement that truths of fact are contingent with the statement that they rest on the principle of sufficient reason. We discover that consistency is purchased at the price of a new, and minimalist, account of contingency.

On the face of it, human beings seem to have some properties that are necessary and others that are contingent. Antoine is necessarily human, but it is a contingent matter whether he is a bachelor or is married. It was

thus that scholastic philosophers distinguished between the essential properties of a substance, and its accidental ones. But this is not at all how
Leibniz saw the matter. He believed that every predicate which was, as a
matter of fact, true of a particular subject was in some way part of its
essence, 'so that whoever understood perfectly the notion of the subject
would also judge that the predicate belongs to it' (*D* VIII).

Consider the history of Alexander the Great, which consists in a series of
truths of fact. God, seeing the individual notion of Alexander, sees
contained in it all the predicates truly attributable to him: whether he
conquered Darius, whether he died a natural death, and so on. The
predicate 'conqueror of Darius' must appear in a complete and perfect
idea of Alexander. A person of whom that predicate was not true would
not be our Alexander but somebody else (*D* VIII).

Leibniz tells us that necessary truths, such as the truths of geometry and
arithmetic, are analytic: 'when a truth is necessary, the reason for it can be
found by analysis, that is, by resolving it into simpler ideas and truths until
the primary ones are reached.' As an example of how this is to be done, we
may take Leibniz's proof that 2+2=4. We start with three definitions: (i)
2=1+1; (ii) 3=2+1; (iii) 4=3+1; and the axiom that if equals are substituted for equals the equality remains. We then demonstrate as follows:

$$2 + 2 = 2 + 1 + 1 (\text{df i})$$
$$= 3 + 1 (\text{df ii})$$
$$= 4 (\text{df iii})^2$$

Now truths of fact are not capable of demonstration of this kind; human
beings, it seems, can discover them only by empirical investigation. But
Leibniz's account of individual notions means that in every statement of
fact the predicate is covertly included in the subject. Hence, statements
of fact are in a sense analytic. But the analysis necessary to exhibit this
would be an infinite one, which only God could complete.

But if statements of fact are from God's point of view analytic, how can
they be contingent? Leibniz answers that the demonstration that their

---

[2] As Frege was later to point out, there is a gap in this proof: Leibniz has tacitly assumed that 2+
(1+1) = (2+1) +1, which depends on the associative law for addition.

predicates belong to their subjects 'is not as absolute as those of numbers or of geometry, but that it supposes the sequence of things that God has freely chosen and which is founded on the first free decree of God, the import of which is always to do what is most perfect' (D XIII). There are two elements in this answer: first, there is no internal contradiction in the notion of an Alexander who was defeated by Darius, such as there is in the notion of a triangle with four sides. Second, the inclusion of the predicate in the notion of *our* Alexander is the result of a free decree of God to create such a person. To be sure, this makes Alexander's conquest in a sense necessary, but only by moral necessity, not metaphysical necessity. God cannot but choose the best, but this is because of his goodness, not because of any limit on his almighty power (T, 367).

The contingency that we are left with seems very slender. There is nothing contingent about the actual Alexander's possession of each of his properties and going through each event in his life. What is contingent is the existence of this particular Alexander, with this particular history, rather than any of the other possible Alexanders that God might have created. This is something that is contingent even from God's point of view: the only necessary existence is God's own existence.

There is clearly a remarkable notion of identity at work here. If I imagine myself with one hair more on my chin than I have, then on Leibniz's terms I am imagining a different person altogether. Leibniz gave considerable thought to the logic of identity, and enunciated two theorems about it. One is that if A is identical with B, then whatever is true of A is true of B, and whatever is true of B is true of A. The other is that if whatever is true of A is true of B, and vice versa, then A is identical with B. The first principle, though commonly known as 'Leibniz's law', was widely accepted both before and after his time. The second, commonly called the principle of the identity of indiscernibles, has always been more controversial: this is the thesis that no two individuals have all their properties in common. Leibniz himself, when he stated in the *Discourse* (IX) that it was not possible for two substances to resemble each other entirely and differ only numerically, described this as 'a notable paradox'.

He could, however, cite authorities in support. Scholastic Aristotelians had held that the principle of individuation, that is to say what distinguished one individual from another, was matter: two peas, however alike, were two peas and not one because they were two different pieces of

Leibniz illustrates the identity of indiscernibles by showing the ladies of the court that no two leaves are exactly similar

matter.[3] As a consequence of this, thinkers like Aquinas had argued that if there were substances that were immaterial—angels, say—then there could be only one of each kind, since there was no matter to distinguish one member of a species from another. Leibniz's doctrine of individual notions or essences forced him to generalize this: all substances, and not just Aquinas' angels, were unique specimens of their kind. He argued that if there were in nature two beings indiscernible from each other, then God would act without sufficient reason in treating one differently from the other (G VII. 393).

Is the principle of the identity of indiscernibles itself necessary or contingent? Leibniz does not seem to have made up his mind. Since, to establish it, he appeals to the principle of sufficient reason, not to that of non-contradiction, it appears contingent; and in a letter he wrote that it was possible to conceive two indiscernible substances, even though it was false to suppose they existed (G VII. 394). In his *New Essays*, however, he says that if two individuals were perfectly alike and indistinguishable there would not be any distinction between them; and he goes on to draw the conclusion that the atomic theory must be false. It was not enough to say that one atom was at a different time and place from another: there must be some internal principle of distinction or there would be only one atom, not two (G V. 214).

Berkeley's Idealism

Leibniz's philosophy is the first systematic presentation since Antiquity of idealism, the theory that reality consists ultimately of mental entities, that is to say immaterial perceivers along with their perceptions. During his lifetime another version of idealism was propounded by Bishop Berkeley. The two systems resemble each other, but there are important differences between them: Leibniz's idealism is a rationalist idealism; Berkeley's is an empiricist idealism. The differences arise from the different starting points of the two philosophers. Before comparing the systems in detail, therefore, we should follow the track of argument by which Berkeley arrives at his destination.

[3] Vol. II, pp. 204–6.

In the second of Berkeley's *Dialogues*, Hylas, having earlier been made to agree that primary and secondary qualities are alike only mental, nonetheless attempts to defend the concept of material substance. His arguments for the existence of matter are swiftly despatched. Matter is not perceived, because it has been agreed that only ideas are perceived. It must, therefore, be something discovered by the reason, not the sense. Shall we say then that it is the cause of ideas? But matter is inert and unthinking; so it cannot be a cause of thought. But perhaps, Hylas pleads, the motions of matter may be an instrument of the supreme cause, God. But matter, having no sensible qualities, cannot have motion or even extension; and surely God, who can act by mere willing, has no need of lifeless tools. Shall we say, as Malebranche did, that matter provides the occasion for God to act? Surely the all-wise one needs no prompting! 'Do you not at length perceive', taunts Philonous, 'that in all these different acceptations of Matter, you have been only supposing you know not what, for no manner of reason, and to no kind of use?' He sums up his argument triumphantly:

Either you perceive the being of Matter immediately or mediately. If immediately, pray inform me by which of the senses you perceive it. If mediately, let me know by what reasoning it is inferred from those things which you perceive immediately. So much for the perception. Then for the Matter itself, I ask whether it is object, *substratum,* cause, instrument or occasion? You have already pleaded for each of these, shifting your notions, and making Matter to appear sometimes in one shape, then in another. And what you have offered hath been disapproved and rejected by yourself. (*BPW*, 184)

If Hylas continues to defend the existence of matter, he does not know what he means by 'matter' or what he means by 'existence' (*BPW*, 187).

I think we must agree that Berkeley has successfully exploded the Lockean notion of substance, with which poor Hylas has been saddled. But suppose that Philonous were to debate not with Hylas but with Aristotle. What answers would he receive? Material substances, he would be told, are indeed perceived by the senses. Take a cat: I can see it, hear it, feel it, smell it, and if I feel so inclined, taste it. It is true that it is not by sense but by intellect that I know what *kind* of substance it is—I know that it is a cat because I have learnt how to classify animals—but that does not mean that I infer by reasoning that it is a cat. So much for material substance; what of matter itself? That too I perceive by the senses, in that the substances we encounter are chunks of matter, matter in this case with the form of cattishness. Prime matter, matter devoid of any form, is indeed not perceptible by any sense; but that is because there is no such thing in reality; prime matter is a philosophical abstraction for the purpose of the analysis of substantial change.[4]

It cannot, of course, be taken for granted that the Aristotelian account of substance and matter can be reconciled with, or adapted to, the progress made by seventeenth-century scientists in the analysis and explanation of motion and change. The point I wish to make here is simply that the traditional notion of substance is not disposed of by Berkeley's demolition of the quite different, internally incoherent, notion propagated by Locke.

The criticism of matter is not in fact essential to the construction of Berkeley's idealism; it merely removes an obstacle to its acceptance. Matter was fantasized in order to be the basis of our ideas. That role in Berkeley's system belongs not to matter but to God. The first premiss of the argument to that conclusion is that human beings know nothing except ideas; and that premiss is stated long before the onslaught on the notion of material substance. The first book of the *Principles* begins thus:

It is evident to any one who takes a survey of the *objects of human knowledge*, that they are either *ideas* actually imprinted on the senses; or else such as are perceived by attending to the passions and operations of the mind; or lastly *ideas* formed by help of memory and imagination. (BPW, 61)

This is surely *not* evident at all. Use the word 'idea', if you wish, in such a broad sense as to make it true that whenever I perceive, remember, or think of X I have an idea of X, and that whenever I learn, believe, or know that *p* I have a corresponding idea. It still does not follow that the objects of all human knowledge are ideas. From the very broad nature of the definition it follows that any cognitive act or state will involve my having ideas; but that does not mean that every cognitive act or state is *about* those ideas, or has those ideas as its *object*. If I see a giraffe, I will, given this terminology, have an idea of a giraffe; but what I see is a giraffe, not an idea. If I think of the larch at the end of my garden, I will, again, have an idea of that tree; but what I am thinking about is the tree, not the idea. To be sure, I can also think of that idea; for instance, I can think that it is a pretty hazy one. But that is quite a different thought, a thought about

---

[4] See vol. I, p. 192.

an idea, not a thought about a tree. In thinking it, I am not thinking that the tree is a pretty hazy one. Ideas, if you must speak of ideas in this way, are the things we think *with*; they are not, in general, the things that we think *about*.

The opening passage quoted from the *Principles* already assumes the idealism that is supposed to be the conclusion of a long argument. Idealism is implicit in the initial confusion between mental acts and their objects. It cannot be said that Berkeley was unaware that this criticism could be levelled. Hylas, near the end of the first Dialogue, makes a distinction between object and sensation. He says:

The sensation I take to be an act of the mind perceiving; besides which, there is something perceived; and this I call the *object*. For example, there is red and yellow on that tulip. But then the act of perceiving those colours is in me only, and not in the tulip. (*BPW*, 158)

Philonous' rejection of this takes a very oblique route. He picks on the word 'act' and proceeds to argue that a sensation—e.g. smelling the tulip—is something passive, not active.

Dubious though that claim is, there is no need for Hylas to controvert it in order to defend his distinction. All he has to do is to substitute the expression 'event in the mind' for 'act of the mind'. But Philonous sails on to his conclusion by substituting the ambiguous word 'perception' for the ambiguous word 'idea', and taking it casually for granted that the object of a perception is a *part* of the perception (*BPW*, 159).

If there is nothing that we can know except ideas, and if ideas can exist only in a mind, then it is not difficult for Berkeley to reach his conclusion that everything that we can know to exist is in the mind of God:

When I deny sensible things an existence out of the mind, I do not mean my mind in particular but all minds. Now it is plain they have an existence exterior to my mind; since I find them by experience to be independent of it. There is therefore some other Mind wherein they exist, during the intervals between the times of my perceiving them: as likewise they did before my birth, and would do after my supposed annihilation. And as the same is true with regard to all other finite created spirits, it necessarily follows that there is an *omnipresent eternal Mind*, which knows and comprehends all things.[5]

---

[5] Berkeley's proof of the existence of God is considered in detail in Ch. 10.

In the final dialogue, Berkeley gives Philonous the task of showing that the thesis that nothing exists except ideas in a finite or infinite mind is something that is perfectly compatible with our common-sense beliefs about the world. This involves a heroic reinterpretation of ordinary language. Statements about material substances have to be translated into statements about collections of ideas: a cherry, for instance, is nothing but a congeries of sensible impressions, or ideas perceived by various senses (*BPW*, 211). It is much easier to do this, Philonous argues, than to interpret them as statements about inert Lockean substrata. 'The real things are those very things I see and feel and perceive by my senses ... A piece of sensible bread, for instance, would stay my stomach better than ten thousand times as much of that insensible, unintelligible, real bread you speak of' (A, 192). Only his own phenomenalist system, Berkeley believes, enables one to say truly that snow is white and fire is hot.

A material substance, then, is a collection of sensible ideas of various senses treated as a unit by the mind because of their constant conjunction with each other. This thesis is, according to Berkeley, perfectly consistent with the use of scientific instruments and the framing of natural laws. Such laws state relationships not between things but between phenomena, that is, ideas, and what scientific instruments do is to bring new phenomena for us to relate to the old ones. If we make a distinction between appearance and reality, what we are really doing is contrasting more vivid ideas with less vivid ideas, and comparing the different degrees of voluntary control that accompany our ideas. There is no hidden reality: everything is appearance. That is the doctrine of 'phenomenalism', to use a word which was not invented until the nineteenth century.

Both Leibniz and Berkeley are phenomenalists in the sense that they agree that the material world is a matter of appearance rather than reality. But they give different accounts of the nature of the phenomena, and different explanations of their underlying causes. For the empiricist Berkeley, ideas are not infinitely divisible, since there is a finite limit to the mind's ability to discriminate by the senses. The rationalist Leibniz, on the other hand, rejects such atomism: the phenomenal world has the properties exhibited by geometry and arithmetic. With this difference in the nature of the phenomena goes a difference in their sustaining causes. For Leibniz, the underlying reality is the infinity of animate monads; for Berkeley, it is the single all-comprehending God.

Hume on Causation

If neither of these two philosophies is in the end credible, this is not due to any lack of ingenuity in their inventors. Rather, the defects in each system can be traced back to a single root: the confused epistemology of ideas, which was bequeathed to rationalists by Descartes and to empiricists by Locke. The philosopher in whose work we can see most fully the consequences of such an epistemology is David Hume. His official system, according to which everything whatever is a mere collection of ideas and impressions, is nothing less than absurd. Nonetheless, Hume's genius is such that despite the distortions and constraints which his system imposed upon him, he was able to make highly significant contributions to philosophy. Nowhere is this more evident than in his treatment of causality.

Prior to Hume, the following propositions about causes were very widely held by philosophers:

1. Every contingent being must have a cause.
2. Cause and effect must resemble each other.
3. Given a cause, its effect must necessarily follow.

The first two propositions were common ground between Aristotelian philosophers and their opponents. Paradigm examples of Aristotelian efficient causes were the generation of living beings and the operation of the four elements. Every animal has parents, and parents and offspring resemble each other: dog begets dog and cat begets cat, and in general like begets like. Fire burns and water dampens: that is, a hot thing makes other things hot and a wet thing makes other things wet; once again, like causes like. Early modern philosophers offered other more subtle examples of causal relations, but they continued to subscribe to propositions (1) and (2).

The third proposition was not quite such a simple matter. Spinoza stated 'Given a determinate cause, the effect follows of necessity' (E I,3), and Hobbes claimed that when all causal elements of a situation are present, 'it cannot be understood but that the effect is produced'. Aristotle, however, was not so determinist as Spinoza and Hobbes were, and he made a distinction between natural causes and rational causes. A natural cause, like fire, was 'determined to one thing'; a rational cause, such as a human being, had a two-way power, a power that could be exercised or not at will. Even in such a case, Aristotle was willing to link the notions of cause and necessity: the possessor of a rational power, if it has the desire to exercise it, does so of necessity.[6]

Hume sets out to demolish all three of the theses set out above. He does so by altering the standard examples of causation. For him, a typical cause is not an agent (like a dog or a stove) but an event (like the rolling of a billiard ball across a table). The change in paradigm is masked by his talking of causes and effects as 'objects'. Strictly speaking, the only events possible in a Humean world are occurrences of ideas and occurrences of impressions; but this rule, fortunately, is not uniformly observed in the discussion. A rule that does hold firm is this: cause and effect must be two events identifiable independently of each other.

In attacking the traditional account of causation, Hume first denies that whatever begins to exist must have a cause of existence:

As all distinct ideas are separable from each other, and as the ideas of cause and effect are evidently distinct, 'twill be easy for us to conceive any object to be non-existent this moment, and existent the next, without conjoining to it the distinct idea of a cause or productive principle. (*T*, 79)

Since the ideas can be separated, so can the objects; so there is no contradiction in there being an actual beginning of existence without a cause. To be sure, 'effect' and 'cause' are correlative terms, like 'husband' and 'wife'. Every effect must have a cause, just as every husband must have a wife. But that does not mean that every event must be caused, any more than that every man must be married.

If there is no absurdity in conceiving something coming into existence without any cause at all, there is *a fortiori* no absurdity in conceiving of it coming into existence without a cause of a particular kind. Anything, Hume says, may produce anything. There is no logical reason to believe that like must be caused by like. 'Where objects are not contrary, nothing hinders them from having that constant conjunction, on which the

---

[6] See G. E. M. Anscombe, 'Causality and Determination', in *Metaphysics and the Philosophy of Mind* (Oxford: Blackwell, 1981), pp. 133–47.

relation of cause and effect totally depends' (*T*, 173). Because many different effects are logically conceivable as arising from a particular cause, only
experience leads us to expect the actual one. But on what basis?

Hume offers three rules by which to judge of causes and effects:

1. The cause and effect must be contiguous in space and time.
2. The cause must be prior to the effect.
3. There must be a constant union betwixt the cause and the effect.
   (*T*, 173)

The third rule is the most important one: 'Contiguity and succession are
not sufficient to make us pronounce any two objects to be cause and effect,
unless we perceive that these two relations are preserved in several
instances.' But how does this take us further? If the causal relationship
was not to be detected in a single instance, how can it be detected in
repeated instances?

Hume's answer is that the observation of the constant conjunction
produces a new impression *in the mind*. Once we have observed a sufficient
number of instances of a B following an A, we feel a determination, when next
we encounter an A, to pass on to B. This is the origin of the idea of necessary
connection which was expressed in the third of the traditional axioms.
Necessity is 'nothing but an internal impression of the mind, or a determination to carry our thoughts from one object to another'. This account enables
Hume to claim that once again the thesis is verified that there is no idea
without an antecedent impression. The felt expectation of the effect when
the cause presents itself, an impression produced by customary conjunction,
is the impression from which the idea of necessary connection is derived.

Hume sums up his discussion by offering two definitions of causation.
The first is this: a cause is 'an object precedent and contiguous to another,
and where all the objects resembling the former are placed in a like relation
of priority and contiguity to those objects that resemble the latter'. In this
definition nothing is said about necessary connection, and no reference is
made to the activity of the mind. Accordingly, we are offered a second
definition that makes the philosophical analysis more explicit. A cause is
'an object precedent and contiguous to another, and so united with it in
the imagination that the idea of the one determines the mind to form the
idea of the other, and the impression of the one to form a more lively idea
of the other' (*T*, 170, 172).

There are problems with both these definitions. Take the second one first. The mind, we are told, is 'determined' to form one idea by the presence of another idea. Is there not a circularity here, since 'determination' is not very different from 'causation'? Remember that Hume's theory of necessary connection is supposed to apply to moral necessity as well as to natural necessity, to mental as well as to physical causation. If we go back to the first definition, we need to look more closely at the notion of *resemblance*. If we took Hume's definition literally we would have to deny such things as that my young son's white mouse was the cause of the disappearance of that piece of cheese in his cage; for all white things resemble my mouse, but not all white things cause cheese to disappear. It must be doubtful whether the notion of *resemblance* could be appropriately refined (e.g. by reference to natural kinds) without some tacit reference to causal concepts.

The Response of Kant

Hume's account of causation deserves, and has received, intense philosophical scrutiny. Kant attacked the idea that temporal succession could be used to define causality; rather, we make use of causal notions in order to determine temporal sequence. More recently it has been questioned whether a causeless beginning of existence is conceivable: here, too, it is arguable that we use causal notions in order to determine when things begin.[7] Nonetheless, Hume introduced a completely new approach to the philosophical discussion of causation, and the agenda for that discussion remains to this day the one that he set.

Kant's response to Hume occurs in the system of principles in the *Critique of Pure Reason*, in a section unhelpfully entitled 'Analogies of Experience'. This section sets out to establish the following thesis: experience is only possible if necessary connections are to be found among our perceptions. There are three stages in the proof, which are called by Kant the first, second, and third analogies. The first two are as follows: (a) If I am to have experience at all I must have experience of an objective realm,

---

[7] See G. E. M. Anscombe, 'Times, Beginnings and Causes', in *Metaphysics and the Philosophy of Mind*, pp. 148–62.

and this must contain enduring substances; (b) If I am to have an experience of an objective realm, I must have experience of causally ordered substances. Each of these stages takes off from reflection on our awareness of time: time considered first as duration, and then as succession. The third analogy, which appears as something of an appendix to the argument offered in the first two, arises from a consideration of coexistence in time. Distinct objects which exist at the same time as each other must coexist in space, and if they do so they must form a system of mutual interaction.

Kant begins by pointing out that time itself cannot be perceived. In a momentary sensation considered as an independent atom of experience, there is nothing to show when it occurs, or whether it occurs before or after any other given inner event. We can only be aware of time, then, if we can relate such phenomena to some permanent substratum. Moreover, if there is to be genuine change, as opposed to mere succession, there has to be something that is first one thing and then another. But this permanent element cannot be supplied by our experience, which is itself in constant flux; it must therefore be supplied by something objective, which we may call 'substance'. 'All existence in time and all change in time have to be viewed simply as a mode of the existence of something that remains and persists' (A, 184).

The conclusion of the first analogy is not altogether clear. Does Kant think that he has shown that there must be one single permanent thing behind the flux of experience—something such as an everlasting quantity of conserved matter? Or is his conclusion simply that there must be at least some permanent things, objective entities with non-momentary duration, such as we commonly take rocks and trees to be? Only the latter, weaker, conclusion is necessary in order to refute empiricist atomism.

The second analogy is based on a simple observation, whose significance Kant was the first philosopher to see. If I stand still and watch a ship moving down a river I have a succession of different views: first of the ship upstream, then of it downstream, and so on. But, equally, if I look at a house, there will be a certain succession in my experiences: first, perhaps, I look at the roof, then at the upper and lower floors, and finally at the basement. What is it that distinguishes between a merely subjective succession of phenomena (the various glimpses of the house) and an objective observation of a change (the motion of the ship downstream)? In the one case, but not the other, it would be possible for me at will to reverse the

In this eighteenth-century picture of Fort William, Calcutta we can easily decide what is stationary and what is moving. But what is it, Kant asks, that tells us this?

order of perceptions. But there is no basis for making the distinction except some necessary causal regularity:

Let us suppose that there is an event which has nothing preceding it from which it follows according to a rule. All succession in perception would then be only in the apprehension, that is would be merely subjective, and there would be no way to determine which perceptions really came first and which came later. We should then have only a play of impressions relating to no object and it would be impossible in our perceptions to make temporal distinctions between one phenomenon and another. (A, 194)

This shows that there is something deeply wrong with Hume's idea that we first perceive temporal succession between events, and then go on to regard one as cause and one as effect. Matters are the other way round: without relationships between cause and effect we cannot establish order in time. Even if we could, Kant goes on, bare temporal succession is insufficient to account for causality, because cause and effect may be simultaneous. Augustine had long ago said that a foot causes a footprint, not the other way round, and Kant echoes him by saying that a ball laid on a stuffed cushion makes a hollow as soon as it is laid on it, yet the ball is the cause and the hollow is the effect. We know this because every such ball makes a dent, but not every such hollow contains a ball.

The third analogy starts from the same point as the second, but moves in the opposite direction:

I can direct my perception first to the moon and then to the earth, or, conversely, first to the earth and then to the moon; and because the perceptions of these objects can follow each other in either order I say that they are coexistent. (B, 258)

But nothing in either perception tells me that the order between them can be reversed, that is, that they coexist with each other. 'Thus,' Kant concludes, perhaps too swiftly, 'the coexistence of substances in space cannot be known in experience save on the assumption of their reciprocal interaction' (B, 258).

Whatever criticisms may be made of details of Kant's analogies, there is no doubt that they establish that the relation between time and causation is much more complicated than Hume imagined, and that Berkeley's abolition of the notion of substance demolishes along with it the ordered sequence of phenomena, held out by virtue of his idealism as the reality of the world.

Whereas Kant, in *The Critique of Pure Reason*, tried to show the futility of claims to knowledge divorced from the conditioned world of experience, Hegel, especially in *The Phenomenology of Spirit*, tried to establish the authenticity of a metaphysics which would provide unconditioned knowledge of the absolute. In one sense, Hegel's idealism marks the high point of metaphysical speculation, and opponents of metaphysics have often chosen gobbets of his text as examples to illustrate the necessary obscurity and futility of any such enterprise. Yet it is surprisingly difficult to select and present passages from his writings which display insights relevant to the topics that have been the concerns of this chapter. This is not because Hegel lacked genius; it is because of the holism that is the dominant characteristic of his thought. At every level, Hegel maintained, parts can only be understood as parts of a whole. We can have no real knowledge even of the smallest item unless we understand its relationship to the entire universe. There is no truth short of the whole truth. Some of his writings can be quarried for nuggets of golden insight, but his metaphysical system must either be taken as a whole or passed by.

The period between Descartes and Hegel was the great age of metaphysical system-building. In the medieval period there were many gifted metaphysicians, but they did not think of themselves as creating a new system; rather, they offered piecemeal improvements to a system already given by the teaching of the Church and the genius of Aristotle. Descartes, Spinoza, Kant, and Hegel, on the other hand, saw themselves as setting out, for the first time, a complete system to harmonize all the fundamental truths that could be known. It cannot be said that any of them succeeded in this gigantic task; but there is much to be learnt from their heroic failures.

In the nineteenth and twentieth centuries, when Western philosophy split into conflicting traditions on the European continent and in the anglophone world, one tradition adopted the medieval pattern and the other followed the lead of the early modern metaphysicians. In Germany and France, philosophers continued to see it as their task to create a new system which would supersede that of their predecessors. In England and the United States, most philosophers contented themselves with the attempt to clarify or amend particular elements within a framework given us by the work of the natural scientists and the language of our everyday lives. But many philosophers have resisted being judged by either paradigm; and the best way to avoid being obsessed with either is a study of philosophy's history over the long term.

7

Mind and Soul

Descartes on Mind

The area of philosophy that underwent the most significant development in the early modern period was the philosophy of mind. This
was due above all to the work of Descartes. Whereas Cartesian physics had a
short and inglorious life, Cartesian psychology was widely adopted and to
this day its influence remains powerful in the thinking of many who have
never read his work or who explicitly reject his system.

Descartes redrew the boundaries between mind and body, and introduced a new way of characterizing the mental. Since his time it has been
natural for philosophers and scientists to structure psychology in a way
quite different from that employed by his Aristotelian predecessors in the
Middle Ages and the Renaissance.[1] This has affected even everyday thinking
about human nature and about the natural world.

The Aristotelians regarded mind as the faculty, or set of faculties, that
mark off human beings from other animals. Dumb animals share with us
certain abilities and activities: dogs, cows, and pigs can all, like us, see and
hear and feel; they have in common with us the faculty or faculties of
sensation. But only human beings can think abstract thoughts and take
rational decisions: they are set off from other animals by the possession of
intellect and will. It was these two faculties which, for the Aristotelians,
essentially constituted the mind. Intellectual activity was in a particular
sense immaterial, whereas sensation was impossible without a material
body.

---

[1] See vol. II, Ch. 8.

For Descartes and those who followed him, the boundary between mind and matter was set elsewhere. It was consciousness, not intelligence or rationality, that was the defining criterion of the mental: the mind is the realm of whatever is accessible to introspection. So the mind included not only human understanding and willing, but also human seeing, hearing, feeling, pain, and pleasure. Every form of human experience, according to Descartes, included an element that was spiritual rather than material, a phenomenal component that was no more than contingently connected with bodily causes, expressions, and mechanisms.

Descartes, like his Aristotelian predecessors, believed that the mind was what distinguished human beings from other animals; but he did so for quite different reasons. For the Aristotelians, the mind was restricted to the intellectual soul, and this was something that only humans possessed. For Descartes, mind extends also to sensation, but only humans had genuine sensation. The bodily machinery that accompanies sensation in human beings may occur also in animal bodies, but in an animal a phenomenon like pain is a purely mechanical event, unaccompanied by any consciousness.

Not many people have followed Descartes in regarding animals as mere machines, but there has been very widespread acceptance of his substitution of consciousness in place of rationality as the defining characteristic of the mental. This has the consequence of making the mind appear a specially private place. The intellectual capacities characteristic of language-users are not marked by any special privacy: another person may know better than I do whether I understand quantum physics or am motivated by ambition. On the other hand, if I want to know what experiences someone is having, I have to give his utterances a special status. If you tell me what you seem to see or hear, or what you are imagining or saying to yourself, what you say cannot be mistaken. Of course it need not be true—you may be lying, or misunderstand the words you are using—but your utterance cannot be erroneous. Experiences, thus, have a certain property of indubitability, and it was this property that Descartes took as the essential feature of thought, and used as the foundation of his epistemological system.[2]

To see the way in which Descartes effects this revolutionary change, we need to go back to the second *Meditation*. Having proved to his own satisfaction that he exists, Descartes goes on to ask: '*What* am I, this I

---

[2] See above, Ch. 4.

whom I know to exist?' The immediate answer is that I am a thing that thinks (*res cogitans*). 'What is a thing that thinks? It is a thing that doubts, understands, conceives, affirms, denies, wills, refuses, which also imagines and feels' (AT VII.28; *CSMK* II.19). As always in Descartes 'thought' is to be understood broadly: thinking is not always to think *that* something or other, and not only intellectual meditation but also volition, sensation, and emotion count as thoughts. No previous author had used the word with such a wide extension, but Descartes did not believe that he was altering the sense of the word. He applied it to unusual items because he believed that they possessed the feature which was the most important characteristic of the usual items, namely, immediate consciousness. 'I use this term to include everything that is within us in such a way that we are immediately conscious of it' (AT VII.160; *CSMK* II.113).

Let us examine in turn the activities that Descartes lists as characteristic of a *res cogitans*. Understanding and conception—the mastery of concepts and the formulation of articulate thoughts—are, for him as for the Aristotelians, operations of the intellect. Thoughts and perceptions that are both clear and distinct are for him operations of the intellect par excellence. The next items, affirming and denying, would have been regarded prior to Descartes as acts of the intellect; but for Descartes the making of judgements is the task not of the intellect but of the will. For instance, understanding the proposition '115+28=143' is a perception of the intellect, but making the judgement that the proposition is true, actually affirming that 115 plus 28 is 143, is an act of will. The intellect merely provides the ideas which are the content on which the will is to make a judgement (AT VII.50; *CSMK* II.34). The mind's consciousness of its own thoughts is not a case of judgement: simply to entertain an idea or set of ideas, without affirming or denying any relation between them and the real world, is not to make a judgement. 'Affirming and denying', then, go not with the preceding items in Descartes' list, 'understanding and conceiving', but rather with the following items, 'willing and refusing'. The will is the faculty for saying 'yes' or 'no' to propositions (about what is the case) and projects (about what to do).

The intellect, then, is the faculty of knowing (*facultas cognoscendi*) and the will is the faculty of choosing (*facultas eligendi*). In many cases the will can choose to refrain from making a judgement about the ideas that the intellect presents. Doubting, too (which comes first in Descartes' list because he is just emerging from his universal doubt), is an act of the will, not of the intellect. However, when the intellectual perception is clear and distinct, doubt is not possible. A clear and distinct perception is one that forces the will, a perception that cannot be doubted however hard one tries. Such is the perception of one's own existence produced by the *cogito*. It is possible, but wrong, for the will to make a judgement in the absence of clear and distinct perception. To avoid error one should suspend judgement until perception achieves the appropriate clarity and distinctness (AT VII.50; *CSMK* II.34).

Descartes believed in the freedom of the will; but to understand his teaching we have to recall the distinction between liberty of indifference (the ability to chose between alternatives) and liberty of spontaneity (the ability to follow one's desires). Descartes placed no great value on liberty of indifference: that was only possible when there was a balance of reasons for and against a particular choice. Clear and distinct perception, which left the will with no alternative to assent, took away liberty of indifference but not liberty of spontaneity: 'If we see very clearly that something is good for us it is very difficult—and on my view impossible, as long as one continues in the same thought—to stop the course of our desires.' The human mind is at its best when assenting, spontaneously but not indifferently, to the data of clear and distinct perception.

So much, then, for the faculties of intellect and will. But among the activities of a *res cogitans*, imagination and sensation are listed also. Here it is that Descartes makes his most striking innovation. For Aristotelians, sensation was impossible without a body, because it involved the operation of bodily organs. Descartes sometimes uses the verb 'sentire' in a similar way, when he has not yet weaned his readers off their Aristotelian prejudices. But within the Cartesian system sensation is strictly nothing other than a mode of thought. We have already met the passage where, striving to emerge from his doubt, he says, 'I am now seeing light, hearing a noise, feeling heat. These objects are unreal, for I am asleep; but at least I seem to see, to hear to be warmed. This cannot be unreal, and this is what is properly called my sensation.' Here he seeks to isolate an indubitable immediate experience, the seeming-to-see-a-light that cannot be mistaken, the item that is common to both veridical and hallucinatory experience. This does not involve any judgement: it is a thought that I can have, while refraining, as part of the discipline of Cartesian doubt, from making any judgements at all. But of course the thought *may* be accompanied by judgement, and a person not yet purified of Aristotelianism will indeed accompany it with the erroneous judgement that there are real things in the world which totally resemble my perceptions (AT VII.437; *CSMK* II.295).

Human sensation is accompanied and occasioned by motions in the body: vision, for instance, by motions in the extremities of the optic nerves. But such mechanical events are only contingently connected with the purely mental thought, and Descartes can be certain of the occurrence of his sensations at a stage when he still doubts whether he has a body and whether there is an external world. It is only after meditation on the veracity of God, and the nature of the faculties God has given him, that he is in a position to pronounce upon the mechanical element involved in the sensations occurring in an embodied mind.

The same mechanical motions may occur in the body of a non-human animal. If we like, we can call these sensations in a broad sense. But an animal cannot have thoughts, and it is thought in which sensation, strictly so called, consists. It follows that, for Descartes, an animal cannot suffer pain, though the machine of its body may cause it to react in a way which, in a human, would be the expression of a pain:

I see no argument for animals having thoughts except that fact that since they have eyes, ears, tongues and other sense-organs like ours it seems likely that they have sensations like us; and since thought is included in our mode of sensation, similar thought seems to be attributable to them. This argument, which is very obvious, has taken possession of the minds of all men from their earliest age. But there are other arguments, stronger and more numerous, but not so obvious to everyone, which strongly urge the opposite.

The doctrine that animals have no feelings and no consciousness did not seem as shocking to Descartes' contemporaries as it does to most people nowadays. But people reacted with horror when some of his followers claimed that human beings, no less than animals, were only complicated machines.

Dualism and its Discontents

In human beings, Descartes argues for a sharp distinction between mind and body. In the sixth *Meditation* he says that he knows that if he can clearly and distinctly understand one thing without another, that shows that the two things are distinct, because God at least can separate them. Since he knows that he exists, but observes nothing else as belonging to his nature other than that he is a thinking thing, he concludes that his nature or essence consists simply in being a thinking thing; he is really distinct from his body and can exist without it. In considering this argument, it is hard to avoid the conclusion that Descartes is confusing 'I can clearly and distinctly perceive A without clearly and distinctly perceiving B' with 'I can clearly and distinctly perceive A without B.'

As a matter of contingent fact, human beings in this world are, Descartes agrees, compounds of mind and body. But the nature of this composition, this 'intimate union' between mind and body, is one of the most puzzling features of the Cartesian system. The matter is made even more obscure, when we are told (AT XI.353; *CSMK* I. 340) that the mind is not directly affected by any part of the body other than the pineal gland in the brain. All sensations and emotions consist of motions in the body which travel through the nerves to this gland and there give a signal to the mind which occasions a certain experience.

Descartes explains the mechanism of vision as follows:

If we see some animal approach us, the light reflected from its body depicts two images of it, one in each of our eyes, and these two images form two others, by means of the optic nerves, in the interior surface of the brain which faces its cavities; then from there, by means of the vital fluids with which its cavities are filled, these images so radiate towards the little gland that is surrounded by these fluids, that the movement that forms each point of one of the images tends towards the same point of the gland towards which tends the movement that forms the point of the other images which represents the same part of this animal. By this means the two images which are in the brain form but one upon the gland, which, acting immediately on the soul, causes it to see the form of this animal. (AT IX.355; *CSMK* I. 341)

To speak of the soul as seeing, or reading off, images in the brain is to imagine the soul as a little human being or homunculus. This is a fallacy that Descartes himself warned against in his *Dioptrics* when he was describing the formation of retinal images. These images, he informed the reader, were part of the process of conveying information from the world to the brain, and they retained a degree of resemblance to the objects from which they originated. 'We must not think', he warned, 'that it is by means of this

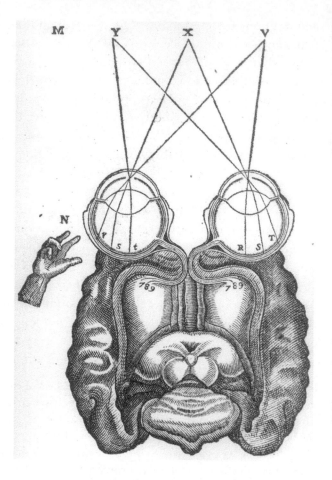

Descartes' diagram, in the *Discourse on Method*, of the mechanics of vision

resemblance that the image makes us aware of the objects—as though we had another pair of eyes to see it, inside our brain.'

But the homunculus fallacy is no less involved in treating the transaction between the soul and the pineal gland as if it was a case of seeing or reading. The interaction between mind and matter is philosophically as puzzling a few centimetres behind the eye as it is in the eye itself. The mind–body problem is not solved, but merely miniaturized, by the introduction of the pineal gland.

Interaction between mind and matter, as conceived by Descartes, is highly mysterious. The only form of material causation in Descartes' physical system is the communication of motion, and the mind is not the kind of thing to move around in space. 'How can soul move body?' Princess Elizabeth asked. Surely, motion involves contact, and contact involves extension, and the soul is unextended. Descartes, in reply, told her to think of weight, of the heaviness of a body which pushed it downward without there being any surface contact involved. But this conception of weight, as Elizabeth was quick to point out, was one that Descartes himself regarded as a scholastic muddle. After a few more exchanges, Descartes was reduced to telling the princess not to bother her pretty head further about the problem.

Elizabeth had, in fact, located the fundamental weakness in Descartes' philosophy of mind. Descartes' system was dualist, that is to say, it was tantamount to belief in two separate worlds—the physical world containing matter, and a psychical world containing private mental events. The two worlds are defined and described in such systematically different ways that mental and physical realities can interact, if at all, only in a mysterious manner that transcends the normal rules of causality and evidence. Such dualism is a fundamentally mistaken philosophy. The incoherence spotted by Princess Elizabeth was to be pointed out with exhaustive patience in later centuries by Kant and Wittgenstein. But Cartesian dualism is still alive and well in the twenty-first century.

Determinism, Freedom, and Compatibilism

In Descartes' own time the most vociferous critic of dualism was the materialist Thomas Hobbes, who denied the existence of any non-extended, spiritual entities like the Cartesian mind. Whereas Descartes exaggerated the difference between humans and animals, Hobbes minimized it. He described human action as a particular form of animal behaviour. There are two kinds of motion in animals, he says, one called vital and one called voluntary. Vital motions include breathing, digestion, and the course of the blood. Voluntary motion is 'to go, to speak, to move any of our limbs, in such manner as is first fancied in our minds'. The operations that Descartes (and the Aristotelians before him) attributed to reason are by Hobbes assigned to the imagination, a faculty common to all animals that is purely material, all thoughts of any kind being small motions in the head. If a particular imagining is caused by words or other signs, it is called 'understanding'. But this too is common to all animals, 'for a dog by custom will understand the call or the rating of his Master, and so will many other Beasts' (L, 3, 10).

The difference between animals and humans here is simply that when a man imagines a thing, he goes on to wonder what he can do with it. But this is a matter of will, not intellect. Not that the will is a faculty peculiar to humans: a will is simply a desire, the desire that comes last at the end of a train of deliberation, and 'beasts that have deliberation must necessarily also have will'. Human and animal desires are alike consequences of mechanical forces. The difference is simply that humans have a wider repertoire of wants, in the service of which they employ their imaginations. The freedom of the will is no greater in humans than in animals.

This thesis caused great offence, and led to a celebrated debate with John Bramhall, a royalist Bishop of Derry who had shared Hobbes' exile.[3] Hobbes insisted, 'Such a liberty as is free from necessity is not to be found in the will either of men or of beasts.' He claimed, however, that liberty and necessity were not necessarily incompatible:

Liberty and Necessity are Consistent: as in the water, that hath not only liberty, but a necessity of descending by the Channel; so likewise in the Actions which men voluntarily do; which, because they proceed from their will, proceed from liberty; and yet, because every act of man's will, and every desire and inclination proceedeth from some cause, and that from another cause, in a continuall chaine, whose first link is in the hand of God, first of all causes, they proceeed from necessity. (L, 140)

'This is a brutish liberty,' Bramhall objected, 'such a liberty as a bird hath to fly when her wings are clipped. Is not this a ridiculous liberty?' Hobbes replied that a man was free to follow his will, but was not free to will. The will to write, for instance, or the will to forbear from writing, did not come upon a person as a result of some previous will. 'He that cannot understand the difference between *free to do it if he will* and *free to will* is not fit', Hobbes snorted, 'to hear this controversy disputed, much less to be a writer in it.'

Hobbes' account of liberty gives him a claim to be the founder of the doctrine called 'compatibilism', the thesis that freedom and determinism are compatible with each other. He presents it in a crude form which, as Bramhall pointed out, fails to do justice to the obvious differences between the modes of action of inanimate agents and of rational agents like human beings. His version depends on a linear model of causation as a series of

---

[3] Published in 1663 as *The Questions Concerning Liberty, Necessity and Chance*, from which the following quotations are taken.

events following in sequence, each linked to the next by a causal relation. Thus my action is preceded and caused by my willing, which is preceded and caused by my deliberation, which is preceded and caused by a series of motions outside my control which terminates ultimately in the primal causation by God. My action is free, because the event which immediately precedes it is an act of will; it is necessitated, because it comes at the end of a series each of whose items is a necessary consequence of its predecesssor.

There are problems with the notion of a series which alternates in this manner between mental and physical events. It is true that for Hobbes mental events (a thought or a will) do not take place, as they did for Descartes, in a spiritual realm outside material space; for him all the motions of the mind are actually motions in the body. But there are further problems, which later philosophers would explore, in simply identifying mental and physical events in this manner. Moreover, in many cases of voluntary behaviour, there is in advance of the action no identifiable mental event to fulfil the causal role that Hobbes' version of compatibilism requires of the will. The pros and cons of compatibilism are better evaluated in the versions developed by later, more sophisticated, thinkers such as Immanuel Kant.[4]

Locke's treatment of the will is already an improvement on Hobbes. We find in ourselves, he says, a power to begin or forbear actions of our minds and bodies 'barely by a thought or preference of the mind ordering, or as it were commanding the doing or not doing such or such a particular action'. This power is what we call the will, and the exercise of such a power—the issuing of such an order—is volition, or willing. An action in obedience to such an order is what is called voluntary. Whenever a man has a power to think, or not to think, to move or not to move, in accordance with the direction of his mind, he is so far free (E, 236–7).

Liberty or freedom requires two things: a volition to act, and a power to act or forbear. A tennis ball is not free, because it has neither of these. A man who falls from a broken bridge has a volition to stop falling, but no power to do so; his fall is not a free action. Even if I have a volition to do something, and am actually doing it, that may not be enough to make my action a free one:

Suppose a man be carried, whilst fast asleep, into a Room, where is a person he longs to see and speak with; and be there locked fast in, beyond his Power to get

⁴ See below, p. 243, and my *Will, Freedom and Power* (Oxford: Blackwell, 1975), pp. 145–61.

out: he awakes, and is glad to find himself in so desirable a Company, which he stays willingly in, i.e. prefers his stay to going away. I ask, Is not this stay voluntary? I think, no Body will doubt it: and yet being locked fast in, 'tis evident he is not at liberty not to stay, he has not freedom to be gone. (*E*, 238)

This shows that an action may be voluntary without being free. Freedom is the opposite of necessity, but voluntariness is compatible with necessity. A man may prefer the state he is in to its absence or change, even though necessity has made it inalterable. But although voluntariness is not a sufficient condition for freedom, it is an essential prerequisite. Agents that have no thought or volition at all are all necessary agents.

What are we to make of the question whether the human will is free or not? Locke tells us that the question is as improper as asking whether sleep is swift or virtue is square. The will is a power, not an agent, and liberty belongs only to agents. When we talk of the will as a faculty, we should beware of personifying it. We can, if we wish, talk of a singing faculty and a dancing faculty; but it would be absurd to say that the singing faculty sings or that the dancing faculty; dances. It is no less foolish to say that the will chooses, or is free.

Here, Locke seems to be avoiding the question that preoccupied Hobbes. On Locke's own account a volition is an act of the mind directing or restraining a particular action. Can we say that the agent is free to perform or forbear such a particular act of the mind? Locke states as a general proposition, that if a particular thought is such that we have power to take it up, or lay it by, at our preference, then we are at liberty. But volition, he says, is not such a thought. 'A man in respect of willing, or the Act of Volition, when any action in his power is once proposed to his Thoughts, as presently to be done cannot be free' (*E*, 245).

It is not just that we cannot, during waking life, help willing something or other; we cannot, Locke says, help the particular volitions that we have. 'To ask whether a Man be at liberty to will either Motion or Rest; Speaking or Silence; which he pleases, is to ask, whether a man can will what he wills'—and this is a question that needs no answer. Here, Locke seems to be guilty of a fallacy which trapped other great philosophers: the invalid argument from the true premiss 'Necessarily, if I prefer X, I prefer X', to the dubious conclusion 'If I prefer X, I necessarily prefer X'.

But Locke has a positive reason for denying liberty to the choices of the will. Every choice to perform an action, he maintains, is determined by a preceding mental state: one of uneasiness at the present state of things.

Uneasiness alone acts on the will and determines its choices. We are constantly beset with sundry uneasinesses, and the most pressing one of those that are removable 'determines the will successively in that train of voluntary actions which make up our lives'. The most we can do is to suspend the execution of a particular desire while we decide whether to act on it would make us happy in the long run. This, Locke says, is the source of all liberty, and this is what is called (improperly) free will. But once the pros and cons have been weighed up, the resulting desire will determine the will (*E*, 250–63).

Locke is aware that the objection can be made to his system that a man is not free at all, if he be not as free to will, as he is to act what he wills. He does not offer a direct answer to this objection; instead he considers at length what are the factors which lead people to make wrong choices. His principal explanation is the same as that given by Plato in the *Protagoras*: that, by the intellectual equivalent of an optical illusion, we misjudge the proportion between present pains and pleasures and future pains and pleasures. He illustrates this with the example of a hangover:

Were the Pleasure of Drinking accompanied, the very moment a Man takes off his Glass, with that sick Stomack, and aking Head, which in some Men are sure to follow not many hours after, I think no body, whatever Pleasure he had in his Cups, would, on these Conditions, ever let Wine touch his Lips; which yet he daily swallows, and the evil side comes to be chosen only by the fallacy of a little difference in time. (*E*, 276)

Locke on Personal Identity

Locke's most influential contribution to the philosophical study of human beings concerned not the freedom of the will, but the nature of personal identity. In discussing identity and diversity, Locke accepts that identity is relative rather than absolute: A may be the same F as B, but not the same G as B. The criterion for the identity of a mass of matter (no particles added and no particles taken away) is not the same as the criterion for the identity of a living being:

In the state of living Creatures, their Identity depends not on a Mass of the same Particles; but on something else. For in them the variation of great parcels of Matter alters not the Identity: An Oak, growing from a Plant to a great Tree, and then lopp'd, is still the same Oak; and a Colt grown up to a Horse, sometimes fat, sometimes lean, is all the while the same Horse: though, in both these Cases, there may be a manifest change of the parts: So that truly they are not either of them the same Masses of Matter, though they be truly one of them the same Oak, and the other the same Horse. (*E*, 330)

The identity of plants and animals consists in continuous life in accordance with the characteristic metabolism of the organism. Human beings are animal organisms, and Locke offers a similar account of 'the Identity of the same *Man*'. (By 'man' of course he means a human being of either sex.) The identity of a human being consists in 'nothing but a participation of the same continued Life by constantly fleeting Particles of Matter, in succession vitally united to the same organized Body'. Only such a definition, he says, will enable us to accept that an embryo and 'one of years, mad and sober' can be one and the same man, without having to accept wildly improbable cases of identity.

So far, Locke's definition of human identity seems sound and straightforward; but it is complicated by his having to position himself with respect to ancient theories of the reincarnation and transmigration of souls, together with Christian doctrines of the survival of disembodied souls and the eventual resurrection of long-dead bodies. We cannot, Locke says, base our account of the identity of a human being on the identity of a human soul. For if souls can pass from one body to another, we cannot be sure that Socrates, Pontius Pilate, and Cesare Borgia are not the same man. Some have supposed that the souls of wicked men—such as the Roman Emperor Heliogabalus—were sent as a punishment after death into the bodies of brutes. 'But yet I think no body, could he be sure that the Soul of Heliogabalus were in one of his Hogs, would yet say that Hog were a man or Heliogabalus' (*E*, 332). A man is an animal of a certain kind, indeed of a certain shape. However rational and intelligent a parrot might turn out to be, it would still not be a man.

However, settling the question of human identity does not yet settle the nature of personal identity. Locke distinguishes the concept *man* from the concept *person*. A person is 'a thinking intelligent Being, that has reason and reflection, and can consider it self as itself, the same thinking thing in different times and places'. Self-consciousness is the mark of a person, and the identity of a person is the identity of self-consciousness. 'As far as this consciousness can be extended backwards to any past Action or Thought, so far reaches the Identity of that Person; it is the same *self* now as it was

Kneller's portrait of John Locke, in Christ Church hall

then; and 'tis by the same *self* with this present one that now reflects on it, that that Action was done' (*E*, 335).

So if we want to know whether A (at this moment) is the same person as B (some time ago) we ask whether A's consciousness extends back to the actions of B. If so, A is the same person as B; if not, not. But what is it for a consciousness to extend backward in time? It seems unobjectionable to say that my consciousness extends backwards for so long as this consciousness had a continuous history. But what makes *this* consciousness the individual consciousness it is? Locke cannot reply that *this* consciousness is the consciousness of *this* human being, because of the distinction he has made between *man* and *person*.

So it seems that Locke must say that my present consciousness extends backwards so far, and only so far, as I remember. He accepts that this means that if I remember the experiences of a human being that lived before my birth, then I am the same person as that man:

Whatever has the consciousness of present and past Actions, is the same Person to whom they both belong. Had I the same consciousness that I saw the Ark and Noah's Flood, as that I saw an overflowing of the Thames last Winter, or as that I write now, I could no more doubt that I, that write this now, that saw the Thames overflow'd last Winter, and that view'd the Flood at the general Deluge, was the same self...than that I that write this am the same *my self* now whilst I write...that I was Yesterday' (*E*, 341)

The converse of this is that my past is no longer my past if I forget it, and I can disown actions I no longer recall. I am not the same person, but only the same man, who did the actions I have forgotten.

Locke believes that punishment and reward attached not to the man, but to the person: it seems to follow that I should not be punished for actions I have forgotten. Locke seems willing to accept this, though the example he chooses to illustrate his acceptance is a very particular case, tendentiously selected. If a man has fits of madness, he says, human laws do not punish 'the mad man for the sober man's actions; nor the sober man for what the mad man did, thereby making them two persons'. But Locke seems unwilling to contemplate the further consequences of his thesis that if I erroneously think I remember being King Herod ordering the massacre of the innocents then I can be justly punished for their murder. A consequence that can be drawn from Locke's definition of a person is that very young infants, who have not yet acquired self-consciousness, are not yet persons and therefore do not enjoy the human rights and legal protections that persons enjoy. Philosophers in later ages have drawn this consequence—some treating it as a *reductio ad absurdum* of Locke's distinction between persons and humans, others treating it as a legitimation of infanticide.

It is not only ethical considerations, however, that may make one hesitate to accept Locke's identification of personality with self-consciousness. The main difficulty—ably presented in the eighteenth century by Bishop Joseph Butler—arises in connection with the role that Locke assigns to memory. If a person, call her Titia, claims to remember doing something, or being somewhere, we can check whether her memory is accurate by investigating whether she actually did the deed or was present on the appropriate occasion. We do this by tracing the history of her body. But if Locke is right, this will tell us nothing about the person Titia, but only about the human being Titia. Nor can Titia herself, from within, distinguish between genuine memories and present images of past events which offer themselves delusively as memories. Locke's account of self-consciousness makes it difficult to draw the distinction between veracious and deceptive memories at all. The distinction can only be made if we are willing to join together what Locke has put asunder and recognize that persons are human beings.

Whatever the merits of Locke's distinction between persons and humans, it does not exhaust the complication of his account of personal identity, because he includes a third category, that of spirits. According to Locke, I am at the same time a man (a human animal), a spirit (a soul or immaterial substance), and a person (a centre of self-consciousness). These three entities are all distinguishable, and Locke rings the changes on various combinations of them. The soul of Heliogabalus translated into one of his hogs gives us a case of one spirit in two bodies. One spirit might be united to two persons: Locke had a friend who thought he had inherited the soul of Socrates, though he had no memory of any of Socrates' experiences. On the other hand, if the present mayor of Queensborough had conscious recall of the life of Socrates, we would have two spirits in one person. Locke proposes more complicated combinations which we need not explore. There are many difficulties, by no means peculiar to Locke's system, in the whole notion of a soul considered as an immaterial, spiritual substance, and few of Locke's modern admirers wish to preserve this part of his theory of personal identity.

The Soul as the Idea of the Body in Spinoza

The relation between soul and body, which was problematic in Descartes and Locke, becomes more obscure than ever when we turn to Spinoza. The way in which Spinoza states it, however, sounds beautifully simple: the soul is the idea of the body. What this means is not obvious; but it is at least clear that Spinoza thinks that in order to understand the soul we have first to understand the body (*Eth*, 40). Human beings are bodies, related to and limited by other bodies; all these bodies are modes of the divine attribute of extension. Every body, and every part of every body, is represented by an idea in the mind of God; that is to say, to every item in the divine attribute of extension there corresponds an item in the divine attribute of thought. The item of divine thought that corresponds to the item of divine extension which is Peter's body is what constitutes Peter's mind. It follows, Spinoza says, that the human mind is part of the infinite intellect of God (*Eth*, 39).

What exactly is the 'correspondence' which constitutes the relationship between an individual soul and an individual body? It is, for Spinoza, nothing less than identity. Peter's soul and Peter's body are one and the same thing, looked at from two different points of view. Thinking substance and extended substance, he has told us, are one and the same substance—namely God—looked at now under one attribute, now under another (*Eth*, 35). The same goes for modes of these attributes. Peter's soul is a mode of the attribute of thinking, and Peter's body is a mode of the attribute of extension: they are both one and the same thing, expressed in two ways. This doctrine is meant to exclude the problem that bedevilled Descartes, namely, how to explain the manner in which soul and body interact. They do not interact at all, Spinoza answers: they are the very same thing.[5]

The human body is composed of a great number of parts, each of them complex and capable of modification by other bodies in various ways. The idea that constitutes the mind is likewise complex, compounded of a great number of ideas (*Eth*, 44). The mind, Spinoza says, perceives absolutely everything that takes place in the body (*Eth*, 39). This rather surprising statement is qualified by a later proposition (*Eth*, 47) which states that the human mind has no knowledge of the body, and does not know it to exist, except through the ideas of the modifications whereby the body is affected. We are left wondering why there may not

---

[5] It is not clear how this metaphysical thesis is to be reconciled with the epistemological thesis that the idea of X is something quite distinct from X; perhaps we have a case of the ambiguity of 'idea of X' identified above on p. 201.

be—as common sense suggests—processes in the body of which the mind is unaware. Why does there have to be an idea corresponding to every bodily event?

Spinoza does indeed agree that there is a lot that we do not know about bodies. The mind, he says, is capable of perceiving many things other than its own body, in proportion to the many ways in which the body is capable of receiving impressions. The ideas which go through my mind when I perceive involve the natures both of my own body and of other bodies. It follows, Spinoza says, that the ideas that we have of external bodies indicate rather the constitution of our own body than the nature of external bodies (*Eth*, 45). Further, the mind only knows itself in so far as it perceives the ideas of the modifications of the body. These ideas are not clear and distinct, and the sum of our ideas does not give us an adequate knowledge of other bodies, or of our own bodies, or of our own souls (*Eth*, 51). 'The human mind, when it perceives things after the common order of nature, has not an adequate but only a confused and fragmentary knowledge of itself, of its own body, and of external bodies' (*Eth*, 51).

Spinoza's account of the soul as the idea of the body gives rise to a question that has perplexed many a reader. What, we may wonder, is supposed to individuate the soul of Peter, and makes it the soul of Peter and not of Paul? Ideas are naturally thought to be individuated by belonging to, or inhering in, particular thinkers: my idea of the sun is distinct from your idea of the sun, simply because it is mine and not yours. But Spinoza cannot say this, since all ideas belong only to God. It must, then, be the content, not the possessor, of the idea that individuates it. But there are ideas of Peter's body in many minds other than Peter's mind: how then can the idea of Peter's body be Peter's soul?

Spinoza responds:

We clearly understand what is the difference between the idea, say, of Peter, which constitutes the essence of Peter's mind, and the idea of the same Peter, which is in another man, say Paul. The former directly expresses the essence of Peter's own body, and involves existence only as long as Peter exists; but the latter indicates the constitution of Paul's body rather than the nature of Peter, and therefore, as long as that disposition lasts, contemplates Peter as present even though Peter may not exist. (*Eth*, 46)

The crucial passage here is the statement that the idea of Peter that is Peter's soul 'involves existence only as long as Peter exists'. Does this mean that Peter's soul goes out of existence when Peter does? This would seem to follow from Spinoza's statements that a human being consists of body and soul, and that body and soul are the same thing under two different aspects. Peter, Peter's soul, and Peter's body should, on this account, come into and go out of existence together. But if we ask whether the soul is immortal, Spinoza does not give a totally unequivocal answer. On the one hand, he says 'our mind can only be said to last as long as our body lasts'—but this remark occurs in a footnote to a proposition that reads 'the human mind cannot be totally destroyed with the body, but something of it remains that is eternal' (*Eth*, 172). But this turns out really only to mean that since our soul is an idea, and all ideas are ultimately in the mind of God, and God is eternal, there never was or will be a time when our soul was totally non-existent. Our life is but an episode in the eternal life of God, and when we die that life persists. This is something very different from the personal survival in an afterlife which was the aspiration of popular piety.

In proclaiming that body and mind are a single thing, Spinoza can perhaps be said to have founded a school that persists to this day: the school that maintains that the relationship between mind and body is one of identity. But his teaching is so entwined with his more general thesis of the identity between God and nature that it is difficult to make exact comparisons between his thesis and that of later identity theorists. It is much easier to place Spinoza in connection with another fundamental thesis of his philosophy of mind, namely, psychological determinism.

Like Hobbes, Spinoza believes that every one of our thoughts and actions is predetermined by a necessity as rigid as the necessity of logical conse-quence. Spinoza indeed believed that the necessity of our lives *was* the necessity of logical consequence, in virtue of his general theory that the order of things and the order of ideas are one and the same. 'All things follow from the eternal decree of God by the same necessity, as it follows from the essence of a triangle, that the three angles are equal to two right angles' (*Eth*, 14). But the upshot is the same for both philosophers: freedom of the will is an illusion begotten of ignorance:

Men are mistaken in thinking themselves free; their opinion is made up of consciousness of their own actions, and ignorance of the causes by which they are determined. Their idea of freedom is simply their lack of knowledge of any cause for their actions. (*Eth*, 53)

Hobbes and many who would later follow him argued that though we are free to do what we will, we are not free to will what we will. Here again, Spinoza goes further: there is no such thing as the will:

When people say that human actions depend on the will, these are mere words to which no idea corresponds. What the will is, and how it moves the body, they none of them know; and when they go on to imagine seats and domiciles for the soul, they provoke ridicule or nausea. (*Eth*, 53)

Here Spinoza's target is Descartes, who located the soul in the pineal gland, and who placed great importance on the distinction between the intellect and the will. For Spinoza, there is no faculty of the will; there are indeed individual volitions, but these are merely ideas, caused by previous ideas, which have in their turn been determined by other ideas, and so on ad infinitum. Activities which Descartes attributed to the will—such as making or suspending judgements—are part and parcel of the series of ideas, they are perceptions or the lack thereof. A particular volition and a particular idea are one and the same thing, therefore will and understanding are one and the same (*Eth*, 63).

Leibniz's Monadology

Spinoza's amalgamation of intellect and will, and his identification of soul and body as aspects of a single substance, were among the elements of his philosophy that were unpicked by Leibniz. But Leibniz did not return to Descartes' system in which mind and matter were the two contrasting elements of a dualistic universe. Instead, he gave mind a status of unprecedented privilege. In the Cartesian partnership of mind and matter, of course, mind had always held the senior position; but for Leibniz, matter is no more than a sleeping partner.

In the *Discourse* Leibniz takes issue with Descartes' fundamental claim that matter is extension:

The nature of body does not consist merely in extension, that is, in size, shape, and motion, but we must necessarily recognize in body something akin to souls, something we commonly call substantial form, even though it makes no change in the phenomena, any more than do the souls of animals, if they have any. (*D*, 12)

The notions of extension and motion, Leibniz went on to argue, were not as distinct as Descartes thought: the notions of these primary qualities contained a subjective element no less than secondary qualities such as colour and heat. This was a theme later to be developed by Berkeley.[6]

Leibniz had two main arguments against the identification of matter with extension. First, if there were nothing in matter but size and shape, he argued, bodies would offer no resistance to each other. A rolling pebble colliding with a stationary boulder would put the boulder into motion without losing anything of its own force. Second, if matter was mere extension, we could never identify individual bodies at all, for extension is infinitely divisible. At whatever point we stop in our division we meet only an aggregate—and an aggregate (e.g. the pair formed by the diamond of the Great Mogul and the diamond of the Grand Duke) is only an imaginary object, not a real being. Only something resembling a soul can confer individual unity on a body and give it a power of activity (D, 21; G II. 97).

For these reasons Leibniz felt compelled to re-admit into philosophy the substantial forms which were so despised by fashionable philosophers, and he adopted a name for them which advertised their Aristotelian origin, namely 'entelechy'. But he differed from contemporary Aristotelians in two ways. First, he thought that while substantial forms were necessary to explain the behaviour of bodies, they were not sufficient; for the explanation of particular phenomena one must have recourse to the mathematical and mechanical theories of current corpuscular science. If asked how a clock tells the time, he said, it would be futile to say they had a horodictic faculty rather than explaining how the weights and wheels worked (D, 10; G V. 61). Second, he thought that in a human being there was not just one substantial form but an infinite number: each organ of the body had its own entelechy, and each organ was, he told Arnauld, 'full of an infinite number of other corporeal substances endowed with their own entelechies' (G II.120).

The great gap which Leibniz saw in Descartes' system was the lack of the notion of *force*. 'The idea of energy or virtue,' he wrote in 1691, 'called by the Germans *Kraft* and by the French *la force*, to explain which I have projected a special science of dynamics, throws a lot of light on the true

---

[6] See above, p. 147.

232

understanding of substance' (G IV.469). It was for this reason that the notion of substantial form had to be rehabilitated. Once the role of force was appreciated, it was matter, not form, that turned out to be illusory. Cartesian extension was a pure phenomenon, he told Arnauld, like a rainbow.[7]

Leibniz was, however, still trapped in Descartes' false dichotomy of mind and matter. Because force could find no place in a world of mere extension, he located it in the realm of the mental. He thought of it as a form of appetition analogous to human desire and volition. This comes out most clearly in the mature form of his philosophy presented in his *Monadology*. The monads or entelechies which are the basis of his system have the properties only of mind. The inert bodies that we see and feel around us are only phenomena, aggregates of invisible, intangible monads. They are not illusory entities—they are, in Leibniz's phrase, well-founded phenomena. But the only true substances are the monads.

Monads are independent, indivisible, and unrepeatable. Having no parts, they cannot grow or decay; they can only be created or annihilated. They can change, but only in the way that souls can change. As they have no physical properties to alter, their changes must be changes of mental states. The life of a monad, Leibniz tells us, is a series of perceptions. A perception is an internal state that is a representation of other items in the universe. This inner state will change as the environment changes, not because of the environmental change, but because of the internal drive or 'appetition' that has been programmed into them by God.

Monads are incorporeal automata; they are everywhere and there are countless millions of them:

There is a world of created beings—living things, animals, entelechies and souls— in the least part of matter. Each portion of matter may be conceived as a garden full of plants and as a pond full of fish. But every branch of each plant, every member of each animal, and every drop of their liquid parts is itself likewise a similar garden or pond. (G VI.66)

The idea that the human body is an assemblage of cells, each living an individual life, was still a new one, though not of course peculiar to Leibniz.

---

[7] Here I am indebted to Daniel Garber, 'Leibniz on Body, Matter, and Extension', *PASS* (2004): 23–40.

The monads that correspond to a human body in the Leibnizian system are like cells in having an individual life-history, but unlike cells in being immaterial and immortal.

We have come a long way from our Cartesian starting point. For Descartes, human minds were the only souls in the created universe; all else was lifeless machinery. For Leibniz, the smallest part of the smallest bug is ensouled—and it has not only one, but myriad souls. We have indeed gone further than Aristotle, for whom only living things had souls. Now there are souls galore behind every stock and stone. What, in this pullulating maelstrom of monads, makes the human mind unique?

For Leibniz, the difference between living and non-living bodies is this. Organic bodies are not mere aggregates of monads: they have a single dominant monad which gives them an individual substantial unity. The dominant monad in a human being is the human soul. All monads have perception and appetite, but the dominant monad in a human being has a more vivid mental life and a more imperious appetition. It has not just perception, but 'apperception', which is self-consciouness, reflexive knowledge of the internal states that constitute perception. Whereas we know of the existence of other monads only by philosophical reasoning, we are aware of our own substantiality through this self-consciousness. 'We have a clear but not a distinct idea of substance,' Leibniz wrote in a letter, 'which comes, in my opinion, from the fact that we have the internal feeling of it in ourselves' (G III.247).

The good of the soul is the goal, or final cause, not just of its own activity, but also of all the other monads that it dominates. The soul does not, however, exert any efficient causality on any of the other monads, nor any of them on any other: the good is achieved in virtue of the harmony pre-established by God in the body and in its environment and throughout the universe. Once again, Leibniz's rehabilitation of Aristotle goes further than Aristotle himself. Final causes were just one of Aristotle's quartet of causes; Descartes had expelled them from science but they are now readmitted and enthroned as the *only* finite causes operative in biology.

In all of this, is any room left for free will? In theory, Leibniz defends a full libertarian doctrine:

Absolutely speaking, our will, considered as contrasted with necessity, is in a state of indifference, and it has the power to do otherwise or to suspend its action altogether, the one and the other alternative being and remaining possible. (*D*, 30)

But human beings, like all agents, finite or infinite, need a reason for acting; that follows from the principle of sufficient reason. In the case of free agents, Leibniz maintains, the motives that provide the sufficient reason for action 'incline but do not necessitate'. But it is hard to see how he can really make room for a special kind of freedom for human beings. True, in his system, no agent of any kind is acted on from outside; all are completely self-determining. But no agent, rational or not, can step outside the life-history laid out for it in the pre-established harmony. Hence it seems that Leibniz cannot consistently accept that we enjoy the liberty of indifference that he described in the *Discourse*. All that is left is 'liberty of spontaneity'—the ability to act upon one's motives. But this, as Bramhall had argued against Hobbes, is an illusory freedom unless accompanied by liberty of indifference.

Berkeley and Hume on Spirits and Selves

In the universe of Berkeley there are only two kinds of things: spirits and ideas. 'The former', he says, 'are *active, indivisible substances;* the latter are *inert,* fleeting, dependent beings, which subsist not by themselves, but are supported by, or exist in minds or spiritual substances' (*BPW*, 98). Since Berkeley's metaphysical system places more weight on the notion of *spirit* than any other philosophy, one would expect that he would give us a full account of the concept; but in fact his philosophy of mind is remarkable jejune. Indeed, he tells us that we have no idea of what a spirit is.

This turns out to be less agnostic than it sounds, because Berkeley is here, as so often, using 'idea' to mean image. He concedes that we do have a notion of spirit in the sense that we understand the meaning of the word. A spirit is a real thing, which is neither an idea nor like an idea, but 'that which perceives ideas, and wills and reasons about them' (*BPW*, 120). Perhaps, for consistency, Berkeley should have said that a spirit was a congeries of ideas, just as he said a body was; but in the case of spirit, unlike body, he is willing to accept the notion of an underlying substance, distinct from ideas, in which ideas inhere. There is no distinction, in Berkeley's philosophy, between 'spirit' and 'mind'; he simply prefers the first term because it emphasizes the mind's immateriality.

235

Georgius Berkeley.S.T.P.
Confecr.Ep.Cleonenfis.
Maii.19.1733.

This portrait of Berkeley as Bishop of Cloyne alludes also to his transatlantic ambitions

How do we know that there are such things as spirits? 'We comprehend our own existence by inward feeling or reflexion, and that of other spirits by reason,' Berkeley tells us; but it is hard to see how he can consistently say either of these things. The only things that I can perceive or reflect upon are ideas; and Berkeley tells us that nothing could be more absurd than to say 'I am an idea or notion'. And the line of reasoning by which he seeks to establish the existence of other minds is broken-backed.

According to Berkeley, when I am looking at my wife, I do not see her at all. All I see is a collection of my own ideas that I have constantly observed in conjunction with each other. I know her existence and that of other people, he tells us, because 'I perceive several motions, changes, and combinations of ideas, that inform me there are certain particular agents like myself, which accompany them, and concur in their production.' But the ideas I see are my ideas, not my wife's ideas; and the ideas for which she provides the substratum are her ideas, to which I have no possible access. Berkeley cannot claim that she 'concurs in the production' of my ideas. No one other than myself or God can cause me to have an idea.

Berkeley's account of causation is minimalist. When we speak of one thing as cause and another as effect we are talking of relations between ideas. 'The connexion of ideas does not imply the relation of cause and effect, but only of a mark or sign with the thing signified. The fire which I see is not the cause of the pain I suffer on my approaching it, but the mark that forewarns me of it.' But how can the ideas which constitute my perception of my wife inform me either of her ideas, which I can never perceive, or of her spirit, which even she does not perceive? The problem of other minds was a *damnosa hereditas* which Berkeley bequeathed to following phenomenalists.

Hume, however, was to show that empiricism presents us with a problem not only about the minds of others but also about our own minds. Solipsism—the belief that only one's own self really exists—was always the logical conclusion of empiricism, implicit in the thesis that the mind knows nothing except its own perceptions. Hume drew out this implication more candidly than previous empiricists, but he went further and reached the conclusion that even the self of solipsism is an illusion.

Since Descartes and Locke, philosophers had conceived sensation not as a transaction between a perceiver and an object in the external world, but as the private perceiving by the mind of some interior perception, impression, or idea. Seeing a horse is really observing a horse-like visual sense-datum; feeling a teddy bear is really observing a teddy-like tactile sense-datum. The relation between a thinker and his thoughts is that of an inner eye to an inner art gallery. Hume follows wholeheartedly in this tradition and endeavours to give purely internal accounts of the differences between different mental activities, events, and states. This comes out particularly clearly in his account of the passions.

The relation between a passion and the mind to which it belongs is conceived by Hume as the relation of perceived to perceiver. 'Nothing', he writes, ' is ever present with the mind but its perceptions or impressions and ideas ... To hate, to love, to think, to feel, to see; all this is nothing but to perceive' (T, 67). One might draw from the passage the idea that loving a woman is one way of perceiving a woman, just as seeing a woman is one way of perceiving a woman; but that is not what Hume means at all. What is perceived when a passion is felt is the passion itself. The mind is represented as an observer which perceives the passions which are present to it.

The self as thus conceived is essentially the subject of such inner observation: it is the eye of inner vision, the ear of inner hearing; or rather, it is supposed to be the possessor of both inner eye and inner ear and whatever other inner organs of sensation may be demanded by empiricist epistemology. It was Hume who had the courage to show that the self, as thus conceived, was a chimera. Empiricism teaches that nothing is real except what can be discovered by the senses, inner or outer. The self, as inner subject, clearly cannot be perceived by the outer senses. But can it be discovered by inward observation? Hume, after the most diligent investigation, failed to locate the self:

Whenever I enter most intimately into what I call *myself*, I always stumble on some particular perception or other, of heat or cold, light or shade, love or hatred, pain or pleasure. I never catch *myself* at any time without a perception and never can observe anything but the perception ... If anyone upon serious and unprejudic'd reflection, thinks he has a different notion of *himself*, I must confess I can reason no longer with him. All I can allow him is, that he may well be in the right as well as I, and that we are essentially different in this particular. He may, perhaps, perceive something simple and continu'd, which he calls *himself*; though I am certain there is no such principle in me. (*T*, 252)

The imperceptibility of the self is a consequence of the concept of it as an inner sensor. We cannot taste our tongue, or see our eyes: the self is an unobservable observer, just as the eye is an invisible organ. But, as Hume shows, the empiricist self vanishes when subjected to systematic empiricist scrutiny. It is not discoverable by any sense, whether inner or outer, and therefore it is to be rejected as a metaphysical monster. Berkeley had maintained that ideas inhered in nothing outside the mind; Hume shows that there is nothing inside the mind for them to inhere in. There is no impression of the self, and no idea of the self; there are simply bundles of impressions and ideas.

Hume showed that the inner subject was illusory, but he did not expose the underlying error which led the empiricists to espouse the myth of the self. The real way out of the impasse is to reject the thesis that the mind knows nothing but its own ideas, and to accept that a thinker is not a solitary inner perceiver, but an embodied person living in a public world. Hume was right that he had no self other than himself; but he was himself not a bundle of impressions, but a portly human being in the midst of eighteenth-century society.

It might be thought that a bundle of impressions was so different from any kind of active agent that it would be idle to discuss whether or not it enjoyed free will. However, Hume goes on to address the topic of liberty and necessity, quite oblivious to his official philosophy of mind. (This is his custom when pursuing a difficult philosophical agenda—an agreeable inconsistency for which we may be grateful.) His general thesis is that human decisions and actions are necessitated by causal laws no less than the operations of lifeless natural agents, and are equally predictable:

Were a man, whom I know to be honest and opulent, and with whom I live in intimate friendship, to come into my house, where I am surrounded with my servants, I rest assured that he is not to stab me before he leaves it in order to rob me of my silver standish . . . A man who at noon leaves his purse full of gold on the pavement at Charing Cross may as well expect that it will fly away like a feather as that he will find it untouched an hour after. (E, 91)

Whatever we do, Hume maintains, is necessitated by causal links between motive, circumstance, and action. Class, among other things, is a great determinant of character and behaviour: 'The skin, pores, muscles and nerves of a day-labourer are different from those of a man of quality: So are his sentiments, actions and manners.' Hume's insistence on determinism leads him to some implausible conclusions: that a group of labourers should go on strike is for him as unthinkable as that an unsupported heavy body will not fall.

Although he believes that human actions are determined, Hume is willing to accept that we do enjoy a certain liberty. Like some of his successors, he was a 'compatibilist', someone who maintains that freedom and determinism are compatible with each other if rightly understood. Our natural

239

reluctance to accept that our actions are necessitated, he believes, arises from a confusion between necessity and constraint:

Few are capable of distinguishing betwixt the liberty of *spontaneity*, as it is call'd in the schools, and the liberty of *indifference*; betwixt that which is oppos'd to violence, and that which means a negation of necessity and causes. The first is even the most common sense of the word; and as 'tis only that species of liberty, which it concerns us to preserve, our thoughts have been principally turn'd towards it, and have almost universally confounded it. (*T*, 408)

Experience exhibits our liberty of spontaneity: we often do, unconstrained, what we want to do. But experience cannot provide genuine evidence for liberty of indifference, that is, the ability to do otherwise than we in fact do. We may imagine we feel such a liberty within ourselves, 'but a spectator can commonly infer our actions from our motives and character; and even when he cannot, he concludes in general, that he might, were he perfectly acquainted with every circumstance of our situation and temper, and the most secret springs of our complexion and disposition' (*T*, 408).

Such talk of 'secret springs' of action is one indication that in discussing this issue Hume has forgotten his official theory of mind and his official theory of causation. Indeed, his very definition of the human will seems incompatible with them. 'By *the will* I mean nothing but the *internal impression we feel and are conscious of, when we knowingly give rise to any new motion of our body, or new perception of our mind*' (*T*, 399). Given his view of causation, we must wonder what right Hume has to talk of our 'giving rise' to motions and perceptions. But if we replace 'we knowingly give rise to any new motion' with 'any new motion is observed to arise', the definition no longer looks at all appropriate.

Kant's Anatomy of the Mind

The anatomy of the mind, as described by Kant, contains many traditional elements. He made a distinction between the intellect and the senses, and between inner sense and the five outer senses. These distinctions, although rejected by some philosophers, had remained commonplaces since the Middle Ages. Kant's only innovation so far was to give novel epistemological functions to traditional faculties. But he went on to draw new distinctions, and to bring new insights to bear on the philosophy of mind.

240

In the *Critique of Judgement* Kant divides the faculties of the human mind into: (a) cognitive powers; (b) powers of feeling pleasure and pain; and (c) powers of desire. By 'cognitive powers' are meant, in this context, intellectual powers, and here Kant makes a threefold distinction between understanding *(Verstand)*, reason *(Vernunft)*, and judgement *(Urteil)*. Understanding is the legitimate operation of the intellect in the conceptualization of experience. That is something that we know from the first critique, where too 'Reason' is used as a technical term for the illegitimate operation of the intellect in transcendental speculation. In the second critique a positive role is given to reason as the arbiter of ethical behaviour. The function of judgement, however, is not clear from the earlier critiques. Previous philosophers had used the word (as Kant himself often does) to mean an assent to a proposition of any kind. In the third critique Kant concentrates on judgements of aesthetic taste. We thus arrive at a trinity of faculties: one (the understanding) which has truth as its object; one (the practical reason) which has goodness as its object; and one (the judgement) which has as its object the beautiful and the sublime (M, 31ff.).

All the operations of the intellect are accompanied by self-consciousness. Kant spells this out most fully in the case of the understanding. The conceptualization of experience involves the union of all the items of awareness in a single consciousness. In a difficult, but original and profound, section of the first critique entitled 'The original synthetic unity of apperception' Kant analyses what is meant by speaking of the unity of self-consciousness (B, 132–43).

It is not possible for me to *discover* that something is an item of *my* consciousness. It is absurd to think of me as being faced with an item of consciousness, then going on to wonder to whom it belongs, and then concluding upon inquiry that it belongs to none other than myself. Through reflection I may become aware of many features of my conscious experience (is it painful? is it clear? etc.) but I cannot become aware that it is *mine*. The self-conscious discoveries that one can make about one's perceptions are called by Kant 'apperceptions'. The point that one does not rely on experience to recognize one's consciousness as one's own is stated thus by Kant: one's ownership of one's own consciousness is not an empirical apperception, but a 'transcendental apperception'.

What unites my experiences in a single consciousness is not experience itself; in themselves my experiences are, as Kant says 'many coloured and diverse'. The unity is created by the *a priori* activity of the understanding making a synthesis of intuitions, combining them into what Kant calls 'the transcendental unity of apperception'. But this does not mean that I have some transcendental self-knowledge. The original unity of apperception gives me only the concept of myself; for any actual self-awareness, experience is necessary.

Kant agrees with Descartes that the thought 'I think' must accompany every other possible thought. Self-consciousness is inseparable from thought, because self-consciousness is necessary to think of thinking, and in advance of experience we attribute to things those properties which are the necessary conditions of our thinking of them. However, Kant disagrees sharply with the conclusions that Descartes drew from his *Cogito*. In the section of the transcendental dialectic entitled 'The paralogisms of Pure Reason' he makes a sustained attack upon Cartesian psychology, and indeed upon *a priori* and rational psychology in general.

Whereas empirical psychology deals with the soul as the object of inner sense, rational psychology treats of the soul as the thinking subject. Rational psychology, Kant says, 'professes to be a science built upon the single proposition *I think*'. It purports to be a study of an unknown X, the transcendental subject of thinking, 'the I or he or it (the thing) that thinks' (A, 343–5).

Our natural drive to go beyond the limits of merely empirical psychology leads us into fallacies—Kant calls them 'paralogisms' or bogus syllogisms. He lists four paralogisms of pure reason which can be crudely summarized as follows: (1) from 'Necessarily the thinking subject is a subject' we conclude 'The thinking subject is a necessary subject'; (2) from 'Dividing up the ego makes no sense' we conclude 'The ego is an indivisible substance; (3) from 'Whenever I am conscious, it is the same I who am conscious' we conclude 'Whenever I am conscious, I am conscious of the same I'; (4) from 'I can think of myself without my body' we conclude 'Without my body I can think of myself'.

In each paralogism, a harmless analytical proposition is converted, by logical sleight of hand, into a contentious synthetic *a priori* proposition. On the basis of the paralogisms rational psychology concludes that the self is an immaterial, incorruptible, personal, immortal entity.

The rational proof of the immortality of the soul is nothing but delusion. But that does not mean that we cannot believe in a future life as a postulate of practical reason. In the present life happiness is clearly not proportioned to virtue; so if we are to be motivated to behave well, we must believe that the balance will be redressed in another life elsewhere. The refutation of rational psychology, Kant claims, is a help, not a hindrance, to faith in an afterlife. 'For the merely speculative proof has never been able to exercise any influence upon the common reason of men. It so stands upon the point of a hair, that even the schools preserve it from falling only so long as they keep it unceasingly spinning round like a top' (B, 424).

The positive element in Kant's philosophy of mind that has had the longest-lasting influence is his treatment of freedom and determinism. His contribution to this topic is placed not in the section of the first critique devoted to rational and empirical psychology, but among the antinomies that purport to show the incoherence of attempts to survey the cosmos as a whole. The third antinomy relates the idea of the world as a single determinist system to the belief in the possibility of free uncaused action. The topic of this antinomy was later eloquently laid out by Tolstoy at the end of *War and Peace*:

The problem of freewill from earliest times has occupied the best intellects of mankind and has from earliest times appeared in all its colossal significance. The problem lies in the fact that if we regard man as a subject for observation from whatever point of view—theological, historical, ethical or philosophic—we find the universal law of necessity to which he (like everything else that exists) is subject. But looking upon man from within ourselves—man as the object of our own inner consciousness—we feel ourselves to be free.

The laws of necessity taught us by reason, Tolstoy thought, forced us to renounce an illusory freedom and recognize our unconscious dependence on universal law.

Kant, on the other hand, thought that determinism and freedom could be reconciled. In the third antinomy, unlike the first two antinomies, both thesis and antithesis, if properly interpreted, are true. The thesis is that natural causality is not sufficient to explain the phenomena of the world; in addition to determining causes we must take account of freedom and spontaneity. The antithesis argues that to postulate transcendental freedom is to resign oneself to blind lawlessness. As Tolstoy was to put it, 'If one man only out of millions once in a thousand years had the power of acting freely, i.e. as he chose, it is obvious that one single free act of that man in violation of the laws would be enough to prove that laws governing all human action cannot possibly exist.'

Kant, like Tolstoy, was a determinist, although he was not a hard determinist but a soft determinist. That is to say, he believed that determinism was compatible with human freedom and spontaneity. The human will, he said, is sensuous but free: that is to say, it is affected by passion but not necessitated by passion. 'There is in man a power of self-determination, independently of any coercion through sensuous impulses.' But the exercise of this power of self-determination has two aspects: empirical (perceptible in experience); and intelligible (graspable only by the intellect). Our free agency is the intelligible cause of sensible effects; and these sensible phenomena are also part of an unbroken series that unfolds in accordance with unchangeable laws. To reconcile human freedom with deterministic nature Kant says that nature operates in time, whereas the human will belongs to a non-phenomenal self that transcends time.

Throughout the centuries theologians had sought to reconcile human freedom with the omniscience of God by saying that God's knowledge was outside time. It was a novelty for a philosopher to seek to reconcile human freedom with the omnipotence of Nature by saying that human freedom was outside time. It is indeed difficult to reconcile Kant's claim that the human will is atemporal with the examples he himself gives of free action, such as his rising from the chair at his desk. But an impressive line of philosophers up to the present day have sought, like Kant, to show that freedom and determinism are compatible with each other. It is surely correct that causal explanation ('I knocked him over because I was pushed') and explanation by reasons ('I knocked him over to teach him a lesson') are two radically different types of explanation, each irreducible to the other. Kant was surely right to emphasize this difference and to believe that it must be the basis of any reconciling project.

The reconciliation between freedom and determinism takes a baroque form in the metaphysics of Hegel. Individual human choices such as Caesar's decision to cross the Rubicon are actually determined by the world-spirit, who uses 'the cunning of Reason' to give effect to its purposes. But the necessity that operates at the level of the individual is an expression of the highest form of freedom, for freedom is the essential attribute of spirit and its ever increasing expression is the guiding force of history.

When Hegel speaks of the world-spirit his references to it are not mere metaphors for the operation of impersonal historical forces. Hegel's spirit resembles Kant's transcendental unity of apperception in being the subject of all experience, which cannot itself be an object of experience. Kant was content to assume that there will be a separate such focus in the life of each individual mind. But what ground, Hegel might ask, is there for such an assumption? Behind Kant's transcendental self stands the Cartesian ego; and one of the first critics of Descartes' *cogito* put the pertinent question: how do you know that it is you who are thinking, and not the world-soul that thinks in you? Hegel's spirit is meant to be a centre of consciousness prior to any individual consciousness. One spirit thinks severally in the thoughts of Descartes and in the thoughts of Kant, perhaps rather as I, as a single person, can simultaneously feel toothache and gout in different parts of myself. But it is difficult to accommodate within either empirical or analytic psychology a spirit whose behavioural expression is the entire universe. Rather than a philosophy of mind, Hegel offers us a Philosophy of Mind.

In respect of the philosophy of the human mind, the thinker who made the most significant contribution in our period was undoubtedly Kant. Throughout the seventeenth and eighteenth centuries, philosophy of mind was made subordinate to epistemology, in consequence of the Cartesian pursuit of certainty. In the course of this pursuit, Descartes and the rationalists undervalued the role of the senses, and the British empiricists eliminated the role of the intellect. It took the overarching genius of Kant to put together again what the partisan energies of his predecessors had shattered, and to give an account of the human mind that did justice to its various faculties. In his work epistemology and philosophical psychology once again meet together, as they had done in the best work of the Middle Ages.

8

Ethics

Histories of ethics often skim swiftly over the sixteenth century. In the high Middle Ages moral philosophy was presented in commentaries on Aristotle's *Nicomachean Ethics* and in treatises on the natural or revealed law of God. In Aquinas' *Summa Theologiae* both elements are combined, but the system is structured around the concept of virtue rather than around the concept of law. It was Aquinas' successors, from Duns Scotus onward, who gave the theory of divine law the central place in presentations of Christian morality.[1] But the medieval tradition in ethics suffered a shock, from which it never recovered, under the impact of the Reformation and the Counter-Reformation.

Both Luther and Calvin emphasized the depravity of human nature in the absence of the divine grace that was offered only through Christianity. For them, the path to human salvation and happiness lay through faith, not through moral endeavour, and there was little scope for any philosophical system of ethics. Aristotle was the enemy, not the friend, of the only possible good life. As for other ancient sages, their teaching could not lead to virtue; as Augustine had insisted, the best it could do was to add a certain splendour to vice.

Catholics did not agree that human possibilities for goodness had been totally extinguished by the Fall, and the Council of Trent declared it a heresy to say that all deeds of non-Christians were sinful. But the disciplinary regulations of that council gave Catholic moral theology a new direction which took it far away from Aquinas' synthesis of Aristotelian and Augustinian ethics. A decree of 1551, strengthening a rule of the

---

[1] See vol. II, pp. 263–77.

Lateran Council of 1215, laid down that all Catholics must make regular confession to a priest. It made a distinction between two classes of sin, mortal and venial: mortal sins were more serious, and if unrepented rendered the sinner liable to the eternal punishments of hell. Under the new rule, a penitent was bound to confess all mortal sins according to their species, number, and circumstances. Henceforth, Catholic moralists focused less on consideration of the virtues than on the specification and individuation of different kinds of sin, and the listing of aggravating or mitigating circumstances.

Casuistry

The decree of Trent fostered a whole new ethical discipline: the science of casuistry. Casuistry in general is the application of moral principle to particular decisions; in particular to 'cases of conscience' where such principles might appear to conflict with each other. In the broad sense, any expert advice given to resolve a particular moral dilemma might count as an exercise of casuistry: for instance, the guidance given to the Emperor Charles V by a group of theologians on the treatment of his new American subjects, or the counsel given to King Charles I by Archbishop Laud on the legality of the impeachment of the Earl of Strafford. But when contemporaries and historians talked of casuistry they commonly had in mind the textbooks and manuals, produced in abundance in the sixteenth and seventeenth centuries, which dealt not with actual decisions, but with imaginary cases, as a guide to confessors and spiritual directors in their dealings with the penitent and the devout.

Although manuals of casuistry were written by theologians from many different religious orders, casuistry became and remained specially associated with the newly founded Counter-Reformation order of the Jesuits, the Society of Jesus. While the Jesuit system of training made provision for more scholarly students to study the moral system of Aquinas, those destined for non-academic work learnt their ethics through the study of cases of conscience, reading manuals of casuistry, listening to lectures from casuists, and practising pastoral care through case conferences. Jesuits were much in demand as confessors, in particular to the great and the good; in 1602 the general of the order felt obliged to issue a special instruction *On the*

This illustration to the Codex Azcatitla shows an Indian being baptized amid a throng of tonsured friars

Confession of Princes. Thus casuistry acquired political as well as ethical importance.

During the sixteenth century the casuists had to face a number of novel moral problems. One of the most important was the relationship of Christians to the original inhabitants of the newly discovered continent of America. Were the Spanish and Portuguese colonists entitled to annex the lands of the indigenous peoples and make them their slaves? The Emperor Charles V called a conference of theologians at Valladolid in 1550 to discuss the issue. His imperial historiographer, Sepulveda, basing his theories on Aristotle's teaching that some men were better fitted to serve than to rule, and were therefore natural slaves, argued that American Indians, who lived a life of rudeness and inferiority, and were ignorant of Christianity, could justly be enslaved and forcibly converted. This position was controverted on the spot by the missionary Bartolome de las Casas, and forcefully attacked in publications by two of the most influential Spanish theologians of the age, the Dominican Francisco de Vitoria and the Jesuit Franscisco Suarez.

In his posthumously published treatises, *De Indis* (1557), Vitoria first of all defended St Thomas' teaching that the forcible conversion of the heathen was unjust, and went on to deny that either the pope or the emperor had any jurisdiction over the Indians. The Indians, he maintained, had ownership and property rights just as if they were Christians: they constituted a genuine political society, and their civil arrangements showed that they enjoyed the full use of reason:

There is a certain method in their affairs, for they have polities which are orderly arranged, and they have definite marriage and magistrates, overlords, laws, and workshops, and a system of exchange, all of which call for the use of reason.[2]

He concluded that there was no justification for confiscating the land and possessions of these heathen peoples on the pretext that they had no genuine ownership of their property. The Jesuit Suarez took a similar line in his discussion of the rights and wrongs of war.[3]

The expansion of overseas exploration and international trade in the sixteenth century forced casuists to examine the ethics of the methods by which maritime ventures were financed. On the basis of certain biblical texts, and of an Aristotelian analysis of the nature of money, Thomas Aquinas had issued a severe condemnation of the taking of interest on loans.[4] There was however an important difference, recognized by Aquinas, between two ways of financing a project. One was by making a loan to an entrepreneur (to be repaid to the lender whether the venture succeeds or not); the other was by buying a share in the enterprise (where the financier bears part of the risk of failure). The first was usury, and it was wicked. The second was partnership, and it was honourable (*ST* 2.2. 78. 2 ad 5).

The prohibition on usury was maintained throughout the Middle Ages: it was repeated by St Antoninus, who in the fifteenth century was archbishop of Florence, a city that was by then home to great banking houses such as the Medici. Antoninus did, however, allow a charge to be made upon a loan in one particular case: if delay in repayment of a loan had led

---

[2] *De Indis Recenter Inventis*, 1.23; quoted by Bull et al., *Hugo Grotius and International Relations* (Oxford: Oxford University Press, 1990), p. 46.

[3] See below, p. 281. It is sad that the views of las Casas, Vitoria, and Suarez did not have more effect on the actual practice of Christian colonizers.

[4] See vol. II, p. 271.

to unforeseen loss to the lender (given the technical name *damnum emergens*). This was seen as compensation for damage inflicted, rather than interest on the loan itself. But this minor relaxation of the prohibition led, over the next century, to its total emasculation at the hands of the casuists.

The first step was the introduction of the notion of opportunity cost. One of the things one gives up when making a loan is the possibility of making profit from an alternative use of the money. So *damnum emergens* is joined by *lucrum cessans* (cessation of gain) as a title to reimbursement. The expansion of capitalism during the sixteenth century multiplied the opportunities for alternative investment, and so casuists were able to argue that in almost every case there would be present one or other of these justifications for charging interest.

The casuists' logic was surely, on their own terms, very dubious. The money which I lend you I could indeed put to other uses: I could lend it to someone else, or I could invest it in a partnership. But on the first supposition, the only gain I am losing by lending to you is a gain which would itself be unlawful, namely, the taking of usury. And on the second supposition, it is not at all sure that I am losing anything by making you the loan. My alternative venture might go wrong and so far from making a profit, I would lose my capital as well. You may turn out to have been doing me a good turn by borrowing from me.

Nonetheless, casuists, some of them hired as consultants by the major banking houses, came out with ever more complicated schemes to circumvent the prohibition on usury. The Duke of Bavaria, in whose dominions such schemes were highly popular, proposed the following case for consideration by a commission of Jesuits in 1580. It is worth quoting in its own terms, for it is framed in the typical format of a 'case of conscience':

Titius, a German, loans Sympronius a sum of money. Sympronius is a person of means, and the money is lent to him for no specific purpose. The conditions are that Titius is to receive annually five florins for every hundred lent, and afterwards have the whole capital back. There is no danger to the capital, and Titius must get his 5%, whether or not Sympronius makes a profit.[5]

The question proposed was: is this contract lawful? The commissioners returned a highly qualified reply, but on its basis the Jesuit order declared

[5] Quoted by Jonsen and Toulmin, *The Abuse of Casuistry* (Berkeley: University of California Press, 1988), p, 189.

the contract morally licit. Henceforth the prohibition on usury was a dead letter among Roman Catholics.

Mysticism and Stoicism

The heyday of casuistry was the century from 1550 to 1650. During that period volumes of casuistry were not, of course, the only guides to life that were published. On the one hand, there were many manuals of devotion which included practical moral advice; on the other hand, some writers urged the merits of ancient ethical texts. As examples of these two tendencies we may consider St John of the Cross and René Descartes.

St John of the Cross (1542–91), the spiritual director of St Teresa of Avila, who reformed the Carmelite order, was a poet and mystic. His work *The Dark Night of the Soul* describes the long and painful ascent which leads to union with God. He describes the ecstasy of the goal in terms of incomprehensible rapture, but he makes clear that the way towards it is through suffering and self-discipline. First one must enter the dark night of the senses; but this is only a kindergarten of preparation for the dark night of the soul, which is itself only the first stage of the mystical ascent. It is thus that he sets out the first steps of the spiritual life:

Strive always to prefer, not that which is easiest, but that which is most difficult;
Not that which is most delectable, but that which is most unpleasing;
Not that which gives most pleasure, but rather that which gives least
Not that which is restful, but that which is wearisome . . .
In order to arrive at having pleasure in everything,
Desire to have pleasure in nothing.
In order to arrive at possessing everything
Desire to possess nothing.
In order to arrive at being everything,
Desire to be nothing.

St John's treatise was the most severe of sixteenth-century devotional guides, and was clearly addressed to a cloistered minority. But similar teaching, in a more emollient form, was presented by the French bishop St Francis de Sales, in his *Introduction to the Devout Life* (1608), the first manual of piety aimed at lay people living a secular life in the world.

Descartes, although an observant Catholic, drew the inspiration of his morality from quite different sources. When he was embarking on his project of all-embracing doubt, he safeguarded himself by drawing up a provisional code of morality, consisting of three principal maxims: first, to obey the laws and customs of his country; second, to be resolute in action once he had taken a decision; third, 'to try always to conquer myself rather than fortune; to change my desires, rather than the order of the world'. This, he says, 'was the secret of those philosophers of old who could withdraw from the dominion of fortune, and, amid suffering and poverty, could debate whether their Gods were as happy as they' (AT VI.26; *CSMK* I.124).

Observing Catholic practice appears only as a subdivision of 'obeying the laws and customs of my country': it is to ancient Stoicism that the young Descartes looks for ethical guidance. It was the same ten years later when he was corresponding with Princess Elizabeth. He repeated his three maxims, and to instruct her on the nature of true happiness, he recommended a reading of Seneca's *De Vita Beata*. In his letters of moral advice, he constantly stresses the role of reason in the moderation of the passions, which make us believe certain goods to be more desirable than they are. 'The true function of reason', he wrote, 'in the conduct of life is to examine and consider without passion the value of all perfections of body and soul that can be acquired by our conduct, so that since we are commonly obliged to deprive ourselves of some goods in order to acquire others, we shall always choose the better' (AT IV.286; *CSMK* III.265).

Descartes worked up some of the ideas of his correspondence with Elizabeth into a *Treatise on the Passions*. This is as much an exercise in speculative physiology as in moral philosophy: an understanding of the bodily causes of our passions, Descartes believed, was a valuable aid to our bringing them under rational control. The detailed examination of the passions, he believed, was the one area in which his own moral philosophy was superior to that of the ancients (AT XI.327–8; *CSMK* I.328–9).

The passion whose description brings out most fully Descartes' moral ideals is the passion of *générosité*, which defies exact translation into English. The *généreux* is no doubt generous, but he is much more than that: he is, we might say with a degree of anachronism, the perfect gentleman. Such people, Descartes tells us:

are naturally led to do great deeds, and at the same time not to undertake anything of which they do not feel themselves capable. And because they esteem nothing more highly than doing good to others and disregarding their own self-interest, they are always perfectly courteous, gracious and obliging to everyone. Moreover, they have complete command over their passions. In particular they have mastery over their desires, and over jealousy and envy, because everything they think sufficiently valuable to be worth pursuing is such that its acquisition depends solely on themselves. (AT XI.448; *CSMK* I.385)

Pascal against the Jesuits

Descartes' *généreux*, tranquil, aloof, and self-sufficient, lives in a different world from the penitents of the casuists, wallowing in a sea of sin and craving advice and absolution from their confessors. But by the time of *The Passions of the Soul* the casuists had brought themselves into great disrepute, which came to a climax with the publication of Pascal's *Lettres Provinciales* in 1655. There were three practices commended by casuists which Pascal was not alone in regarding as scandalous: equivocation, probabilism, and the direction of intention. We will consider each in turn.

Traditional Christian teaching strictly forbade lying: Augustine and Aquinas agreed that deliberately stating a falsehood was always sinful. It was not always obligatory to utter the whole truth, but even to save the life of an innocent person, one must never tell a lie. This doctrine appeared harsh to many in the sixteenth century. In the England of Queen Elizabeth it was a capital crime for a priest or Jesuit to enter the country, and Catholic missionaries had to move about secretly, often concealing themselves in hideaways in country mansions. If government officials raided a house in search of priests, was it lawful for the host to deny that there was a priest in the house?

In 1595 the leader of the English Jesuits, Father Henry Garnet, in an anonymous pamphlet entitled *A Treatise of Equivocation or Against Lying and Fraudulent Dissimulation*, answered this question in the affirmative. The master or mistress of the house should say 'There is no priest in the house,' and mean 'There is no priest in the house about whom anyone is bound to tell you.' This was not a lie, he argued, because a lie was a case of saying one thing while believing another. In this case, the spoken proposition did correspond to the proposition in the mind of the speaker; it was simply that the utterance revealed only part of it. But it was common ground

Fr Henry Garnet S.J. on the scaffold before being executed for complicity in the Gunpowder Plot

among theologians that one did not have to tell *the whole truth* when that would damage an innocent third party. Hence, equivocation of this kind was perfectly lawful.

Garnet's version of equivocation shocked many of his fellow casuists. Others had been prepared to defend equivocation in the sense of giving an answer which contained words which were genuinely ambiguous. But it was a different matter to alter completely the natural sense of a spoken sentence by a totally private addition or subtraction of words ('mental reservation' as it came to be called). Equivocation of this kind, many felt, was worse than lying, piling hypocrisy upon deceit. After he had been tried and executed for complicity in the Gunpowder Plot of 1605, Garnet became for English Protestants the paradigm of the deceitful Jesuit. In Shakespeare's *Macbeth*, after the murder of Duncan, a drunken porter imagines he is keeper of the gates of hell. Among those who knock to be admitted:

Faith, here's an equivocator, that could swear in both the scales against either scale, who committed treason enough for God's sake, yet could not equivocate to Heaven: O, come in, equivocator. (II.iii)

Garnet's defence of mental reservation was a minority opinion even among casuists. But there was a second-order moral principle, widely held by casuists, which gave a special significance to minority opinions. Suppose that moralists disagree with each other whether a particular action is sinful or not: is it lawful to perform it? One school of thought answered that one must take the least dangerous course, and refrain; that was called 'tutiorism', from the Latin word *tutior* meaning 'safer'. Another school of thought said that one could perform the action only if a majority of authorities regarded it as lawful. This was 'probabiliorism', which maintained that one must follow the more probable opinion. But there was a third theory, popular with many casuists, which held that even a less probable opinion could lawfully be followed, provided that it was probable at all. To be 'probable' it was sufficient that the opinion was maintained by someone in a position of authority, even though he might have the majority of experts against him. This was the doctrine of 'probabilism'. It was first propounded in 1577 by a Dominican commentator on St Thomas, Bartolomeo Medina of Salamanca, who wrote 'if an opinion is probable, it is licit to follow it, even though the opposite opinion is more probable'.[6]

The use of probabilism was perhaps not so very different from the common practice in business and politics today of shopping around among lawyers until one finds one who is willing to advise that the course of action one has decided on is perfectly legal. But to thinkers like Pascal it

---

[6] Quoted in Jonsen and Toulmin, p. 164.

seemed to eat away the foundation of all religious morality. The variety of opinions among moralists upon important issues, which pious people might well reagrd as a scandal, turns out, on the probabilists' assumptions, to be a great boon. 'I now see the purpose', he says to a fictional Jesuit, 'of the conflicts of opinion between your Doctors on every topic. One of them will always serve your turn, and the other will do you no harm' (*LP* V. 51). Some casuists went so far as to say that an opinion could be made probable by being propounded even by a single moralist, provided he was a person of weight. This meant, as Pascal saw it, that any Johnny-come-lately who had got himself a chair in moral theology could overturn the teaching of all the Fathers of the Church.

In his attack on the laxity which, he alleged, Jesuit confessors encouraged in their clients, one of the targets that Pascal singled out for attack was the practice of 'direction of intention'. The imaginary Jesuit in his book says: 'Our method of direction consists in proposing to oneself, as the end of one's actions, a permitted object. So far as we can we turn men away from forbidden things, but when we cannot prevent the action at least we purify the intention.' Thus, for instance, it is allowable to kill a man in return for an insult, even though the Bible tells us not to return evil for evil. 'All you have to do is to turn your intention from the desire for vengeance, which is criminal, to the desire to defend one's honour, which is permitted.' Duelling is prohibited, but if one is challenged one may turn up at the place designated, not with the intention of fighting a duel, but to avoid being thought a coward; and then, if threatened by one's opponent, one may of course kill him in self-defence.

Such direction of intention, obviously enough, is simply a performance in the imagination which has little to do with genuine intention, which is expressed in the means one chooses to one's ends. It was this doctrine, and Pascal's attack on it, which brought into disrepute the doctrine of double effect, according to which there is an important moral distinction between the intended and unintended effects of one's action. If the theory of double effect is combined with the practice of direction of intention, it becomes no more than a hypocritical cloak for the justification of the means by the end.

There was, however, hypocrisy on both sides of this controversy over casuistry. Pascal, in the *Provinicial Letters*, poses as a man of the world shocked by the excessive laxity of Jesuit confessors. In fact, as a Jansenist, he saw not

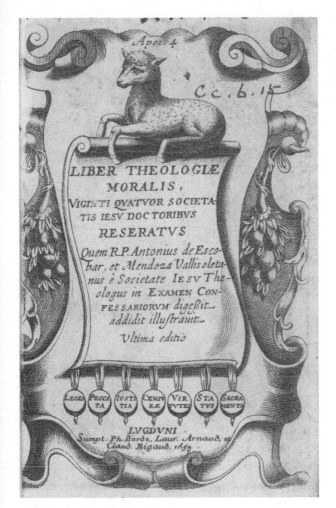

The title page of Escobar's *Moral Theology*, a notorious classic of casuistry

only the Jesuits, but any moralists willing to make the slightest concession to human weakness, as tools of Satan. He and his friends at Port Royal saw themselves as a small privileged elect, chosen to walk on the difficult path to salvation while the great mass of mankind hurtled on its way to damnation.

There is an odd similarity between Port Royal in the seventeenth century and Bloomsbury in the twentieth century. In each case a small group of upper-class intellectuals—ascetics in the one case, hedonists in the other—saw themselves as uniquely enlightened in a world of philistines. Each group contained writers of great literary skill, and each group fostered artists of talent. On the fringe of each group there stood out a great mathematical philosopher: Bertrand Russell in the case of Bloomsbury; Blaise Pascal in the case of Port Royal. Each group flared for a while in the limelight, and then gradually faded into obscurity, leaving behind a musty odour of exquisite spiritual snobbery.

Spinoza's Ethical System

No one could ever accuse Spinoza of having belonged to a clique. A solitary thinker of great intellectual courage, he devised an elaborate, elegant, and demanding ethical system. Like Descartes, he gives an important role in ethics to the detailed examination of the passions, which occupies the third book of the *Ethics*. But both the philosophical substructure and the practical conclusions of his analysis of the emotions are very different from Descartes', so that the resulting ethical system is unlike any other of modern times.

The metaphysical basis of Spinoza's ethical system is a principle of existential inertia. Everything, so far as it can by its own power, endeavours to persevere in its own being. This self-perpetuating endeavour in each thing constitutes its very essence (*Eth*, 75). Applied to men and women, this general principle means that the fundamental motive of human action is self-preservation. Desire is defined by Spinoza as the self-conscious endeavour to preserve the existence of soul and body. We are conscious not only of this appetite for existence, but also of any increase or diminution in our powers of action: consciousness of such an increase constitutes pleasure; consciousness of diminution constitutes pain (*Eth*, 77). Desire, pleasure, and pain are the three fundamental human drives: all the other emotions, such as love, hatred, hope, and fear, are derived from them.

There are, however, two different kinds of emotions, passive and active. There are passive emotions, or passions, in which we 'toss to and fro like waves of the sea driven by contrary winds' (*Eth*, 103). In the passive emotions, modifications of the body give rise to corresponding ideas in the mind—ideas which will be inadequate and confused. But there are also active emotions arising from the mind's own endeavour to increase its understanding by conceiving clear and distinct ideas. Active emotions are derivable only from desire and pleasure; pain, which is the mark of a reduction in human power, physical and mental, cannot give rise to an active emotion. Actions arising from active emotions are expressions of strength of character (*fortitudo*). Strength of character, when it is expressed in self-perserving actions, is called 'courage' (*animositas*); when expressed in actions aiming at the good of others, it is called 'nobility' (*generositas*).

The notion of nobility, which is introduced at the end of Book Three of the *Ethics*, appears at first sight to conflict with the ruthlessly egoistical analysis of the passions which occupies most of the book. We are told, for instance, 'He who conceives that someone he hates is in pain will feel pleasure' (*Eth*, 82), and that 'if we conceive that anyone delights in an object that only one person can possess, we will try to prevent the person in question from gaining possession of it' (*Eth*, 87). Apparently cynical remarks of this kind are often shrewd: for instance, 'if a man begins to hate what he once loved but loves no more, he will regard it with greater hatred than if he had never loved it' (*Eth*, 90). But only a rare remark prepares the way for the notion of nobility: for instance, 'Hatred is increased when it is reciprocated, but hatred can be destroyed by love' (*Eth*, 93).

The reconciliation of egoism and altruism is carried out by Spinoza in the fourth and fifth books of the *Ethics*: 'On Human Bondage' and 'On Human Freedom'. The overarching theme of these books is this: we are in bondage to the extent that we feel passive emotions, and we are free to the extent that we feel active emotions. An emotion ceases to be a passion once we achieve a clear and distinct idea of it, which means an understanding of its causes. Paradoxically, the key to liberation is the appreciation of the necessity of all things. We cannot avoid being determined, but moral progress consists in the replacement of external determination by internal determination. What we need to do is to take a God's eye view of the whole necessary natural scheme of things, seeing it 'in the light of eternity'.

Not all passions can be turned into emotions, but those that cannot may be eliminated. Hatred, for instance, is a passive emotion, being a form of pain. But once I understand that the actions of others are determined, I will cease to feel hatred to those that do me harm. The passions of different people may conflict with each other, but people who are guided by reason and feel emotion rather than passion will find themselves in agreement (*Eth*, 132). Self-preservation remains the underlying drive, prior to any virtue (*Eth*, 127). Nonetheless, we ought to want virtue for its own sake, for there is nothing more useful for us which might serve as its goal. This is how egoism and altruism are to be reconciled. There is scope for nobility when self-preservation is enlightened by the realization of one's own place as a part of the great whole which is Nature:

To man there is nothing more useful than man—nothing, I repeat, more excellent for preserving their being can be wished for by man, than that all should so in all points agree that the minds and bodies of all should form, as it were, one single mind and one single body, and that all should, with one consent seek what is useful to them all. Hence, men who are governed by reason—that is, who seek what is useful to them in accord with reason—desire for themselves nothing, which they do not also desire for the rest of mankind, and consequently are just, faithful, and honourable in their conduct. (*Eth*, 125)

In 'On Human Bondage' Spinoza goes through the emotions, telling us which ones are good and which are bad ('good' and 'bad' for him, of course, simply mean what is conducive or non-conducive to self-preservation). Mirth, for instance, is a good thing, which we cannot have too much of; melancholy, however, is always bad (*Eth*, 138). (Spinoza recommends music as a cure for melancholy (*Eth*, 115).) Desires for non-competitive goods should be preferred to desires for goods that can be possessed by one person only. The highest good is one that is common to all who follow virtue, one in which all can equally rejoice. 'The mind's highest good is the knowledge of God, and the mind's highest virtue is to know God' (*Eth*, 129). God, of course, is for Spinoza the same as Nature, and the more we increase our knowledge of Nature the more we rejoice. This joy, accompanied by the thought of God as cause, is called by Spinoza 'the intellectual love of God'.

Spinoza's ideal human, a free person absorbed in the intellectual love of God, is no less subject to determinism than someone who is in bondage to the basest passions. The difference is that the free man is determined by causes that are internal, not external, and that are clearly and distinctly perceived. One of the effects of the clear and distinct perception of the human condition is that time ceases to matter. Past, present, and future are all equal to each other. We naturally think of the past as what cannot be changed, and the future as being open to alternatives. But in Spinoza's deterministic universe, the future is no less fixed than the past. The difference, therefore, between past and future should play no part in the reflections of a wise man: we should not worry about the future nor feel remorse about the past.

One passion which must altogether disappear in a free man is the passion of fear. Fear can never be a rational emotion; its object is future evil, and for Spinoza both the future and evil are ultimately unreal. The free man has only positive motives: he eats well and takes healthy exercise because he enjoys doing so, not in order to postpone his death. 'A free man thinks of death least of all things; and his wisdom is a meditation not on death but on life' (*Eth*, 151).

It is difficult not to admire the beauty of Spinoza's ethical writing; it is equally difficult to accept it as offering a real guide to living. Spinoza is a victim of his own success: he has woven his ethics so tightly to his metaphysics that it is difficult to swallow the one without the other. Bertrand Russell, who totally rejected Spinoza's metaphysics, but thought him the one really admirable human being in the history of philosophy, made a gallant effort to draw a practical moral from the *Ethics*:

Spinoza's principle of thinking about the whole, or at any rate about larger matters than your own grief, is a useful one. There are even times when it is comforting to reflect that human life, with all that it contains of evil and suffering, is an infinitesimal part of the life of the universe. Such reflections may not suffice to constitute a religion, but in a painful world they are a help towards sanity and an antidote to the paralysis of utter despair. (*HWP*, 562)

Hume on Reason, Passion, and Virtue

For Spinoza, as for Socrates in the ancient world, all wrongdoing is a result of ignorance: vicious conduct is ultimately a failure of reason. At the opposite pole stands David Hume: for him, reason has nothing at all to do with the distinction between right and wrong, between virtue and vice. Reason's only function is a technical one: to assist us in the achievement of the goals set by our passions. In the evaluation of our goals, reason has no place. ''Tis not contrary to reason to prefer the destruction of the whole world to the scratching of my finger. 'Tis not contrary to reason for me to chuse my total ruin, to prevent the least uneasiness of an Indian or person totally unknown to me' (*T*, 416). Reason can neither adjudicate nor control passion; a passion can be conquered only by another, stronger, passion. Why then do people—and not only philosophers—talk so much about the conflict between reason and passion? Hume's answer is that they mistake for reason what is actually a gentle, non-violent, passion:

There are certain calm desires and tendencies which, tho' they be real passions, produce little emotion in the mind, and are more known by their effects than by the immediate feeling or sensation. These desires are of two kinds; either certain instincts originally implanted in our natures, such as benevolence and resentment, the love of life, and kindness to children; or the general appetite to good, and aversion to evil, consider'd merely as such. When any of these passions are calm, and cause no disorder in the soul, they are very readily taken for the determinations of reason. (*T*, 417)

Moral judgements are calm passions of this kind: they are not ideas, but impressions. Morality is more properly felt than judged of. Virtue gives us pleasure, and vice pain: 'An action or sentiment or character is virtuous or vicious; why? because its view causes a pleasure or uneasiness of a particular kind.' But of course not every action or person or thing that gives us pleasure is virtuous: wine, women, and song may be pleasant but the pleasure they give is not the special pleasure taken by the moral sense. Well, what are the marks of the *particular* kind of pleasure involved in favourable moral judgement? Hume offers two: that it should be disinterested and that it should involve approbation. These seem insufficient to mark off moral from aesthetic judgement. Surely we need to distinguish one from the other if morality is not simply to be a matter of taste.

Hume offers us no general criterion adequate to differentiate moral judgement, but proceeds to investigate individual virtues. The two most important are benevolence and justice. Benevolence is universally admired: we all esteem those who relieve the distressed, comfort the afflicted, and are generous even to strangers. But in a natural state, benevolence extends only to those who in one way or another are close to us. 'There is no such passion in human minds, as the love of mankind, merely as such, independent of personal qualities, of services, or of relation to ourself' (*T*, 481). Benevolence alone, then, cannot be the foundation of justice; of our obligation to repay our debts even to strangers and enemies. We must conclude that justice is not a natural virtue, but an artificial one.

Human beings are impotent outside society; but society is unstable unless social rules are observed, in particular property rights. What we need is a convention entered into by all members of society to leave everyone in possession of the external goods acquired by their fortune and industry. Justice is founded therefore on utility, on self-interest broadly interpreted:

Instead of departing from our own interest, or from that of our nearest friends, by abstaining from the possessions of others, we cannot better consult both these interests, than by such a convention; because it is by that means we maintain society, which is so necessary to their well-being and subsistence, as well as to our own. (*T*, 489)

It is because it is based on a convention, entered into for the sake of utility, that justice is an 'artificial virtue'.

Natural virtues, such as meekness, charity, clemency, or generosity, are not based on utility, but arise from a more fundamental feature of human nature: sympathy. The passions of each human being are reflected in other human beings, as strings resonate in harmony. A difference between natural and artificial virtues is this: that individual acts of benevolence do good, whereas it is only the entire system of justice that promotes happiness. 'Judges take from a poor man to give to a rich; they bestow on the dissolute the labour of the industrious; and put into the hands of the vicious the means of harming both themselves and others. The whole scheme, however, of law and justice is advantageous to the society.' It is because of this advantage to society that we esteem justice; but justice is only a means to an end:

Now as the means to an end can only be agreeable, where the end is agreeable; and as the good of society, where our own interest is not concerned, or that of our friends, pleases only by sympathy: It follows, that sympathy is the source of the esteem which we pay to all the artificial virtues. (*T*, 577)

In an appendix to the second Enquiry, Hume takes some pains to argue against those who claim that benevolence is only a disguised form of self-love. Even animals show disinterested benevolence; so why should we doubt the genuineness of human gratitude and friendship and maternal love? In thus rejecting the long philosophical tradition of eudaimonism—the thesis that the ultimate goal of all one's actions is one's own happiness—Hume was, probably unwittingly, following in the footsteps of his compatriot Duns Scotus.[7] But whereas Scotus thought that the innate motive independent of self-love was a love of justice, Hume saw the motive of benevolence as even more deeply rooted in human nature.

[7] See vol. II, p. 272.

Kant on Morality, Duty, and Law

Kant, although he presented a very different system of ethics, agreed with Hume in the rejection of eudaimonism. Happiness, he argues in the *Groundwork*, cannot be the ultimate purpose of morality:

Suppose now that for a being possessed of reason and will the real purpose of nature were his preservation, his welfare, or in a word his happiness. In that case nature would have hit on a very bad arrangement by choosing reason in the creature to carry out this purpose. For all the actions he has to perform with this end in view, and the whole rule of his behaviour, would have been mapped out for him far more accurately by instinct; and the end in question could have been maintained far more surely by instinct than it ever can be by reason. (*G*, 395)

The overarching concept in Kantian morality is not happiness, but duty. The function of reason in ethics is not to inform the will how best to choose means to some further end; it is to produce a will that is good in itself, and a will is good only if it is motivated by duty. Good will, for Kant, is the only thing that is good without qualification. Fortune, power, intelligence, courage, and all the traditional virtues can be used to bad ends; even happiness itself can be corrupting. It is not what it achieves that constitutes the goodness of a good will; good will is good in itself alone:

Even if, by some special disfavour of destiny, or by the niggardly endowment of stepmotherly nature, this will is entirely lacking in power to carry out its intentions, if by its utmost effort it still accomplishes nothing, and only good will is left...even then it would still shine like a jewel for its own sake as something which has its full value in itself. (*G*, 394)

Good will is the highest good and the condition of all other goods, including happiness.

If a will is good only when motivated by duty, we must ask what it is to act out of duty. A first answer is to say that it is to act as the moral law prescribes. But this is not enough. Kant distinguishes between acting in accordance with duty, and acting from the motive of duty. A grocer who chooses honesty as the best policy, or a philanthropist who takes delight in pleasing others, may do actions that are in accord with duty. Such actions conform to the moral law, but they are not motivated by reverence for it. Actions of this kind, however correct and amiable, have, according to Kant, no moral worth. Worth of character is shown only when someone does good not from inclination but from duty. A man who is wholly wretched and longs to die, but preserves his own life solely out of a sense of duty—that is Kant's paradigm of good willing (*G*, 398).

Happiness and duty, therefore, are for Kant not just different but conflicting motives. Aristotle had taught that people were not really virtuous as long as virtuous action went against the grain. *His* paradigm of a virtuous man was somebody who thoroughly enjoyed carrying out his virtuous endeavours. But for Kant it is the painfulness of well-doing that is the real mark of virtue. If virtue brings happiness, that must only be as a by-product. 'The more a cultivated reason concerns itself with the aim of enjoying life and happiness, the farther does man get away from true contentment' (*G*, 395). We should not take the Bible seriously when it tells us to love our neighbour: it is cold, unfeeling, charitable assistance that is really commanded (*G*, 399).

The way to test whether one is acting out of a sense of duty is to inquire into the maxim, or principle, on which one acts; that is to say, the imperative that guides one's action. An imperative may take a hypothetical form: 'If you wish to achieve so-and-so, act in such-and-such a way.' Such an imperative enjoins an action as a means to a particular end. Thus, the maxim of the honest grocer may be the hypothetical imperative: 'If you wish to keep your customers, do not overcharge them.'

A person who acts out of duty, however, is obeying not a hypothetical imperative, but a categorical imperative, which commands: 'No matter what you wish to achieve, act in such-and-such a way.' The categorical imperative of duty is an overarching imperative which discriminates between virtuous and vicious hypothetical imperatives. It is thus formulated by Kant: 'Act only according to a maxim which you can at the same time will to become a universal law.'

Kant gives several examples to illustrate the operation of the categorical imperative. Suppose that I am tempted to get out of a difficulty by making a promise I have no intention of keeping, and I then wonder whether such a lying promise can be reconciled with duty:

I have then to ask myself 'Should I really be content that my maxim (the maxim of getting out of a difficulty by a false promise) should hold as a universal law (one valid both for myself and others)? And could I really say to myself that every one may make a false promise if he finds himself in a difficulty from which he can extricate himself in no other way?' I then become aware at once that I can indeed will to lie, but I can by no means will a universal law of lying; for by such a law there could properly be no promises at all. (*G*, 403)

A second example is this. A well-to-do person is asked to help some others who are suffering hardship. He is tempted to respond: 'What does this matter to me? Let everyone be as happy as Heaven wills or as he can make himself. I won't do him any harm, but I won't help him either.' But when he considers the categorical imperative he comes to realize that he cannot will 'never harm but never help' as a universal maxim because in many situations he will himself need help and sympathy from others (*G*, 423).

These two examples illustrate two different ways in which the categorical imperative operates. In the first case, the vicious maxim cannot be universalized because its universalization leads to contradiction: if no one keeps promises, there is no such thing as promising. In the second case, there is nothing self-contradictory in the idea of no one ever helping anyone else; but no one could rationally *will* to bring about such a situation. Kant says that the two different kinds of case correspond to two different kinds of duties: strict duties (like that of not lying) and meritorious duties (such as that of helping the needy) (*G*, 424).

Kant argues that the categorical imperative rules out suicide. But it is not clear how it does so, in the formulation he has given. There is nothing self-contradictory in the prospect of universal suicide; and someone disgusted with the human race might well applaud the prospect. Kant has, however, a different formulation of the categorical imperative which does not appeal to universalizability: 'Act in such a way that you always treat humanity, whether in your own person or in the person of any other, never simply as a means, but always at the same time as an end.' This formulation is more effective in ruling out suicide, since it can be argued that to take one's own life is to use one's own person as a means of bringing to an end one's discomfort and distress. It also clearly rules out slavery, and in *On Perpetual Peace* Kant argues that it rules out aggressive wars. However, it is hard to see exactly what else it excludes, since we all every day make use, as means to our own ends, of other people from dustmen to solicitors. We need more enlightenment about what it is to treat people 'at the same time as an end'.

What Kant tells us is that as a human being I am not only an end in myself, but a member of a kingdom of ends. In rationally choosing my maxims, I am proposing universal laws; but so too is every other rational being. Universal law is law which is made by rational wills like mine. 'There arises', Kant tells us, 'a systematic union of rational beings under common objective laws—that is a kingdom.' A rational being is subject only to laws that are made by himself and yet are universal: the moral will is autonomous, giving to itself the laws that it obeys. In the kingdom of ends, we are all both legislators and subjects. The idea of the autonomy of the moral will is very attractive; but one wonders how Kant can be so confident that the operation of all the different rational choices of maxim will produce a single system of universal laws. Can we, as he cheerfully tells us to do, 'abstract from the personal differences between rational beings, and also from all the content of their private ends' (G, 433)?

'In the kingdom of ends', Kant tells us, 'everything has either a price or a worth'. If it has a price, something else can be put in its place as a fair exchange; if it is beyond price and is unexchangeable, then it has worth. There are two kinds of price: market price, which is related to the satisfaction of need, and fancy price, which is related to the satisfaction of taste. Morality is above and beyond either kind of price:

Morality, and humanity so far as it is capable of morality, is the only thing which has worth. Skill and diligence in work have a market price; wit, imagination, and humour have a fancy price; but fidelity to promises and benevolence based on principle (not on instinct) have an intrinsic worth. (G, 435)

Kant made room, in the kingdom of ends, for a sovereign or head who was (like the members) a legislator, but who (unlike the members) was not subject to law and did not act out of duty. This sovereign is no doubt God, but he is given no special role in the determination of the moral law. Kant's successors in later centuries, who have been attracted by the idea of the autonomous will as the moral legislator, have quietly dropped the sovereign, and turned the kingdom of ends into a republic of ends, in which no legislator is privileged over any other.

Hegel's Ethical Synthesis

We noticed earlier that Kant's ethics stood at an opposite pole from Aristotle's. For Aristotle the overarching ethical concept was that of happiness, which was the ultimate goal of every fully rational human

In this portrait Hegel radiates the self-confidence appropriate to a philosopher whose thought represented the highest point of human self-consciousness

action. Kant dethroned happiness and put in its place duty, the necessary motive of any action of moral worth. For Aristotle virtue was exhibited in the joy that a good man took in his good actions; for Kant the measure of virtue was the cost in painful effort of its exercise.

Hegel saw Aristotelian ethics and Kantian ethics as thesis and antithesis to which he should offer a synthesis. Like Aristotle he saw the foundation of ethics as a concept of human flourishing; but he defined this in terms of free self-actualization, which accorded with Kant's emphasis on the autonomy of the moral life. Unlike Kant, however, he gave pride of place in moral theory not to the notion of duty, but the notion of right: in Hegel, as in Aristotle, obedience to law takes second place to the free expression of what is best in each person's human nature.

Hegel's great innovation in moral philosophy was that he injected a social and historical element into the notion of 'human nature'. The aims and capacities which an individual can pursue and develop depend on the social institutions within which she lives, and these institutions will vary in different places and times. Rights, which are the basic elements in Hegel's ethics, are claims to exercise one's individual choice within an 'external sphere'—and this sphere is to a large extent defined by the form of the society to which one belongs. Hegel demonstrates this in a famous passage of the *Phenomenology of Spirit* which sets out how individual self-consciousness develops as a consciousness of one's role in relation to others. The example of a social relation he chooses to illustrate the point is that of master and slave.

Initially a master is fully self-conscious, but sees his slave as a mere thing. The slave is conscious of his master, but sees his own self only in his relation to the master's purposes. The master recognizes selfhood only in himself, and the slave recognizes it only in his master. However, as the slave is set to work to produce benefits for the master, the relationship changes. As his labour transforms matter into useful products, the slave becomes aware of his own power, but finds his goals still limited by the master's commands. The master, on the other hand, sees his own self-consciousness as limited through his inability to find a responsive self-consciousness in the slave. The relationship denies to each of them a full measure of self-consciousness (*PG*, 178–96).

Hegel traces through history attempts to remove the obstacles to self-consciousness set by the master–slave relationship. Stoicism encouraged people to accept their social position as a matter of cosmic necessity, to be accepted with tranquillity: both the slave Epictetus and the Emperor Marcus Aurelius embraced Stoicism. But looking within and turning one's back on society does not really resolve the contradictions implicit in the master–slave relationship. It leads on to the second form of false consciousness, the sceptical attitude which outwardly conforms to society's demands while inwardly denying the reality of the norms which society proclaims. The contrast between inner and outer attitudes becomes intolerable, and consciousness passes into a third false stage, which Hegel calls 'The Unhappy Consciousness', and which he regards as typical of medieval Christendom.

In the unhappy consciousness the contradictions of the master–slave relationship are recreated within a single individual self. A person is conscious of a gap between an ideal self and his own imperfect self, the latter a false self, the former a true but as yet unrealized self. The ideal self is then projected into another world and identified with a God of which the actual self is no part. Thus a person's consciousness is divided, and he becomes 'alienated' from it. This concept of alienation—of treating as alien something with which by rights one should identify—was to have a powerful future among Hegel's disciples.

All such forms of false consciousness represent an attempt to interiorize a problem that can only be solved by a change in social institutions. The realization of this is what accounts for the emphasis that Hegel places on rights. A person has an inalienable right to life and to freedom from slavery, and to a minimum of personal property; only societies that protect these rights can provide a context for individual human flourishing (PR, 46).

Rights are necessary because an individual person can only express herself as a free spirit by giving herself an external sphere of freedom. A right is an entitlement to property interpreted in a broad sense; for Hegel, a person's body, life, and liberty are his property no less than material things. Some rights, like the right to the products of one's labour, can be given up; but no one can relinquish her total freedom by accepting slavery.

Besides rights to property Hegel recognizes two other forms of right: rights of contract and rights of punishment. The former are embodied in the civil law, and the latter in the criminal law. Hegel's view of punishment is retributive: it is an annulment of wrongdoing, implicitly willed by the criminal himself since his crime was itself a violation of the universal will (PR, 99–100).

The theory of rights, important though it is for Hegel, is only one of three sections of his ethics. The other two are the theory of morality (Moralität) and of uprightness (Sittlichkeit). Morality incorporates the Kantian elements of Hegel's system, and uprightness the Aristotelian elements. Morality is defined largely in formal terms; uprightness is described in more concrete examples. Morality is related to duty, and uprightness is related to virtue.

For Hegel, morality is concerned mainly with the motives of the moral agent. Hegel distinguishes between purpose (Absicht) and intention (Vorsatz). The purpose is the overarching motive that relates an action to my welfare; the intention is the immediate end to which I choose a means. (Thus, in taking a particular medication my intention might be to lower my cholesterol level; my purpose is to keep in good health.) Intention is, for Hegel, defined in terms of knowledge: unforeseen consequences of my actions are not intentional. A good purpose is essential if an action is to be morally good.

Hegel resembles Kant in the emphasis he places on the importance of purpose, or ultimate motive. But he does not agree with him that duty is the only morally worthy purpose, and he does not appeal to the principle of universalizability as the criterion of moral acceptibility. Kant's formula of universal law, he complains, allows in some highly suspect maxims (*PR*, 148).

The mere belief that one's purpose is good does not suffice to render an action morally correct. Following one's conscience is indeed necessary, but not sufficient, for virtuous behaviour. Hegel stands at a distance from those subjectivists, before him and after him, who have claimed that the individual conscience is the ultimate court of appeal. Here, as elsewhere, Hegel is well aware of the social context of private judgement.

When we turn to the third section of Hegel's ethical system, uprightness, the social element becomes clearly dominant. For uprightness consists of self-harmony in one's social life; it concerns the concrete, external aspect of ethical behaviour, and this must take place in an institutional setting. This section of the *Philosophy of Right* examines the nature of three social structures in which individuals find themselves: the family, civil society, and the state. Its exposition belongs, therefore, rather to the succeeding chapter on political philosophy than to the present chapter on ethics.

The period covered by this volume is an instructive one for anyone who wishes to inquire to what extent metaphysics is a guide to ethics. Of the great seventeenth-century metaphysicians, Descartes produced an ethical system which, despite the recent respectful attention of scholars, is generally regard as too jejune to be a key to life, while Spinoza devised an ethics which is so closely interwoven with his metaphysics that it can give guidance only to those who share his cosmic outlook. On the other hand, two great philosophers of the eighteenth century still exercise substantial influence on moral philosophy, precisely because their ethics stands at a distance from metaphysics. Hume insisted that moral prescriptions should be quite separate from any judgements of fact, whether physical or (if such were possible) metaphysical: an 'ought' never followed from an 'is'. Kant, on the other hand, though the greatest metaphysician of them all, created a moral system that demands no commitment whatever to other areas of his philosophy. Despite, or perhaps because of, this his contribution to moral philosophy went far beyond that of any other of the philosophers we have been considering. His ethics of duty remains to this day the main competitor to the eudaimonistic virtue ethics of Plato and Aristotle, and to the consequentialist utilitarian ethics that became the most influential moral system of much of the nineteenth and twentieth centuries.

9

Political Philosophy

Machiavelli's Prince

Two works of the decade 1511–20 mark the beginning of modern political philosophy: Machiavelli's *Prince* and More's *Utopia*. Both books are very different from the typical scholastic treatise which seeks to derive, from first principles, the essence of the ideal state and the qualities of a good ruler. One is a brief, stylish, how-to manual; the other is a work of romantic fantasy. The two works stand at opposite ends of the political spectrum. A Machiavellian prince is an absolute autocrat, while Utopia holds out a blueprint for democratic communism. For this reason, the two treatises can be regarded as setting out the parameters for subsequent debate in political philosophy.

It should be said, however, that *The Prince* was not Machiavelli's only political work. He also wrote discourses on Livy in which he set out recipes for republican government parallel to his recipes for monarchical rule. In the course of those discourses he enunciates the following principle:

When a decision is to be taken on which the whole safety of one's country depends, no attention should be paid either to justice or injustice, to kindness or cruelty, to praise or shame. All other considerations should be set aside, and that course adopted which will save the life and preserve the freedom of one's country.[1]

Salus populi suprema lex—'the welfare of the people is the highest law'—was not a wholly new doctrine. Cicero had proclaimed it in theory and acted

---

[1] Quoted in Janet Coleman, *A History of Political Thought from the Middle Ages to the Renaissance* (2000), p. 248.

on it in practice. In *The Prince*, however, it is not only the welfare of the state, but also the welfare of its ruler, which trump all other considerations. The autocratic ruler can, in the appropriate circumstances, ignore legality, morality, and public opinion.

Drawing on his experience as an official and diplomat, and on his reading of ancient history, Machiavelli describes how provinces are won and lost and how they can best be kept under control. If a prince is to take over a state that has been free and self-governing, he must destroy it utterly; otherwise the memory of liberty will always goad the subjects into rebellion. Once in power a prince must strive to appear, rather than to be, virtuous. He should desire to be accounted merciful rather than cruel, but in reality it is safer to be feared than to be loved.

But in order to feared, it is not necessary to make oneself hated. A prince may be feared without being hated:

so long as he does not meddle with the property or with the women of his citizens and subjects. And if constrained to put any to death, he should do so only when there is reasonable justification and manifest cause. But above all, he must abstain from the property of others. For men will sooner forget the death of their father than the loss of their patrimony. (*P*, ch. 17)

Nothing is more important for a prince than to appear to have the virtues of mercy, good faith, humanity, integrity, and piety, and he should never let a word leave his mouth which is not full of those estimable qualities. But in fact, in order to preserve the state, he will frequently be constrained to violate faith and to sin against charity, humanity, and religion. More people will see and hear his admirable professions than will feel the pain of his unscrupulous practice, and thus he will maintain his rule and win his subjects' praise (*P*, ch. 18).

In particular, a prince need not keep a promise when keeping it is hurtful to him and when the reasons for the promise have been removed. He should imitate a fox, no less than a lion, and he will never lack for plausible reasons to cloak a breach of faith. But how will anyone believe princes who constantly break their word? History shows that it is simply a matter of skill in deception. Anyone who has a mind to deceive will have no trouble finding people who are willing to be deceived.

The cool cynicism of Machiavelli's teaching is impressive. Not only does he recommend to princes absolute unscrupulousness; his advice is based on the assumption that all their subjects are gullible and guided solely by self-interest. Some have been shocked by the book's immorality; others have found its lack of humbug refreshing. Few, however, have been persuaded to admire the models held up by Machiavelli, such as Pope Alexander VI and his son Cesare Borgia. Alexander is praised as the arch dissembler: 'No man was ever more effective in making promises, or bound himself by more solemn oaths, or observed them less.' Cesare, who worked by bribery and assassination to appropriate central Italy for the Borgias, and failed to do so only through an unpredictable piece of ill-luck, is saluted as a paradigm of political skill: 'Reviewing thus all the actions of the Duke, I find nothing to blame; on the contrary it seems proper to hold him as an example to be imitated' (P, ch. 18).

The history of the papal states under the Borgia pope, or under his enemy and successor the warrior Pope Julius II, is hard to reconcile with the brief chapter of The Prince devoted to ecclesiastical princedoms. Princes who are churchmen, Machiavelli says, have states that they do not defend and subjects that they do not govern; yet their undefended states are not taken from them, and their ungoverned subjects do not and cannot think of throwing off their allegiance. 'Accordingly, only such princedoms are secure and happy' (P, ch. 11).

More's Utopia

It is hard to know whether this remark was meant ironically, or was a shameless pitch to secure employment in Rome under the new Medici Pope Leo who had succeeded Julius. The passage finds a parallel in More's Utopia, where it is observed that treaties are always solemnly observed in Europe, partly out of reverence for the sovereign pontiffs:

Which, like as they make no promises themselves, but they do very religiously perform the same, so they exhort all princes in any wise to abide by their promises; and them that refuse or deny so to do, by their pontifical power and authority they compel thereto. (U, 116)

Here the intention must surely be ironical. More was willing to die in defence of the papal office; but he was not willing to deceive himself about the perfidy of some of its sixteenth-century holders.

Direct, oblique, and ironical criticism of vicious practices and institutions is a regular feature of *Utopia*. The work—a dialogue between More, just returned from a diplomatic mission to Flanders, Peter Gilles, the town clerk of Antwerp, and a fictitious navigator named Raphael Hythlodaye— is divided into two books. In the first of these, social criticism is direct and pointed; in the second, a mocking mirror is held up to reveal the distortions of contemporary society.

Hythlodaye, we are told in the first book, had been a Portuguese companion of the navigator Amerigo Vespucci, from whom the newly discovered continent of America had taken its name. Left behind by Vespucci in Brazil, he had travelled home via India and had visited many different countries, of which the most remarkable had been Utopia. More and Gilles are anxious to hear him describe it, but before doing so Hythlodaye makes some observations about practices in England. The execution of thieves, he complains, is too harsh a penalty and insufficient as a deterrent to those for whom starvation is the only alternative to robbery. It is altogether unjust that one man should suffer the loss of his life for the loss of someone else's money. Theft should be attacked by removing its cause, which is poverty. This is due to the avarice of noblemen, drones who live on the labour of others: they drive out poor farmers to enclose land for sheep-rearing, which puts up the price of both wool and food.

Hythlodaye presents two arguments against the death penalty for theft. First, it is a violation of the divine command 'Thou shalt not kill'. Second:

Everyone knows how absurd and even dangerous to the commonwealth it is that a thief and a murderer should receive the same punishment. Since the robber sees that he is in as great danger if merely condemned for theft as if he were convicted of murder as well, this reason alone impels him to murder one whom otherwise he would only have robbed ... There is greater safety in putting the man out of the way and greater hope of covering up the crime if he leaves no one left to tell the tale. (*U*, 30)

This argument was to be repeated by reformers until the death penalty for theft was abolished by Parliament in the nineteenth century.[2] But it is the second rather than the first book of *Utopia* that was to make More famous: for it is there that we read the description of the fictitious commonwealth.

---

[2] See, for instance, Macaulay's *Notes on the Indian Penal Code*, in his *Collected Works* (London, 1898), XI.23.

'Utopia' is a Latin transliteration of a Greek name. The Latin 'U' may represent a Greek ου, in which case the name means 'Nowhereland'. Or it may represent a Greek ευ, in which case the name means 'Happyland'. The ambiguity is probably intentional.

Utopia is an island, shaped like a crescent moon, 500 miles long and 200 across at its broadest part. It contains fifty-four cities of 6,000 households apiece, each with its own agricultural hinterland. The farms are worked by the city-dwellers who are sent according to a rota, in batches of twenty, to spend two-year stints in the country. Every year each city sends three elders to meet in a senate in the capital, Amaurot. As described, Amaurot resembles More's London, with one startling difference: there is no such thing as privacy or private property. All houses are open and no door is ever locked.

Every citizen, male or female, in addition to farming learns a craft such as clothworking or carpentry. Only scholars, priests, and elected magistrates are exempt from manual labour There are no drones, and everyone must work, but the working day is only six hours long. How do the Utopians satisfy their needs while working so few hours? It is easy to work this out if you consider how many people in Europe live in idleness:

First, almost all the women which be the half of the whole number: or else, if the women be somewhere occupied, there most commonly in their stead the men be idle. Besides this, how great and how idle a company is there of priests and religious men, as they call them; put thereto all rich men, specially all landed men, which commonly be called gentlemen and noblemen—take into this number also their servants: I mean all that flock of stout bragging swashbucklers. Join to them also sturdy and valiant beggars, cloaking their idle life under the colour of some disease or sickness. (U, 71–2)

Work in Utopia is made light not only by the many hands, but by the simplicity of the needs they serve. Buildings, being communal, are well maintained and do not need constant alteration at the whim of new owners. Clothes do not demand great labour in their manufacture, since Utopians prefer coarse and sturdy wear of undyed cloth.

A big difference between Utopia and Plato's Republic is that the family household is the primary unit of society. Girls, when they grow up, move to the household of their husbands, but sons and grandsons remain in the same household under the rule of the oldest parent so long as he is fit to govern it. No household may contain less than ten or more than sixteen

Frontispiece of the first edition of More's *Utopia*

adults; excess numbers are transferred to other households who have fallen below quota. If the number of households in the city exceeds 6,000, families are transferred to smaller cities. If every city in the island is fully manned, a colony is planted overseas. If the natives there resist settlement, the Utopians will establish it by force of arms, 'for they count this the most just cause of war, when any people holdeth a piece of ground void and vacant to no good and profitable use, keeping others from the use and possession of it which, notwithstanding, by the law of nature, ought thereof to be nourished and relieved' (*U*, 76).

Each household, as has been said, is devoted to a single craft. The households' produce is placed in storehouses in the city centre from which any householder can carry away, free of charge, whatever he needs. The Utopians make no use of money; they employ gold and silver only to make chamber pots and fetters for criminals. Internal travel is regulated by passport; but any authorized traveller is warmly welcomed in other cities. But no one, wherever he may be, is fed unless he has done his daily stint of work.

The women of the households take turns in preparing meals, which are eaten in a common hall, with the men sitting with their backs to the wall facing the women on the outer benches. Nursing mothers and children under five eat apart in a nursery; the children over five wait at table. Before dinner and supper a passage is read from an edifying book; after supper there is music and spices are burnt to perfume the hall. 'For they be much inclined to this opinion: to think no kind of pleasure forbidden, whereof cometh no harm' (*U*, 81).

Utopians indeed are no ascetics, and they regard bodily mortification for its own sake as something perverse. However, they honour those who live selfless lives performing tasks that others reject as loathsome, such as road-building or sick-nursing. Some of these people practise celibacy and are vegetarians; others eat flesh and live normal family lives. The former, they say, are holier, but the latter are wiser.

Males marry at twenty-two and females at eighteen. Premarital intercourse is forbidden, but before the marriage 'a grave and honest matron showeth the woman, be she maid or widow, naked to the wooer; and likewise a sage and discreet man exhibiteth the wooer naked to the woman'. A man would not buy a colt without thorough inspection, the Utopians argue, so it is the height of foolishness to choose a partner for life without having seen more than a face (*U*, 110). In principle, marriage is lifelong, but adultery may break a marriage and in that case the innocent, but not the adulterous, spouse is allowed to remarry. Adultery is severely punished and if repeated incurs the death penalty. On rare occasions, divorce by consent is permitted.

Apart from family law, the Utopians have few laws and no lawyers. Their laws are stated simply enough to need no interpretation, and they think it better that a man should plead his own case and tell the same story to the judge that he would tell to his own attorney.

The Utopians are not pacifists, but they regard war as a matter of necessity rather than of glory: it is justified in order to repel invaders or to liberate peoples oppressed by tyranny. If a Utopian is killed or maimed anywhere, they send an embassy to determine the facts and demand the surrender of wrongdoers; if this is refused, they forthwith declare war. But they prefer to win a war by bribery or assassination rather than by battle and bloodshed; if a pitched battle abroad cannot be avoided they employ foreign mercenaries to fight it for them. In wars of defence in the home-land, husbands and wives stand in battle side by side. 'It is a great reproach and dishonesty for the husband to come home without his wife, or the wife without her husband' (*U*, 125).

The final chapter of Hythlodaye's account concerns Utopian religion. Most Utopians worship a 'godly power, unknown, everlasting, incompre-hensible, inexplicable, far above the capacity and reach of man's wit', which they call 'the father of all'. Utopians do not impose their religious beliefs on others, and toleration is the rule. A Christian convert who proselytized with hellfire sermons was arrested, tried, and banished, 'not as a despiser of religion, but as a seditious person and raiser up of dissension among the people' (*U*, 133). But toleration has limits: anyone who professes that the soul perishes with the body is condemned to silence and forbidden to hold public office. Suicide on private initiative is not permitted, but the incur-ably and painfully sick may, after counselling, take their own lives. Reluc-tance to die is taken as a sign of a guilty conscience, but those who die cheerfully are cremated with songs of joy. When a good man dies 'no part of his life is so oft or gladly talked of, as his merry death'.

There are priests in Utopia—persons of extraordinary holiness 'and therefore very few'. There are thirteen, in fact, in every city, elected by popular vote in secret ballot. Women as well as men may become priests, but only if they are widows of a certain age. The male priests marry the choicest wives. Priests, male and female, take charge of the education of children, have the power to excommunicate for immoral behaviour, and serve as chaplains to the army. On great festivals they wear vestments made from birds' feathers, like those of American Indian chiefs. The service culminates in a solemn prayer in which the worshippers thank God that they belong to the happiest commonwealth and profess the truest of all religions (U, 145).

Like the Platonic Republic, Utopia alternates attractive features with repellent ones, and mixes practicable institutions with lunatic devices. Like Plato, More often leaves his readers to guess how far he is proposing serious political reforms, and how far he is simply using fantasy to castigate the follies and corruption of actual society.

Just and Unjust Wars

When discussing the Utopians' attitude to war, More states: 'Their one and only object in war is to secure that which, had it been obtained beforehand, would have prevented the declaration of war' (U, 120). Such a maxim would rule out all demands for unconditional surrender, and other forms of mission creep. But More, who was himself involved as a politician in more than one of Henry VIII's wars, did not work out systematically the ethical principles which make the difference between just and unjust wars. This was done later in the century by the Jesuit theologian Francisco Suarez.

Suarez, developing ideas to be found in Aquinas, summarizes the classic theory of the just war as follows:

For war to occur honourably several conditions must be observed, which can be reduced to three heads. First, it must be declared by a lawful authority; second, there must be just cause and title; third, the proper means and proportion must be observed in its inception, prosecution and victory. (*De Caritate*, 13. 1.4)

The condition of lawful authority means, for Suarez, that wars may be waged only by sovereign governments. Individuals and groups within a state have no right to settle their differences by force of arms. The pope, however, as a supranational authority, has the right to intervene to settle disputes between Christian sovereigns.

281

Two kinds of just cause are recognized by Suarez. If one's country is attacked, one has the right to defend it in arms. But it can also be legitimate to wage an offensive war: a sovereign may order an attack on another state if that is the only way to remedy a grave injustice to oneself or one's allies. But hostilities may be initiated only if there is good hope of victory; otherwise the recourse to arms will fail to remedy the injustice which provided the initial ground for war.

The third condition has three elements. Before beginning war, a sovereign must offer the potential enemy the opportunity to remedy the evil complained of. Only if he fails to do so may he be attacked. In the course of the war, only such violence must be used as is necessary to achieve victory. After the war, compensation and just punishment may be exacted, and wartime wrongdoers may be executed.

The second of these elements, Suarez says, rules out deliberate attacks on innocent people. But who are the innocent? Suarez gives a definition that is narrower than that of some of his successors. Children, women, and those unable to bear arms are declared innocent by the natural law, and positive law rules out attacks on ambassadors and clerics. But all others, Suarez maintains, are legitimate targets. 'All other persons are considered guilty, for human judgement looks upon those able to take up arms as having actually done so' (13.7.10). Suarez accepts too that in war it is likely that some innocent people will be killed as part of the collateral damage inflicted in the course of an attack. What is ruled out is the deliberate targeting of the innocent.

Suarez sees his rules as primarily binding on sovereigns: it is they who have the duty to satisfy themselves that, on the balance of probabilities, the war they are contemplating is a just one. A regular soldier, ordered to fight, can assume that the war is just unless it is manifestly unjust; and even a mercenary volunteer can put the burden of the inquiry on to the commander of his brigade.

Suarez's teaching on the morality of warfare was taken over without acknowledgement and given much wider circulation by Hugo Grotius, a polymath Dutch lawyer and diplomat who published in 1625 a celebrated treatise, *De Iure Belli et Pacis* ('On the rights and wrongs of war and peace'). This set the doctrine of the just war in the context of a moral theory which was deliberately designed to be detachable from the notion of divine law. This did not at all mean that Grotius was an unbeliever, but his experience of the wars of religion, and the frustration of his own efforts in aid of Christian unification, led him to conclude that particular religious beliefs were an unreliable foundation for a sound international order.

Hobbes on Chaos and Sovereignty

Suarez and Grotius saw warfare as a sometimes necessary deviation from a natural order in which states would coexist harmoniously within a consensual moral framework. The most famous political philosopher of the seventeenth century, Thomas Hobbes, had a directly contrary view of the nature of politics: the natural state of free human beings was one of perpetual warfare, and it was the prime task of the moral philosopher to justify the consent of individuals to live in peaceful subjection to a government. To this he devoted his masterpiece *Leviathan*.

Hobbes draws a sombre picture of the natural condition of mankind. Men are roughly equal in their natural powers of body and mind. 'From this equality of ability, ariseth equality of hope in the attaining of our ends. And therefore if any two men desire the same thing, which nevertheless they cannot both enjoy, they become enemies.' Whether they are seeking pleasure, or aiming simply at self-preservation, men find themselves in competition with each other. Each man distrusts his competitors and fears attack, so he seeks by anticipation to overpower them. Each man seeks praise from his companions, and resents any sign of dispraise. 'So that in the nature of man, we find three principal causes of quarrel. First, competition; secondly diffidence; thirdly glory' (*L*, 82 3).

Unless and until there is a common power to keep men in awe, there will be constant quarrelsome and unregulated competition for goods, power, and glory. This can be described as a state of war: a war of every man against every man. In such conditions, Hobbes says, there can be no industry, agriculture, or commerce:

no knowledge of the face of the earth; no account of time; no arts; no letters; no society; and, which is worst of all, continual fear and danger of violent death; and the life of man, solitary, poor, nasty, brutish and short. (*L*, 84)

Some readers may think this picture too gloomy; surely there was never such a time of universal war. Perhaps not throughout the world, Hobbes

Piero di Cosimo's representation of a state of mankind when life was nasty, brutish, and short

admits, but we can see instances of it in contemporary America; and even in civilized countries, men are always taking precautions against their fellows. Let the reader consider that 'when taking a journey, he arms himself, and seeks to go well accompanied; when going to sleep, he locks his doors; when even in his house, he locks his chests; and this when he knows there be laws and public officers' (L, 84).

Hobbes insists that in describing the primeval state of war, he is not accusing human beings in their natural state of any wickedness. In the absence of laws there can be no sin, and in the absence of a sovereign there can be no law. In the state of nature, the notions of right and wrong, or justice and injustice, have no place. 'Where there is no common power, there is no law: where no law, no injustice. Force, and fraud, are in war the two

cardinal virtues.' Likewise, there is no property or ownership, 'but only that to be every man's, that he can get; and for so long, as he can keep it' (*L*, 85).

Philosophers are accustomed to speak of a natural law (*lex naturalis*) and a right of nature (*ius naturale*). It is important, Hobbes insists, to distinguish between laws and rights. A right is a liberty to do or forbear doing something. A law is a command to do or forbear something. In a state of nature there are, strictly speaking, neither laws nor rights. But there are 'laws of nature': principles of rational self-interest; recipes for maximizing the chances of survival. And because there is a necessity of nature that each man desires his own good, there is a right of nature that every man may preserve his own life and limbs with all the power he has. Since he has a right to this end, he has a right to all necessary means to it, including a right to the bodies of others (*L*, 87).

As long as men retain this right, no man has security of living out his natural life. Rational self-interest, therefore, urges a man to give up some of the unfettered liberty conferred by this right in return for equal concessions by others. Thus there is a law of nature:

That a man be willing, when others are so too, as far forth, as for peace, and defence of himself he shall think it necessary, to lay down this right to all things; and be contented with so much liberty against other men, as he would allow other men against himself. (*L*. 87)

This and other laws of nature lead men to transfer all their rights, except that of basic self-defence, to a central power which is able to enforce the laws of nature by punitive sanctions.

Among the other laws of nature (Hobbes lists nineteen in all), the most important is the third 'that men keep their covenants made'. A covenant, for Hobbes, is a particular form of contract. A contract is a transfer of right to another in consideration of a reciprocal benefit. A covenant is a contract in which—unlike immediate buying and selling—there is an element of trust. At least one party to a covenant leaves the other party to perform his part of the bargain at a later time. Without the third law of nature, Hobbes says, 'covenants are in vain and but empty words; and the right of all men to all things remaining, we are still in the condition of war'. It is this law that is the foundation of the notions of justice and injustice; for injustice is precisely the failure to perform a covenant; and whatever is not unjust is just (*L*, 95–6).

But covenants do not bind where there is a fear of non-performance on either part, as there is bound to be in the state of nature. 'Therefore before the names of just, and unjust can have place, there must be some coercive power, to compel men equally to the performance of their covenants, by the terror of some punishment, greater than the benefit they expect by the breach of their covenant.' Before the establishment of a commonwealth there is no such power: 'Covenants, without the sword, are but words, and of no strength to secure a man at all' (*L*, 95–6, 111).

The only way to set up a common power is for men to 'confer all their power and strength to one man, or one assembly of men, that may reduce all their wills, by plurality of voices, unto one will'. Each man must say to every other man 'I give up my right of governing myself, to this man, or to this assembly of men, on this condition, that thou give up thy right to him and authorise all his actions in like manner.' The central authority then personifies the entire multitude, and the multitude united in a single person is called a Commonwealth. 'This is the generation of that great Leviathan, or to speak more reverently, of that mortal god, to which we owe under the immortal God our peace and defence'. The covenant made by the members of the commonwealth sets up a sovereign, and makes all the covenanting members his subjects.

There may seem to be a vicious circle in Hobbes' account. He says that there cannot be binding covenants, unless there is a sovereign to enforce them; and there cannot be a sovereign unless he is set in office by a binding covenant. To solve this difficulty, we must appreciate that the covenant and the sovereign come into existence simultaneously. The sovereign is not himself a party to the covenant, and therefore cannot be in breach of it. It is his function to enforce, not only the original covenant that constitutes the state but individual covenants that his subjects make with one another.

Although Hobbes made no secret that he was himself a royalist, he deliberately left it open in his political theory whether the sovereign should be an individual or an assembly. Had he not done so, he could hardly with consistency have returned in 1652 to an England ruled over by Parliament. But whether the sovereign authority is a monarchy, an aristocracy, or a democracy, *Leviathan* insists that its rule must be absolute. A sovereign cannot forfeit his power, and no subject can accuse his sovereign of injustice. Because the sovereign personifies the multitude, every subject is the author of every action of the sovereign, and so he cannot make any complaint about such actions. 'No man that hath sovereign power can justly be put to death, or otherwise in any manner by his subjects punished. For seeing every subject is author of the actions of his sovereign; he punisheth another, for the actions committed by himself' (*L*, 118).

The sovereign is the source of law and of property rights. He has the right to determine what means are necessary for the defence of the commonwealth, and it is his prerogative to make war and peace with other nations. He is the arbiter of all contested lawsuits, and it is for him to decide what opinions and doctrines may be maintained within the commonwealth. He alone has the power to appoint, and to reward and punish, all ministers and magistrates. If the sovereign is a monarch, he has the right to dispose of the succession to the throne (*L*, 118–20).

Finally, the sovereign is supreme in matters of religion. It is for the sovereign, and not for any presbytery or bishop, to determine which books are to be accepted as Holy Scripture and in what way they are to be interpreted. The insolent interpretations of fanatical sectaries have been the cause of civil war in England, but the greatest usurpation of sovereignty in the name of religion is to be found in Rome. 'If a man will consider the originall of this great Ecclesiastical Dominion, he will easily perceive, that the Papacy is no other, than the Ghost of the deceased Roman Empire, sitting crowned upon the grave thereof' (L, 463).

Under a Hobbesian sovereign, what liberty is left to the subject? Liberty is no more than the silence of the law: the subject has liberty to do whatever the sovereign has not regulated by law. Thus, a subject has liberty to buy and sell, to choose his abode, his diet, and his trade; parents have liberty to educate their children as they think fit. But does a subject ever have liberty to disobey a sovereign's command? One might expect Hobbes to answer 'Never!'—to do so would be to disobey oneself. But in fact he allows ample scope for civil disobedience:

If the sovereign command a man (though justly condemned) to kill, wound, or maim himself; or not to resist those that assault him; or to abstain from the use of food, air medicine, or any other thing, without which he cannot live; yet hath that man the liberty to disobey. (L, 144)

A subject cannot be compelled to incriminate himself, nor is he bound in justice to fight as a soldier at his sovereign's command. Allowance must be made, Hobbes says, for natural timorousness, not only in women but in men 'of feminine courage'. To avoid battle may be cowardly, but it is not unjust. The one occasion when military service is obligatory is when the defence of the commonwealth requires the enlistment of all who are able to bear arms. Finally, 'the obligation of subjects to the sovereign is understood to last as long, and no longer, than the power lasteth, by which he is able to protect them'. Accordingly, if the sovereign fails to fulfil his principal function, that of protecting his subjects, then their obligation to him lapses.

The theory of commonwealth presented in Leviathan is an original and powerful intellectual system whose structure has been reflected in the work of political philosophers from Hobbes' day to our own. The system is not totalitarian, in spite of its emphasis on absolute sovereignty, because within it the state exists for the sake of the citizens, not the other way round. Despite his loyalty to Stuart sovereigns, Hobbes did not believe in the doctrine of the divine right of kings propounded by the founder of that dynasty, King James I. For him, the rights of the sovereign derive not from God but from the rights of those individuals who renounce them to become his subjects. In this doctrine, Hobbes' closest precursor was Marsilius of Padua, who had insisted in the fourteenth century that the laws enacted by rulers derived their legitimacy, not directly from God, but only through the mediation of the citizens' consent.[3] But Hobbes is the first philosopher to derive the legitimacy of a ruler directly from a covenant of the citizens, without any authorization by God over and above his role as the ultimate cause of human nature.

Spinoza's Political Determinism

The political theory put forward by Spinoza in his *Tractatus Theologico Politicus* in 1670 resembles that of Hobbes in *Leviathan* two decades earlier. Both philosophers were determinists, and both started from a view of human nature as fundamentally egoistic. 'It is the sovereign law and right of nature', Spinoza tells us, 'that each individual should endeavour to preserve itself as it is, without regard to anything but itself.' When Spinoza talks of natural laws, he does not mean a set of commands or principles that human beings are obliged to obey: he means rather the underlying natural regularities that determine the behaviour of all things, living or inert. Fishes have natural rights no less than men, and in the context of the eternal order of nature humans are no more than a speck (E I. 200–13).

An individual's natural rights are not determined by reason but by desire and power; everyone, wise or foolish, has a right to whatever he wants and can get; nature prohibits only what no one wants and no one can achieve. However, it is better for men to live according to laws and dictates of reason, for every one is ill at ease in the midst of enmity, hatred, anger, and deceit, even though all these are legitimate in the state of nature. So men must make an agreement to be guided by reason, to repress harmful desires, and to do as they would be done by.

But an agreement between one individual and another, Spinoza maintains, is only valid as long as it is useful; I can break any promise once it ceases to be to my advantage to keep it. It is necessary, therefore, to back up contracts with the threat of some greater evil than the evil which will tempt

[3] See vol. II, p. 93.

men to break it. This can only be achieved 'if each individual hands over the whole of his power to the body politic, which will then possess sovereign natural right over all things'. This power, like Hobbes' sovereign, will be bound by no laws, and everyone will be bound to obey it in all things.

But the rights of the sovereign in civil society, like the rights of the individual in a state of nature, extend only so far as his power. If he lacks the power to enforce his will, he lacks also the right. For this reason the transfer of power from individual to state can never be complete: a sovereign cannot command the inner affections of the subject (E I. 214). Here Spinoza explicitly dissociates himself from Hobbes: no man's mind can possibly lie wholly at the disposition of another, for no one can willingly transfer his natural right of free reason and judgement or be compelled to do so. In a democracy, which Spinoza believed to be the most natural form of government, 'no one transfers his natural right so absolutely that he has no further choice in affairs, he only hands it over to the majority of a society, whereof he is a unit. Thus all men remain, as they were in the state of nature, equals' (E II. 368). Moreover, Spinoza offers a more positive reason than Hobbes does for subjecting oneself to the sovereignty of the state. It is not simply for security from attack by others; it is also to provide the context for a life of full self-realization.

From his abstract theory of the state, combined with reflections upon history, especially that of the Hebrews, Spinoza derives a number of quite specific political conclusions. One is that it always leads to trouble if the clergy are given political power. Another is that good governments will allow freedom of religious belief and philosophical speculation. Everyone should be free to choose for himself his basic creed, because laws directed against mere opinion only irritate the upright without constraining any criminal. Finally, Spinoza warns that once you set up a monarchy, it is very difficult to get rid of it. In proof of this he points to the recent history of England, where the dethronement of a lawful king was followed by the rule of a much greater tyrant.

Locke on Civil Government

Spinoza was writing after the restoration of King Charles II, and it was in his reign that the theory of divine right of kings became a major issue for

English philosophers. In 1680, the year after the death of Hobbes, a book called *Patriarcha, or the Natural Power of Kings* was published. This had been written years earlier by a royalist landowner, Sir Robert Filmer, who had died during the commonwealth. It compared the monarch's power over the nation to a father's power over his family. The king's authority, it claimed, derived by patriarchal descent from the royal authority of Adam, and should be free of all restraint by elected bodies such as Parliament. Filmer's book presented an easy target for the most politically influential philosopher of the age, John Locke.

Like Hobbes, Locke in his *Two Treatises of Civil Government* takes his start from a consideration of the state of nature. Filmer's great error, he maintains, is to deny that by nature men are free and equal to each other. In the natural state, men live together without any earthly superior. 'All men', he maintains, 'are naturally in that state and remain so till by their own consents they make themselves members of some politic society' (*TG*, 2, 15).

Locke's view of the state of nature is much more optimistic than Hobbes. It is not a state of war, because everyone is aware of a natural law which teaches that all men are equal and independent, and that no one ought to harm another in his life, liberty, or possession. This law is binding prior to any earthly sovereign or civil society. It confers natural rights, notably the rights to life, self-defence, and freedom. No one can take away a right to life, whether his own or others'; and no one can take away the right to liberty by enslaving himself or another.

What of property in the state of nature? Is the whole earth the common possession of mankind, as earlier political theorists had argued, or did God assign different portions of it to different peoples and families? Or is there no such thing as private property prior to all organized society?

Locke's answer is ingenious. What gives a title to private property, even in a state of nature, is labour. My labour is undoubtedly my own; and by mixing my labour with natural goods, by drawing water, clearing forests, tilling the soil, and collecting fruit, I acquire a right to what I have worked on and what I have made of it. But my right is not unlimited: I am entitled only to such fruits of my labour as I can consume, and only to the amount of land that I can cultivate and use (*TG*, 5, 49). However, what I have thus acquired I can pass on to my children; the right of inheritance is natural and precedes any civil codification.

For Locke, then, unlike Hobbes, property rights precede and do not depend upon any covenant. However, in the state of nature men have only a precarious hold on their property. Other men, although aware of the teachings of nature, may transgress them, and there is no central authority to discipline them. Individuals have a theoretical right to punish; but they may lack power to do so, and it is unsatisfactory for everyone to be judge in his own case. It is this that leads to the institution of the state, by the only possible means, namely, by men agreeing together to give up some of their natural liberty 'to join and unite into a community for their comfortable, safe, and peaceable living one amongst another, in a secure enjoyment of their properties and a great security against any that are not of it' (*TG*, 8, 95).

Individual members of society therefore transfer whatever powers they have to enforce the law of nature to a central authority. A government has more power, and can be expected to be more impartial, in enforcing individuals' property rights than any isolated individual could hope to be. The existence of a central government, set up by consent, gives authority to two institutions whose legitimacy was doubtful in the mere state of nature: namely, the enclosure of land, and the institution of money. These institutions make it lawful to produce and enjoy more than is necessary for one's immediate subsistence, and this in turn benefits the whole of society.

The citizens hand over to a legislature the right to make laws for the common good, and to an executive the right to enforce these laws. (Locke was aware of good reasons for separating these two branches of government.) The legislature and executive may take several differen forms: it is for a majority of the citizens (or at least of the property owners) to decide which form to adopt. But a problem arises if—as Locke believed—the power of enforcing the laws includes the right to exact capital punishment. The initial contractors can hand over only what rights they have, but no one has, by the natural law, the right to commit suicide. How then can anyone confer on anyone else the right—even a conditional right—to kill him? Surely only God can confer such a right; and this was one of Filmer's arguments for deriving the authority of sovereigns directly from God.

This, however, was only one of the objections that Locke's contemporaries and successors could make to his theory of social contract. The most common was that there were no records of any such contracts ever being made. Locke offered some implausible historical examples, but more important was his distinction between explicit and implicit consent. The maintenance of any government, he insisted, depended on the continuing consent of the citizens in each generation. Such consent, he admits, is rarely explicit, but implicit consent is given by anyone who enjoys the benefits of society, whether by accepting an inheritance or merely by travelling on the highway. He can always renounce his consent by migrating to another country, or going into the wilderness to live in the state of nature.

The principal way in which Locke's social compact differs from Hobbes' convention is that the governors, unlike Hobbes' sovereign, are themselves parties to the initial contract. They hold their powers as trustees for the community, and if the government breaches the trust placed in it, the people can remove or alter it. Laws must fulfil three conditions: they must be equal for all; they must be designed for the good of the people; and they must not impose any taxation without consent. 'The supreme power cannot take from any man any part of his property without his consent.' A ruler who violates these rules, and governs in his own interest, rather than for the common good, is then at war with his subjects and rebellion is justified as a form of self-defence. When he published his *Treatises* Locke obviously had in mind the autocratic rule of the Stuart kings and the Glorious Revolution of 1688.

Locke's system is not original and is not consistent, as many later critics were to point out. It combines uneasily elements from medieval theories of natural law and post-Renaissance theories of voluntary confederation. Nonetheless, it was very influential, and its influence continued among people who had ceased to believe in theories of the state of nature and the natural law that underpinned them. The Founding Fathers of the United States drew heavily on the *Second Treatise* to argue that King George III, no less than the Stuart monarchs, had by arbitrary government and unrepresentative taxation forfeited his claim to rule and made himself the enemy of his American subjects.

Montesquieu on Law

The American Constitution also owed much to the French philosopher, Montesquieu, who was nearly sixty years Locke's junior. Montesquieu assembled a great mass of geographical, historical, and sociological data, of uneven reliability, on which to construct a theory of the nature of the state. 'Men', he tells us, 'are governed by many factors: climate, religion, law, the precepts of government, the examples of the past, customs, manners; and from the combination of such influences there arises a general spirit.' The general spirit of a particular society finds its expression in the laws appropriate for it; it creates 'the spirit of the laws', which was the title of Montesquieu's political treatise.

Montesquieu believed that there were fundamental laws of justice established by God, which preceded actual human legislation in the same way as the properties of triangles preceded their codification by geometers. But these universal principles were not in themselves sufficient to determine the appropriate structure for particular societies. It is not possible to single out a particular set of social institutions as suitable for all times and places: the government should be fitted to the climate, the wealth, and the national character of a country.

Aristotle had studied a wide variety of constitutions and classified them into three kinds: monarchy, aristocracy, and democracy.[4] Montesquieu, likewise, after his sociological inquiries, comes up with a threefold classification, but his types are republican, monarchical, and despotic. (With a bow to Aristotle, he divides republics into democratic and aristocratic republics (EL II.1).) Each type of state is marked by a dominant characteristic: virtue, honour, and fear, respectively.

Such are the principles of the three governments; which does not mean that in a certain republic people are virtuous, but that they ought to be. This does not prove that in a certain monarchy people have a sense of honour, and that in particular despotic states people have a sense of fear, but that they ought to have it. Without these qualities a government will be imperfect (EL III.2).

In a despotic state, rule is by the decree of the ruler, backed up not by law but by religion or custom. In a monarchy, government is carried on by a hierarchy of officials of varied rank and status. In a republic, all the citizens need to be educated in civic values and trained to carry out public tasks.

Republics, we are told, suit cold climates and small states; despotism suits large states and hot climates. A constitution suitable for Sicilians would not suit Scotsmen, since, *inter alia*, sea-girt islands differ from mountainous

---

[4] See vol. I, p. 82ff.

mainlands. Montesquieu's own preference, however, is for monarchy, and particularly the 'mixed monarchy' he discerned in England.

The feature that Montesquieu admired in the British Constitution, and that found its way into the American Constitution, was the principle of the separation of powers. After the revolution of 1688 Parliament had achieved sole legislative power, while leaving in practice considerable executive discretion to the king's ministers, and judges became very largely free of governmental interference. There was not—and is not to this day—to be found in British constitutional law any explicit statement that the legislative, executive, and judicial branches of government should not be combined in a single person or institution, or any formulated theory of checks and balances. Nonetheless, Montesquieu's benign interpretation of the Hanoverian system, in which the power of a sovereign's ministers essentially depended on the consent of Parliament, had a lasting influence on constitution makers in many parts of the world.

The separation of powers was important, Montesquieu believed, because it provided the best bulwark against tyranny and the best guarantee of the liberty of the subject. What, then, is liberty? 'Liberty', Montesquieu replies, 'is a right of doing whatever the laws permit' (EL XI.3). Is that all, we may wonder; doesn't a citizen of a tyranny enjoy that much freedom? We must first remember that for Montesquieu a despot ruled not by law but by decree: only an instrument created by an independent legislature counts as a law. Secondly, in many countries, including the France of Montesquieu's own time, citizens have often been at risk of arbitrary arrest for actions that were perfectly legal but were regarded as offensive by those in power.

Montesquieu offered another, more substantial, definition of liberty. It does not consist in freedom from all restraint, but 'in the power of doing what we ought to will and in not being constrained to do what we ought not to will' (EL XI.3). This link between liberal social institutions and an idealized form of the individual will was developed into a substantial political theory by Jean-Jacques Rousseau in his *Social Contract*.

Rousseau and the General Will

When Rousseau begins by saying 'Man is born free, and he is everywhere in chains,' those who have read his earlier works on the corrupting effect of civilization are likely to assume that the chains are those of social institutions, and that we are about to be encouraged to reject the social order. Instead, we are told that it is a sacred right which is the basis of all other rights. Social institutions, Rousseau now thinks, liberate rather than enslave.

Like Hobbes and Locke, Rousseau begins with a consideration of human beings in a state of nature. His account of such a state is, in accordance with his earlier thoughts about the noble savage, more optimistic than Hobbes'. In a state of nature men are not necessarily hostile to each other. They are motivated by self-love, to be sure, but self-love is not the same as egoism: it can be combined, in both humans and animals, with sympathy and compassion for one's fellows. In a state of nature a man has only simple, animal, desires: 'the only goods he acknowledges in the world are food, a female, and sleep; the only ills he fears are pain and hunger'. These desires are not as inherently competitive as the quest for power in more sophisticated societies.

Rousseau agrees with Hobbes, against Locke, that in a state of nature there are no property rights and therefore neither justice nor injustice. But as society develops from its primitive state, the lack of such rights begins to be felt. Economic cooperation and technical progress make it necessary to form an association for the protection of individuals' persons and possessions. How can this be done while allowing each member of the association to remain as free as he was before? The *Social Contract* provides the solution by presenting the concept of the general will.

The general will comes into existence when 'each of us puts his person and all his power in common under the supreme direction of the general will, and, in our corporate capacity, we receive each member as an indivisible part of the whole' (*SC* 1. 6). This compact creates a public person, a moral and collective body, the state or sovereign people. Every individual is both a citizen and a subject: as a citizen he shares in the sovereign authority, and as subject owes obedience to the laws of the state.

Rousseau's sovereign, unlike Hobbes' sovereign, has no existence independent of the contracting citizens who compose it. Consequently, it can have no interest independent of theirs: it expresses the general will and it cannot go wrong in its pursuit of the public good. Men lose their natural liberty to grasp whatever tempts them, but they gain civil liberty, which permits the stable ownership of property.

In this contemporary etching Rousseau appears more proud of his opera, *Le Devin du Village*, than of the *Social Contract*, which is tossed to the ground

But what is the general will, and how is it to be ascertained? It is not the same as the unanimous will of the citizens: Rousseau distinguished between 'the general will' and 'the will of all'. An individual's will may go contrary to the general will. 'There is often considerable difference between the will of all and the general will. The latter is concerned only with the common interest, the former with interests that are partial, being itself but the sum of particular wills' (SC 3. 3). Should we say then that the general will should be identified with the will of the majority of the citizens? No, the deliberations of a popular assembly are by no means infallible: voters may suffer from ignorance, or be swayed by individual self-interest.

It appears to follow that even the general will is not ascertainable even by a referendum, and this seems to make it an abstraction of no practical value. But Rousseau believed that it could be determined by plebiscite on two conditions: first, that every voter was fully informed, and second, that no two voters held any communication with each other. The second condition is laid down to prevent the formation of groups smaller than the whole community. 'It is essential,' Rousseau wrote, 'if the general will is to be able to express itself, that there should be no partial society within the State, and that each citizen should think only his own thoughts' (SC 2. 3). So not only political parties but religious groups also must be banned if the general will is to find expression in a referendum. It is only within the context of the entire community that the differences between the self-interest of individuals will cancel out and yield the self-interest of the sovereign people as a whole.

Rousseau is no devotee in principle of the separation of powers. The sovereignty of the people, he says, is indivisible: if you separate the powers of the legislative and executive branches you make the sovereignty chimerical. However, a practical division of responsibility follows from his requirement that the sovereign people should legislate only on very general matters, leaving executive power concerning particular issues in the hands of a government which is an intermediary between subjects and sovereign. But the government must always act as a delegate of the people, and ideally a popular assembly should meet at regular intervals to confirm the constitution and to renew or terminate the mandate of the holders of public office.

The type of arrangement here proposed by Rousseau seems practicable only in a Swiss canton or a city-state like Geneva. But he insisted, like Montesquieu, that one cannot specify a single form of government as appropriate to all circumstances. However, an issue of much wider application is raised by the theory of the general will. A citizen in a Rousseauian state gives his consent to all the laws, including those that are passed in spite of his opposition (*SC* 4. 2). What, in such a polity, are the rights of dissident minorities?

Rousseau says that the social compact tacitly includes an undertaking that whoever refuses to submit to it may be constrained by his fellow citizens to conform to it. 'This means nothing other than that he shall be forced to be free.' If I vote against a measure which then triumphs in a poll, this shows that I was mistaken about where my true good, and my genuine freedom, were to be found. But the freedom that an imprisoned malefactor enjoys is only the rather rarefied freedom to be a reluctant expression of the general will.

In spite of his concern with the general will, Rousseau was not a wholehearted supporter of democracy in practice. 'If there were a people of gods, they would govern themselves democratically. But a government of such perfection is not suitable for human beings' (*SC* 3. 4). In a direct democracy where rule is by popular assembly, government is likely to be fractious and inefficient. Better have an elective aristocracy in which the wise govern the masses: 'there is no point in getting twenty thousand men to do what a hundred select men can do ever better' (*SC* 3. 1). Aristocracy demands fewer virtues in the citizens than democracy does—all that it requires is a spirit of moderation in the rich and of contentment in the poor. Naturally, the rich will do most of the governing: they have more time to spare.

This seems a tame and bourgeois conclusion to a book that began by calling mankind to throw off its chains. Nonetheless, the concept of the general will had an explosive revolutionary potential. Examined closely, the notion is theoretically incoherent and practically vacuous. It is not true as a matter of logic that if A wills A's good and B wills B's good, then A and B jointly will the good of A and B. This remains true, however well informed A and B may be, because there may be a genuine, unavoidable incompatibility between the goods of each.

It is precisely the difficulty of determining what the general will prescribes that made the notion of the general will such a powerful tool in the hands of demagogues. Robespierre at the height of the French revolutionary terror could claim that he was expressing the general will, and forcing citizens to be free. Who was in a position to contradict him? The conditions Rousseau laid down for the general will's expression were that every citizen should be fully informed and that no two citizens should be allowed to combine with each other. The first condition could never be fulfilled outside a community of gods, and the second condition of its nature demands a totally tyranny to enforce.

For better or worse, the *Social Contract* became the bible of revolutionaries, and not only in France; Rousseau's influence was enormous. Napoleon, never one to underestimate his own importance, attributed to Rousseau an equal responsibility with himself for the gigantic changes that Europe underwent as the eighteenth century turned into the nineteenth. 'Who can tell', he asked as he approached death, 'whether the world would be a better place if Rousseau and I had never lived?'

Hegel on the Nation-State

Rousseau's notion of the general will was taken up, in different ways, by Kant and Hegel. Kant sought to give it a non-mythical form as a universal consensus of moral agents each legislating universal laws for themselves and for all others. Hegel transformed it into the freedom of the world-spirit expressing itself in the history of mankind.

There seems a vast difference, Hegel realized, between his thesis of the evolution of the spirit into ever greater freedom and self-consciousness, and the dismal spectacle presented by actual history. He accepted that nothing seemed to happen in the world except as the result of the self-interested actions of individuals; and he was willing to describe history as the slaughterhouse in which the happiness of peoples, the wisdom of states, and the virtues of individuals are sacrificed. But the gloom, he maintained, is not justified; for the self-interested actions of individuals are the only means by which the ideal destiny of the world can be realized. 'The Ideal provides the warp, and human passions the woof, of the web of history.'

Human actions are performed in social contexts, and self-interest need not be egoistic. One can find self-fulfilment in the performance of social roles: my love of my family and my pride in my profession contribute to my happiness without being forms of selfishness. Conversely, social institutions are not a restraint on my freedom: they expand my freedom by giving a wider scope to my possibilities of action. This is true of the family, and it is true also of what Hegel calls 'civil society'—voluntary organizations such as clubs and businesses. It is true above all of the state, which provides the widest scope for freedom of action, while at the same time furthering the purposes of the world-spirit *(Weltgeist)*.

Ideally, a state should be so organized that the private interests of the citizens coincide with the common interests of the state. In respect of history, states and peoples themselves count among the individuals who are, unconsciously, the instruments by which the world-spirit achieves its object. There are also some unique figures, great men like Caesar or Napoleon, who have a special role in expressing the will of the world-spirit, and who see the aspects of history which are ripe for development in their time.

Such people, however, are the exception, and the normal development of the world-spirit is through the spirit of particular peoples or nations, the *Volksgeist*. That spirit shows itself in the culture, religion, and philosophy of a people, as well as in its social institutions. Nations are not necessarily identical with states—indeed, when Hegel wrote, the German nation had not yet turned itself into a German state—but only in a state does a nation become self-conscious of itself.

The creation of the state is the high object for which the world-spirit uses individuals and peoples as its instruments. A state for Hegel is not just a coercive instrument for keeping the peace or for protecting property: it is a platform for new and higher purposes which extend the liberty of individuals by giving a new dimension to their lives. The state, as the incarnation of freedom, exists for its own sake. All the worth, all the spiritual reality which the individual citizen possesses, he possesses only through the state. For only by participating in social and political life is he fully conscious of his own rationality, and of himself as a manifestation, through the folk-spirit, of the world-spirit. The state, Hegel says, is the divine Idea as it exists on earth.

The divine Idea, however, is not yet fully realized. The German spirit, Hegel believed, was the spirit of a new world in which absolute truth would be realized in unlimited freedom. But even the kingdom of Prussia was not the last word of the world-spirit. Given Hegel's constant preference for wholes over their parts, one might expect that in his scheme of things nation-states would eventually give way to a world-state. But Hegel disliked the idea of a world-state, because it would take away the opportunity for war, which was a necessary stage in the dialectic of history. War, for him, was not just a necessary evil, but had a positive value as a reminder of the contingent nature of finite existence. It was 'the condition in which we have to take seriously the vanity of temporal goods and things' (PR, 324). Accordingly, Hegel attacked Kant's quest for perpetual peace. The future of humanity, Hegel predicted, lay neither in Germany nor in a united world, but rather in America, 'where, in the ages that lie before us, the burden of the world's history shall reveal itself'—perhaps in a great continental struggle between North and South.

The history of Germany for a century and more after Hegel's death brought upon his political philosophy a barrage of obloquy. His glorification of the state as an end in itself, his belief in the cosmic role of the German people, and his positive evaluation of warfare can hardly avoid a share of the responsibility for the two World Wars that disfigured the twentieth century. It is true that the Prussian model that he commended was a constitutional monarchy, and that the nationalism he preached was at some remove from the totalitarian racism of the Nazis. Nonetheless, his philosophical career, like Rousseau's, is a reminder of the disastrous consequences that can flow from flawed metaphysics. One can believe that the state has an intrinsic value of its own only if we think of it as in some way personal, and indeed a higher form of person than an ordinary human individual. And one can rationally believe this only if one accepts some version of Hegel's metaphysical doctrine that there is a world-spirit whose life is lived through the interplay between the folk-spirits that animate the nation-states.

For those who are interested in the history of philosophy for the sake of the light it can cast on contemporary concerns, the period from Machiavelli to Hegel is the heyday of political philosophy. The political institutions of the ancient and medieval world are too distant from our own for the reflections upon them of ancient and medieval philosophers to have much to offer to contemporary political philosophy. On the other hand, as we shall see in the next volume, the political evaluations of the great philosophers of the nineteenth century owe as much to the nascent disciplines of economics and sociology as they do to the conceptual concerns that remain as the abiding core of pure political philosophy.

10

God

Molina on Omniscience and Freedom

The problem of reconciling human freedom with God's foreknowledge of human actions had baffled all the great scholastics of the Middle Ages. Thomas Aquinas maintained that God foresaw what we would do because all our actions were present to him in the single moment of eternity. Duns Scotus complained that this solution would work only if time was fundamentally unreal. Instead, he proposed that God knew creatures' actions by knowing what he himself had decreed from all eternity. Ockham objected that such knowledge would provide foreknowledge of human actions only if our actions were predetermined and therefore unfree. He himself offered no solution to the problem: divine foreknowledge was just a dogma to be blindly believed. Peter de Rivo had tried to preserve freedom while accepting divine omniscience by denying that future contingent propositions had any truth-value to be known even by God; but this was a weasel way out and was condemned by the Church. Lorenzo Valla, Erasmus, and Luther were no better able than their predecessors to reconcile liberty and omniscience. All were reduced to quoting the Pauline text with which every theologian sooner or later admits his bafflement on this topic: 'Oh, the depth of the riches both of the wisdom and knowledge of God! How unsearchable are his judgments and his ways past finding out!' (Rom 11: 35).[1]

A novel and highly ingenious solution to the problem was proposed at the end of the sixteenth century by the Jesuit Luis Molina. Molina agreed

---

[1] See vol. II, pp. 298–301.

with Ockham in rejecting the accounts of Aquinas and Scotus, and he accepted the Church teaching that future contingent propositions had truth-values. His innovation was to suggest that God's knowledge of the future depended on God's knowledge of the truth-values of counterfactual propositions. God knows what any possible creature would freely do in any possible circumstances. By knowing this and by knowing which creatures he will create and which circumstances he will himself bring about, he knows what actual creatures will in fact do.

Molina made a distinction between three kinds of divine knowledge. First, there is God's natural knowledge, by which he knows his own nature and all the things that are possible to him either by his own action or by the action of free possible creatures. This knowledge is prior to any divine decision about creation. Then there is God's free knowledge: his knowledge of what will actually happen after the free divine decision to create certain free creatures and place them in certain particular circumstances. Between these two kinds of knowledge there is God's 'middle knowledge': that is, his knowledge of what any possible creature will do in any possible circumstances. Because middle knowledge is based on creatures' own hypothetical decisions, human autonomy is upheld; because middle knowledge is prior to the decision to create, God's omniscience about the actual world is preserved.

What Molina called 'circumstances', or 'orders of events', later philosophers have called 'possible worlds'. So Molina's theory is essentially that God's knowledge of what will happen in the actual world is based on his knowledge of all possible worlds plus his knowledge of which possible world he has decided to actualize. Before creating Adam and Eve God know that Eve would yield to the serpent and Adam would yield to Eve. He knew this because he knew all kinds of counterfactuals about Adam and Eve: he knew what they would do in every possible world. He knew, for instance, whether Adam, if tempted by the serpent directly rather than via Eve, would still have eaten the forbidden fruit. The weak point in Molina's solution is his assumption that all counterfactual propositions—propositions of the form 'If A were to happen, B would happen'—have truth-values. Undoubtedly, some such propositions, e.g. 'if the earth were to crash into the sun, human life would cease to exist,' are true; other such propositions, e.g. 'if the Great Pyramid were hexagonal, it would have seventeen sides,' are false; but when we ascribe truth-values to such propositions we do so on the basis of logical or natural laws. Matters are different when we construct counterfactuals about free agents. There is no general principle of conditional excluded middle which runs 'Either (if A were to happen B would happen), or (if A were to happen B would not happen').

Descartes, in answer to a query from Princess Elizabeth, offered a reconciliation between divine foreknowledge and human freedom that in some ways resembles Molina's. He wrote:

Suppose that a King has forbidden duels, and knows with certainty that two gentlemen of his kingdom who live in different towns have a quarrel, and are so hostile to each other that if they meet nothing will stop them from fighting. If this King orders one of them to go on a certain day to the town where the other lives, and orders the other to go on the same day to the place where the first is, he knows with certainty that they will meet, and fight, and thus disobey his prohibition: but none the less, he does not compel them, and his knowledge, and even his will to make them act thus, does not prevent their combat when they meet being as voluntary and free as if they had met on some other occasion and he had known nothing about it. And they can be no less justly punished for disobeying the prohibition. Now what a King can do in such a case, concerning certain free actions of his subjects, God, with His infinite foresight and power does infallibly in regard to all the free actions of all men. (AT IV.393; *CSMK* III.282)

Descartes does not, however, say like Molina that God knows what our actions will be because he has already seen what we would do in all possible worlds; he goes on to say that God knows what we will do because he has determined what desires he will give us and what circumstances he will place us in. But this takes away the point of the parallel with the king of his parable. It is only because all the other actions of the duellists that have formed their characters are independent of the king's desires and control that he can plausibly be said not to be responsible for their final duel, and to be entitled to punish them for disobeying his prohibition. If every action of every human being is stage-managed by God just as much as the final act in the duellists' drama it is hard to see how God himself can avoid being responsible for sin.

Descartes' Rational Theology

Descartes' principal contributions to philosophical natural theology are in two different areas. First, he refashioned the traditional concept of creation. Second, he revived a version of the ontological argument of God's existence.

Theologians have commonly distinguished between creation and con-servation. In the beginning, God created heaven and earth, and from day to day he keeps heaven and earth in being. But his conservation of the universe does not involve fresh acts of creation: beings, once created, have by themselves a tendency to keep on existing, unless interfered with. They have a kind of existential inertia.

Descartes rejected this, when, in the third *Meditation*, he was inquiring about his own origin:

All the course of my life may be divided into an infinite number of parts, none of which is in any way dependent on the other; and thus from the fact that I was in existence a short time ago it does not follow that I must be in existence now, unless some cause at this instant, so to speak, produces me anew. (AT VII.50; *CSMK* II.334)

One's life is not a continuous duration, but rather is built up out of instants, in the way in which movement in the cinema is built out of a series of stills. The cause that Descartes has in mind in this passage is, of course, God. So for him there is no distinction between creation and conservation: at each moment I am created anew by God. In physics, Descartes opposed atomism; since matter was identical with extension, and extension was infinitely divisible, there could be no indivisible parts of matter. But the doctrine of continuous creation seems to involve a certain metaphysical atomism: history is built up out of an infinite number of time slices, each of which is quite independent of its predecessor and its successor.

The passage we have been considering occurs in the third *Meditation* when Descartes was offering a proof of God's existence from the occurrence in his own mind of an idea of God.[2] But in the fifth *Meditation* he offers a different proof of God's existence, which since the time of Kant has been famous under the title 'the ontological argument'. The argument was already adumbrated in the *Discourse on Method*:

I saw quite well that, assuming a triangle, its three angles must be equal to two right angles; but for all that, I saw nothing that assured me that there was any triangle in the real world. On the other hand, going back to an examination of my idea of a perfect Being, I found that this included the existence of such a Being; in

---

[2] See p. 37 above.

the same way as the idea of a triangle includes the equality of its three angles to two right angles ... Consequently, it is at least as certain that God, the perfect Being in question, is or exists, as any proof in geometry can be. (AT VI.36; *CSMK* I.129)

Expanding on this in the fifth *Meditation*, Descartes says that reflecting on the idea he has of God, a supremely perfect being, he clearly and distinctly perceives that everlasting existence belongs to God's nature. Existence can no more be taken away from the divine essence than the sum of the angles can be taken away from a Euclidean triangle. 'It is not less absurd to think of God (that is, a supremely perfect being) lacking existence (that is, lacking a certain perfection) than to think of a hill without a valley' (i.e. an uphill slope without a downhill slope).

To see that this argument is not a simple begging of the question of God's existence, we have to recall that Descartes believed in a Platonic world of essences independent both of the real world and the world of the mind.[3] 'When I imagine a triangle, it may be that no such figure exists anywhere outside my thought, or never has existed; but there certainly is its determinate nature, its essence, its form, which is unchangeable and eternal. This is no figment of mine, and does not depend on my mind.' Theorems can be proved about triangles whether or not anything in the world is triangular; similarly, therefore, theorems could be stated about God in abstraction, whether or not there exists any such being. One such theorem is that God is a totally perfect being, that is, he contains all perfections. But existence itself is a perfection; hence, God, who contains all perfections, must exist.

The vulnerable point in the argument is the claim that existence is a perfection. This was siezed upon by Pierre Gassendi, author of the fifth set of Objections to the Meditations. 'Neither in God nor in anything else is existence a perfection, but rather that without which there are no perfections ... Existence cannot be said to exist in a thing like a perfection; and if a thing lacks existence, then it is not just imperfect or lacking perfection, it is nothing at all.' Descartes had no ultimately convincing answer to this objection, and it was later to be pressed home conclusively by Immanuel Kant and Gottlob Frege.[4]

---

[3] See p. 185 above.
[4] See below, p. 325.

GOD

Pascal and Spinoza on God

Continental philosophers in the century of Descartes moved on from his treatment of God's existence in two different directions. Blaise Pascal abandoned the quest for a demonstration: our natural reason was so limited and so corrupt that any such attempt must be futile. Instead, he urged informal considerations that should prompt us to believe in the absence of proof. Baruch Spinoza, on the other hand, offered his own version of the ontological argument, giving it the most thoroughly formalized presentation it had ever received.

Pascal admits that by the natural light of reason we are incapable not only of knowing what God is, but even if there is a God at all. But the believer is not left without resource. He addresses the unbeliever thus:

Either God exists or not. Which side shall we take? Reason can determine nothing here. An infinite abyss separates us, and across this infinite distance a game is being played, which will turn out heads or tails. Which will you bet? (*P*, 680)

You, the unbeliever, perhaps prefer not to wager at all. But you cannot escape: the game has already begun and all have a stake. The chances, so far as reason can show, are equal on either side. But the outcomes of the possible bets are very different. Suppose you bet your life that God exists. If you win, God exists, and you gain infinite happiness; if you lose, then God does not exist and what you lose is nothing. So the bet on God is a good one. But how much should we bet? If you were offered three lives of happiness in return for betting your present life, it would make sense to take the offer. But in fact what you are offered is not just three lifetimes but a whole eternity of happiness, so the bet must be infinitely attractive. We have been assuming that the chances of winning or losing a bet on God are fifty-fifty. But the proportion of infinite happiness, in comparison with what is on offer in the present life, is so great that the bet on God's existence is a solid proposition even if the odds against winning are enormous, so long as they are only finite.

Is it true, as Pascal assumes, that one cannot suspend judgement about the existence of God? In the absence of a convincing proof either of theism or of atheism, is not the rational position that of the agnostic, who refuses to place a bet either way? Pascal claims that this is tantamount to betting against God. That may be so, if in fact there is a God who has commanded

Pascal's time gambling was highly fashionable. It would have been rash, however, to bet in the company represented in this genre painting by George de la Tour

us under pain of damnation to believe in him; but that should be the conclusion, not the starting point of the discussion.

What is it, in fact, to bet one's life on the existence of God? For Pascal, it meant leading the life of an austere Jansenist. But if reason alone can tell us nothing about God, how can we be sure that that is the kind of life that he will reward with eternal happiness? Perhaps we are being invited to bet on the existence, not just of God, but of the Jansenist God. But then the game is no longer one in which there are only two possible bets: someone may ask us to bet on the Jesuit God, or the Calvinist God, or the God of Islam. Pascal's ingenious apologetic does not succeed in its task; but it does draw attention to the fact that it is possible to have good reasons for believing in a proposition that are quite separate from reasons that provide evidence for its truth. This consideration was to be developed in more elaborate ways by later philosophers of religion such as Søren Kierkegaard and John Henry Newman.

Spinoza, on the other hand, was not at all a betting man: he liked his reasons as cut and dried as possible. The existence of God, he believed, could be shown to be as plain to see as the truth of any proposition in Euclid. To show this he presented his own version of the ontological argument, set out in geometrical form, in the first book of his *Ethics*.

Proposition 11 of that book reads: 'God, a substance consisting of infinite attributes, each of which expresses an eternal and infinite essence, necessarily exists.' The description here given of God is derived from the sixth of the series of definitions set out at the beginning of the book.

The proof of proposition 11 is by *reductio ad absurdum*:

If you deny this, conceive, if you can, that God does not exist. Therefore (by Axiom 7) his essence does not involve existence. But this (by Proposition 7) is absurd. Therefore, God necessarily exists. Q.E.D. (*Eth*, 7)

If we look up Axiom 7, we find that it says that if a thing can be conceived as non-existing its essence does not involve existence. Proposition 7 is more controversial: existence is part of the nature of a substance. To prove this, Spinoza tells us that a substance cannot be produced by anything else, and so must be its own cause; that is to say, its essence must involve existence. But why cannot a substance be produced by something else—by another substance? We are referred to Proposition 5 (there cannot be two or more substances with the same attribute) and to Proposition 3 (if A is to be the cause of B, A must have something in common with B). These in turn rest on Definition 3, the initial definition of substance as 'that which is in itself and is conceived by itself, so that its concept can be formed independently of the concept of any other thing' (*Eth*, 1).

Two elements in Spinoza's argument are counterintuitive. Are we not surrounded in life by cases of substances giving rise to other substances, most conspicuously living things generating other living things? And why should we accept the claim that if B is the cause of A, then the concept of B must be part of the concept of A? It is not possible to know what lung cancer is without knowing what a lung is, but is it not possible to know what lung cancer is without knowing what the cause of lung cancer is? Spinoza is identifying causal relationships and logical relationships in a manner that is surely unwarranted. But it is not, of course, inadvertent: the equivalence of the two kinds of consequence, logical and causal, is a key element of his metaphysical system. But it is not argued for: it is smuggled in through the original definition of substance.

Spinoza's initial set of definitions includes also a novel definition of God as containing an infinite number of attributes. Since we are told that we can only know two of these attributes, namely thought and extension, these infinite attributes play little further part in the system. Once Spinoza has proved to his satisfaction the existence of God he goes on to derive a number of properties of God that belong to traditional theism: God is infinite, indivisible, unique, eternal, and all-comprehending; he is the first efficient cause of everything that can fall within his comprehension, and he is the only entity in which essence and existence are identical (*Eth*, 9–18). But he also describes God in highly unorthodox ways. Although in the *Tractatus* he had campaigned against anthropomorphic concepts of God, he nonetheless states that God is extended, and therefore is something bodily (*Eth*, 33). God is not a creator as envisaged in the Judaeo-Christian tradition: he does not choose to give existence to the universe, but everything that there is follows by necessity from the divine nature. He is free only in the sense that he is not determined by anything outside his own nature, but it was not open to him not to create or to create a world different from the one that we have (*Eth*, 21–2). He is an immanent and not a transcendent cause of things, and there is no such thing as the purpose of creation.

Spinoza's innovations in natural theology are summed up in the equation of God with Nature. Although the word was not invented until the next century, his theism can be called 'pantheism', the doctrine that God is everything and everything is God. But, like every other element in his system, 'Nature' is a subtle concept. Like Bruno, Spinoza distinguishes *Natura Naturans* (literally, 'Nature Naturing', which we may call 'active nature') and *Natura Naturata* ('Nature Natured', which we may call 'passive nature'). The infinite attributes of the single divine substance belong to active nature; the series of modes that constitute finite beings belong to passive nature. Just as the finite beings that make up the tapestry of the universe cannot exist or be conceived without God, so too God cannot exist or be conceived of without each of these threads of being. Most significantly, we are told that intellect and will belong not to active nature but to passive nature. Hence, God is not a personal God as devout Jews and Christians believed.

Does this mean that God does not love us? Spinoza, as we have seen, believed that intellectual love for God was the highest form of human activity. But he went on to say that a man who loves God should not endeavour that God should love him in return. Indeed, if you want God to love you, you want him to cease to be God (*Eth*, 169–70). However, God can be said to love himself, and our love of God can be seen as one expression of this self-love. In this sense God's love for men is exactly the same thing as men's intellectual love of God.

The Optimism of Leibniz

When Leibniz visited Spinoza in 1676 one of the topics they discussed was Descartes' ontological argument for the existence of God. Descartes had argued that God is by definition a being who possesses all perfections; but existence is a perfection, therefore God possesses existence. Leibniz thought this argument had a dubious premiss: how can we know that the idea of a being possessing all perfections is a coherent idea? He wrote a paper for Spinoza in which he tried to make good this defect. He defined a perfection as a 'simple quality which is positive and absolute'. Incompatibility, he argued, could only arise between complex qualities which, when analysed, might be shown to contain contradictory elements. But a simple quality is unanalysable. Accordingly, there is nothing impossible in the notion of a being containing all simple qualities, that is to say an *ens perfectissimum* (G VII.261–2).

Leibniz, having added this rider, accepted the ontological argument. He did not question the idea that existence is a perfection—the premiss that, to Gassendi at the time, and to many philosophers from Kant to the present day, has seemed the really vulnerable point in Descartes' reasoning. This is surprising, for as we have seen in his own system existence is something quite different from all the predicates that attach to a subject and constitute its definition.[5]

Leibniz gives a new twist also to the cosmological proof which argues to God as the first cause of the universe. He does not assume that a series of finite causes must itself be a finite series: he says, for instance, that an infinity of shapes and movements, present and past, form part of the efficient cause of his writing the *Monadology*. But each element in this series

---

[5] See above, p. 197.

is a contingent entity which does not have in itself a sufficient reason for its existence. The ultimate reason must be found outside the series, in a necessary being, and this we call God (G VI.613). Clearly, this argument stands or falls with the principle of sufficient reason.

Leibniz offers two other proofs of God's existence, one traditional and one novel. One is the argument from eternal truths, which goes back to St Augustine.[6] It runs as follows. Minds are the regions in which truths dwell; but logical and mathematical truths are prior to human minds, so they must have a *locus* in an eternal divine mind. The second, new, argument depends on the theory of the pre-established harmony: 'This perfect harmony of so many substances that have no communication with each other can only come from a common cause' (G IV.486). This argument, of course, will convince only those who have accepted Leibniz's system of windowless monads.

Unlike Spinoza, Leibniz believed that God was totally distinct from nature, and that he had freely created a world of free creatures. Before deciding to create, God surveys the infinite number of possible creatures. Among the possible creatures there will be many possible Julius Caesars; among these there will be one Julius Caesar who crosses the Rubicon and one who does not. Each of these possible Caesars acts for a reason, and neither of them will be necessitated to act. When, therefore, God decides to give existence to the Rubicon-crossing Caesar he is making actual a freely choosing Caesar. Hence, our Caesar crossed the Rubicon freely.

What of God's own choice to give existence to the actual world we live in, rather than the myriad other possible worlds he might have created? Leibniz answers that God, as a rational agent, chose to create the best of all possible worlds. In the eighth chapter of the first part of his *Theodicy* he says that God's supreme wisdom, conjoined with infinite goodness, could not have failed to choose the best. A lesser good is a kind of evil, just as a lesser evil is a kind of good; so God must have chosen the best world under pain of having done evil. If there were no best world, he would not have chosen to create at all. It may appear that a world without sin and suffering would have been better than ours, but that is an illusion. If the slightest existing evil were lacking in the present world, it would be a different world. The eternal truths demand that physical and moral evil are possible, and therefore many of the infinitely many possible

[6] See vol. II, pp. 278–80.

worlds will contain them. For all we can show to the contrary, therefore, the best of all worlds is among those that contain evils of both kinds (G VI.107ff).

Leibniz was not the first to claim that our world was the best possible—already in the twelfth century Abelard had maintained that God had no power to make a better world than the one he had made.[7] But Leibniz distinguished his position from Abelard's by saying that other worlds besides the actual one are possible—metaphysically possible. The necessity which obliged God to choose the best world was a moral, not a metaphysical, necessity: he was determined not by any lack of power, but by the infinity of his goodness. Thus Leibniz can claim, in the *Discourse* (*D*, 3), that God creates the world freely: it is the highest liberty to act perfectly, according to sovereign reason. God acts freely because although he cannot create anything but the best he need not have created at all.

Leibniz believed that his theory solved the traditional problem of evil: why does an omnipotent and loving God permit sin and suffering? He points out that not all things that are possible in advance can be made actual together: as he puts it, A and B may each be possible, but A and B may not be compossible. Any created world is a system of compossibles, and the best possible world is the system that has the greatest surplus of good over evil. A world in which there is free will that is sometimes sinfully misused is better than a world in which there is neither freedom nor sin. Thus the existence of evil in the world provides no argument against the goodness of God.

One is inclined to make to the 'optimism' of Leibniz the kind of objection that he made to Descartes' ontological argument. How do we know that 'the best of all possible worlds' expresses a coherent notion? Leibniz himself offered a proof that there was no such thing as the fastest of all possible motions. If there is such a velocity, imagine a wheel rotating at such a rate; if you stick a nail in the wheel to project out from its circumference, the nail will rotate even faster, which shows the absurdity of the notion (G IV. 424). If the alleged best possible world contains evil E, can we not imagine a world similar in all other respects but lacking E? And if God is omnipotent, how could it be impossible for him to bring such a world into being?

---

[7] See vol. II, p. 296.

The God of Berkeley

We have seen that Leibniz found much to approve in Berkeley's early writings. The admiration, however, does not seem to have been reciprocated. Berkeley was scornful of Leibniz's ontological argument for the existence of God. On the other hand he offered a new proof of his own—a 'direct and immediate demonstration' of the being of God—which could be regarded as a gigantic expansion of the argument from eternal truths borrowed by Leibniz from St Augustine. In the dialogue, having established to his satisfaction that sensible things cannot exist otherwise than in a mind or spirit, he continues:

Whence I conclude, not that they have no real existence, but that, seeing they depend not on my thought, and have an existence distinct from being perceived by me, there must be some other Mind wherein they exist. As sure, therefore, as the sensible world really exists, so sure is there an infinite omnipresent Spirit who contains and supports it. (*BPW*, 175)

Thus, not only do the august truths of logic and mathematics dwell as ideas in the mind of God, so does the most everyday empirical truth, such as the fact that there is a ladybird walking across my desk at this moment. Berkeley is not simply saying that God knows such humble truths—that had long been the majority opinion among theologians. He is saying that the very thing that makes such a proposition true is nothing other than a set of ideas in God's mind—God's idea of the ladybird and God's idea of my desk. This was indeed an innovation. 'Men commonly believe that all things are known or perceived by God, because they believe the being of a God, whereas I on the other side immediately and necessarily conclude the being of a God, because all sensible things must be perceived by Him' (*BPW*, 175).

If we grant to Berkeley, for the sake of argument, that the sensible world consists only of ideas, there still seems to be a flaw in his proof of God's existence. One cannot, without fallacy, pass from the premiss 'There is no finite mind in which everything exists' to the conclusion 'therefore there is an infinite mind in which everything exists'. It could be that whatever exists exists in some finite mind or other, even though no finite mind is capacious enough to hold every existent. Few would be convinced by the following parallel argument. 'All humans are citizens; there is no nation state of which everyone is a citizen; therefore there is an international state of which everyone is a citizen.'

Perhaps Berkeley is really intending to argue that if things existed only in finite minds, their existence would be patchy and intermittent. The horse in his stable would exist while he was looking at it, and again when his groom was attending to it, but would go out of existence in between whiles. Only if there is an infinite, omnipresent, omnitemporal mind will continuous existence be guaranteed. This is the theme of a famous pair of limericks in which Ronald Knox tried to summarize Berkeley's contention:

> There was a young man who said, 'God
> Must think it exceedingly odd
>   If he finds that this tree
>   Continues to be
> When there's no one about in the Quad.'

Reply:

> Dear Sir, your astonishment's odd
> *I* am always about in the Quad.
>   And that's why the tree
>   Will continue to be
> Since observed by
>   Yours faithfully,
>   GOD.

The God whose existence is allegedly proved by Berkeley's route seems different in an important respect from the God of traditional theism. If objects when perceived by no finite spirit are kept in existence by God's perceiving them, there must be in God's mind ideas of all perceptible things—not only objects like desks and ladybirds, but also colours, shapes, smells, pleasures, pains, and all kinds of sense-data. But Christian thinkers had commonly denied that God enjoyed sense-experience. The psalmist asked: 'Is the inventor of the ear unable to hear? The creator of the eye unable to see?' These rhetorical 'questions expecting the answer no' were given a 'yes' answer by Thomas Aquinas and a multitude of other theologians. Commenting on the text 'the eyes of the Lord are on the just,' Aquinas wrote, 'Parts of the body are ascribed to God in the scriptures by a metaphor drawn from their functions. Eyes, for example, see, and so when

316

"God's eye" is spoken of, it means his power to see, even though his seeing is an intellectual and not a sensory activity' (Ia 3.1 ad 3).

For Aristotelians it was clear that God had no senses or sensory experience, because in order to see, hear, feel, taste, or otherwise sense it was essential to have a body, and God had no body. However, since Descartes had made popular the idea that the key element in human sensation was in fact a purely mental event, the matter was no longer so clear-cut. But Berkeley is anxious to avoid the conclusion that God has sense-experience.

In the third dialogue Hylas, the opposition spokesman, says that it would follow from Berkeley's theory that God, the perfect spirit, suffers pain, which is an imperfection. Berkeley's mouthpiece, Philonous, replies as follows:

That God knows or understands all things, and that he knows, among other things, what pain is, even every sort of painful sensation, and what it is for creatures to suffer pain, I make no question. But that God, though he knows and sometimes causes painful sensations in us, can himself suffer pain, I positively deny . . . No corporeal motions are attended with the sensations of pain or pleasure in His mind. To know everything knowable is certainly a perfection; but to endure or suffer or feel anything by sense is an imperfection. The former, I say, agrees to God, but not the latter. God knows, or hath, ideas; but His ideas are not conveyed to him by sense as ours are. (*BPW*, 202–3)

It is difficult to see how this is consistent with Berkeley's epistemology. Among the ideas we encounter are those of hot and cold, sweet and sour. If all ideas are ideas in the mind of God, then these ideas are somehow in the mind of God. If God nonetheless does not feel sensations, then the possession of such ideas is insufficient for sensation. But if that is so, then Berkeley's account of ordinary human sensation is quite inadequate.

Hume on Religion

Unlike Berkeley, Hume made a lasting, if negative, contribution to natural theology. His critical observations on the arguments for the existence of God, and his discussion of the role of miracles in establishing the authority of a revelation, have remained points of departure for both theist and atheist philosophers of religion. We may consider first the essay on miracles which was inserted as section ten of the *Inquiry*, having no counterpart in the earlier *Treatise*.

A miracle, for Hume, is a violation of a law of nature: he gives as examples of miracles a dead man coming back to life, or the raising of a house or ship into the air. Surprisingly, he does not deny that miracles are possible— he does not, like some of his followers, argue that if an apparently miracu- lous event were proved to have happened that would not show that a law had been violated, but that we had oversimplified our statement of the law. What he is really interested in is not whether miracles can be done, but whether they can be seen to be done. For his target is the use of miracles by apologists to claim supernatural authorization of a particular religious message.

The first part of the essay ends with the following statement:

No testimony is sufficient to establish a miracle unless the testimony be of such a kind that its falsehood would be more miraculous, than the fact, which it endeavours to establish . . . When anyone tells me that he saw a dead man restored to life, I immediately consider with myself whether it be more probable that this person should either deceive or be deceived, or that the fact, which he relates, should really have happened . . . If the falsehood of his testimony would be more miraculous than the event which he relates; then, and not till then, can he pretend to command my belief or opinion. (W, 212)

Hume is not ruling out that a miracle could be proved, any more than he ruled out that a miracle could happen. Indeed, he tells us that given the appropriate unanimity of testimony, he would himself be prepared to believe what he regards as a miracle, namely, a total darkness over the whole earth for eight days. We may find this surprising. On his own definition a miracle is a violation of the laws of nature, and someone's being deceived or deceiving could never be a violation of a law of nature; therefore the evidence against a miracle must always be stronger than the evidence for it. But we must remember that according to Hume's account of the human will, a human action can be just as much a violation of a law of nature as any physical event.

Hume is surely right that if it is claimed that an event E has happened which is a violation of a law of nature, then the probability that E happened must be in inverse proportion to the evidence that if E happened it would be a violation of the law. For the evidence that if E happened it would be a violation of the law is *eo ipso* evidence that E didn't happen. But surely Hume must have overstated his case. Otherwise it would never be possible for scientists to correct a mistaken belief about a natural law. Faced with a claim by a colleague that his experiments have revealed a counter-example to the law, they should, on Hume's showing, discount the evidence on the grounds that it would be less of a miracle for the experimenter to be lying or mistaken than for the law to be violated.

In the second part of the essay Hume offers three de facto arguments to show that miracles never have been established on evidence full enough to meet his standards. First, he states categorically that no miracle has been sufficiently attested by sufficiently good witnesses who have much to lose and can be easily detected if fraudulent. Second, he evokes the credulity of the human race, as shown in the numerous imposture miracles subsequently detected. Third, he maintains that supernatural and miraculous stories abound chiefly among ignorant and barbarous nations. Each of these contentions can be, and has been, contested on straightforward historical grounds.

More interesting is his fourth argument, which is based on the undoubted fact that miracles are claimed to have been wrought in aid of religions which contradict each other. If a miracle proves a doctrine to be revealed by God, and consequently true, a miracle can never be wrought for a contrary doctrine. Hence, every story of a miracle wrought in support of one particular religion must be a piece of evidence against any story of a miracle wrought in favour of a different religion.

Hume considers three examples to illustrate his point: the cure of a blind and lame man by the emperor Vespasian, reported in Tacitus; Cardinal de Retz's account of a man who grew a second leg by rubbing an amputated stump with holy oil; and the miracles wrought at the tomb of a devout Jansenist, the Abbé Paris. The three cases are of uneven interest: the evidence for the first two miracles is no more than a few hundred words, but for the third there are volumes and volumes of authenticated testimony. Hume describes the events thus:

The curing of the sick, giving hearing to the deaf, and sight to the blind, were everywhere talked of as the usual effects of that holy sepulchre. But what is more extraordinary: many of the miracles were immediately proved on the spot, before

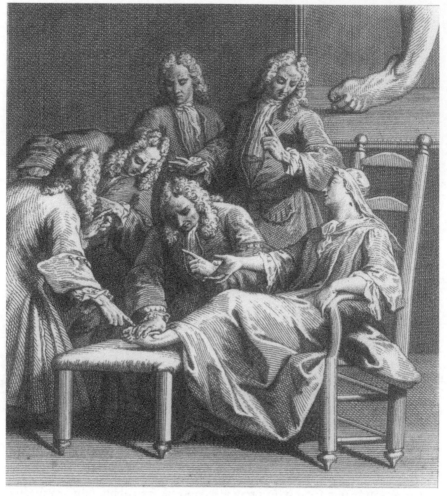

One of the Jansenist healings cited by Hume in his treatise on miracles

judges of unquestioned integrity, attested by witnesses of credit and distinction, in a learned age, and on the most eminent theatre that now is in the world. (W, 220)

Hume's picture is a little overdrawn, and is not quite consistent with his earlier point that miracles are only reported in barbarous contexts. But historians of undoubted Catholic piety confirm the main lines of his account of these miracles wrought in support of a heresy that had been repeatedly condemned by the popes. It seems to me that this final argument does establish Hume's case that a miracle cannot be proved in such a way as to be the foundation of a religion. Not, of course, that theists have ever thought that it could be so, in the sense of showing that God exists; they have only claimed that if we know from elsewhere that God exists we know that he is almighty and that it is in his power to work miracles, perhaps in order to authenticate one sect rather than another.

Do we know of God from other sources—from the traditional arguments, for instance? Hume believed that there was no being whose nonexistence implied a contradiction: accordingly, he had little sympathy with the ontological argument for the existence of God. But he makes no direct onslaught on it; his most relevant remarks occur in the section of the *Treatise* in which he is trying to establish the nature of belief. In arguing that belief was not an idea, he claimed that when, after conceiving something, we conceive it is existent, we add nothing to our first idea:

Thus when we affirm, that God is existent, we simply form the idea of such a being, as he is represented to us; nor is the existence, which we attribute to him, conceiv'd by a particular idea, which we join to the idea of his other qualities, and can again separate and distinguish from them...When I think of God, when I think of him as existent, and when I believe him to be existent, my idea of him neither encreases nor diminishes. (*T*, 94)

It is correct that believing and conceiving need not differ in content: if I believe that God exists and you do not we are disagreeing, in Hume's terms, about the same idea. But having a thought about God and believing that God exists are two quite different things—an atheist who says 'if there is a God, then he is a brute or braggart' expresses, in his if-clause, the thought that God exists without assenting to it. And Hume is wrong to say that there is no concept of existence distinct from the concept of the existing thing—if that were so, how could we judge that something does *not* exist? But it is true, and important, that the concept of existence is quite a different kind of concept from the concept of God or the concept of a unicorn. To say that unicorns exist is to make a statement of a quite different logical form from the statement that unicorns are difficult to tame. Hume's insight here was given more precise and accurate form by later philosophers such as Kant and Frege, who used it in a definitive demolition of the ontological argument.

The argument from design is treated more fully and respectfully by Hume. His *Dialogues Concerning Natural Religion* feature three characters,

Cleanthes, Philo, and Demea. It is a tribute to Hume's skill in composition that it is not easy to identify which of the three is the spokesman for his own views. Of the three, Demea is the character presented least sympathetically; but scholars have been willing, on both internal and external grounds, to identify both Philo and Cleanthes as mouthpieces for their author. It is remarkable that both of them take seriously the argument from design.

In the second part, Cleanthes compares the universe to a great machine divided into an infinite number of smaller machines:

All these various machines, and even their most minute parts, are adjusted to each other with an accuracy, which ravished into admiration all men, who have ever contemplated them. The curious adapting of means to ends, throughout all nature, resembles exactly, though it much exceeds, the productions of human contrivance; of human designs, thought, wisdom and intelligence. Since there-fore the effects resemble each other, we are led to infer, by all the rules of analogy, that the causes also resemble; and that the Author of Nature is somewhat similar to the mind of man; though possessed of much larger faculties, proportioned to the grandeur of the work, which he has executed. (W, 116)

Philo is critical of this argument, but he too, in the final section of the dialogues, and after a detailed presentation of the problem of evil as a counterbalance to the argument from design, is willing to say that a divine being 'discovers himself to reason in the inexplicable contrivance and artifice of Nature' (W, 189). But his assent to natural theology is very guarded. He is willing to agree that the cause or causes of order in the universe probably bear some remote analogy to human intelligence; but his agreement is hedged about with conditions. However, provided: (1) that 'this proposition be not capable of extension, variation or more particular explication'; (2) that 'it afford no inference that affects human life or can be the source of any action or forbearance'; and (3) that 'the analogy, imperfect as it is, can be carried no farther than to the human intelligence', then he is prepared to accept the conclusion of the argument from design. 'What can the most inquisitive, contemplative, and religious man do more than give a plain, philosophical assent to the proposition as often as it occurs; and believe that the arguments on which it is established exceed the objections which lie against it' (W, 203).

This probably represents Hume's own position. It is clear that Hume enjoyed annoying the clergy, and that he detested Christianity itself, despite the ironical compliments to it which he scatters throughout his works. But with respect to the existence of God he was an agnostic, not an atheist. It was not until the triumph of Darwinism in the next century that an atheist could feel confident that he had an effective antidote to the argument from design.

Kant's Theological Dialectic

The third chapter of Kant's transcendental dialectic is entitled 'The Ideal of Pure Reason': its principal topic is a critique of rational theology, the attempt to establish by pure reason the existence of a transcendent God. Kant begins with the claim that all possible proofs of God's existence must fall into one of three classes. There are ontological arguments, which take their start from the *a priori* concept of a supreme being; there are cosmological proofs, which argue from the general nature of the empirical world; and there are proofs based on particular natural phenomena, which we may call 'physico-theological proofs'. In every kind of proof, Kant says, reason 'stretches its wings in vain, to soar beyond the world of sense by the mere might of speculative thought' (M, 346).

The ontological argument, as Kant sets it out, begins with a definition of God as an absolutely necessary being. Such a being is a thing whose non-existence is impossible. But can we really make sense, he asks, of such a definition? Necessity really belongs to propositions, not to things; and we cannot transfer the logical necessity of a proposition such as 'a triangle has three angles' and make it a property of a real being. Logical necessity is only conditional necessity; nothing is absolutely necessary:

To suppose the existence of a triangle and not that of its three angles is self-contradictory; but to suppose the non-existence of both triangle and angles is perfectly admissible. The same holds true of the concept of an absolutely necessary being. If you think away its existence, you think away the thing itself with all its predicates, and there is no question of any contradiction. (M, 348)

If the ontological argument is valid, then 'God exists' is an analytic proposition: 'exist' is a predicate that is tacitly contained in the subject 'God'. But Kant insists that all statements of real existence are synthetic: we cannot derive actual reality from pure concepts. We might object that we can at least argue from concepts to non-existence: it is because we grasp the concepts *square* and *circle* that we know there are no square circles. If 'square circles do not exist' is analytic, why not 'there is a necessary being'?

Kant's real objection to the ontological argument is not that 'God exists' is a synthetic proposition, but that it is not a subject–predicate proposition at all. 'God is omnipotent' contains two concepts linked by the copula 'is'. But:

If I take the subject, God, with all its predicates including omnipotence and say 'God is' or 'There is a God' I add no new predicate to the concept of God, I merely posit or affirm the existence of the subject with all its predicates: I posit the object corresponding to my concept. (M, 350)

Existential propositions do not, in fact, always 'posit', because they may occur as subclauses in a larger sentence (as in 'If there is a God, sinners will be punished'). But it is true that neither the affirmation nor the supposition of God's existence adds anything to the predicates that make up the concept of God. This point is correct whether or not any particular concept of God is coherent or not (as Kant thought *necessary being* was not). Even if we allow that God is possible, there remains the point that Kant memorably expressed by saying that a hundred real dollars contain no more than a hundred possible dollars.

Echoing Hume, Kant says: 'By however many predicates we may think a thing—even if we completely determine it—we do not make the least addition to the thing when we further declare that this thing *is*. Otherwise it would not be exactly the same thing that exists, but something more than we had thought in the concept; and we could not, therefore, say that the exact object of my concept exists' (M, 350). It must always be illegitimate to try to build existence—even possible existence—into the concept of a thing. Existence is not a predicate that can enter into such a concept.

Abelard in the twelfth century, and Frege in the nineteenth century, urged us to rephrase statements of existence so that 'exists' does not even look like a predicate. 'Angels exist' should be formulated as 'Some things are angels'. This has the advantage that it does not make it appear that when we say 'Angels do not exist' we are first positing angels and then rejecting them. But it does not settle the issues surrounding the ontological argument, because the problems about arguing from possibility to actuality return as questions about what counts as 'something': are we including in our consideration possible as well as actual objects? Thus some recent philosophers have tried to restate the ontological argument in a novel way, by including possible objects within the range of discussion. A necessary being, they argue, is one that exists in all possible worlds. So defined, a necessary being must exist in our world, the actual world. Our world would not exist unless it were possible; so if God exists in every possible world he must exist in ours.

Kant is surely right to insist that whether there is something in reality corresponding to my concept of a thing cannot itself be part of my concept. A concept has to be determined prior to being compared to reality, otherwise we would not know *which* concept was being compared and found to correspond, or maybe not correspond, to reality. *That* there is a God cannot be part of what we mean by 'God'; hence, 'there is a God' cannot be an analytic proposition and the ontological argument must fail.

However, Kant overestimated the force of his criticism. He maintained that the refutation of the ontological argument carried with it the defeat of the much more popular proof of God's existence from the contingency of the world. That argument is briskly set out by Kant:

If anything exists, an absolutely necessary being must also exist. Now I, at least, exist. Therefore an absolutely necessary being exists. The minor premise contains an experience, the major premise the inference from their being any experience at all to the existence of the necessary. The proof therefore really begins with experience and is not wholly *a priori* ontological. For this reason, and because the object of all possible experience is called the world, it is entitled the *cosmological* proof. (A, 605)

Kant argues that the appeal to experience here is illusory; the force of the cosmological derives only from the ontological argument. For what is meant by 'necessary being'? Surely, a being in whom essence involves existence, that is to say, a being whose existence can be established by the ontological argument. But here Kant ignores the possibility of a different definition of 'necessary being' as meaning a being which can neither come into nor go out of existence, and which cannot suffer change of any kind. Such in fact was the standard account of necessary being given by medieval philosophers who, like Kant, rejected the ontological argument. Such a being may well be regarded as sufficiently different from the caused, variable, and contingent items in the world of experience to provide the necessary stable grounding for our fragile and fleeting cosmos.

However, Kant has a further criticism of the cosmological argument which is independent of his claim that it is the ontological argument in disguise. All forms of the cosmological argument seek to show that a series of contingent causes, however prolonged, can be completed only by a necessary cause. But if we ask whether the necessary cause is, or is not, part of the chain of causes, we are faced with a dilemma. If it is part of the chain, then we can ask, in its case as in others, why it exists. But we cannot imagine a supreme being saying to itself 'I am from eternity to eternity, and outside me there is nothing save what is through my will, *but whence then am I?*' (A, 613). On the other hand, if the necessary being is not part of the chain of causation, how can it account for the links in the chain that end with the existence of myself?

The argument for God's existence that Kant treats most gently is the physico-theological proof, which he says must always be mentioned with respect and which he himself states with great eloquence:

This world presents to us such an immeasurable spectacle of variety, order, purpose and beauty, shown alike in its infinite extent and in the unlimited divisibility of its parts, that even with such knowledge as our weak understanding can acquire we encounter so many marvels immeasurably great that all speech loses its force, all numbers their power to measure, our thoughts lose all precision, and our judgement of the whole dissolves into an amazement whose very silence speaks with eloquence. Everywhere we see a chain of effects and causes, of ends and means, regularity in coming into and going out of existence. Nothing has of itself come into the condition into which we find it, but always points behind itself to something else as its cause; and this in its turn obliges us to make the same inquiry. The whole universe would thus sink into the abyss of nothingness unless over and above this infinite chain of contingencies one assumed something to support it—something that is original and independently self-subsistent, and which not only caused the origin of the universe but also secures its continuance. (A, 622)

The argument thus presented seems to combine several of the traditional proofs of God's existence—the argument to a first cause, for instance, as well as the argument from design. There is no doubt that everywhere in the world we find signs of order, in accordance with a determinate purpose, apparently carried out with great wisdom. Since this order is alien to the individual things which constitute the world, we must conclude that it must have been imposed by one or more sublime wise causes, operating not blindly as nature does, but freely as humans do. Kant raises various difficulties about the analogies that the argument draws between the operation of nature and the artifice of human skill; but his real criticism of the proof is not to deny its authority but to limit its scope. The most the argument can prove is the existence of 'an *architect* of the world who is always very much hampered by the adaptability of the material in which he works, not a *creator* of the world to whose idea everything is subject'. Many religious believers would be very content to have established beyond reasonable doubt the existence of such a grand architect.

However, Kant did not say his last word about God in the *Critique of Pure Reason*. In his second critique he sets out a number of postulates of practical reason; assumptions that must be made if obedience to the moral law is to be made a rational activity. The postulates turn out to be the same as the traditional topics of natural metaphysics: God, freedom, and immortality. We have an obligation to pursue perfect goodness, which includes both virtue and happiness. We can only have an obligation to pursue something if it is possible of achievement: '*Ought*', Kant said memorably, 'implies *can*.' But only an all-powerful, omniscient God could ensure that virtue and happiness can coincide—and even such a God can do so only if there is a life after the present one. Hence, it is morally necessary to assume the existence of God.

Kant insists that there is no inconsistency between this claim and his denial in the first critique that speculative reason could prove the existence and attributes of God. The postulation of God's existence demanded by the moral life is an act of faith. Already in a preface to the first Critique Kant had marked out the difference between the two approaches to theology, and claimed that his critical approach to metaphysics was actually a necessary condition of a morally valuable belief in God's existence:

I cannot even assume God, freedom and immortality for the sake of the necessary practical use of my reason unless I simultaneously deprive speculative reason of its pretension to extravagant insights ... Thus I have to deny knowledge in order to make room for faith. The dogmatism of metaphysics—the idea that it is possible to make progress in the subject without criticizing pure reason—is the true source of that dogmatic unbelief which is at odds with morality. (B)

The architect of the cosmos, portrayed in William Blake's *The Ancient of Days*

Kant's postulation of God as a condition of moral behaviour is an elaboration of a strategy first laid out by Pascal, namely, that we should believe that God exists not because we have reason to think that 'God exists' is true, but because it is a proposition that is good for us to believe.

The Absolute of Hegel

Hegel was fond of using Christian language. For instance, he divides the history of Germany into three periods: the period up to Charlemagne, which he calls the Kingdom of the Father; the period from Charlemagne to the Reformation, which he calls the Kingdom of the Son; and finally the period from the Reformation to the Prussian monarchy, which is the Kingdom of the Holy Ghost or Spirit. From time to time he refers to the absolute as God and his statement that the absolute is the Thought that thinks itself recalls a phrase of Aristotle that was often employed by Christian thinkers as an approach to a definition of God. But on examination it turns out that the absolute is something very different from the Christian God.

God as conceived by Christian tradition is an eternal, unchanging, being whose existence is quite independent of the existence of the world and of human beings. Before Adam and Abraham existed, God already existed in the fullness of self-awareness. Hegel's absolute, on the other hand, is a spirit who lives only through the lives of human beings, and the self-awareness of the absolute is brought about by the reflection of philosophers in the everyday world. Spirit, however, is not simply reducible to the totality of human thinking; the absolute has purposes which are not those of any human thinker and which human activity unconsciously serves. But the spirit's plan of the universe is not something imposed from outside by a transcendent creator; it is an internal evolution programmed by a cosmic equivalent of DNA.

Hegel saw his system as a rational, scientific, presentation of truths conveyed symbolically by religion. Philosophy and religion covered the same area as each other:

The objects of philosophy are upon the whole the same as those of religion. In both the object is Truth, in that supreme sense in which God and God only is the

Truth. Both in like manner go on to treat of the finite worlds of Nature and the human Mind, with their relation to each other and to their truth in God.

In both philosophy and religion mankind aims to make its own the universal cosmic reason: religion does this by worship; philosophy by rational reflection.

Initially, religion presents us with myths and images. Thus in classical Antiquity Homer and Hesiod created the pantheon of Greek gods and goddesses. The first reaction of philosophy to myth and image is to explode their pretensions to literal truth: thus Plato denounces the theology of the poets and the sculptors. This pattern repeats itself in other cultures. The Jewish and Christian narratives, for instance, are mocked by the philosophers of the Enlightenment. But this antagonism between religion and anti-religious philosophy is superseded in the true, Hegelian, philosophy which accepts both faith and reason as different methods of presenting a single eternal truth.

What philosophy presents in thought, religion presents in images. What appears in Hegel's system as the objectification of the concept in Nature is presented in the great monotheistic religions as the free creation of a world by a transcendent God. The Hegelian insight that the finite spirit is a moment in the life of infinite spirit is expressed in Christianity by the doctrine that in Christ God became incarnate in a human being. But philosophy does not render religion superfluous: 'The form of Religion is necessary to Mind as it is in and for itself; it is the form of truth as it is for all men, and for every mode of consciousness.' Hegel proudly proclaimed that he was a Lutheran and intended to remain one (*LHP*, I.73).

Hegel's attitude to Christian doctrines, then, was one of sympathetic condescension. So too was his attitude to traditional proofs of the existence of God. But if God is the absolute, and the absolute is all being, then God's existence hardly needs proof. That is Hegel's version of the ontological argument. 'It would be strange', he wrote, 'if the concrete totality we call God were not rich enough to include so poor a category as being, the very poorest and most abstract of all' (*Logic* 1975, 85). For him, the real proof of the existence of God is the Hegelian system itself in its entirety.

The early modern period was a testing time for natural theology. It underwent criticism not only from philosophers who became increasingly sceptical of elements of religious tradition, but also from theologians who wished to downgrade the claims of natural religion to make room for faith. The Enlightenment philosophers sought to downgrade and perhaps eliminate the input of theological doctrines into the areas of epistemology, psychology, biology, ethics, and politics. The French Revolution and its aftermath led European thinkers to re-evaluate both traditional religion and the Enlightenment programme. In the nineteenth century, as we will observe in the next volume, this led to both an intensification of the challenge to religion from admirers of the sciences, and a reactive response from the religious intelligentsia.

CHRONOLOGY

LIST OF ABBREVIATIONS
AND CONVENTIONS

General

HWP	Bertrand Rusell, *History of Western Philosophy*
PASS	*Supplementary Proceedings of the Aristotelian Society*
ST	Thomas Aquinas, *Summa Theologiae*, cited by part, question, and article
CHSCP	*The Cambridge History of Seventeenth-Century Philosophy*, ed. D. Garber and M. Ayers

Luther

E	*Erasmus-Luther: Discourse on Free Will*, ed. E. F. Winter (London: Constable, 1961), cited by page
WA	Weimarer Ausgabe, the standard edition of his works.

Machiavelli

P	*Il Principe*, cited by chapter

Montaigne

ME	*Essais*, cited by page in the Flammarion edition of 1969

More

U	*Utopia*, cited by page in the edition of E. Surtz (New Haven, Conn.: Yale University Press, 1964)

Ramus

L	*Peter Ramus: The Logike 1574* (Menton: Scolar Press, 1970), cited by page

Suarez

DM	*Disputationes Metaphysicae* = vol. 25 of *Opera Omnia* (Hildesheim: Olms, 1965), cited by disputation, section, and article

LIST OF ABBREVIATIONS AND CONVENTIONS

Bacon

B   Oxford Authors *Bacon*, cited by page

Descartes

AT   The standard edition of Adam and Tannery, cited by volume and page

CSMK   The 3-volume standard English translation, cited by volume and page

Hobbes

L   *Leviathan*, cited by page in the Oxford World Classics edition, ed. J. C. A. Gaskin

G   *Human Nature and De Corpore Politico*, ed. J. C. A. Gaskin (Oxford World Classics, 1994), cited by page

Locke

E   *Essay on Human Understanding,* cited by page in the Oxford edition by P. H. Nidditch

T   *Two Treatises on Government,* cited by page in the Yale University Press edition of 2003

Pascal and Malebranche

EM   *Essai de la Metaphysique*, ibid.

LP   *Lettres Provinciales*, ed. H. F. Stewart (Manchester: Manchester University Press, 1919), cited by page

P   Pascal's *Pensées*, cited by the number in the Oxford World Classics edition

R de V   *De la Recherche de la Verité* in *Oeuvres Complètes de Malebranches*, ed. André Robinet (Paris: Vrin, 1958–84)

TNG   Malebranche's *Treatise on Nature and Grace,* cited by page of the Oxford translation of 1992

Spinoza

CPS   *The Cambridge Companion to Spinoza*, ed. D. Garett (Cambridge: Cambridge University Press, 1996)

E   References are given by page to Curley's Penguin translation of the *Ethics* (1996)

Ep   References are to the letters edited by A. Wolf

334

LIST OF ABBREVIATIONS AND CONVENTIONS

Leibniz

A *The Leibniz Clarke Correspondence*, ed. H. G. Alexander (Manchester: Manchester University Press, 1956)

D References to the *Discourse on Metaphysics* are to the Manchester edition of 1988

G References are given by volume and page to the Gerhardt edition of the complete works.

T *Theodicy*, trs. E. M. Huggard (Lasalle, Ill.: Open Court Press, 1985)

Berkeley

BPW References are given by page to *Berkeley's Philosophical Writings*, ed. D. A. Armstrong (New York: Collier Macmillan, 1965)

Hume

T *Treatise of Human Nature*, ed. S. Bigge and P. H. Nidditch; references are given by book, part and, section.

E *Enquiry Concerning Human Understanding*, by the same editors; references are given by page numbers

W *Hume on Religion*, ed. R. Wollheim (London: Collins, 1963)

Smith and Reid

I Thomas Reid, *Inquiry and Essays*, ed. R. E. Beanblossom and K. Lehrer

TMS Adam Smith, *Theory of Moral Sentiments* (Oxford: Oxford University Press, 1976), cited by page .

The Enlightenment

PD Voltaire, *Philosophical Dictionary*, ed T. Besterman (Harmondsworth: Penguin, 1971), cited by page

EL Montesquieu, *Esprit des lois*, ed. G. Truc (Paris: Payot, 1945)

Rousseau

SC References to the *Social Contract* are by chapter and paragraph

Kant

A Reference by page number to the first edition of the *Critique of Pure Reason*

B   Reference by page number to the second edition of the *Critique of Pure Reason*

G   *Groundwork of the Metaphysics of Morals* cited by page of the Akademie edition

M   *Critique of Judgement*, ed. J. H. Meredith (Oxford: Oxford University Press, 1978)

Hegel

LHP   *Lectures on the History of Philosophy*, trs. E. S. Haldane and F. H. Simpson, 1966

PG   *The Phenomenology of Spirit*, trs. A. V. Miller, cited by page

PR   *Philosophy of Right*, trs. H. B. Nisbet, ed. A. Wood (Cambridge: Cambridge University Press, 1991), cited by page

BIBLIOGRAPHY

General works

BENNETT, JONATHAN, *Locke, Berkeley, Hume: Central Themes* (Oxford: Oxford University Press, 1971).

COPLESTON, FREDERICK, *History of Philosophy*, 9 vols. (London: Burns Oates and Search Press, 1943–7).

COTTINGHAM, JOHN, *The Rationalists* (Oxford: Oxford University Press, 1988).

CRAIG, E. G., *The Mind of God and the Works of Man* (Oxford: Oxford University Press, 1987).

GARBER, DANIEL and AYERS, MICHAEL, *The Cambridge History of Seventeenth-Century Philosophy*, 2 vols. (Cambridge: Cambridge University Press, 1998).

GRIBBIN, JOHN, *Science, a History 1543–2001* (Harmondsworth: Penguin, 2002).

KENNY, ANTHONY, *The God of the Philosophers* (Oxford: Clarendon Press, 1979).

——, *The Metaphysics of Mind* (Oxford: Clarendon Press, 1989).

KNEALE, WILLIAM and KNEALE, MARTHA, *The Development of Logic* (Oxford: Clarendon Press, 1979).

POPKIN, R. H., *The History of Scepticism from Erasmus to Spinoza* (Leiden: Gorcum van Assen, 1979).

SCHMITT, CHARLES B., and SKINNER, QUENTIN, *The Cambridge History of Renaissance Philosophy* (Cambridge: Cambridge University Press, 1988).

WOOLHOUSE, R. S., *The Empiricists* (Oxford: Oxford University Press, 1988).

——, *Descartes, Spinoza, Leibniz: the Concept of Substance in Seventeenth-Century Metaphysics* (London: Routledge, 1993).

Sixteenth-Century Philosophy

COLEMAN, JANET, *A History of Political Thought from the Middle Ages to the Renaissance* (Oxford: Blackwell, 2000).

COPENHAVER, B. P. and SCHMITT, CHARLES B., *Renaissance Philosophy* (Oxford: Oxford University Press, 1992).

MCCONICA, JAMES, *Renaissance Thinkers* (Oxford: Oxford University Press, 1993).

MACHIAVELLI, NICCOLÒ, *Il Principe* (Milano: Mondadori, 1994).

MORE, THOMAS *Utopia*, ed. Edward Surtz (New Haven, Conn.: Yale University Press, 1964).

Descartes

The standard edition is that of Adam and Tannery, 12 volumes in the revised edition of Vrin/CRNS, Paris, 1964–76. The now standard English translation is that in 3 volumes published by Cambridge University Press in 1985 and 1991, the first two edited by J. Cottingham, R. Stoothoff, and D. Murdoch, and the third edited by the same and A. Kenny. A very convenient French edition is the single volume Pleiade text, ed. A. Bridoux (Paris: Gallimard, 1973). A lively English translation of selected texts is that by E. Anscombe and P. T. Geach, *Descartes, Philosophical Writings* (London: Nelson, 1969).

COTTTINGHAM, JOHN, *The Cambridge Companion to Descartes* (Cambridge: Cambridge University Press, 1992).

——(ed.), *Descartes: Oxford Readings in Philosophy* (Oxford: Oxford University Press, 1998).

——, *Descartes* (Oxford: Blackwell, 1986).

CURLEY, EDWIN, *Descartes against the Sceptics* (Oxford: Blackwell, 1978).

DAVIES, RICHARD, *Descartes, Belief, Scepticism and Virtue* (London: Routledge, 2001).

FRANKFURT, HARRY, *Demons, Dreamers and Madmen* (Indianapolis: Bobbs-Merrill, 1970).

GARBER, DANIEL, *Descartes' Metaphysical Physics* (Chicago: University of Chicago Press, 1992).

GAUKROGER, STEPHEN, *Descartes: An Intellectual Biography* (Oxford: Clarendon Press, 1995).

KENNY, ANTHONY, *Descartes* (New York: Random House, 1968; reprinted by Thoemmes, 1993).

ROZEMOND, MARLEEN, *Descartes's Dualism* (Cambridge, Mass.: Harvard University Press, 1998).

WILLIAMS, BERNARD, *Descartes: the Project of Pure Inquiry* (Harmondsworth: Penguin, 1978).

WILSON, MARGARET, *Descartes* (London: Routledge and Kegan Paul, 1976).

Hobbes

The complete works of Hobbes were edited by W. Molesworth between 1839 and 1845, in 11 volumes of English works and 5 volumes of Latin works. Oxford University Press is producing a modern edition of his works, but so far only the following volumes have appeared: *De Cive* (1984), *Writings on Common Law and Hereditary Right* (2005), and the correspondence, edited in 2 volumes by Noel Malcolm (1994). There are convenient editions of *Leviathan* (1996) and *Human Nature and De Corpore Politico* (1999) by J. C. A. Gaskin (Oxford World Classics).

AUBREY, JOHN, *Brief Lives*, ed. Oliver Lawson Dick (Harmondsworth: Penguin, 1962; London: Folio Society, 1975).

GAUTHIER, DAVID, *The Logic of Leviathan* (Oxford: Oxford University Press, 1969).

OAKESHOTT, MICHAEL, *Hobbes on Civil Association* (Oxford: Oxford University Press, 1975).

RAPHAEL, DAVID D., *Hobbes, Morals and Politics* (London: Routledge, 1977).

BIBLIOGRAPHY

SORELL, TOM, *Hobbes* (London: Routledge 1986).

——, *The Cambridge Companion to Hobbes* (Cambridge: Cambridge University Press 1996).

TUCK, RICHARD, *Hobbes* (Oxford, Oxford University Press, 1989).

WARRENDER, HOWARD, *The Political Philosophy of Hobbes* (Oxford: Oxford University Press, 1957).

Locke

The Clarendon edition of the works of John Locke is planned to occupy 30 volumes, which will include his diaries and letters. The series is approaching completion (Oxford: Oxford University Press, 1975–) and all the major works are already published. The edition of the *Essay Concerning Human Understanding* by P. H. Nidditch (1975) was brought out in paperback in 1975. A convenient paperback of *Two Treatises on Government* and *A Letter Concerning Toleration* (ed. Ian Shapiro) was produced by Yale University Press (New Haven, Conn.) in 2003.

AYERS, MICHAEL, *Locke*, 2 vols. (London: Routledge, 1991).

CHAPPELL, VERE, *The Cambridge Companion to Locke* (Cambridge: Cambridge University Press, 1994).

CRANSTON, MAURICE, *John Locke: a Biography* (Oxford: Oxford University Press, 1985).

DUNN, JOHN, *The Political Thought of John Locke* (Cambridge: Cambridge University Press, 1969).

——, *Locke* (Oxford: Oxford University Press, 1984).

MACKIE, JOHN, *Problems from Locke* (Oxford: Oxford University Press, 1976).

ROGERS, G. A. J., *Locke's Philosophy: Content and Context* (Oxford: Oxford University Press, 1974).

WOOLHOUSE, R. S., *Locke* (Brighton: Harvester, 1983).

YOLTON, JOHN, *John Locke and the Way of Ideas* (Oxford: Oxford University Press, 1956).

——, *John Locke: Problems and Perspectives* (Cambridge: Cambridge University Press, 1969).

——, *Locke, an Introduction* (Oxford: Blackwell, 1985).

——, *A Locke Dictionary* (Oxford: Blackwell, 1993).

Pascal and Malebranche

The best complete edition of the works of Pascal is *Oeuvres Complètes*, ed. Louis Lafuma (Paris: Éditions du Seuil, 1963). The numbering of the *Pensées* in this edition is the one commonly used. There is an edition of *Les Provinciales* by H. F. Stewart (Manchester: Manchester University Press, 1919), and a translation by A. J. Krailsheimer (Harmondsworth: Penguin, 1967). A new translation of the *Pensées* by Honor Levi has appeared in Oxford World Classics (Oxford University Press, 1995). The standard edition of Malebranche is *Oeuvres Complètes*, ed. André Robinet, in 20 vols (Paris: Vrin, 1958–84). There is an English translation of the *Treatise on Nature and Grace* by Patrick Riley (Oxford: Clarendon Press, 1992).

BIBLIOGRAPHY

KRAILSHAIMER, ALBAN, *Pascal* (Oxford: Oxford University Press, 1980).

McCRACKEN, C. J., *Malebranche and British Philosophy* (Oxford: Oxford University Press, 1983).

MESNARD, J., *Pascal, His Life and Works* (London: Collins, 1952).

NADLER, STEVEN, *Malebranche and Ideas* (Oxford: Oxford University Press, 1992).

Spinoza

The standard edition is *Spinoza Opera*, ed. Carl Gebhardt, 4 vols. (Heidelberg: Carl Winter, 1925). A convenient 2 vol. English translation is *The Chief Works of Benedict de Spinoza*, translated by R. H. M. Elwes (New York: Dover, 1951). A new edition of the Collected Works in English is being published by Princeton University Press, edited and translated by Edwin Curley, of which the first volume appeared in 1985. A Penguin translation of the *Ethics* was published in 1996. His correspondence, edited and translated by A. Wolf, was published in 1928 and reprinted (London: Frank Cass) in 1966.

BENNETT, JONATHAN, *A Study of Spinoza's Ethics* (Indianapolis: Hackett, 1984).

CURLEY, EDWIN, *Spinoza's Metaphysics: An Essay in Interpretation* (Cambridge, Mass.: Harvard University Press, 1969).

DELAHUNTY, R. J., *Spinoza* (London: Routledge and Kegan Paul, 1985).

DONAGAN, ALAN, *Spinoza* (Chicago: Chicago University Press, 1988).

HAMPSHIRE, STUART, *Spinoza* (Harmondsworth: Penguin, 1951).

WOLFSON, HARRY A., *The Philosophy of Spinoza*, 2 vols. (Cambridge, Mass.: Harvard University Press, 1934).

Leibniz

The current standard edition of the philosophical writings is *Die Philosophischen Schriften*, in 7 vols. ed. C. I. Gerhardt (Hildesheim: Olms, 1963). In due course this will be replaced by the German Academy edition, *Samtliche Schriften und Briefe* (1923–). English editions of his writings include: *G. W. Leibniz: Philosophical Papers and Letters* (Dordrecht: Reidel, 1969); *G. W. Leibniz: Discourse on Metaphysics and related Writings*, ed. and trs. R. Martin and others (Manchester: Manchester University Press, 1988); *Leibniz: Philosophical Writings*, ed. and trs. G. H. R. Parkinson (London: Dent, 1973); *Leibniz: Logical Papers*, ed. and trs. G. H. R. Parkinson (Oxford: Clarendon Press, 1966); *Theodicy*, trs. E. M. Huggard (Lasalle, Ill.: Open Court Press, 1985); *Monadology and other Philosophical Essays*, trs. P. and A. M. Schrecker (Indianapolis: Bobbs-Merrill, 1965).

ADAMS, ROBERT, *Leibniz: Determinist, Theist, Idealist* (Oxford: Oxford University Press, 1994).

ARIEW, ROGER, *The Cambridge Companion to Leibniz* (Cambridge: Cambridge University Press, 1995).

BROWN, STUART, *Leibniz* (Brighton: Harvester Press, 1984).

ISHIGURO, HIDE, *Leibniz's Philosophy of Logic and Language* (London: Duckworth, 1972).

MATES, BENSON, *The Philosophy of Leibniz: Metaphysics and Language* (Oxford: Oxford University Press, 1986).

PARKINSON, G. H. R., *Logic and Reality in Leibniz's Metaphysics* (Oxford: Oxford University Press, 1965).

RUSSELL, BERTRAND, *A Critical Exposition of the Philosophy of Leibniz*, 2nd edn. (London: Allen and Unwin, 1937).

Berkeley

Berkeley's works have been published in 9 volumes by A. A. Luce and T. E. Jessop (Edinburgh: Thomas Nelson, 1948–57). His *Principles* and *Dialogues* have appeared in Oxford World Classics (Oxford: Oxford University Press, 1999).

BERMAN, D., *George Berkeley: Idealism and the Man* (Oxford: Clarendon Press, 1994).

MARTIN, C. B. and ARMSTRONG, D. M. eds., *Locke and Berkeley: A Collection of Critical Essays* (New York: Doubleday, 1968).

PITCHER, GEORGE, *Berkeley* (London: Routledge and Kegan Paul, 1977).

URMSON, JAMES, *Berkeley* (Oxford: Oxford University Press, 1982).

WARNOCK, GEOFFREY, *Berkeley* (Harmondsworth: Penguin, 1953).

WINKLER, K., *Berkeley, An Interpretation* (Oxford: Oxford University Press, 1989).

Hume

The most complete current edition is *The Philosophical Works of David Hume*, ed. T. H. Green and T. H. Grose (London: Longman Green, 1875). The Clarendon Press is publishing a new edition, in which the *Enquiries* are edited by Tom Beauchamp (1999, 2001) and the *Treatise* is edited by D. and M. Norton (2006). Convenient editions of the main works are *Treatise of Human Nature*, ed. L. A. Selby Bigge and P. H. Nidditch (3rd edn.; Oxford: Oxford University Press, 1978), and *Enquiry Concerning Human Understanding*, ed. L. A. Selby Bigge and P. H. Nidditch (2nd edn.; Oxford: Oxford University Press, 1978). *Hume on Religion*, ed. Richard Wollheim (London: Collins, 1963), is a useful selection, including *The Natural History of Religion* and *Dialogues Concerning Natural Religion*.

AYER, ALFRED J., *Hume* (Oxford: Oxford University Press, 1980).

FLEW, ANTONY, *Hume's Philosophy of Belief* (London: Routledge and Kegan Paul, 1961).

KEMP SMITH, NORMAN, *The Philosophy of David Hume* (London: Macmillan, 1941).

PEARS, DAVID, *Hume's System* (Oxford: Oxford University Press, 1990).

STRAWSON, GALEN, *The Secret Connexion* (Oxford: Clarendon Press, 1989).

WRIGHT, J. P., *The Sceptical Realism of David Hume* (Manchester: Manchester University Press, 1983).

Smith and Reid

A Glasgow edition of the works of Adam Smith is being produced by Oxford University Press; his *Theory of Moral Sentiments* was published in this series in 1976. *The Wealth of Nations* has appeared in Oxford World Classics, ed. K. Sutherland (Oxford: Oxford University Press, 1993). Reid's *Essays on the Intellectual Powers of Man* and *Essays on the Active Powers of the Human Mind* are available in modern reprints (Cambridge, Mass.: MIT Press).

LEHRER, KEITH, *Thomas Reid* (London: Routledge, 1989).
RAPHAEL, D. D., *Adam Smith* (Oxford: Oxford University Press, 1985).

The Enlightenment

Several of Voltaire's works are conveniently available in French in the Flammarion collection (Paris, 1964–), and in English translations in Oxford World Classics, and in Penguin Classics, which published his *Philosophical Dictionary*, ed. T. Besterman, in 1971. Rousseau's works are similarly available from Flammarion, and his *Discourse on Political Economy* and the *Social Contract* are in English in Oxford World Classics; his *Confessions* was published as a Penguin Classic in 1966. Lessing's *Laocoon* was published in a translation by E. A. McCormick in 1962, in the Library of Liberal Arts (Indianapolis: Bobbs-Merrill).

WADE, I., *The Intellectual Development of Voltaire* (Princeton, NJ: Princeton University Press).
WOKLER, R., *Rousseau* (Oxford: Oxford University Press, 1995).

Kant

The standard critical edition of Kant is the Akademie edition (*Kant's Gesammelte Schriften*), published in 29 vols. since 1900 (Berlin: Reimer/de Gruyter). A convenient German pocket edition in 12 vols. was published by Insel Verlag (Wiesbaden, 1956). A Cambridge edition of Kant's works in English was begun in 1991, with the publication of *Metaphysics of Morals* (ed. M. Gregor); the *Critique of Pure Reason*, ed. and trs. Paul Guyer and A. W. Wood, was published by Cambridge University Press in 1998. Among earlier translations still used are *The Critique of Practical Reason*, trs. Lewis White Beck (Indianapolis: Bobbs-Merrill, 1956) and *The Critique of Judgement*, trs. J. C. Meredith (Oxford: Oxford University Press, 1978)

BENNETT, JONATHAN, *Kant's Analytic* (Cambridge: Cambridge University Press, 1966).
———, *Kant's Dialectic* (Cambridge: Cambridge University Press, 1974).
CAYGILL, HOWARD, *A Kant Dictionary* (Oxford: Blackwell, 1994).
GUYER, PAUL, *Kant and the Claims of Knowledge* (Cambridge: Cambridge University Press, 1987).

——— (ed.), *The Cambridge Companion to Kant* (Cambridge: Cambridge University Press, 1992).

KITSCHER, PATRICIA, *Kant's Transcendental Psychology* (Oxford: Oxford University Press, 1990).

KÖRNER, STEPHAN, *Kant* (Harmondsworth: Penguin, 1955).

O'NEILL, ONORA, *Constructions of Reason: Explorations of Kant's Practical Philosophy* (Cambridge: Cambridge University Press, 1989).

PATON, H. J., *The Moral Law* (London: Hutchinson, 1955).

SCRUTON, ROGER, *Kant* (Oxford: Oxford University Press, 1982).

STRAWSON, PETER, *The Bounds of Sense* (London: Methuen, 1966).

WALKER, RALPH, *Kant* (London: Routledge and Kegan Paul, 1978).

WOOD, ALLEN, *Kant's Rational Theology* (Ithaca, NY: Cornell University Press, 1978).

Hegel

The Deutsche Forschungsgemeinschaft has been bringing out a critical edition of Hegel's works since 1968 (Hamburg: Meiner). The most convenient German edition to use is the *Werkausgabe* in 20 vols. ed. E. Moldenhauer and K. Michel (Frankfurt: Suhrkamp, 1969–72). Among English translations of Hegel's works are *Logic,* trs. William Wallace (Oxford: Oxford University Press, 1975); *Phenomenology of Spirit,* trs. A. V. Miller (Oxford: Oxford University Press, 1977); *Lectures on the History of Philosophy,* trs. E. S. Haldane and F. H. Simpson (3 vols. London: Routledge, 1966); *Philosophy of Right,* trs. H. B. Nisbet, ed. Allen Wood (Cambridge: Cambridge University Press, 1991).

FINDLAY, J. N., *Hegel: A Re-examination* (London: George Allen and Unwin, 1958).

INWOOD, MICHAEL, *Hegel* (London: Routledge and Kegan Paul, 1983).

KAUFMANN, WALTER, *Hegel: A Re-examination* (Garden City, NY: Doubleday, 1965).

POPPER, KARL, *The Open Society and its Enemies* (London: Routledge and Kegan Paul, 1966).

ROSEN, MICHAEL, *Hegel's Dialectic and its Criticism* (Cambridge: Cambridge University Press, 1982).

SOLOMON, ROBERT, *In the Spirit of Hegel* (Oxford: Oxford University Press, 1983).

TAYLOR, CHARLES, *Hegel* (Cambridge: Cambridge University Press, 1975).

——— , *Hegel and Modern Society* (Cambridge: Cambridge University Press, 1979).

WALSH, W. H., *Hegelian Ethics* (London: Macmillan, 1969).

ILLUSTRATIONS

ILLUSTRATIONS

INDEX